Adrienne M. Shore

THE CRIME *of* GALILEO

THE CRIME *of* GALILEO

By

GIORGIO DE SANTILLANA

THE UNIVERSITY OF CHICAGO PRESS
Chicago & London

The University of Chicago Press, Chicago 60637
The University of Chicago Press, Ltd., London

Published 1955. Midway Reprint 1976
Printed in the United States of America

International Standard Book Number: 0-226-73481-1
Library of Congress Catalog Card Number: 55-7400

LUDOVICO AND ANNA

DIAZ DE SANTILLANA

XXVIII DEC. MCMLIII

Q. B. F. S.

PREFACE

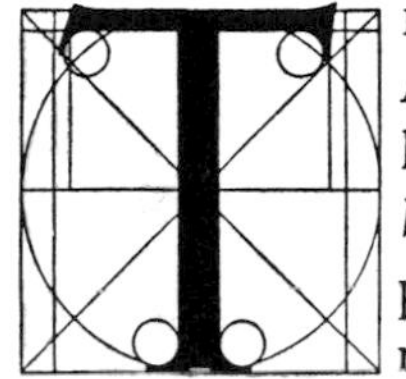

HIS work is not the result of a plan aforethought. As I tried to clear up the astonishingly complex background of Galileo's *Dialogue on the Great World Systems*,[1] I was drawn to the drama which played a decisive part in that fateful event of modern history, the secularization of thought. It seemed strange to me that, after so much research and controversy, the story of events as I found it should make so little sense. As I worked, it became clear that a large area of the puzzle had remained oddly disassembled to the present day, by what looks like an inexplicable tacit agreement between the warring factions.

Galileo did not come to grief as "the scientist" facing a religious credo. He was far from standing in the role of a technician of science; had he done so, he would have escaped all trouble. Everyone knows that his discoveries went unchallenged. Those of Descartes did too. And so did Descartes himself. But then, as he admitted, he "went forth under a mask," whereas Galileo is the man without a mask. Both his friends and his enemies saw in him a unique type of creative personality, whose essential achievement might very well be conceived to stand or fall with him. He was a classic type of humanist, trying to bring his culture to the awareness of the new scientific ideas, and among the forces that he found aligned against him religious fundamentalism was by no means the strongest.

It is difficult to see the actual shape of the conflict in these matters so long as we remain under the spell of a misunderstanding tacitly accepted by both sides: the idea of the scientist as a bold "freethinker" and "progressive" facing the static resistance of conserva-

---

1. Galileo Galilei, *Dialogue on the Great World Systems.* The Salusbury translation. Revised, annotated, and with an Introduction by Giorgio de Santillana. Chicago: University of Chicago Press, 1953.

tism. This may well be the aspect on the level of personalities, for it is usually the scientist who shows the freer and more speculative mind in contrast with prejudiced opponents. But the core of the thing is different: there the scientist appears more often than not as the conservative overtaken by fast-moving social forces. He usually has the Law and the Prophets on his side.

This ought to become immediately clear if we think of contemporary events. The tragedy of the geneticists in Russia, with its lamentable apologies and recantations, is a faithful rehearsal of the Galileo story; yet we could not accuse the Soviet government of clinging to ancient superstitions or of underestimating the pressing need for science and technology. And lest our straining for beams make us overlook our own domestic gnats, we may perceive in the Oppenheimer case a parallel which is a shade too close for comfort. In such vastly different climates of time and thought, whenever the conflict comes up, we find a similarity of symptoms and behavior which points to a fundamental relation.

True, the Oppenheimer case is very different from Galileo's as to context. Today there is a tendency not to suppress physics but rather to exploit it; a tendency to act not on deep philosophic differences but on mere issues of expediency. Yet, as the story unfolds before the public, the exact analogy in structure, in symptoms and behaviors, shows us that we are dealing with the same disease. Through the little that we are allowed to know, we can discern the scientific mind as it has ever been—with its free-roaming curiosity, its unconventional interests, its detachment, its ancient and somewhat esoteric set of values (it is the scientist, we may remember, who is reproached with having brought the concept of "sin" into modern contexts)—surprised by policy decisions dictated by "Reasons of State" or what are judged to be such.

It might be a mere game of tally, but it is tempting to establish a one-to-one correspondence between the actors of the two dramas three centuries apart and to follow them through parallel convolutions. One might say, for instance: for "Holy Office" read "AEC Board," for "Caccini" read "Crouch," for "Lorini" read "Borden," for "S.J." (*Societas Jesu*) read "SAC" (Strategic Air Command), for "Report of the Preliminary Commission" read "Gray-Morgan Majority Report," for "Grienberger" read "Teller," for "certain German mathematicians" read "a certain Dr. Malraux," and so on. As for the hooded figure of Michelangelo Segizi de Lauda, the craftsman of iniquity, the number of high-placed contestants in public life and in the Communications Empire would make it invidious to choose.

The two chief figures of authority, too, are remarkably similar in their complex motivations. But the chairman of the Atomic Energy Commission wrote out his own résumé of the case, which turned out to be also the decision, whereas it will appear reasonably proved in this work that Urban VIII's decision was based on a deliberately arranged résumé which was submitted to him in order to lead him astray.

There is no doubt that the ecclesiastical figures of the seventeenth century come out ahead of their modern counterparts. After all, the question revolved at that time around metaphysical and cosmological questions of such majestic import that even the gravest moral errors committed in defense of the traditional view may appear today as concern for the ultimate salvation of mankind. The findings of our contemporary authorities, in their absent-mindedness, are much closer to the prosecutor's conclusion against Lavoisier: "La République n'a pas besoin de savants." And, as then, science has to keep silence.

But parallels are at best an invitation to thought, and this one should not be pushed too far. What I think can be brought out in all these cases is that—at least when the question reaches the higher echelons—it is not so much a matter of "science" versus "prejudice" as of the classic question coming up again: "What *is* the scientist?" It is usually the scientist who is taken by surprise by a redefinition of his activities coming from outside. And the result is always one more turn racked up on the old screw. By subjecting the scientist as a cultural being to the administrative suspicion that usually attaches to questionable adventurers in international traffics, we have simply brought one step further the process of secularization of thought.

So much is sure, that in the seventeenth-century episode the seeming paradox comes out with full force: within the specific frame of Western Christendom the actual conflict reveals Galileo, like all free men, seeking a support in established custom, credit, and tradition, while Urban VIII, like all organizers of power, becomes the unwitting tool of the streamlined, the "efficient," and the new.

This may not be conformable, I readily admit, to the perspective set up by current historiography, largely built up as it is on hindsight. But this is how it was experienced, more or less consciously, by the actors of the drama; and that ought to be a not wholly negligible aspect of historical reality.

Galileo may be excused for wondering why his discoveries were dubbed alarming "novelties," since science was only supposed to discover things that must have been eternally so. What appeared to him much more of a "novelty" was the way in which authorities had taken to handing down administrative decisions in a field in which they were not supposed to have any competence. It was to him a startling interpretation of that other new thing which might be called the Tridentine Amendment to the immemorial constitutions of Christendom.

In thinking of Galileo's universe, an image that comes to mind is the bare, strong interior of the Pazzi Chapel in Florence, that meeting point of Christ and geometry. If we try to populate it in our fancy, it will have to be a singular mixture of characters from Ghirlandaio and Mantegna, with some disdainful personages of Titian or Bronzino to represent the intellectual ruling class. After all, Galileo had been born way back in 1564; the world of his conceptions is still that of the sixteenth century. He has at best, of the seventeenth, the "Edwardian" or Jacobean coloring of its beginnings.

Far from that is Pope Urban's world—the splendor of the "sumptuous palaces" of the Barberinis in the renovated Capital, the magnificent declaratory flights of Borromini's façades, the colossal grip of Bernini's colonnades, the noisy massiveness and ornamental flourish of St. Peter's. It is space-embracing organization against delicate permanence. The contrast would not be more marked between Grand Central Terminal and a New England town common.

In his concern with enduring things, in his confessional simplicity, Galileo spans the centuries. Through him, what we call science is speaking out unequivocally for the first time; yet there lives in him a spirit more ancient and ample than that of the ecclesiastical statesman in Rome. It is the spirit of ecumenic and conciliar Christianity which warns and exhorts with the dignity of a Father of the early centuries. The contrast between the theological style of his epistles and that of the official apologetic literature is enough to tell the story. The elaborate baroque formulas of submissiveness do not prevent the reader from feeling that here is someone like Ambrose, Augustine, or Bonaventure, reprehending sleepy shepherds and degenerate epigones. He speaks in the name of the community of the faithful which joins the ancient dead to the yet unborn. He is not simply the consulting astronomer; he is the adviser in matters of natural philosophy and metaphysics who requests to be heard, and, if, as he intimates, it is holiness of intention and gravity of counsel that make authority, he deserves heeding no less than Aquinas himself.

He was not wrong either, as a matter of record. The content of his spurned and incriminated theological letters has become official Church doctrine since 1893. Had there been in Rome, at the time of the first crisis of 1616, a youthful Aquinas to take up his lead, instead of an aged Bellarmine—but there was no Aquinas, and there was no time.

The whole drama turns out to be in the nature of a surprise encounter for both sides. Both the authorities and the scientist had the mutual impression of being ambushed, and in neither case was it true. The ambush, in so far as there was one, had been carefully laid by third parties, who carefully exploited the critical situation of the times. But Galileo never felt himself in the figure of an innovator and a rebel. As the central figure of accepted science, as the acknowledged leader of his culture in thought and expression, not last as a perfectly orthodox representative of metaphysical Christianity, he could not but stand his ground, in growing bewilderment, until administrative violence established a quietus, leaving everybody, including the authorities themselves, in a state of utter confusion.

The confusion goes on unremittingly even today, for the Galileo affair is far from dead, and every decade brings a new "line" and new suggestions meant to explain it away, just as it brings a repetition of the ancient rationalist war whoops. The side that stands for the authorities neither is, nor by any means has been, all Catholic. One of the most irresponsible and widely used accounts came from a Protestant publicist of the eighteenth century, Mallet du Pan, and a popular prejudiced version from the pen of another Protestant, Sir David Brewster. Some of the silliest accusations against Galileo have been accredited by the antireligious French Encyclopedists. On the other hand, some of the more honest efforts to restore the facts are due to professedly Catholic historians like L'Epinois and Reusch.

Since names have been mentioned, I should add, to honor them, those of scholars who, belonging to neither camp, labored to attain an impartial view of the situation: mainly Emil Wohlwill, Th. H. Martin, Karl von Gebler, and Antonio Favaro. Most of the literature through which one has to wade deserves no mention at all. It ranges from average casual incompetence to prevarication and plain filth. Let it go back to whence it came. There is no common measure between the policy problems of long ago—the motives, the hesitation, the eventual refusal, of men who felt intrusted with the fate of millions of people who pray—and the gratuitous distortions that later and self-appointed apologists scattered abroad in their name. The long-drawn-out polemic is not strictly, I hope to have made it clear, one between the confessional and the anticonfessional faction. It has been made to look like that; in reality it is a confused free-for-all in which prejudice, inveterate rancor, and all sorts of special and corporate interests have been the prime movers. Those who dragged and keep dragging the Church into it are no candid souls. As L'Epinois says rightly, the Church has all to gain and nothing to lose from the truth.

As far as I can make out, the unsolved state of the puzzle is due to this: that the "freethinkers" are only too glad to put the Roman Church as a whole under accusation in the affair, while inside the ecclesiastic hierarchy powerful corporate interests are ready to accept the terrain chosen by the attackers rather than have some of their long-deceased members stand under the spotlight of history. Thus, they are willing to involve the Church in this quarrel, with the inevitable consequences that they have to resort to laborious smoke screens, devious implications, and all sorts of unfair tactics.

Did, indeed, the conflict have to take place at all under this form? It has been known for a long time that a major part of the Church intellectuals were on the side of Galileo, while the clearest opposition to him came from secular ideas. It can be proved further (or at least I hope I have done so) that the tragedy was the result of a plot of which the hierarchies themselves turned out to be the victims no less than Galileo—an intrigue engineered by a group of obscure and disparate characters in strange collusion who planted false documents in the file, who later misinformed the Pope and then presented to him a misleading account of the trial for decision.

The real story affords a fascinating insight into the way in which such decisions actually take place and in which the ponderous state machinery is set into motion by what seem to be Reasons of State and perhaps later become so, but originate really as a constellation of accidents and personal motives. An objective account ought to be more relevant to a decent understanding than all the innuendoes, diversions, and stage sets invented around it on both sides. By pinpointing the culpability of a few individuals, it tends to absolve a far greater number who had stood hitherto under the darkest suspicions, and among them the Commissary-General of the Inquisition himself, who conducted the trial. Once recognized, the facts should lead us forward to the problems of present reality and disperse this perennial battle with windmills.

I want to express my gratitude to Father Robert Lord, S.J., Father Joseph Clark, S.J., and Professor Edward Rosen for their criticism and their helpful suggestions; to Miss Elizabeth Cameron and Mrs. Nancy Chivers for their invaluable assistance in preparing the manuscript.

GIORGIO DE SANTILLANA

MASSACHUSETTS INSTITUTE OF TECHNOLOGY

TABLE OF CONTENTS

LIST OF ILLUSTRATIONS

INTRODUCTION

Our fight is against some devilry that lies in the very process of things.

H. BUTTERFIELD

CIENTIFIC endeavor and social authority, in one form or another, are characteristics of man's life on this planet that are expected to endure for as long as we can see ahead. In this essay, which aims at analyzing their complex relations, we intend to go at length into the episode which provides, as it were, a grand overture to their conflict in the modern age, namely, the trial of Galileo and the circumstances that brought it about. But, as we work out the general conditions attendant on such a conflict, we shall not pass in silence what similarities and dissimilarities occur with the further phase of conflict which is being played out in our time.

In fact, if one is still fascinated by the details of an episode which is three centuries old, it is mainly because the trial provides a demonstration piece such as could hardly be found elsewhere. We are going to offer no apology for dwelling on the past. Sometime, when other now well-guarded archives are open, and the historical point of view is sufficiently remote, historians may be able to anatomize the events of the present day with something resembling objectivity. Even so, we may be prepared to find it dull reading, for the modern state produces its own kind of dreary setting and ever worsening prose, while the events surrounding Galileo's trial remain a Baroque production as articulate and spectacular as a painting by Veronese, peopled with amply gesturing characters who continually and irresistibly "compose" in the eloquent seventeenth-century style.

It has become a set piece in history to present Pope Urban VIII and his counselors as the bigoted oppressors of science. It would be possibly more accurate to say that they were the first bewildered victims of the scientific age. They had come into collision with a force of which they had not the faintest notion. In that sense, they are almost the polar opposite of the "progressive" rulers of the twentieth century, who are, one and all, bigoted believers in "scientism" while dealing with science in a no less highhanded manner. Still, the dramatic shape remains the same.

"Our fight," Professor Butterfield lately wrote, "is against some devilry that lies in the very process of things, against something that we might even call demonic forces existing in the air. The forces get men into their grip, so that the men themselves are victims in a sense, even if it is by some fault of their own nature—they are victims of a sort of possession."

These words are not written by a poet or a Doctor of Divinity but by one of the ranking historians of our time. We feel encouraged by them to face the problem in a somewhat similar spirit, if it be understood that his words are to apply to all participants without exception.

Galileo Galilei was born in Pisa in 1564, the year in which Michelangelo died and Shakespeare came into the world. He sprang of an old Florentine family whose main stem had borne the name of Buonaiuti. His rather singular Christian name comes of an old Tuscan custom of duplicating the surname in the first-born, as, for example, in Braccio Bracci or Pazzino de' Pazzi. His father Vincenzio Galilei was a musician and composer.

The boy had a happy childhood and received his first education from the friars of Vallombrosa; in 1581 he entered the University of Pisa as a student of medicine and philosophy. His natural bent, however, as well as a disinclination toward the natural philosophy then taught in the schools, drew him to geometry and mechanics. At nineteen, he is said to have discovered the isochronism of the pendulum; at twenty-two, he invented his hydrostatic balance. Archimedes, who had but recently become known in the full Latin translation, became his scientific model. He decided to create a mathematical science which should do for the motion of bodies what Archimedes had achieved for statics. The Greek endeavor had broken down on the theory of motion, and Galileo had to struggle for many years with the suasive theories he had been taught out of Aristotle as well as with his own preconceptions. It was only after twenty years of searching and false starts that he was able to give, in 1604, the correct law of the motion of falling bodies.

A first lectureship in his own University of Pisa had not been a happy experience, as he had aroused antagonism in the faculty. He left after three years, in 1592, to take up a vacancy in the ancient University of Padua under the jurisdiction of the Venetian Republic. The salary was 180 florins a year, later increased to 520. Cremonini, the "great philosopher" of the university and a straightforward pedant, earned 2,000. This goes to show what academic authorities thought of the importance of mathematics; the chair of "mathematics" then covered the teaching of geometry, astronomy, military engineering, and fortification.

Galileo's success as a lecturer and humanist with students from all parts of Europe brought him international renown. He published in that period treatises on mechanics, spherical geometry, and fortifications. But a new and fascinating subject had meanwhile begun to hold his attention: the Copernican theory. Nicolaus Copernicus had published in Germany many years previously, in 1543, a treatise on the *Revolutions of the Celestial Orbs*, dedicated to Pope Paul III, which went counter to the established theories. The natural philosophy of Aristotle, as well as the astronomy of Ptolemy adopted both by the universities and by the Church, taught that the Earth was at the center of things and that the heavens revolved around it in twenty-four hours, together with the Sun, Moon, and planets. Copernicus, taking up some hints of half-forgotten theories of the Greeks, had suggested that this might come of an optical illusion and that the whole geometrical device worked out by Ptolemy made more rational sense if the Sun were placed in the center of the universe, and the Earth among the planets, covering its orbit in one year, as the Sun had been supposed to do, as well as turning on itself in twenty-four hours.

The great treatise of Copernicus had been known for a half-century, but in all this time it had aroused mostly skepticism.

A few romantic and daring spirits had been captured by the new idea, but they could not master the difficult details of the system. Official astronomy, represented by the great Tycho Brahe, had declared against it, and Tycho had advanced instead a compromise system of his own in which the Earth remained at the center of things. The philosophers of the schools dismissed Copernicus because his theory could not be reconciled with their physics. The Protestants were against him because they felt he cast doubt upon the literal truth of Scripture. As for the Catholic hierarchies, they held Copernicus in respect as a church man and scholar, but they considered his system as one more of those ingenious mathematical devices which could lay no claim to physical reality. Mathematics was rated at the time as a thing for technicians and *virtuosi*, as they were called, with no claim to philosophical relevance; and the mystical and metaphysical speculations of some adventurous minds who searched for the "divine secret" in proportion and number were not such as to compel the assent of responsible scholars. Added to this, the Churchmen derived some good reasons for their reserve from the book of Copernicus himself, which had come to them provided with a spurious preface written really by Osiander, a Protestant clergyman, which disclaimed any pretension of physical validity for the theory.

Galileo, who had been maturing in those years since 1585 a completely new natural philosophy based on mathematics, saw the book in a very different light. To him it made excellent physical sense and showed the way to a truer cosmology. He admitted as much to his friends in 1597. But, knowing that one would have "to mold anew the brains of men" before bringing them over to his point of view, he decided to bide his time. He knew he had no proof as yet which would look convincing to the unprepared mind. The proof came to him by a stroke of luck, with the discovery of the telescope in 1610, which also established his name in the mind of the public at large as that of the leading scientist of his time. And this is where our story begins.

I

THE DAYS OF DISCOVERY

These novelties of ancient truths, of new worlds, new systems, new nations, are the beginning of a new era. Let God not make delay, and let us for our small part do all we can.

CAMPANELLA

I

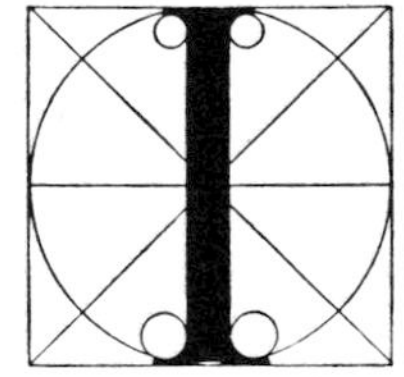

N MARCH, 1610, Galileo announced to the world, in his *Message from the Stars*, the discovery of the telescope. "That universe," as he was to say later, "that I enlarged a hundred and a thousand times from what the wise men of all past ages had thought" was not only bringing in its message new and unimagined things in heaven. It was also bringing new ideas to the mind of its discoverer.

Others might think that here was "a new America in the skies" and more magnificence of stars. To the explorer himself, the *Nuncius sidereus*[1] brought a very clear decision: Copernicus had been right in making the Earth a planet and not the center of the universe. Galileo had divined as much long ago, while engaged in his less-known work in mechanics. No one could have guessed then his ultimate aim; but, as he sought the laws of missiles and falling bodies, he had told himself he would not show his hand in cosmology until he could come forward as an entirely new type of

1. This was the title of the pamphlet in its original Latin.

Copernican—not the mere astronomer but "the astronomer philosophical," the physicist of the skies. The sudden discovery of the telescope had decided the matter for him, since it brought unexpected observational confirmation to his theory while it catapulted him into fame and fortune. He was now forty-five years of age. The work of his life lay ahead of him.

On May 7, 1610, two months after the publication of his *Message*, he wrote a long letter to his faithful friend Belisario Vinta, the Florentine secretary of state. He spoke of all the great plans he would be able to carry through, once relieved of the obligation of teaching in Padua, and of his desire to serve the Grand Duke:

"I have many and most admirable plans and devices; but they could only be put to work by princes, because it is they who are able to carry on war, build and defend fortresses, and for their regal sport make most splendid expenditure, and not I or any private gentleman. The works that I intend to bring to a conclusion are principally two books on the *System* or *Constitution of the World*, an immense design, full of philosophy, astronomy, and geometry. Then there are three books *On Motion*, a science entirely new. . . ."[2]

This is the first explicit mention of the project to which he had previously only alluded: a work of natural philosophy establishing the Copernican systems in the light of the new discoveries in astronomy and physics after two decades of thought given to the problem. What he needed now was a "perfect state of quiet of mind."

For twenty years he had struggled along in an underpaid position, harassed with the financial needs of his relatives, compelled to eke out his salary by tutoring and boarding students and giving extra hours to what people really expected of a man of his profession: the theory of fortifications, "saps, mines, gabions, palisadoes, ravelins, half-moons, and such trumpery." Apart from that,

2. This letter, as well as all further texts whose source is not otherwise specified, is to be found in the National Edition of Galileo's *Works*, by Antonio Favaro, in twenty volumes. The correspondence is arranged in strict chronological order, so that the date constitutes a sufficient reference.

universities did not have much to offer to a mathematician. The learned profession, in this decline of the Renaissance, had come upon dull times. The outlook was shrinking under the impact of the religious tension; it was as though learning had lost its point. Had it not been for the presence of Fabricius of Acquapendente, the great anatomist, and a few jurists, consultors of the Venetian Republic and worthy successors of the learned Bellario, Galileo would have found it difficult to put up with the self-importance of his Paduan colleagues; and too rare were the escapes he could allow himself into the cosmopolitan atmosphere of Venice twenty miles away, where he and Fabricius were always welcomed by the small senatorial circle gathering for free conversation in the famous counting-house of Ca' Morosini.

True, fame had come now with his discoveries, and his salary had been raised to one thousand florins. But Galileo had made up his mind long since. It was not so much, as has been suggested at times, that he wanted his little revenge on the scholars of Tuscany who had refused him a post in his early days; he had enough weighty reasons without that and had stated some of those in his letter to Vinta. In the secretary of state he had the right kind of friend who could understand him.[3] Under Vinta's stewardship the little Tuscan principality, less than a million in population but still not forgetful of the glories of the past centuries, had embarked on a bold economic policy aimed at fighting the prevalent economic depression of the times. Canals had been dug, vast stretches of land had been reclaimed in the provinces of Siena, Arezzo, and Grosseto, and the new port of Leghorn, with its shipyards and arsenal, had been built up out of nothing. Vinta had even underwritten a venture in Brazilian colonization to be directed by two Englishmen, Dudley and Thornton. It was through Vinta that Galileo had prevailed on the Grand Duke to accept the dedication of the still con-

3. The closeness between the two men shows throughout their correspondence, even conducted as it is in the formal official tone. At one point Vinta is quoted back in direct speech: "Galileo, nelle cose tue tratta con me e non con altri"—a significant phrase both in the meaning and in the form of address.

troversial satellites of Jupiter in the name of the House of Medici, a master-stroke of scientific diplomacy.

Galileo had good reason, then, to feel that this was the place for him. He wanted to be back in his own native country, amid people of his own speech and friends of his own choosing.

There were risks, he was willing to admit. It was not completely safe to exchange the rigid contractual obligations of such a state as the Republic of Venice for the personal favor of a monarch. As his faithful Sagredo (who was later to become a character in his *Dialogue on the Great World Systems*) wrote with the wisdom of a Venetian aristocrat: "Where will you find the same liberty as here in Venetian territory, where a contract makes you the master of those who command? . . . If not ruined, you may be harried by the surging billows of court life and by the raging winds of envy. . . . Also, your being in a place where the authority of the friends of Berlinzone,[4] from what I am told, stands high gives me great cause for worry."

But the die had been cast. In June, 1610, Galileo resigned his position in Padua, and by September he was in Florence, where he took up his new post.

Truly, he was not overmuch concerned with the dangers of Jesuit power, spanning the continents over his head in vast political machinations; for he himself had never been interested in the jurisdiction of princes, and he did not want to share the quarrel of the Venetian state against the Holy See. On his own account, he knew the Jesuits as modern-minded humanists, friends of science and discovery. Those he feared were the professors.

The "immense design" was indeed one of the main reasons which urged him to his fateful emigration. What he thought, and could not say for various reasons, was that, if he was to challenge the universities with decisive pronouncements, it was better to do so as

---

4. "Messer Rocco Berlinzone" was a nickname for the Jesuits. The Society had been expelled from Venetian territory for political intrigue in 1606 by decree of the Senate. They had been previously banished from France in 1594 but were allowed to return by Henry IV. They were expelled both from France and from Spain in 1767 and finally suppressed by Pope Clement XIV in 1776. That suppression was revoked only in 1814.

"a patrician of Florence, chief philosopher and mathematician to His Most Serene Highness," a friend and protégé of the monarch to whom he had dedicated the satellites of Jupiter, than as a penurious lecturer harried by a faculty council which might decide that the subject of his teaching must remain unchanged in the program.

The project intimated in the *Starry Message* had been slowly changing shape in his mind. The reaction to the telescope, among the learned and semilearned, had been discouraging. He had felt a solid front building against him, from his alma mater of Pisa to Bologna and Padua. The man who should have helped him most, Magini, the professor of astronomy in Bologna, had cast aside the mask of friendship and agitated against him among the bookish Aristotelians. If help had not come from outside, he would have found himself in serious difficulties, his new planets "extirpated from the sky," as Magini had promised. "My dear Kepler," Galileo wrote to the man who had always upheld the cause, "what would you say of the learned here, who, replete with the pertinacity of the asp, have steadfastly refused to cast a glance through the telescope? What shall we make of all this? Shall we laugh, or shall we cry?"

Even before the Jesuit astronomers and more than they, it was public opinion which had helped him. His own printers in Padua had subscribed for an ode to him; writers celebrated the telescope in tracts and in verse both Latin and vernacular, elegiac, pindaric, playful, epigrammatic; in language courtly, precious, and popular; in odes, blank verse, sonnets, octaves, and terza rima. The new discoveries were argued about at princely dinner tables and by the people on the steps of the cathedral. They were frescoed by Cigoli in the very cupola of Santa Maria Maggiore in Rome. The leading poets of the day, Marino and Chiabrera, brought their contributions. From England came news that the telescope had invaded philosophy and the metaphysical lyric.[5] "And who," wrote a pro-

---

5. Cf. Leonardo Olschki, *Geschichte d. neusprachlichen wissenschaftlichen Litteratur,* Vol. III: *Galilei und seine Zeit* (1927). On the effect in English circles see M. H. Nicholson, "The Telescope and Imagination," *Modern Philology,* 1935, and *Studies in Philology* (1935); and F. Johnson, *Astronomical Thought in Renaissance England* (1937).

fessor of philosophy, La Galla, as a prelude to his own underhanded disparagement, "who, even plunged in deepest sleep, would not be awakened by the rumor of this new miracle, which has spread throughout his world?" This was support from new quarters, such as Copernicus had never had. Even from this point of view, the Court was a much better center of operations.

The "Medicean stars" had been cleverly placed under the protection of the Grand Duke, for, once the House of Medici had accepted the dedication, it became mandatory for them to exist; and they were indeed the strategic key point of the operation. Anyone looking at Jupiter through a telescope saw right there, in the visual field, a solar system demonstrated on a small scale.

The face of the Moon seen through the telescope was perhaps more impressive, but one had to follow a train of thought to see what it implied; the valleys, peaks, and ridges like to those of the Earth seen on a celestial body showed that there is no basic difference in physical constitution; and with this the whole official distinction between celestial and terrestrial was obliterated—to anyone who cared to think.

Then, close on each other, the telescope had brought two new decisive discoveries: the phases of Venus and the "companions" of Saturn. Galileo had written to Giuliano de' Medici, the Florentine ambassador in Prague, in 1610: "I am anxiously waiting for what il Sig. Keplero may have to say about the new marvels. . . . He and the rest of the school of Copernicus have good reason for boasting that they have shown themselves excellent philosophers; however much it has been their lot, and may be hereafter, to be regarded by the philosophers of our times who philosophize on paper, with an universal agreement, as men of no intellect and little better than absolute fools."

The ambassador duly forwarded the request to Kepler ("Il Sig. Gleppero," as he called him), and the reaction came back prompt and vivid. "My dear Galileo," wrote Kepler, "I must tell you what occurred the other day. My friend the Baron Wakher von Wachenfels drove up to my door and started shouting excitedly from his carriage: 'Is it true? Is it really true that he has found stars moving around stars?' I told him that it was indeed so, and only then did he step into the house." Kepler left it prudently unsaid that his good friend Wakher was hoping for a proof of Bruno's intimations of infinity and of the plurality of the worlds, for not only were those ideas dangerous but he, Kepler, did not incline to them. But there was enough in the discoveries, notwithstanding his own reserves about the untested new instrument, to call forth his characteristic enthusiasm: "What now, dear reader, shall we make out of our telescope? Shall we make it a Mercury's magic-wand with which to cross the liquid ether, and, like Lucian, lead a colony to the uninhabited evening star? Or shall we make it Cupid's arrow, which, entering by our eyes, has pierced our inmost mind and fired us with a love of Venus?"

But vested learning, unimpressed by the new discoveries, went on considering the Copernicans as "men of no intellect." In fact, rancor and disdain of the doctors could only be increased by the "unfair" easy successes of their opponents in society. This is what Galileo had foreseen all along. As early as 1597, thirteen years before, he had written to Kepler: "Like you, I accepted the Copernican position several years ago and discovered from thence the causes of many natural effects which are doubtless inexplicable by the current theories. I have written up many reasons and refutations on the subject, but I have not dared until now to bring them into the open, being warned by the fortunes of Copernicus himself, our master, who procured for himself immortal fame among a few but stepped down among the great crowd (for this is how foolish people are numbered), only to be derided and dishonored. I would dare publish my thoughts if there were many like you; but, since there are not, I shall forbear."

The discoveries of the telescope, Galileo had thought for a while in 1610, would change all this by providing irrefutable proof to any man in good faith. Perhaps the time had come. . . . But a few months were enough to undeceive him. Certain doctors, who at least had the courage of their convictions, did actually and steadfastly refuse to look through the telescope, as has been recounted many times. Some did look and professed to see nothing; most of them, however, gave it the silent treatment or said that they had never gotten around to looking through it but that they knew already that it would show nothing of philosophical value. One maintained that it was impossible that the ancients should not have had such instruments, since they had excelled in everything, and that their silence on the subject implied an unfavorable judgment of their performance. Another affirmed right away, although he had not yet seen a telescope, that the invention was taken from Aristotle. "Having his works brought, he turned to the place where the philosopher gives the reason why, from the bottom of a very deep well, one may see the stars in heaven at noonday. . . . 'See here,' says he, 'the well, which represents the tube, see here the gross vapours, from whence is taken the invention of the crystals, and see here lastly the sight fortified by the passage of rays through a diaphanous but more dense and obscure medium.' "[6] But surely, said still another, this did not mean that Aristotle approved of such devices, for it could be shown from the text of the philosopher that his conclusions were derived from unaided sight and that therefore instruments could be of no use for the study of heavenly things; but that if, on the other hand, there really happened to be discovered something new in the heavens, it too could be figured out of the text of Aristotle with only the use of a little ingenuity. Galileo's comments rose to heights of scorn:

"O most profound Doctor, this! that can command me; for he will not be led around by Aristotle, but will lead him by the nose and make him speak as he pleases! See how important it is to learn to seize an opportunity. Nor is it seasonable to have to do with Hercules while he is enraged and beside himself but when he is telling merry tales among the Maeonian damosels. Ah, unheard-of sordidness of servile minds! to make themselves willing slaves, to receive as inviolable decrees, to engage themselves to seem satisfied and convinced by arguments of such efficacy and so manifestly conclusive that they themselves cannot resolve whether they were written to that purpose or serve to prove the assumption in hand!

---

6. This and the following quotation are from the *Dialogue on the Great World Systems* (English trans.; Chicago: University of Chicago Press, 1953 [henceforth cited simply as "*Dialogue*"]), pp. 122 and 125; but they belong to sections which were written long before 1630, probably at the time of the polemic with Magini. We know, besides, that such sarcastic remarks were frequently uttered by Galileo from the start of his polemic with the schools.

. . . What is this but to make an oracle of a wooden image and to run to that for answers, to fear it, to reverence and adore it?"

Such lamentable intellectual contortions were a proof indeed that his enemies were ready to go to any lengths; and out of that grew clear and present danger, for Galileo soon realized that the learned coalition, embittered by the feats of this slight "optical reed" which threatened to undo whole libraries of ponderous folios, patrimonies of vested intellectual interests—and the very art of academic disputation which brought them their stipends—was ready to hurl Holy Scripture itself at him. This was, in the academic custom of the time, a distinctly unfair means of attack: not only because it brought about the intervention of ecclesiastical authority in philosophical disputes but also because it gave the rowdies among the monks another pretext to inflame the populace against learning. But, like many a politician before and since, these men preferred to aggravate the incoherence of public opinion in order to dissimulate their own.

II

A young religious fanatic, Francesco Sizi, was prompted to fire the opening gun[7]—a popgun at best—with his *Dianoia astronomica* (1610). The argument, apart from some curious explanations about lenses, is not very different from that of Dr. Slop: "Why, Sir, are there not seven cardinal virtues?—seven mortal sins?—seven golden candlesticks in Moses?—seven heavens?—'Tis more than I know, replied my uncle Toby.—Are there not seven wonders of the world?—seven days of the creation?—seven plagues?" And also, added Sizi—and this was taken from Tycho's ideas—seven metals in al-

7. We say "prompted," because Magini was behind it (see the letter of Sertini, August 7, 1610 [Ed. Naz., X, 411]). Magini had also encouraged Martin Horky's hate-mad pamphlet, which backfired on its author. Since Father Müller (Adolf Müller, S.J., *Galilei und die Katholische Kirche* [1910]) chose to quote its personal remarks, it might be well to give an idea of this kind of polemic, leaving it in Latin as Gibbon does with his most impolite quotes: Galileo, says Horky, was unpopular in Bologna "quia capilli decidunt, tota cutis et cuticula flore Gallico scatet, cranium laesum, in cerebro delirium, optici nervi, quia nimis curiose et pompose scrupula circa Jovem observavit, rupti. . . ."

chemical theory? Therefore, there can be no more than seven planets in heaven, and the new ones revealed by the lenses of the "perspicil"[8] are an optical illusion. Sizi's pamphlet is clearly inspired by the cabalistic theories of Pico della Mirandola and is much more excusable in its mystical passion than Lodovico delle Colombe's *Contro il moto della terra,* circulated soon after; for Colombe's academic arrogance is manifest in his Aristotelian arguments, which he combines with a lot of pretentious geometrical nonsense; and yet he, who claims to be speaking in the name of natural reason, does not refrain from quoting a whole lot of scriptural passages which put the Copernicans in a difficult position for arguing back. Father Benedetto Castelli, a monk of Montecassino, Galileo's favorite disciple, had written that, if Venus could be shown to have phases, it would convince everybody. Now the phases had been discovered, and this was the result. "In order to convince those obdurate men," Galileo wrote back to Castelli, "who are out for the vain approval of the stupid vulgar, it would not be enough even if the stars came down on earth to bring witness about themselves. Let us be concerned only with gaining knowledge for ourselves, and let us find therein our consolation."

But such beautiful ivory-tower attitudes could hardly last longer than a melancholy afternoon. It was not in Galileo's nature to retreat into solitude. Now that certainty had been reached, the motives for silence that he had explained to Kepler no longer were valid. In fact, Kepler's impassioned reply, those many years back, must have been strongly present to his mind:

> I could only have wished that you, who have so profound an insight, would choose another way. You advise us, by your personal example, and in discreetly veiled fashion, to retreat before the general ignorance and not to expose ourselves or heedlessly to oppose the violent attacks of the mob of scholars (and in this you follow Plato and Pythagoras, our true preceptors). But after a tremendous task has been begun in our time, first by Copernicus and then by many very learned mathe-

---

8. The telescope had been called *occhiale* by Galileo, and in Latin it became *perspicillum, arundo optica,* etc. The Greek name of *telescope* was suggested later by Demisiano, a member of the Lyncean Academy (cf. Rosen, "The Naming of the Telescope," *Isis,* 1947).

maticians, and when the assertion that the Earth moves can no longer be considered something new, would it not be much better to pull the wagon to its goal by our joint efforts, now that we have got it under way, and gradually, with powerful voices, to shout down the common herd, which really does not weigh the arguments very carefully? Thus perhaps by cleverness we may bring it to a knowledge of the truth. With your arguments you would at the same time help your comrades who endure so many unjust judgments, for they would obtain either comfort from your agreement or protection from your influential position. It is not only your Italians who cannot believe that they move if they do not feel it, but we in Germany also do not by any means endear ourselves with this idea. Yet there are ways by which we protect ourselves against these difficulties. . . .

Be of good cheer, Galileo, and come out publicly. If I judge correctly, there are only a few of the distinguished mathematicians of Europe who would part company with us, so great is the power of truth. If Italy seems less a favorable place for your publication, and if you look for difficulties there, perhaps Germany will allow us this freedom.

This, Galileo decided, was exactly what he was going to do—and from Florence. The time had come when he could build up a tidal wave of opinion and sweep the new ideas into acceptance. But, for that, he must by-pass the universities and address himself in the vernacular to the intelligent public at large. This involved no doubt a sacrifice of the international value of Latin, but Galileo did not care to mark himself as an exclusive member of the light-shy and scattered republic of scholars; he had written enough satirical rhymes in his time against the nervous blinking doctor, lost in the public thoroughfare, entangled in his robe, who makes for the safety of his study like a frightened cat for a hole.[9] He felt right at ease in the street, in the square, and at the dining table, and he knew he could handle Italian better than most.

He states his reasons straightforwardly in a letter to Paolo Gualdo of May, 1612:

I notice that young men go to the universities in order to become doctors or philosophers or anything so long as it is a title and that many

---

9. Galileo's poetry, like Maxwell's and Minkowski's, is almost nowhere to be found in print, although the rhymes of the latter two are part of the physicists' secret lore. We think we ought to reproduce here, for

go in for those professions who are utterly unfit for them, while others who would be very competent are prevented by business or their daily cares which keep them away from letters. Now these people, while provided with a good intelligence, yet, because they cannot understand what is written in *baos* [a word coined by the comic playwright Ruzzante to indicate the learned language], retain through life the idea that those big folios contain matters beyond their capacity which will forever remain closed to them; whereas I want them to realize that nature, as she has given them eyes to see her works, has given them a brain apt to grasp and understand them.

We are reminded of Copernicus in his dedication. There are many, he had told the Pope seventy years before, who despise science unless it pays; there are others who, although they have taken up the study of philosophy, are worse than useless in it because of their stupidity and behave like drones among the bees. There is still another kind of chatterers, he adds, but to these he will give no thought whatever; it is those who would maliciously and rashly use passages of Scripture to contradict him. This kind of opposition he considers negligible. Did not Lactantius, "a great ecclesiastical writer but a poor mathematician, say childish things about the shape of the Earth, deriding those who had discovered it to be a sphere?"

Like Galileo, Copernicus had foreseen resistance not at all from

---

those who can read Italian, this portrayal of the doctor in the Bernesque manner:

Tu non lo vedi andar se non pe' chiassi
Per la vergogna, o ver lungo le mura,
E in simili altri luoghi da papassi.
E par ch' ei fugga la mala ventura;
Volgesi or da man manca or da man destra
Come un che del bargello abbia paura.
Pare una gatta in una via maestra
Che sbalordita fugga le persone
Quando è caduta giù dalla finestra,
Che se ne corre via carpon carpone
Tanto che la s'imbuchi e si difenda,
Perchè le spiace la conversazione....

Perchè la toga non ti lascia andare,
Ti s'attraversa t'impaccia t'intrica,
Ch' è uno stento a poter camminare:
E però non par ch' ella si disdica
A quei che fanno le lor cose adagio
E non han troppo a grado la fatica.
Anzi han per voto lo star sempre in agio,
Come a dir frati o qualche prete grasso,
Nemici capital d'ogni disagio.

the Church authorities but from vested academic interests. Their common judgment corresponds to the decline of the traditional universities in that era of transition. But from here on the two men diverge. The delicate and retiring soul of Copernicus wanted his subject to be kept among scientific initiates, and he wished that the Pythagorean privacy of research could be restored. "Mathematics are for mathematicians," he reminded gravely, and no one should apply himself to these studies who has not purified his soul. But, then, his theory did appeal only to the abstract intellect. As Galileo says admiringly: "Not being able to solve a number of grave difficulties, yet notwithstanding by other significant occurrences he was induced to confide so much in what reason dictated to him as to affirm confidently that the structure of the universe could have no other figure than that which he designed himself." But, he goes on, "since it has pleased God in our age to vouchsafe to human ingenuity the admirable invention of perfecting our sight by multiplying it as much as forty times," any good mind now can grasp the new truth without the need for Copernicus' daring genius.

Was this Galileo's appeal to the common people, as has been so often said? Hardly. He no more believed that the masses as such were capable of independent judgment than Voltaire was to do, or Samuel Johnson, for that matter. This ought to be made clear, since it has been more than once misrepresented. He had himself explained to Kepler how unwise it had been for Copernicus to be persuaded to step down among the multitude, "for so indeed are foolish people numbered," only to be derided and dishonored. He naturally believed, like Machiavelli, that nostalgic republican, that few are those who can think and that the rest are sheep. Such, too, had been the judgment of their common forebears who had run the free cities of Tuscany; and, like them, he believed that the "vulgar" are much more easily swayed by superstition and violent emotions than by reasonable argument. He knew only too well that the real manipulators of those passions were the rabble-rousing preachers and demagogues, who could turn magic words of fright or authority "into clubs wherewith to crush the endeavors of science." But he also believed, quite classically, that in all walks of life, from the highest to the lowest, there arise men who can think by themselves and who are the natural elite. The last centuries had proved how freely and powerfully such men could shape civilization; it was to them that he was making his appeal, as the "open ruling class," and it was bound to antagonize the interlocking caste interest of the custodians of wisdom.

Whether he realized it or not, he had there on its way a movement bound to cause violent reaction in the measure in which it shook the old edifice to its foundations. It is still maintained in our day[10] that Galileo's fatal mistake lay in his rash indiscretion, his insistence on throwing open to the common people, by writing in the vernacular, a question which was far from being settled and could only, in that form, give scandal to the pious, whereas the proper approach would have been to write elaborate tomes in Latin and then patiently wait for the appraisal of the scholars and theologians. This disingenuous argument has long ago been pinned down in a little popular rhyme: "Cet animal est très méchant, quand on l'attaque, il se défend." The learned apologists seem to forget that their late learned colleagues of the universities had quickly appraised the new theories and decided to make short work of them. Not only that, but, fearing their own power might not be enough, they enlisted, as we shall see, the aid of a few ecclesiastics hardly deserving of the title of theologians in order to create the decisive scandal which would result in a ban. Those particular gentlemen were perfectly willing to deliver their sermons in Italian, or, rather, let us say, in a vernacular as close to Italian as the language of the Hearst press is to English.

Thus, it was not at all a question of the tranquillity of the masses. It was well understood on all sides that Galileo was not writing for the masses. He was writing in literary style upon philosophical subjects for the open ruling class, which included prelates, princes, gentlemen, and men of business; and this could not but threaten the caste privileges of the average literati. Hence he was made out to be, like Socrates, a "poisoner of the people." Terms were coined rapidly to designate his kind: "free mind," "proud curiosity," "*esprit fort*," "lovers of novelties," "those Florentine minds which are too subtle and curious," in order to cast suspicion on such activities as could not lawfully be impeached. The strange paradox

---

10. See, e.g., Müller, *op. cit.*, and the *Catholic Encyclopedia* (New York: Appleton, 1910), art. "Galileo."

of the drama is that those frightened clerics were dealing at last with what they had tried in vain to shape through the late Middle Ages, the orthodox natural philosopher. In him the junction *had* been effected between science and humanism. In Galileo's thinking there is nowhere to be detected the cold sneer of Valla, or the impenetrable and disdainful aloofness of Leonardo, or the dodge of the "double truth" so freely used by Pomponazzi and the Averroists, or the perilous fantasies of Pico or Campanella. He wants to act as a consultant of the theologians in natural philosophy and help them understand correctly the new discoveries. The simple fact is that these were much too upsetting for unprepared minds, even for such minds as John Donne's.

III

It must be admitted that Galileo the man corresponded as little to the clichés of his epoch concerning the Philosopher as he would to those of our time concerning the Scientist.

"He who gazes highest," he will say without false modesty, "is of highest quality; and the turning to the great volume of Nature, which is the proper object of philosophy, is the way to make one look high; in which book, although whatsoever we read, as being the work of Almighty God, is most proportionate: yet notwithstanding, that is more absolute and noble wherein most greatly is revealed his art and skill. The constitution of the universe, among all things of Nature that fall within human comprehension, may, in my opinion, be set in first place; for as in regard of universal extent it excels all others, it ought as the rule and standard of the rest to go before them in nobility." These are lofty words, worthy of a Cambridge Platonist. But the marking of "the great volume of Nature" as the proper object of all philosophy will tell us that here is no contemplative temperament, although in his work the rigor and detachment of thought remain undeviating, free of the facile enthusiasms and the turgid fancies of his contemporaries.

At a time when force of style was held to be in conceits, the Galilean style strikes an independent note which goes back to the Machiavellis and Albertis and the master-craftsmen of his own Florentine past. His thought has the same unconcerned, secure, and apparently effortless *démarche* of the ordering mind amid unfolding realities. In the perpetual dialogue that is his life, his need is for equals, and he is willing to admit that company is all: "It is a great sweetness," he says, "to go wandering and discoursing together amid truths."

The "togetherness" implied in these words is a deeply social realization, away from caste and rank—and also from the prestige of the wizard in technique—even such a one as Socrates had been twenty centuries earlier; it is the free togetherness of thinking men going through unreckoned time toward an ultimate clarification. "Man's intellect," Bovillus had said, "achieves itself in time; it goes from change to change until it has become all things." This was the Platonic hint, understandable to all. Here it is firmly turned from romantic identification to the development of a clear operating abstraction.

For if it could be abstract, Galileo's thought never became otherworldly. He followed with the same keen interest the elegant turning of verse, the knowledgeable tending of a vineyard, or the experienced handling of mechanical problems in the Venice arsenal. "Among those," he wrote, "who have trained themselves over the years to solve the most difficult problems of their craft, there are bound to be some of comprehensive knowledge and very strong intelligence." It was among such men, both high and low, that he would find congenial company; a joyous convivial temperament with all the passions of the amateur and the gourmet, he would plunge with equal zest into a literary argument, a difficult legal case, a well-appointed dinner party, a new "natural effect," or a good wench. Both in work and in pleasure, he drove his vigorous frame to the limits of endurance.

There was still too much Renaissance in the air to have people condemn him for his lack of Puritanism. What the learned class reproached him with were rather his virtues: his unconstrained and direct approach to intellectual problems, his discarding the erudite polysyllabic vestment of thought that was so conveniently used by others to cloak their lack of originality. Typically enough, he never thought up the present Greek names for his instruments. The telescope he named *occhiale*, "eyeglass"; the microscope, *occhialino;* the hydrostatic balance, *bilancetta*, "little balance." In his very indulgences he stood for the uncomplicated and genuine as much as he did in his scientific style. His own gentle and candid Benedetto Castelli, who led throughout uncomplainingly the penurious existence of a miserably underpaid and underfed monk, knew well how to share with his master the simple but epicurean delights of good wine, good cheese, and good figs; their scientific correspondence is interlaced with fanciful excursions and glad exclamations about the very special barrels and parcels that they send in gift to each other.

It becomes rather easy to understand why Galileo should have found his warmest partisans among writers, artists, and enlightened amateurs, while he had most of the professional scholars aligned against him. The latter he could only drive to obloquy by his bantering tone and the light irony of his polemic, whereas the former found in him a protector of the open mind and the "wise ignorance." Typical of them was Ludovico Cigoli, the painter, who had become his unofficial representative in Rome, a man who dearly loved a good fight. Thus, he wrote in 1611 that Kepler's *Dioptrics* had reached the city and was proving a valuable ally: "This is going to discomfit further all the satraps and stuffed robes of learning. . . . I love to see them stuck, silent with popping eyes, that if I had to portray the figure of ignorance I would not draw it otherwise. . . . Kepler should be in all the bookshops, and I wish you would come to his help with your works, so *they* may burst, and that your writings should be around to hound them even in the stalls of the marketplace [*su per le pancaccie*]." Another time, after the *Letters on the Solar Spots,* he writes: "Try to let the booksellers have it freely; it would make the Pigeon League[11] die with rage if they could not look at a stall without finding them. . . . By the way, I have an idea for an emblem those pedants could put on their shingle: A fireplace with a stuffed flue, and the smoke curling back to fill the house in which are assembled people to whom dark comes before evening."[12]

11. The "Pigeon League" was the Peripatetic coalition headed by Lodovico delle Colombe, of which more later. Since *colombe* means "doves," Galileo's friends often called Colombe "the pigeon."

12. A line which had become a familiar proverb: "Gente a cui si fa notte innanzi sera."

Cigoli's scorn might be thought to be that of the unlettered man toward scholarship, but, as a successful and respected painter, Cigoli did not have to contend with any feelings of inferiority; and his judgment is as independently founded as that of a true Renaissance artist. As he watches with attention and concern the attitude of Father Clavius, the Jesuit astronomical authority, he reports to Galileo that Clavius cannot reconcile himself to the idea that there can be real mountains in the Moon and is trying to explain what is observed by certain differences of density inside the polished and pellucid body of the satellite: "He really seems to believe this kind of explanation, and I find no excuse for him except that a mathematician, however great, without the help of a good drawing, is not only half a mathematician, but also a man without eyes."[13]

Leonardo might have spoken thus concerning the knowledge of nature. The man who knows how to see is also the man who can understand the use of the new instruments. It is the Renaissance mind with its irrepressible vitality which is carrying on the fight against Scholasticism; it is only such temperaments (and they are found in the Church as well as among the laity) who could feel cheerfully at ease in the shimmering world of new facts, new hints, "intelligence" brought from afar.

It was not left for Galileo to choose. From 1611 on, his literary activity takes the form of tracts, pamphlets, letters, dialogues, and comments. From the systematic treatise it veers off into *littérature d'occasion*, stylistic elegance, rhetorical ingenuity, and indefatigable oral persuasion. Against the unnatural coalition of his opponents, whom he considered a grubby lot, he turned, as Copernicus had done, to the leaders of the social and spiritual order.[14]

---

13. Letter to Galileo, August 11, 1611. The theory went on being propounded for many years, and Galileo still had to cope with it in his *Dialogue*, pp. 96 ff.

14. Copernicus' work had been announced before its publication, in 1533, by Johannes Widmanstetter to Pope Clement VII, who had approved of the ideas. It had been sponsored by Cardinal Schönberg, then president of the Commission on the Calendar; and Tiedemann Giese, the bishop of Kulm, assisted its publication.

The first thing, of course, was to secure an indorsement of his discoveries from the Jesuit astronomers in Rome, who were the experts of the Vatican in such matters. This would put an end to the sly attempts of his academic enemies to drag the controversy onto the ground of religious taboos. He did not expect, surely, the Roman astronomers to come over bag and baggage to the new theories. That was not their way. But he trusted them, once they had the facts, to draw the consequences on their own and to clear the ground quietly for any coming changes.

Hence he did not tarry in Florence. He had barely settled down when, with the end of the winter season of 1611, he was again on his way to Rome.

Things went as well as he had anticipated. Soon he was writing to Filippo Salviati, the friend who was later to become the chief character in his *Dialogue:* "I have been received and feted by many illustrious cardinals, prelates, and princes of this city, who wanted to see the things I have observed and were much pleased, as I was too on my part in viewing the marvels of their statuary, paintings, frescoed rooms, palaces, gardens, etc." Monsignor Piero Dini writes to Cosimo Sassetti: "He is converting unbelievers one after another; for there are still a few capons who, that they may not know about the satellites of Jupiter, refuse even to look; and if I meet any of them, I want to hear what he has to say. The Lord Cardinal Bellarmine asked the Jesuits for an opinion on Galileo, and the learned Fathers sent the most favorable letter you could think of, and they are great friends of his; in this Order there are very great men, and the most outstanding are here." The Pope himself had given audience to the astronomer and showed him benevolence. On the part of a Pontiff like Paul V, "so circumspect and reserved," writes a contemporary, "that he is held for somber," this was a signal recognition indeed.

The Jesuit astronomers, or at least Clavius and Grienberger, had been shaken in their strict Ptolemaic faith. It had been a difficult decision for old Father Clavius, the author of the Gregorian calendar reform and the undisputed leader of Jesuit astronomy, to yield to the new things in the skies. In the beginning he had laughed at them and said that this new-fangled instrument would have first to put them there in order to see them; but, after looking through

Galileo's best telescope, he had surrendered with good grace. This alone was worth the trip to Rome. But there was another important gain: Galileo was made a member of the new Accadèmia dei Lincei (the "Lynceans," or "lynx-eyed")[15] and established a firm friendship with its founder, Prince Federico Cesi.

The Roman environment was not the most favorable to natural science. But the frail and earnest young nobleman, averse by temperament from the pursuits usual to men of his station, had used his wealth and influence to gather around him some friends interested in the new fields of learning. His own taste went toward botany, and his life's work was to be dedicated to the Central American flora; but what united these men of very disparate interests, and as yet without a productive method of work, was the same urge which caused the rise of such groups all over Europe: the sterility of the universities, the inadequacy of their curriculum, and the resistance of official scholarship to the new ideas. The common endeavor of the Lynceans was, as Cesi put it, "to fight Aristotelianism all the way," which of course implied looking somewhere else for a philosophical inspiration; and, of the respected systems, it could only be Plato's. Just while the "scientific-minded" Jesuits, their friends, were battening down the hatches and tying up their theory to the most guaranteed commonplaces of Peripatetic doctrine, some Lynceans revived a strain of romantic Renaissance Platonism which opened their imagination to intellectual adventure.

Thus we see rehearsed again the paradox of naturalists refusing to acknowledge the greatest naturalist of antiquity and turning for guidance to the prophet who had taught the flight from nature. But, then, we have seen the reasons for it already. Aristotle had been degraded by his epigones into a master of quibbles, and his system had been adopted by educators not so much for its capacity to organize information as for its capacity to dispose of it.

Notwithstanding his youth, Federico Cesi was and remained the natural leader of the Lyncean group. The Roman world respected him not only for his title but for his quiet and mature judgment.

---

15. The mythological reference is to Lynceus the Argonaut, noted in that earliest company of pioneers for his keenness of sight.

He became the spokesman of Galileo and was to be his adviser and support in the difficult period ahead.

Galileo was then absorbed in the "Atlas-like" undertaking of determining the periods of the satellites of Jupiter, which the Jesuits had tried in vain to work out, and hundreds of observations date from that year. But his main task he considered to be that of educating opinion, mainly through letters addressed to men in positions of influence. Therefore, he proceeded gradually, leaving the Copernican conception aside and touching only on those conclusions for which direct evidence was overwhelming, like the mountains of the Moon. Through this approach (which is also that used later in the First Day of the *Dialogue*), he could hope to dismantle the Aristotelian position without arguing about its main tenets; he could show that all the conventional talk about perfect globes and jewel-like celestial substances was a literary commonplace rather than a considered philosophical conclusion.[16]

Still, he had few illusions about the receptiveness of people even to these simple ideas. He was only hoping they would sink in very gradually. The very same ones who hailed his discoveries balked at considering their consequences; and, whenever he felt too confident in his logic, his friends were there to remind him. Thus Paolo Gualdo, whom he trusted, wrote him in May, 1612:

> As to this matter of the Earth turning round, I have found hitherto no philosopher or astrologer who is willing to subscribe to the opinion of Your Honor, and much less a theologian; be pleased therefore to consider carefully before you publish this opinion assertively, for many things can be uttered by way of disputation which it is not wise to affirm.

But, when he received this warning, Galileo had already made a new discovery which he felt ought to give pause even to the most obdurate. On observing the spots on the Sun, which had only recently been found, he showed that they belonged to the solar globe itself and were not dark bodies moving around it, as suggested by Father Scheiner. With this, the Sun's rotation was established—and

16. Letter to Gallanzoni, June 16; to Cigoli, October 1, 1611. Gallanzoni was the secretary of Cardinal Joyeuse, and the fourteen-page letter is obviously meant for the Cardinal himself and also for Bellarmine.

also its deviation from the established canons of perfection and immutability. "This novelty," he wrote to a friend, "may well be the funeral, or rather the last judgment, of pseudo-philosophy."

The *Letters on the Solar Spots*, published in 1613, after Galileo's return to Florence, and under the sponsorship of the Accademia dei Lincei, is Copernican throughout. It is the first open admission that the new theory is the only one for which the telescopic discoveries make sense.

Fortified by official recognition, he sees the road open ahead for the great change. In this meridian hour of his life he concludes triumphantly his third and final Solar Letter: "Saturn and Venus bring in marvelous manner their contribution to the harmony of the great Copernican system, whose complete discovery favorable winds assist, with such shining escort showing the way, that we need fear darkness and adverse storms no longer."

This was written on December 1, 1613. Three weeks earlier the clergy had launched its first open attack.

II

DOMINI CANES

A throwen Evangelist indeed, full of throward Divinitie: Surely, if there were no more than his unmannerly manner, it is enough to disgrace the whole matter thereof.

KING JAMES I, "APOLOGIE"

I

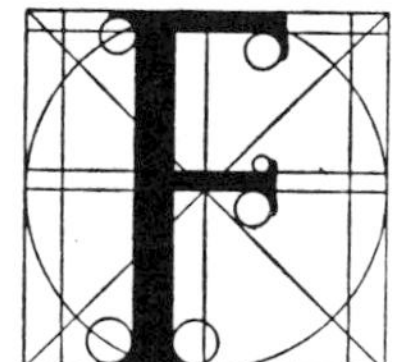

ATHER LORINI of the Dominicans, professor of ecclesiastical history in Florence, was the man who took the initiative. Preaching on All Souls' Day, 1613, he inveighed against the new theories in unbecoming terms. Hauled up for this breach of custom, he wrote a fumbling letter of apology: he had never mentioned science in his sermon, he asserted. "It was only later, in a discussion, and in order not to stand there like a log, that I said a couple of words to the effect that the doctrine of that Ipernicus, or whatever his name is, was against Holy Scripture."

So the monks were on the warpath after all; Cigoli had been right in warning, a year before, about their goings-on in Rome. But that was to be expected. Monks always agitated about something: incomes, privileges, books, jurisdiction, personal quarrels, or the resistance of some official to their everlasting claims. Galileo had taken the precaution of "checking signals" in the Vatican. Cardinal Conti, beseeched for guidance, had written him in July, 1612, that "the statements of Holy Scripture were against rather than for the Aristotelian principle of the unalterability of the heavens, but that the case was different with the Pythagorean doctrine of the Earth's revolution." Some kind of "progressive" motion was admissible, on the word of a learned doctor who had spoken of *imperceptibilis motus*, but a rotation did not seem to agree with Scripture unless it was assumed that it merely adopted the customary mode of expression. But, Conti added, that was a method of interpretation to be employed only in case of the greatest necessity; Didacus à Stunica's pro-Copernican suggestions had not been generally accepted.[1]

This meant, in sum, that the authorities were open to persuasion if someone produced an adequate "necessity." It was exactly what Galileo felt he could do in the next few years. He could ignore the monks as well as a certain hostile activity that he knew to be centered in the archbishopric of Florence. So long as he had the favor of the Roman Curia, the road was still open ahead.

There was one thing, however, that Galileo did not know. Cardinal Bellarmine himself, the chief theologian of the Church, was keeping an eye on him. He had heard much about the scientist in Rome; he had even looked through the telescope. All this had brought the Copernican issue to his attention. What the discoveries could mean was not clear to him, and he was not a man to form hasty judgments. But Bellarmine was no friend of "novelties" or of sensations that were not edifying. There was confusion enough in the world already. Sixteen years earlier it had been his grievous task to frame the decision which led Giordano Bruno to his death at the stake. Admittedly, there was little else that he could have done, for Bruno remained throughout, and to his last moment, an impenitent apostate from the Church. But this, he concluded, was what the "Pythagorean" exaltation could lead men into; and here now was the same Pythagorean astronomy cropping up again, albeit in more respectful garb. It was sure that Galileo had been making a sensation in Rome.

---

1. Didacus à Stunica (Diego de Zuñiga), a Spanish monk, had written a commentary on Job's passage: "He that hath suspended the Earth above the void." Galileo had also thought of this passage, as appears from his marginal comments to Colombe. The "learned doctor" of the Cardinal's letter is obviously Nicholas of Cusa.

One can see from the dates what took place in Bellarmine's mind. On April 24, 1611, he asked Father Clavius whether the discoveries were serious, and was answered that they were. A few days later he gave audience to Galileo and tried, during the exchange of the usual civilities and protestations, to form an opinion of the man. On May 17, as we know now from the secret archives, at a meeting of the Congregation of the Holy Office,[2] he introduced a small item on the agenda: "Let it be seen [*videatur*] whether in the proceedings against Doctor Cesare Cremonini there is a mention of Galileo, professor of philosophy and mathematics." That is all, and it led nowhere; Cremonini himself was never brought to trial. But in its very irrelevance the item is revealing. Cremonini had nothing to do with Galileo except that he quarreled with him. He was a hidebound Aristotelian, one of the few who had really refused to look through the telescope.[3] But Cremonini was a nuisance, and Galileo

2. The Congregations functioned as the equivalent of our Cabinet and Senate committees, but each of them also headed a department. When the Pope was not in the chair, they met at the residence of one or another member. The Congregation of the Holy Office was the most important, as it corresponded more or less to our National Security Council. Its members at the time were the Cardinals Bellarmine, Veralli, Centino detto d'Ascoli, Taberna (di S. Eusebio), Mellini, Gallamino (d'Aracoeli), Bonsi (di S. Clemente), and Sfondrati (di S. Cecilia), "by the mercy of God, cardinals of the Holy Roman Church, Inquisitors-General throughout the Christian Commonwealth against heretical pravity."

3. Cremonini stands in history books as the abstract figure of the pedant, but he was a vivid and colorful personality in his time. The successor of Francesco Zabarella, he had become the leading light of Paduan philosophy as a powerful and systematic teacher of the true Peripatetic doctrine, which, of course, involved a disbelief in the immortality of the individual soul. He had strongly defended the privileges of the university against the attempts of the Jesuits at gaining a foothold in teaching and was twice challenged by the Inquisition, which he disregarded from his position of immunity guaranteed by the Venetian state. Hence it was thought more politic not to press the case against him. His salary of two thousand florins was higher than anyone else's and twice what Galileo had been granted in recognition of his discoveries. He lived in state, with "many servants, two coaches and six horses." As to his personal attitude toward Galileo, it is best expressed

looked as though he might become another. This is known, in the language of the modern state, as spotting by Objective Characteristics. A few months later the Cardinal said confidentially to the Tuscan ambassador: "Whatever the respect we owe to the Grand Duke, if Galileo had stayed longer, it could not but have come to his being called to account."[4]

This, in his mind, had nothing to do with the scientific issue, toward which he always preserved what he felt to be an open attitude. But his position was so far from what we still fondly call our modern one that only the subsequent developments can make it clear. To Galileo himself, it was difficult to gauge and remained so to the last.

II

Galileo's friends were giving conflicting advice. Some were telling him to go on with his discoveries and renounce the cosmological controversy; others, that this was the time to come forward with convincing demonstrations and get the Jesuit experts on his side. True enough, old Father Clavius was wavering, in those last months of his life, in his Ptolemaic position;[5] and the others, Grienberger, van Maelcote, Lembo, ought not to have been hard to persuade. Father Campanella, the generous and ever bellicose con-

---

in a letter of Paolo Gualdo: "Having met him on the street, I told him: 'Mr. Galileo is exceedingly sorry that you wrote a whole great book about heaven while refusing to see his stars.' He replied: 'I don't believe that anyone but he saw them, and besides, that looking through glasses would make me dizzy. Enough, I don't want to hear any more about it. But what a pity that Mr. Galileo has gotten involved in these entertainment tricks, and has forsaken our company, and his safe haven of Padua. He may yet come to regret it.' "

4. "A qualche giustificatione de' casi suoi." This came out only four years later, in a letter by Guicciardini dated December 5, 1615. Galileo's letter to Gallanzoni, which had been shown to Bellarmine, had obviously made no impression at all.

5. It was Kepler who pointed out later that there was evidence of hesitation in Clavius' comments on Sacrobosco, written shortly before his death in 1612. This is confirmed by Father Kircher's admissions (see n. 6, p. 290). But the Jesuits had other lines of retreat, as will be shown on p. 37.

fusionist, wrote to him from his dungeon in Naples (those were happy times when one could keep up a philosophical correspondence from the prisons of the secret police): "All the philosophers of the world receive the law from your pen, for in truth it is impossible to philosophize without an assured system of the world as we expect it from you. . . . Arm yourself with perfect mathematics, leave for heaven's sake all other business, and think only of this one; for you do not know if you will be dead tomorrow."

This was what Galileo would have liked to do, but, as far as we can penetrate through his pretexts, he did not feel ready for a "showdown." The astronomical proofs were brilliant, but he knew better than anybody else that the Copernican hypothesis would remain what it had been for its inceptor—a formal diagram to be accepted on purely optical and kinematic grounds, without a natural philosophy in which to frame it. What Galileo needed was a Newton, and he did not have him; he had only Copernicus, an unconventional, imaginative, mystical mathematician. He had also Kepler, to be sure, "Caesar's astronomer" and a brave fighter, but a dangerous fantast and, as misfortune would have it, a Protestant as well. Against the physical principles of conventional cosmology, which were always brought out against him, he needed an equally solid set of principles—indeed, more solid—because he did not appeal to ordinary experience and common sense as his opponents did. He did not want to stand in the eyes of his enemies as one of "these mathematicians who come forward with claims to new natural theories while themselves devoid of all philosophy." That was why he had always insisted that he had spent more years in the study of philosophy than months in the study of mathematics.

It must be admitted that his opponents had a strong point: the theories of the astronomers had never made any sense physically, and this still applied to both camps. The ancient astronomers had had the good sense to present only abstract mathematical models (Figs. 1 and 2). This man Copernicus, they were being told now, took his ideas as physical truth. But, then, how did he account for the epicycles which still crowded his diagram, a full thirty-four of them?[6] He must have been thinking that, through some special grace,

6. For an explanation of the problem see chap. iii.

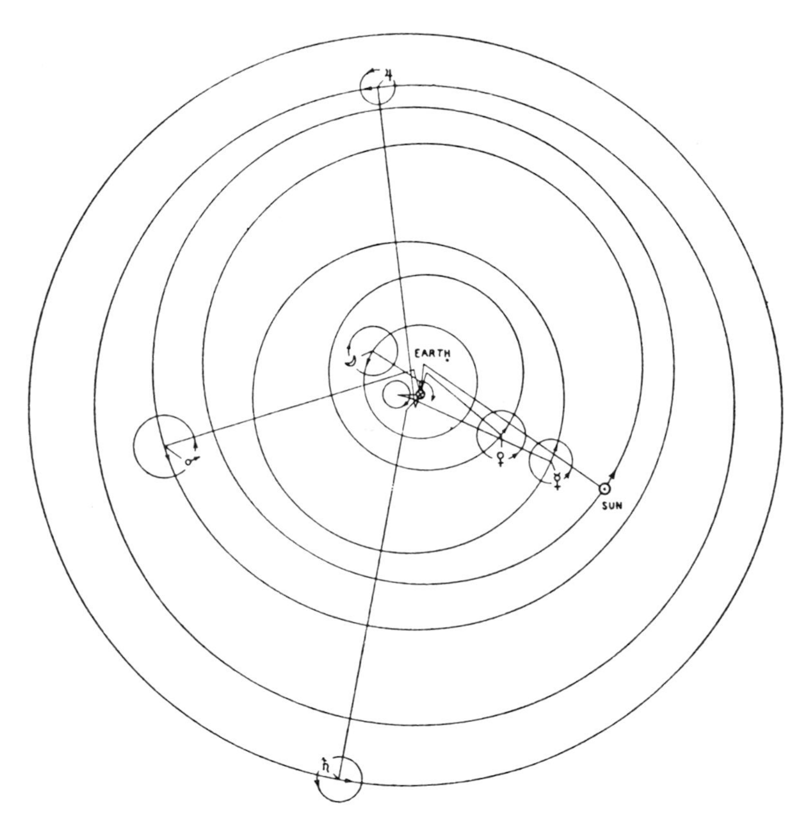

Fig. 1.—The Ptolemaic System

These drawings have been designed to point out how similar in complexity were the Ptolemaic and Copernican systems. Even a cursory glance convinces one that neither system is essentially simpler geometrically than its competitor. Drawings cannot be made accurate in radial dimensions, but special care has been taken properly to orient the centers of the planetary orbits relative to the zodiac. Thus, if one traces in the Ptolemaic diagram the radial line from the Sun to the point under "A" in "EARTH," the point which is the center of the Sun's orbit, it is seen to be between the centers ot rotation of Venus and Mars, precisely as Ptolemy's geocentric theory requires. The relative senses of rotation of the epicycles on their deferent circles and the planets on the epicycles are indicated by the arrows. The planetary distances remain arbitrary, which is not so in Copernicus.

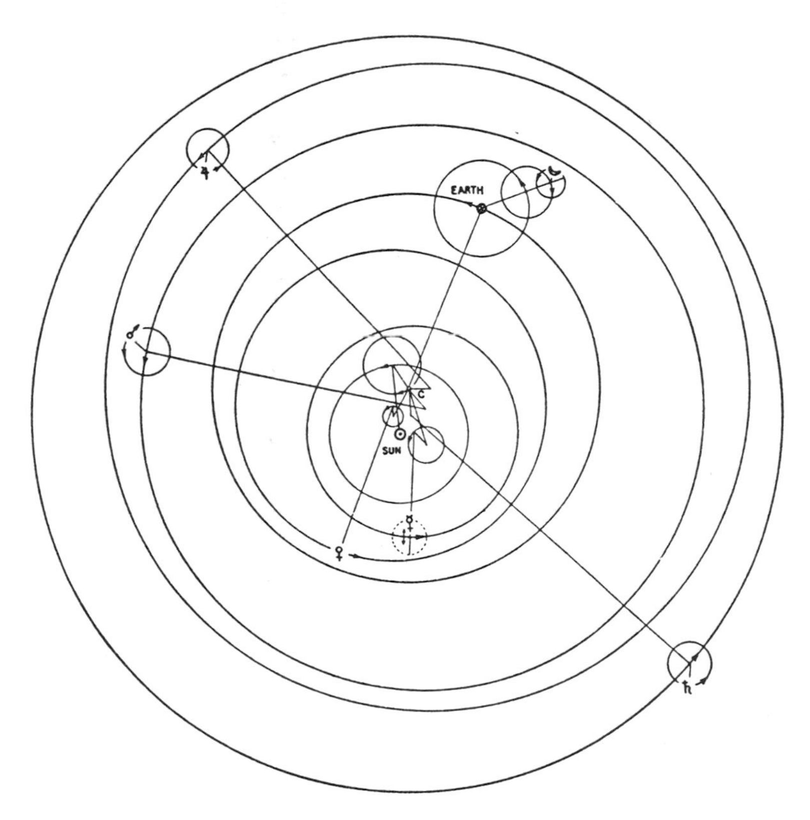

FIG. 2.—THE NEW SYSTEM AS CONCEIVED BY COPERNICUS

In the Copernican system the Sun appears in the center of the stage, but the actual momentary centers of rotation of the planets cluster around the momentary center *C* of the Earth's orbit. In this system Mercury was handled in a unique fashion, librating on the center of an epicycle instead of traveling on the epicycle. The planetary symbols are as follows:

☉	Sun	⊕	Earth
☿	Mercury	♂	Mars
♀	Venus	♃	Jupiter
☾	Moon	♄	Saturn

Drawings are by the courtesy of Dr. W. D. Stahlman (see also p. 68).

abstract circles move by themselves. In fact, he did. He had no better explanation than that. With the insouciance of genius, he had left it to his successors to fill in the gaps in his theory.

The Aristotelians—at least some intelligent ones, who disregarded their master's halfhearted attempt at a mechanism of spheres—could well claim that here was shown the soundness of Aristotle's general policy which eschewed such constructions. Always intent on tidying up the world, it was enough for them to demonstrate the immutable nature of heavenly substance and then assign to it figure and local motion; whereas in terrestrial substance, always in process, much more complex forms of motion and becoming occurred. They might have said of heaven as Pascal was to say later of physics: "One should say: 'It is done by figure and movement; but to say which, and to construct the mechanism, is pointless, for it is difficult and uncertain and laborious.' " The Aristotelians might have added: "and impossible." For the heavens are not to be reached, and what we can know of them is strictly limited. The philosopher should legislate about general principles and attributions in the universe and leave the astronomer to present a variety of abstract models (had not Tycho come out with a new one?) adequate for "saving the phenomena" without involving the philosopher in his impossible suppositions; in the same way as local motion on earth should be classified into a few types, such as natural and violent, and further details left "to the mechanician or other inferior artist." The heavens remain inaccessible, even with the telescope, and we know already far too much about tricky optical effects. Should we now subvert the vast and documented discourse of the schools, which allows us to account in orderly manner for nature and life and the soul itself—and fits in so handsomely with revealed Truth—to launch ourselves in a sea of paradoxes and unnatural conclusions, simply because a man has come forward with two lenses in a length of pipe?

The argument, as we have suggested, is not so empty as it looks. We may understand such a predicament better by referring to modern problems. Cosmology is, and is expected to remain, a conjectural science, for it ought to be safe to say that we shall never know anything final about the universe as a whole and that, in fact, as Galileo thought, the range of acknowledged ignorance will grow with the advance of science. Comte wanted to forbid such speculations no longer than a century ago. Supposing now that the ruling section of public opinion decided that such speculations are in some essential way dangerous for social stability, it is easy to see what would follow. In an unmetaphysical society like ours the universe is a matter of small concern, and economic orthodoxy has replaced the religious, but the response to an alert in that field is just as prompt or even more so.

To the above-mentioned reasons of high policy, Galileo knew that he could not yet oppose any adequate ones of his own. He did have a natural philosophy, too, which would provide most of the answers, but it was contained in his dynamics and was not yet sufficiently organized. (It was to be concluded later—too late to be of any help—in the *Discorsi* of 1638.) He knew he could eventually prove that motion in the heavens obeys the same laws as motion on earth, that those laws are mathematical, for the book of Nature is written in the form of equations and not in the pattern of a discourse made up of predicative sentences, where nouns represent substances and adjectives qualities. That book with seven seals, once deciphered, brought startling conclusions: there is no difference between heaven and earth; we are in heaven, and heaven is on earth. The pleasing "architectonic" disposition of substances makes way for the grandiose and mysterious unity of mathematical law, which starts from first principles unknown to us and leads toward conclusions unforeseeable; but we must follow it wherever it leads us, trusting that God and Nature know better than we do what is best.

Before Galileo could come forward in the open field with such a disturbing philosophy, he felt he needed an organized physics to support his contentions. The "immense project" became more and more immense. Perhaps it ought to be preceded, rather than followed, by the books *On Motion*. This is what we can infer of his thoughts, as he gave dilatory answers to his friends who urged him to come out with his *System of the World*.

III

For the present, he felt he had better go on with his semijournalistic activity, shaking his opponents' system at the weakest points, converting men of influence, creating a favorable climate of opinion.

In friendly discussion he knew he could be invincibly persuasive. He could skirt delicate points by choosing his terrain; he could surprise and carry away by bold admission. Thus to Prince Cesi, who had said that he would gladly favor the Copernican system if only it removed the excentrics and the epicycles, he replies: "We should not desire that Nature should adjust to that which seems to us best arranged and ordered, but we ought rather to adjust our intellect to her works, since they are certainly most perfect and admirable, and all other constructions would reveal themselves eventually as devoid of elegance, incongruous, and puerile. . . . If anyone wants to deny the epicycles, he must deny the paths of the satellites of Jupiter. . . . Excentrics exist, for what else is the path of Mars according to the best observations?"[7]

Thus he was trying to overcome his friend's doubts, hoping that he would not notice that the official epicycles were something entirely different, not, as with Jupiter, the paths of real satellites moving around a real planet, but mere geometric devices moving around imaginary centers—but, then, there were so many things of which he was certain without being able yet to prove them that a little illusionism appeared excusable.[8] As he put it, one does not pull down a perfectly good house just because the fireplace happens to smoke.

It should be added, too, that he had to confront some more dangerous illusionisms on the other side. The Jesuits, always polite, had shown a certain tendency to retreat out of reach; and it was unfortunately Tycho Brahe himself who had provided the easiest way out. They had their own reasons. We are apt to forget that anti-Aristotelianism had been for long a very confused movement indeed. Ramus, the opponent of the schools, had called in 1569 for

---

7. Letter to Cesi, June 30, 1612.

8. The Aristotelians were undoubtedly right on this point. The epicycles would not fit in with any system of natural philosophy, and it is one of the strangest mysteries of that history why Galileo should have refused the proffered help of Kepler with his theory of elliptical orbits. The excentricity of Mars is present in his thought, the ideas of Kepler are being discussed among his friends, but nothing happens (see pp. 169–70 and n. 10 to same).

an astronomy without theories based *ab initio* on observation. Tycho, then in his early twenties, could well reply that theories were necessary to give direction to observation. He eventually suggested a theory which saved most phenomena by having the planets revolve around the Sun, and the Sun in its turn around an unmoved Earth. It was another purely geometrical scheme which left untouched the foundation of official philosophy and the sayings of Scripture. This made Galileo's task all the more difficult, and it explains the bitterness that he later manifests against Tycho in the *Dialogue*. He refused to consider even for a moment the Tychonic variant as a "third system." To him it was a miserable red herring brought in at the last moment. But he could not prevent the Jesuits from thinking—or at least saying—that, if this geometrical device solved one half of the difficulties, a further device might possibly solve the remaining half. This was not a real excuse, but it could be very helpful to minds that did not know which way to turn. In his letter to Clavius of March 12, 1610, Galileo had carefully spelled out the reasons which made the Tychonic system hopelessly obsolete.[9] That system could be proved to withstand the telescope as little as did the Ptolemaic. But there is no persuading someone who chooses not to be persuaded.

Another welcome occasion to strike at an undefended flank soon offered itself. One hot day in August, 1612, Galileo was sitting at the Grand Duke's table with other learned gentlemen, and the talk came around, as it would, to the virtues of ice. A doctor explained that ice is heavier than water, being water condensed, and that it floats only due to its peculiar shape, just as needles or metal foils

---

9. Tycho's main astronomical reason (apart from his frivolous physical ones [see pp. 13 and 62]) had been that he had not been able to detect a stellar parallax of even a half-minute, which removed the stars to a distance of at least eight million semidiameters of the Earth; whereas the last circle of Saturn did not go beyond twelve thousand. This, in turn, given the *apparent* stellar diameters, would have made the stars each greater than the solar system. Moreover, Tycho had insisted that the planets shone by their own light, which made them different from the Earth. Now the telescope showed the apparent stellar diameters to have been due to irradiation, and it showed Venus to be dark where the Sun did not strike it.

will at times be supported on the water's surface. Galileo interposed some pointed remarks, and the controversy was on. It developed into a long polemic in which Aristotelian professors plunged with fury and at one meeting almost came to blows with some opponents. Cardinal Maffeo Barberini himself, on a visit, participated with delight and came out openly on Galileo's side. Out of the polemic, at the Grand Duke's urging, was born the *Discourse on Floating Bodies,* in which Galileo brought his fundamental contribution to hydrostatics on the Archimedean model. Acting as usual in the thick of events, he had not lost sight of his goal. The professors had been shown up as dimwits and retreated in a rage to write learned commentaries. Meanwhile, Galileo had dug the foundation for his physics a little deeper.

The "Galileisti" were growing in number too. He noticed that since his *Discourse* many gentlemen of Florence had taken up the study of mathematics, "for without it the mind lacks the wings to raise itself to the contemplation of Nature."[10] It was indeed difficult to resist the lure of the new discoveries. "O much-knowing perspicil," Kepler exclaimed, "more precious than any scepter! He who holds thee in his right hand is a true king, a world ruler. . . ."

There were some—there are even now—inclined to feel that the empire had been won by a freak of chance. It was not quite so. First of all, the construction of a working telescope involved advanced physical thinking. The mere discovery that two lenses brought things nearer had really been a freak of chance for an optician's boy. But the crude lenses that were used for eyeglasses could have showed nothing at all in the sky, and it was Galileo who had come upon the idea of a method whereby they could be ground correctly by checking them upon a star—and then had focused his instrument on Jupiter. Let us imagine the telescope in the hands of a Giambattista della Porta or some such known contemporary, and we shall understand how much its importance was a matter of the intellectual personality of its author. As Olschki rightly remarks:

"The domination that Galileo's thought exercised over all the branches of knowledge and application was not so much the result of his many-sidedness, as of his great capacity for the 'common

10. Ed. Naz., IV, 445.

touch,' and of his personal influence on the intellectual formation of generations which saw in him an incarnation of wisdom, a leader and master figure. They did so because in his achievements and thoughts they could recognize a concern of the whole of mankind, and not only the fruit of the learned efforts of a specialist. The reproaches of vainglory, self-importance and impatience, which are still raised against him today for leaving his study for the public scene, fall by the wayside if we consider him in his own world, and show themselves as petty judgments or hypocrisy."[11] We may add —as the results of an enmity that will not abate.

Galileo ought indeed to be considered, as we have tried to show, as the last great leader of the Renaissance; his appeal to the people continues Leonardo's struggle against the preconceptions of the learned and the "Halls of Vain Disputation." It was still the world of the Renaissance which was around him, with its curiosity and excitement, its vivid controversies, its violent involvement in high quarrels, its popular juries on art, and its interest in technology; it was the social surge of the new times that was providing him with its power.[12]

The whole system of the schools was in danger. This explains the sudden jelling of the opposition into a kind of mutual defense league, ready for anything. They realized that there was no time to lose in compromising their dangerous enemy by a *fait accompli.* The first step, they decided, was to hurt him at Court, where his strength lay, by arousing against him the strict piety of the Grand Duchess Dowager, Madama Cristina of Lorraine. In March, 1613, with a confessor and a Peripatetic professor, Boscaglia, working together in strange collusion, the occasion was brought about at a Court dinner in Pisa, at which Father Castelli was challenged by the Grand Duchess on the orthodoxy of the Copernican theory. Castelli, candid soul, rose to the bait and answered spiritedly, using his authority as a theologian. The Grand Duchess was appeased.

---

11. Leonardo Olschki, *Geschichte d. neusprachlichen wissenschaftlichen Litteratur,* Vol. III: *Galilei und seine Zeit* (1927).

12. "The learned are plagued by those eager for knowledge, just as the rich are by the poor who press at their door" (letter of Nozzolini, Ed. Naz., VI, 598).

But, as he discussed the incident with his master, Galileo realized that he owed it to his disciple, and to the Grand Duchess, to step forward and take the responsibility of a seriously considered statement which should protect their good names against these organized provocations. In the upright Benedictine soul of Castelli there was also the will, shared by Galileo, not to let a gang of blackmailers compromise the Church for their own convenience.

The "conspiracy" of which Galileo so often speaks is not imagined. It called itself a "League." There were several men in the outfield, engaged in more or less concerted action, like Boscaglia, Coresio, and D'Elci in Pisa, the astronomer Magini in Bologna, Grazia and the Archbishop in Florence, and a number of nameless Dominicans in Rome. But the aggressive leadership belonged to the Lorini-Caccini-Colombe triumvirate, of which more later. Of the tie-up between Colombe and Father Caccini we have positive proof in letters addressed by Matteo Caccini to his brother: "It was a silly thing [for Tommaso] to get himself embroiled in this business by these pigeons [*colombi*]."[13]

IV

Galileo, on the other hand, was too shrewd not to understand that his enemies were trying to draw him onto controversial ground. His reply in the form of a *Letter to Castelli* (December 13, 1613), to be circulated among their friends, was a model of restraint and dialectical skill.[14]

Galileo reminds his readers first that Scripture, although absolute and inviolable truth itself, has always been understood to speak figuratively at many points, as when it mentions the hand of God or

---

13. See pp. 104 and 114.

14. It reached Francis Bacon by way of Toby Matthews, who wrote from Brussels: "I presume to send you the copy of a letter, which Galileo, of whom I am sure you have heard, wrote to a monk of my acquaintance. . . . To an Attorney-General in the midst of a town, and such a one, as is employed in the weightiest affairs of the kingdom, it might seem unseasonable for me to interrupt you with matter of this nature. But I know well enough, etc."

the tent of heaven, and that it is our duty to understand it so that the two truths, that of God's Nature and that of God's Writ, never appear to be in conflict. Why, then, should Holy Writ be used to support the opinions of certain fallible philosophers against others, to the jeopardy of its authority? "For who would set a limit to the mind of man? Who would dare assert that we know all there is to be known? Therefore, it would be well not to burden the articles concerning salvation and the establishment of the Faith—against which there is no danger that valid contradiction ever may arise—with official interpretations beyond need; all the more so, when the request comes from people of whom it is permitted to doubt that they speak under heavenly inspiration, whereas we see most clearly that they are wholly devoid of that understanding which would be necessary, I will not say to refute, but first of all to grasp the demonstrations offered by science."

Scripture, he goes on, deals with natural matters in such a cursory and allusive way that it looks as though it wanted to remind us that its business is not about them but about the soul and that, as concerns Nature, it is willing to adjust its language to the simple minds of the people. And, indeed, adds Galileo with a brilliant dialectical turn, it is obvious that the word about Joshua stopping the Sun in Gibeon cannot have been meant literally if we take the official geocentric interpretation; for it is admitted, with Ptolemy, that the diurnal motion of the Sun as well as of the stars and planets depends on the *primum mobile*. Therefore, if the whole of the heavenly movements was not to be deranged, it must be understood that Johsua stopped the *primum mobile*. On the other hand, by adopting the Copernican theory, we might even understand the words literally; for, if we admit that their revolution is impressed on the planets by the Sun, which is in the center, we might conceive that, by stopping the Sun, Joshua stopped the whole solar system for three hours without disarranging the respective positions.

Needless to say, this is quick fencing rather than sound science. Faced with people who thought only dialectically, Galileo has to be something of a sophist, too, in order to gain attention. He attacks first by showing that the official Greek theory does not really fit the Bible story as believed; then he suggests that a more modern theory might possibly fit better. Since there is really none that does, he has to invent something. But the rather Keplerian idea adopted here of a magnetic rotational force emanating from the Sun denied his own theory of planetary motion as inertial, and, also, it did not in the least explain the daily rotation of the Earth. With all that, the suggestion is not at all on the dead level of casuistic bad faith current among his opponents. It is a brilliant intuition of unknown forces from which it was hoped that some day an explanation of the Holy Text would come, since an explanation there had to be, which to Galileo was axiomatic. It was not science, but neither was it bad fiction. It was faith in conciliation and hope in science.

V

Unfortunately, he provided exactly the opportunity that his enemies had been waiting for. They proclaimed everywhere that he had assailed the authority of Scripture and that he had tried to meddle in theological matters. Few had seen the letter; many came to think they knew what it said. The Bishop of Fiesole wanted to have Copernicus jailed and had to be informed that the good man had been dead for quite some time. Father Tommaso Caccini, a Dominican monk with several acquaintances in the "League," who had already been disciplined by the Archbishop of Bologna as a scandal-maker, saw an excellent occasion for fresh scandal. On December 20, 1614, he preached a sermon in Santa Maria Novella on the text, "Ye men of Galilee [*viri Galilaei*], why stand ye gazing up into heaven?" announcing that mathematics was of the Devil, that mathematicians should be banished from Christian states, and that these ideas about a moving Earth were very close to heresy, as Serrarius himself averred and many another learned text.

Educated opinion has made merry ever since over the antics of Father Thomas. There are one or two things, however, which seem to have escaped attention in his rather artless performance. One is that, although it was not infrequent to have preachers in their zeal upbraid academic learning and the pride of universities,[15] it was

---

15. These motifs were stressed in Counter-Reformation preaching up to our days as a countermeasure to the growth of secular thought:

not done to start shouting heresy and damnation from the pulpit until and unless the correct position has been defined by Rome; and it was well known instead that the authorities were keeping an open mind about the new discoveries. Another is that Caccini, although a man of no intellectual interests, was not an illiterate for all that. He had just then entered his candidacy for the title of Bachelor of Arts. He knew what stood under the heading of mathematics in the order of studies. Now mathematics, were it only because of its limited attributions, had always been theologically white as wool. Whatever trouble there was came from philosophy, which comprised physics and which might come up with all sorts of godless deviations like Averroism, atomism, pantheism, and even Pythagoreanism. But that was not "mathematics."

In order to make it understood that he was concerned with the system of the world, Galileo had had to explain that he was really a philosopher; and he had moved Vinta to state as much explicitly in his official title at Court, which made him out to be "chief philosopher and mathematician to His Most Serene Highness." If Caccini's object had really been the heliocentric theory, his language habits would have caused him to speak of "the new philosophy which puts all in doubt." He said instead that mathematics and mathematicians were all of them of the Devil, and he said it because he knew that "mathematicians" stood mostly for astrologers in the popular mind. The loose usage of the word went back to late antiquity, and princes had kept "court mathematicians" ever since for no other real purpose than the casting of horoscopes. Kepler knew it only too well; although he sincerely believed in astrology, it annoyed him to be paid only for that. Now, since the Order of Preachers had appointed themselves "watchdogs of the Faith," it was only natural that they should go after magicmongering and vain curiosity in the spirit of the Apostolic instruction: *Increpa illos*

"Diceva bene ar Caravita er prete:
Li libri so' invenzione der demonio,
Dunque, fijoli mii, no' li leggete."

G. G. Belli

("The priest said it well at the Caravita oratory: books are an invention of the Devil; therefore, my children, don't read them.")

dure. Caccini had cast himself in that most natural role, the better to promote the confusion between the new ideas, which were even then applying for orthodox and approved standing, and all sorts of subversive and discredited stuff. Seventeen years later, when the campaign started again against Galileo, certain anonymous but well-trained gentlemen in Rome were to resort to the same opening move: They spread the rumor that Galileo had astrologically predicted the Pope's death.

There was no chance that any of these charges could be made to stick in court, but that mattered little. The master-plan, conceived apparently by Lodovico delle Colombe in the interests of the academic group, was simple but effective: Have the friars create a scandal and uproar centered around the person of Galileo and thus compel the Roman authorities, always very sensitive on the subject of "scandal," to take for reasons of public order the measures that they seemed reluctant to take on grounds of theory. The name of "provocateur" had not been invented yet, but the dodge was as old as the world.

The sermon worked according to plan. Florentine opinion had been accustomed for centuries to the ways of the friars; it regarded them with a variety of feelings not all friendly, and it talked of them mainly as ubiquitous, innumerable, and largely self-invited dinner guests. For one Savonarola or San Bernardino, it had decided, there were lots of fakes; and it had coined a number of easygoing disrespectful proverbs to cover the situation.[16] What shocked public opinion now and caused it to take notice was that, in his eagerness to "get into the act," Father Thomas had tackled not the usual small fry but a popular member of the ruling class, a personal friend of the Grand Duke, and a renowned scholar whose discoveries had been applauded by the Pope and the cardinals. In the carefully graded society of the time this was clearly a major social solecism unless—as gossip promptly suggested—Caccini could count on some powerful backers who kept in the shadows. But who could

---

16. Galileo's own youthful burlesque poetry that we have given on p. 16 quotes one of those in the last verse. The doctors, he says, have undertaken to live at ease, "no less than if they were friars or fat priests, capital enemies of all and any discomfort."

they be? Speculation and rumor went buzzing through Florence. The effect had been obtained.

Father Maraffi, Preacher-General of the Dominicans, wrote a letter of apology to Galileo. "Unfortunately," he added, "I have to answer for all the idiocies [*bestialità*] that thirty or forty thousand brothers may and do actually commit." But Galileo was this time alarmed. Some Dominicans might be on his side, but their headquarters in Rome was definitely not. They had been working against him since his visit to Rome, and he knew how close Dominicans were to the Inquisition personnel.

He thought seriously of writing and asking for redress. But Prince Cesi and his older friend, Piero Dini, archbishop of Fermo, urgently advised him to let the matter drop. Cardinal Bellarmine was not too favorably inclined. They might take occasion of his request in Rome, he warned, to consult whether or not the further spread of this opinion should be permitted or condemned. In that case, it would probably be condemned, as the Peripatetic school was in the majority there; besides, it was very easy to prohibit or suspend by simple administrative procedure.

Galileo understood that this was exactly what the compeers of the "League" had been working toward, so he held his peace. But the operation against him went into its second phase according to plan. The opening moves had been to draw him into a theological controversy and then to counterattack by creating a scandal. In the meantime Lorini, the character who had first entered the list against "Ipernicus," had not been inactive. Having secured a copy of the *Letter to Castelli*, he dispatched it on February 7, 1615, to the Inquisition by way of Cardinal Sfondrati, who was on its board. He added the following comments on the "Galileists," never mentioning Galileo by name:

All our Fathers of this devout convent of St. Mark are of opinion that the letter contains many propositions which appear to be suspicious or presumptuous, as when it asserts that the language of Holy Scripture does not mean what it seems to mean; that in discussions about natural phenomena the last and lowest place ought to be given to the authority of the sacred text; that its commentators have very often erred in their interpretation; that the Holy Scriptures should not be mixed up with anything except matters of religion . . . ; that in Nature philosophical and astronomical evidence is of more value than holy and divine (which passages your Lordship will find underlined by me in the said letter, of which I send an exact copy); and finally that, when Joshua commanded the Sun to stand still, we must understand that the command was addressed only to the *primum mobile,* as this itself is the Sun. . . . Ever mindful of our vow to be the "black and white hounds" of the Holy Office . . . when I saw that they expounded the Holy Scriptures according to their private lights and in a manner different from that of the common interpretation of the Fathers of the Church; that they strove to defend an opinion which appeared to be quite contrary to the sacred text; that they spoke in slighting terms of the ancient Fathers and of St. Thomas Aquinas; that they were treading underfoot the entire philosophy of Aristotle which has been of such service to Scholastic theology; and, in fine, that to show their cleverness they were airing and scattering broadcast in our steadfastly Catholic city a thousand saucy and irreverent surmises; when, I say, I became aware of all this, I made up my mind to acquaint your Lordship with the state of affairs, that you in your holy zeal for the Faith may, in conjunction with your most illustrious colleagues, provide such remedies as will appear advisable. . . . I, who hold that those who call themselves Galileists are orderly men and good Christians all, but a little overwise and conceited in their opinions, declare that I am actuated by nothing in this business but zeal for the sacred cause.

Lorini had displayed suitable priestly charity by describing the errant characters as "good Christians all, but a little overwise and conceited in their opinions" (*un poco saccenti e duretti nelle loro opinioni*). In his heart, however, he felt otherwise; they were black souls who did not deserve justice, let alone mercy, and nothing should be left undone for their destruction. His indomitable zeal thought nothing of boldly forging a couple of heresies in his "exact" copy of the letter at the most opportune spots. Galileo had written: "There are in Scripture words which, taken in the strict literal meaning, look as if they differed from the truth." Lorini wrote instead: "which are false in the literal meaning." Galileo had written: "Scripture does not refrain from overshadowing [*adombrare*][17] its

17. The word *adombrare* is used here in the old sense, as in Dante, *Purg.*, XXXI, 144, and not in the more current sense, which is also to be found in the English "to adumbrate."

most essential dogmas by attributing to God qualities very far from and contrary to His essence." Lorini changed "overshadowing" into "perverting" (*pervertire*). The startled Inquisitor was bound to comment: "Such words as 'false' and 'perverting' sound very bad" (fol. 341^r).[18] They were about the only points where he found fault with the text, which otherwise seemed orthodox enough. Even so, he added, they might be construed innocently within the general context. Lorini's attempt had misfired.

The report set the machinery in motion nonetheless. The Holy Office, ever careful, wrote on the twenty-sixth of February, 1615, to the Archbishop of Pisa and the Inquisitor there, instructing them to secure a signed copy of the *Letter to Castelli*, "in a skilful manner," without arousing attention. The Archbishop accordingly showed a sudden interest in the doctrinal problem and asked to see the letter, which pleased Castelli greatly. But Galileo's reflexes of prudence unfortunately stood in the way. To Castelli's repeated requests for authorization, he first replied with silence; he then sent him an unsigned copy with strict orders not to let it out of his hands.[19] The Archbishop had it read to him and diplomatically professed himself satisfied.

This first reconnaissance had yielded almost nothing; it is closed by a routine annotation dated March 13. But the third phase of the combined operation came in with perfect timing to give the Inquisitors a new and more promising start. Caccini had arrived in Rome and had promptly approached the Holy Office by way of the Cardinal of Aracoeli, who was on its board. At the next weekly sit-

---

18. The documents of the Inquisition file are to be found in Vol. XIX of Favaro's National Edition of Galileo's *Works*. But, as they have also been reproduced by L'Epinois and Berti in their earlier publications of the dossier, we refer to them by the number of the actual folio, which is to be found in all three works.

19. This was prudence with respect to the Archbishop and the use he might make of his words, not with respect to the Vatican, for Galileo had already forwarded the true text of the letter by way of Dini, on February 16, 1615; but it was disregarded. Some modern historians like Monsignor Marini, who were apparently acquainted with Galileo's writings only from police reports, found in the term "perverting" further proof of Galileo's arrogance.

ting of the Congregation, which took place on March 19, his request was granted: "Sanctissimus gave orders for the examination of Father Thomas Caccini, who, the Cardinal of Aracoeli says, is informed concerning the errors of Galileo and begs to testify on them for the exoneration of his conscience."

Caccini was called in the next day, March 20, and unburdened his soul. What came out would hardly deserve the honor of history; but, as it provided the principal evidence in the whole affair, it should stand on record. The city of Florence, Caccini revealed, was full of "Galileists" publicly holding impious discourses inspired by their master: such things as that God is not a self-existent being but an accident; that God is a sentient being who can laugh and weep; that the miracles performed by the saints are not real miracles. Caccini managed to suggest that such abominations were only natural coming from a man who had written *Letters on the Solar Spots,* which was full of damnable matter, who belonged to "a certain Academy of the Lincei," who was a friend of the infamous Sarpi,[20] and who corresponded with German mathematicians.—

20. Sarpi is Milton's "Padre Paolo, the great unmasker of the Trentine Council," who "observed that the primitive councils and bishops were wont only to declare what books were not commendable, passing no further but leaving it to each one's conscience to read or lay by" (*Areopagitica*). Paolo Sarpi (1552–1618) had been a friend of Sixtus V and Bellarmine, but the controversy of the Venetian interdict had driven them apart. The Curia excommunicated him, and its agents tried to kidnap him and even to assassinate him in 1607. He remained to the end the consultant of the Venetian Republic and the leader in the fight of the state against the claims of the Vatican, as he defended the ancient and republican *libertas Ecclesiae* against the Jesuits and papal absolutism. "The new name of blind obedience invented by Loyola," he wrote, "was ever unknown to the Church and to all good theologians; it removes the essential feature of virtue which is operating by certain knowledge and choice, it exposes to the risk of offending God, and it does not excuse him who has been deceived by the spiritual ruler."

Needless to say, Galileo's friendship with Sarpi implied no connection whatever with the latter's religious and political activities. Sarpi was one of the great scholarly minds of his time; he had been keenly interested in Galileo's physical theories and had even collabo-

How did he know all this?—He had been told by Lorini and by a certain Jesuit, who also told him that Galileo had barely escaped arrest by the Inquisition when he was in Rome in 1611. He was speaking out of pious zeal, he averred, and would not like to have it known. But Father Lorini was the man who could tell them more. He even could show a copy of a certain letter that Galileo had written to Father Castelli.—Under cross-examination, Caccini began to hedge. About Galileo's Copernican opinions, the Bishop of Cortona would confirm. As to the godless propositions quoted, he stated he had learned them from his friend, Father Ximenes,[21] who said he had heard it from some of "them," several times.—And specifically from whom?—Well, he could only remember the name of one. It was something like Attivanti—youngish, dark beard, thin face. He had heard him disputing with Father Ximenes. He could not produce proof, but he was sure the man was a Galileist, for he had also upheld Galileo's theories. Father Ximenes would know. This, in any case, he could say for sure, that Galileo taught these two propositions: that the Earth moves and that the Sun does not.—Did he know Galileo?—No, he had never met him.—Did he have anything against this other man Attivanti?—Nothing at all. There was nothing in his heart but love for everybody. He spoke out of Christian zeal.—Witness dismissed.

---

rated in his experiments. He was sure that Copernicanism would be accepted eventually as true and stated as much in a written opinion to the Venetian Senate after the prohibition of 1616. All of this did not concern Caccini. The mere mention of Sarpi was an effective smear, and he knew it would stick in Rome.

21. The technique must be again admired. Caccini states that Lorini gave him the *Letter to Castelli* to read; therefore, he knows that Galileo's position is exactly the contrary. "The literal understanding of Scripture," it is said there, "would lead to grave heresies and even to blasphemies, such that God has hands and feet and eyes, that He is subject to bodily affections such as anger, repentance, hatred, and even forgetfulness and ignorance." But, by calling in Ximenes as an independent source, who can be supposed not to know about Galileo's text, he gives himself full latitude. The whole deposition is such an interminable mass of twists and innuendoes and double talk that a summary does no justice to it.

It took quite some time to locate Father Ximenes, a Spaniard, for he was traveling; but, when he was called in (November 13), he picked up the ball with great deftness. Yes, he said, quite true, there was this lamentable scandal caused by the Galileists.—Who were they?—He did not know very well. There was this one man, Giannozzo Attavanti, a parish priest he knew, who had said terrible things. He was sure he had not really meant them; he was no heretic, surely, not informed enough to have a serious opinion. He must have picked them up from Galileo or from some Galileist.—What did he say?—He said that God is an accident and that there is no substance of things or continuous quality but that everything is a discrete quantity composed of vacua (*sic*); that God is sensitive, that He laughs and weeps. "But I do not know whether they speak from their opinion or someone else's."—Did they say that the miracles ascribed to saints were not real miracles?—No, he had never heard that.—Where and when had he heard these opinions?—From this young man, Attavanti, several times, both upstairs and downstairs in the Monastery of Santa Maria Novella. He had begged him not to speak thus, had represented to him the enormity of his sayings, but still he thought the man was not giving his own opinion but Galileo's.—Witness dismissed.

Attavanti was called in on the next day and questioned about the damnable propositions. He answered with assurance. Father Ximenes, he said, can tell you how it happened. We were practicing disputation for our theses, he and I, and I held the contrary part, *addiscendi gratia*. We had taken the section on absolutes, of Aquinas' *Contra Gentes*, where these questions occur.[22] Ximenes will tell you that it was so. This other man must have eavesdropped and imagined something, because another time, as I was telling Ximenes

22. The investigator dropped of his own initiative the proposition about things being made up "of vacua," whatever that may mean. Caccini had not mentioned it, and he seems to have concluded that Ximenes invented it for good measure. The other proposition about the miracles had been given by Caccini and not by Ximenes, so only two propositions were left: those concerning the substance and the attributes of God, which do actually occur in Aquinas. The compeers had gotten their signals slightly mixed over that unfortunate interval of eight months that had elapsed since Caccini's deposition in March.

about the motion of the Earth, he came in from the next room, screaming that this was heretical and that he was going to deliver a sermon about it, as he subsequently did. That is all there is to it. —Did he know Galileo?—Yes, I have met him a few times. We talked about philosophical matters, like the motion of the Earth and the Sun standing still in Gibeon.—What did he know of his theological opinions?—I hold him to be a very good Catholic, otherwise the Grand Duke would not have him around.—Did he have anything against Caccini?—I never talked with him before or after. I did not even know him by name.—Witness dismissed.

The evidence was forwarded to Rome. The official who read it in the last days of November must have used his own judgment about this *roba fratina,* as it was currently called even inside the administration. The still unsuspecting Attavanti had obviously been used as a dupe in a confidence game by the two associates. Nothing much there.[23] But the first part was relevant. He marked in the margin with vertical strokes of his pen several points: *Letters on the Solar Spots, Lincei, German mathematicians, Sarpi, Galileists, propositions.* He went on farther down and underlined Attavanti's words: *very good Catholic, otherwise the Grand Duke would not have him around.*

Then there comes a note in the file, dated November 25, 1615, which transcribes the decision of the Congregation taken on that day: "See the *Letters on the Solar Spots* by the said Galilei." On the next sheet, but dated three months later, comes the convocation of the Qualifiers on February 23.

At this point we should like to show here by an example how shots are called, and how history happens to be written, on this difficult subject. We shall take no less a historian than Father J. Brodrick, S.J., who stands out among his confreres for charm of style, cultivated taste, and discriminating scholarship, as well as for the genuine Christian warmth which pervades his work. Now Father Brodrick gives the following considered judgment on Caccini's deposition, which he discusses briefly but omits to analyze:

---

23. The marks made by the examiner are clear in the manuscript. They have been noted, at least most of them, in L'Epinois's edition of the documents of the trial.

"All the signs point to Caccini having been a very good and honest, if somewhat hot-headed man. As we are asked to accept so much on the evidence of Galileo's friends, why should we not be allowed to believe one of his foes for a change?"[24] This is a somewhat vain question. Anyone will accept this or that detail of the deposition.[25] It is we rather who should ask: Why does Father Brodrick ask the reader to believe on his word as a historian that Caccini was a good and honest man? No one doubts the author's Christian motives, but he need not ask why historians who want to get at the facts have taken to relying rather more on the estimate of the situation provided by Galileo and his friends. In this particular case, Galileo never got to know Caccini's deposition; he never even was told that Caccini had denounced him to the Holy Office. But, when Caccini came to pay him a "courtesy" visit in Rome a few months later, he wrote back to Florence: "That person was with me for over four hours, with many demonstrations of humility, and tried to persuade me that he had not been the original mover of the other activity here. . . . but from all his discourses I discovered a very great ignorance, no less than a mind full of venom and devoid of charity." From all we know now out of the secret archives and so many other sources, Galileo had guessed exactly right.

---

24. J. Brodrick, *The Life and Work of Blessed Robert Francis, Cardinal Bellarmine, S.J.* (1928), II, 353.

25. The single point brought out from the deposition is that the Galileists tried to persuade a Jesuit favorably inclined to Copernicanism to preach a counter-sermon to Caccini and did not succeed. Father Brodrick seems to find this move very wicked. In any case, he might have found it duly acknowledged in Wohlwill's account among others, including a small detail that Caccini had omitted, viz., that the unnamed Jesuit had been willing but was apparently prevented from speaking by Archbishop Marzi Medici. In very much the same vein, Father Brodrick asks us to understand (p. 355) that Lorini's letter is "not an official denunciation of Galileo, Lorini himself writes Cardinal Sfondrati that he did not wish it be considered as such, but merely as a private piece of information for the guidance of the authorities." The *distinguo* is quite interesting, but it may leave a few people puzzled. One runs up against this kind of thing all the time; we have gone into this one particular case only so that we may be excused from further discussing and polemicizing.

VI

The goings-on we have described took place in deepest secrecy, but Galileo was man of the world enough to know that somewhere things had been set in motion. Cesi had advised him to lie low and wait for the clouds to disperse, but he knew what was at stake and decided to take a calculated risk. He sought out intercessors. He wrote in February, 1615, and then again on March 23, to his friend, Monsignor Dini, asking him to have his letters reach the Jesuit mathematicians, also Cardinal Bellarmine, and, if possible, the Pope himself. This time, he inclosed an authentic copy of the *Letter to Castelli* in order to have all his cards on the table.

In these later missives there is no longer the quiet irony of the early one. They are urgently pleading to have any decision suspended; and, since the *Letter to Castelli*, he says, was written in haste, he is asking for more time to give a considered philosophical statement. Meanwhile, he shows himself very much concerned with what Dini had told him—that heliocentrism might be ruled to be acceptable as a simple mathematical hypothesis. This might appease the mathematicians, he says, but is absolutely contrary to what Copernicus had meant and tried to show. He had held his system to be physically true, evidence had since accumulated in his favor, and it would be disastrous if the Church froze the situation by decreeing that physics and mathematics must be kept in separate compartments and controlled by the literal sense of Scripture.

But since Bellarmine, in a conversation with Dini, had quoted the Psalmist as proving beyond doubt that the Sun moves and had said that he would like to know what Galileo thought of it, Galileo finds himself compelled to move again into theological territory to confront him—not for discussion among the public, he protests humbly, but only as a brief submitted to the authorities. A ray of light from heaven may come even to the ignorant if the intention is pure. He is offering his thoughts to his mother, the Church; let them be destroyed if such is her infallible decision. He will gladly submit.

After this premise Galileo suggests that it might be consonant with Scripture to conceive of the great forces of Nature, light and heat, as finding their proper focus in the Sun, located in the middle.

There must have been, he says, some primeval force spread over the universe in the beginning, for Scripture speaks of the Spirit moving upon the face of the waters, even before the firmament was made, and it says of God: "Thou hast made the Light and the Sun," speaking as of two distinct entities. From the most ancient sages to Dionysius the Areopagite, there seems to be a consensus about light as the original power, closest in nature and analogy to God.

Now the Cardinal had referred to Psalm 19; Galileo does not try to by-pass the famous text but faces it resolutely to seek therein, even as his opponents had done, a confirmation of his own views:

> The heavens declare the glory of God; and the firmament sheweth his handiwork.
>
> Day unto day uttereth speech, and night unto night sheweth knowledge.
>
> There is no speech nor language where their voice is not heard.
>
> Their line is gone out through all the earth, and their words to the end of the world. In them hath he set a tabernacle for the sun.
>
> Which is as a bridegroom coming out of his chamber, and rejoiceth as a strong man to run a race.
>
> His going forth is from the end of heaven, and his circuit unto the ends of it: and there is nothing hid from the heat thereof.
>
> The law of the Lord is perfect, converting the soul: the testimony of the Lord is sure, making wise the simple.

This is, however, the King James Version. The Vulgate says: "in Sole posuit tabernaculum suum," which is more amenable. If the Sun is the tabernacle *for* the power of God, then, suggests Galileo, that power is clearly represented here by the light and the heat which circulate in the universe, fecundating it throughout. It is they, rather than the Sun, who can be aptly called the "bridegroom" and the "strong man running his course." This he supports with sundry subtle reasons, such as that the bridegroom "cometh out of his chamber," a simile which does not fit very well the doings of a tabernacle whose only function is to sit still. Similar ideas about that text (but Galileo did not know it) had come to Copernicus, too; he had erased them from the first draft of his text, fearing that they might look too markedly "Pythagorean." This kind of speculation stemmed from the great epoch of medieval Christianity, which had found a theme in the "Metaphysics of Light" brought over from Neo-Platonism into mystical theology. If Galileo had found St.

Bonaventure instead of St. Robert Bellarmine[26] still in the seat of theological authority, he might have become a pillar of the Church. But those times were over. Bellarmine was in authority, a masterful Scholastic mind charged with keeping the Church in line with the decisions of the Council of Trent, and as a Jesuit regretfully resolved never again to disregard the *sinistra cura.*[27]

---

26. Bellarmine was beatified by Pius XI on May 13, 1923, and canonized in 1930.

27. Cf. Dante, *Parad.*, XII, 125:

> "Io son la vita di Bonaventura
> da Bagnoregio, che nei grandi uffici
> sempre posposi la sinistra cura."

III

PHILOSOPHICAL INTERMEZZO

And, oh, it can no more be questioned
That Beautie's self, Proportion, is dead.
JOHN DONNE

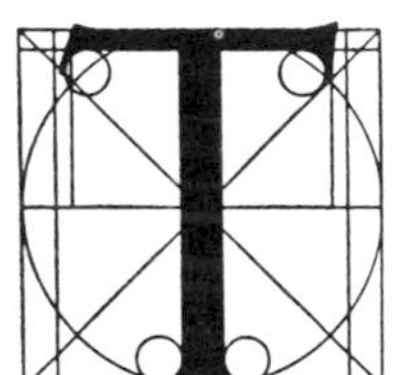

THE controversy had thus reached the higher echelons. It would be only fair at this point not to let the mind dwell on the futile or ridiculous aspects of the conflict and to consider the issue of old versus new in its full dimensions. Galileo's vocal opponents were third-rate Scholastics, but their arguments rested upon a most important doctrine, and it was the groundwork of that which was put in question.

The philosophical synthesis taught in the schools was essentially worked out by many generations from Aristotle, in which the Church and the larger part of the lay scholars agreed.[1] All things and all

1. The dissenters, Averroists and Aristotelians of the stricter observance, among whom was Cremonini, did disagree only in points which had nothing to do with the present issue, like the eternity of the world and the immortality of the soul. There was a "scientific" school trying out its own way, in which Pomponazzi and Zabarella had distinguished themselves; but in the alignment of ideas that we are considering their influence was against Galileo. They still belonged to the Aristotelian circle of thought, with Stoic influxes, and they were at one with the other "independents" on the anti-mathematical issue, as well as against the consensus of humanists. The fact that they were considered "scientific" in their own way did nothing to help the term, since

activities found their natural place in that system. God and Nature are ample enough and opulent enough to afford a niche for all the endless diversity that makes up finite existence. Above the single sciences is philosophy itself, a rational discipline which seeks to formulate the universal principles of all the sciences. It leads to the knowledge of the First Cause. Above that is theology depending on revelation, the end point of the whole system: faith is the fulfilment of reason.

Physics, the "science of Nature," found its place in the structure without difficulty. The universe forms a hierarchy reaching from God down to the lowest being. Every being acts under the internal urge of its own nature, seeking the "good" natural to its kind; and that good is one form of perfection which finds its place in the scale according to its degree. No matter how lowly it may be, no being is wholly lacking in value, for it has its station, its duties, and its rights, through which it contributes to the perfection of the whole. The essence of the scheme is subordination to an end. But, within that hierarchy, the "nature of things" is a tolerant and liberal constitution. All beings of a kind have an essence in common, but they do not cease to be individual "substances." Of all men, all nettles, all cats, there are no two exactly alike, yet they remain true to their essence.

It was, indeed, all one science, as it should be. What else is the science of Nature, a man of that time would have said, if not to know how the natural substances go toward their appointed ends in an ordered way?

The idea of an *order* is paramount. Not the order of the abstract formula but that of a multitude of varied beings whose behaviors coexist and mesh in a vast symphony, the order of the seed that becomes a tree according to the rhythm of the seasons, and then again earth and then life again, with a dim perception of its own purpose.

> Birds sigh for the air
> Soul for it knows not where—

Pomponazzi's books were publicly burned for impiety. Thus, they could only add to the confusion in the public mind about the meaning of science.

And what, then, could the ambition of science be, except to describe that order and its goals, in a vast discourse, as natural history does even today, but revealing the eternal scale of values underlying it?

In that order a very clear distinction seems to impose itself upon all who are not blind—that which severs the things of heaven from those here below. The stars last forever, whereas on earth all is change and passing-away; the skies turn around us everlastingly, while on earth anything let free will fall to the ground and stop. Thus, there must be an essential difference of nature between the two realms, and practically all philosophers had been agreed that nothing under the Moon can be similar to celestial things.

What things are in heaven, or why they are that way, cannot be guessed, except by raising the soul to contemplate those other entities beyond time that are of its own nature, such as the Beautiful and the Good, which seem to be, as it were, reflected in the perfections of heaven. To explain the order of things on this earth, we may appeal to our close experience of them. But the heavenly order seems to be the mirror of a pure metaphysical or aesthetic thought; it will be, in Plato's words, a moving image of eternity. The very matter of heaven will in deliberate fancy be conceived as such an image, whether it be ethereal crystal or subtle fire; the absolute geometric regularity of its orbs will scan the over-all rhythm that is followed by the life of perishable nature here below.

> . . . the rest
> From Man or Angel the great Architect
> Did wisely to conceal, and not divulge
> His secrets, to be scanned by them who ought
> Rather admire. Or, if they list to try
> Conjecture, he his fabric of the Heavens
> Hath left to their disputes—perhaps to move
> His laughter at their quaint opinions wide
> Hereafter, when they come to model heaven,
> And calculate the stars; how they will wield
> The mighty frame; how build, unbuild, contrive
> To save appearances; how gird the sphere
> With centric and eccentric scribbled o'er,
> Cycle and epicycle, orb in orb.

How wise God had been in setting right at this point the Pillars of Hercules of discovery was very clear to Milton: so clear that he did not feel he had to explain or to hedge on the spectacularly unauthorized commitment—even a generation after Galileo. The fact is that the placement of the Earth at the separate center of things is not for Aristotle, or for Milton, a purely astronomical solution or a mere complement of the system. It is the actual foundation of Aristotle's cosmology, which he has chosen after having carefully discussed and rejected the opinions of those "ancients," as he calls them, who made out the Earth to be a planet. It is on this foundation that he has built the elaborate and closely knit structure of his physics. To undermine it at any point, his followers will contend, would "tend to the subversion of all natural philosophy and to the disorder and upsetting of heaven and earth and the whole universe."

It is thus, at least, that Doctor Simplicio will exclaim against the new ideas in Galileo's *Dialogue.* But Simplicio, although invented to serve the author's convenience, is hardly a caricature; he is merely a composite portrait. Galileo makes fun of him in so far as he identifies the welfare of the universe with that of his own school, but the premise underlying the protest he is not far from conceding himself; it is, in fact, explicitly stated in the very opening sentences of the *Dialogue* as a point of general agreement: The universe cannot but be perfect, a thing of beauty and proportion, a totally ordered whole, otherwise Creation would make no sense, and there would be no point to philosophy.

The principle seemed to Galileo himself so obvious, in a way, that it prevented him from following his discoveries to their logical end. He who had discovered the principle of inertia always refused to think of a straight inertial path, because it would have been "disorderly." Natural motion, according to him, cannot be other than circular, since it is intended to keep things in their proper order. Thus, Aristotle, too, had been on common-sense ground when he stated the principle that all things tend toward their proper position in the order. It is this way of being in time and space—which will be no more than free fall in the stone, but growth in the plant, intelligent action in man—that Aristotle calls "motion." The way in which these individual searches for each thing's "proper good" combine and co-operate can be constructed into a system which reveals the order whereby all things tend toward the Supreme Good.

Motion could be defined, hence, as the instrument for this eternal process. But it is even more than that; it is the process itself: the simple word has a rich and multiple content, equivalent to what we would call in modern words "universal becoming."

The technical definition of motion in the Aristotelian language might possibly not convey as much to the modern mind: "Motion is the passage of what is in potency to what is in act, in so far as it is in potency." This definition was to be held up to ridicule by Descartes, who maintained that it made no sense in any language. And so indeed it does not for the type of scientific mind that Descartes represents; but, then, for that scientific mind, motion is understood already as something simpler and clearer, the change of position undergone by a body with respect to other bodies. It is not an activity; it is a state. With it goes the whole Cartesian mechanical universe, a universe of simple location where matter is described only by size, relative place, and movement, where nothing "happens," but everything goes on shifting around blindly according to inertial law. Even animals become, in that world, pure automats; all the world is dead except for the immortal soul of man.

Old-fashioned indeed with respect to that is the conception of Aristotle and its phrasing; yet in essence it says nothing stranger about reality than the word of the poet to man: Become what thou art. The ancient universe is, as it were, a vast republic of gods, men, animals, plants, and things realizing their respective natures and coming to rest in their appointed places, as the eternal forms embody themselves perpetually in new matter according to the heartbeat of life and death.

A limited universe, it is inevitably bounded on all sides as an organism should be; and the space inside it a qualitative field, so to speak, where each being has a proper place and where the place corresponds to the full realization of that being, neither more nor less as each organ has a place in the body. In that universe there are several ways to move and act, of which the shifting of place is only one; there is also growth, shrinking, and change of quality and aspect. All these are "motions." But such a universe is also one where things really "come to be," where the word "realization" has a meaning, whereas in a purely mechanical universe it has none; for it is axiomatic in the Cartesian conception that inert matter only, barely, manages to subsist, identical to itself, by God's decree. Such a harsh simplification as that of Descartes was necessary, it would appear, for clearing the way to the vaster and subtler constructions of science. But one can understand the puzzlement of Goethe, and Keats, and so many of their time, of how anyone could ever accept such an image of reality stripped of its color, variety, and life.

As far as mechanics went, however, Galileo was right in seeing there the weakest point of the Aristotelian system—so weak that it dragged down the rest along with it. In a system patterned on life, centered on the Earth, the motion that is simply a shifting of place becomes the most flat and uninteresting aspect of the general process; it serves only to take things where they should be and function. The stone can express its nature only in one way—by getting to its proper place. Hence the only thing that it knows how to do is to fall. It is the ultimate poverty of being, far below what can be achieved by the poorest fungus. It can change in no way by itself, except in position. We ought to see, then, why the Aristotelian found it absurd to look just in that most blind and uncouth of events, the fall of matter, for a mathematical clarity that he knew he could not find in the so much more important process of the growth of a living being. "Please consider," he would have said, "that mathematics cannot apply to change in any form, for it concerns only what is static or abstract. You may hope to find it perchance in the accomplished form, where Platonists are always searching for it, in the mysteries of divine proportion; but how could you expect to discover it at the most confused and shapeless point of being, in the nascent act, in the urge of pure possibility toward realization, whether it be the sprouting of the seed or the fall of the stone? If you ever find geometry in nature, it will not be there; it will be at the opposite farthest removed from it, in the immobile and accomplished crystal. And this alone ought to show you how right we are. But even the crystal that you find in Nature will express geometry only imperfectly, because Nature, being life, has no use for rigid abstract perfection. See how even the hardest metal sphere will never touch a marble plane on one point only, as geometry would have it."

To this, Galileo, mindful of Archimedes, replied, as we have his words in the *Dialogue:* "Do you admit that any piece of rock has the shape, the weight, the size it happens to have to the greatest degree of precision imaginable? Yes, surely. Why then you ought to see that number and precision appear in nature at levels that you refuse to consider." But his opponents went on refusing to consider, for it would have only upset them uselessly. To be inside the frame of thought of Aristotle meant to have banished number, weight, and measure from philosophical significance. "Mathematics," said the schools, "cannot concern motion, for motion is always toward a given good; and there is no mention of the good in mathematics."

This was, needless to say, only the metaphysical justification. But the strength of the schools did not lie in such arguments; it lay in the earthy obviousness of the principles from which they started. It was the mathematicians who had been, through history, dreamers of wonderful dreams and searchers for mystical hidden harmonies. Reality was surely much closer to what we all know and "understand," to the familiar simplicity of life and organism. It is on this level of life that the Aristotelian position becomes common sense itself. In all things that count, function seems to be clearly marked; we live in a world of distinctive purposes. At a time when all that man dealt with was provided, so to speak, ready-made by Nature, from food to timber and simple tools, when the very word "force," outside of magic, could mean only laborers, horses, or oxen, it cannot be denied that a vitalist explanation found itself at the center of gravity of thought.

"To ignore movement is to ignore Nature." The principle seemed sound enough. And where did one see on earth a motion that went on by itself forever? Even the flowing of streams needed the sun and the rain; one was led from one cause to a larger cause up to the First Cause; one always found an action caused by another action. Man knew only too well from himself that movement is the result of an effort against a resistance; the strength must come from somewhere, and, as it is spent, it leaves behind real change, namely, fatigue and wear.

We see again thought focused on the idea of a process. Something new is always coming in; something is being lost. The familiar images are those of a man carrying a burden, of a cart being pulled along on a rutted road. It would look, then, as though all were clear to the mind so long as it does not move out of the patient works and days. But what of the stone that is hurled from the hand? Common sense here suggests a kind of energy that it picks up and then loses quickly until it falls to the ground.

At this point, unfortunately, the Aristotelian is no longer free to adopt immediate common sense, for he is a prisoner of the mesh of concepts that he has built up already in order to have a proper theory. He will say, then, that spontaneous motion, being an attribute of substance, cannot be transferred. It is axiomatic that attributes are nontransferable. A man who happens to be blond and blue-eyed has no way of transferring these attributes to a man who is not. He can only beget another man who is. And spontaneous motion is no more transferable than blondness or blue eyes.

Yet, there were the facts. Any small boy could prove to Aristotle conclusively that a rock could be thrown to good purpose. Hence Aristotle was compelled to suppose that the rock was urged on its way by something still in contact with it, and it had to be the circumambient air. His disciples admitted discreetly that this was not the strongest point in the master's theory; but, so long as nothing better showed up, they had to accept it bravely as the only way to save the intangible principles.

Galileo had learned this theory at the time when he was a student in Pisa, and he saw at once that there was no way to save it. Casting overboard the intangible principles, he went back, as Hipparchus the astronomer and a number of Parisian doctors had done before him, to the more natural idea of an *impetus* received by the missile. But this idea, too, stemmed from a vitalistic imagination. The missile was supposed to have been "fed" a certain amount of force that it dispersed on its way. To work out the idea meant to find one's self up against the old difficulties. As late as 1587, in his early graduate years, Galileo was still trying out analogies with the heat of an iron bar or the sound of a bell, which dissipate into space. His ingenious efforts in theory and experiment (for it was at this time that he dropped bodies from the Leaning Tower of Pisa with completely deceptive results) came to nothing. The whole idea of impetus was a dead end.

It was about at this time, as far as we can make out, that Galileo became interested in the new Copernican ideas. But as he already had a problem on his mind, a flash of creative imagination brought things together. Here was a case very similar to that of the flywheel which his master Benedetti had already shown to be the most intractable by the old theories. A flywheel whirling on the spot suggests the idea that, barring resistances, it might go on forever, and even better in a void. The mind is led to conceive of a sphere suspended in the void, turning without friction—and why should that not be the Earth? What emerged out of it in its pure state, so to speak, was the new idea of *inertia*—an idea prodigiously abstract and even unnatural for minds working with the ordinary material of experience, and one that Galileo himself had not been able to extract previously.

Now suddenly everything had become clear. If the Earth could be such a sphere, why could not the orbs of the planets obey some such inertial law? What had looked absurd in the Copernican doctrine became now a hint in its favor; for Copernicus, while "making of the Earth a star," had attributed to it motions which seemed incompatible with its nature so "eminently heavy and terrestrial," as the doctors said. If now it appeared that celestial bodies might move owing to just such a nature, the system of the world could cease to be a dreamy geometrical diagram and become a physical reality. A "natural philosophy" began to outline itself which encompassed both heaven and the Earth, with the planets subject to the same physical laws that we can study here below—in fact, with no above or below, since we ourselves are a planet among many.

A wide and wild guess it was, no doubt, in those years around 1590: a perilous leap of the imagination into uncharted regions. No one but Galileo, and at the other end of Europe, Kepler, could see how it could make sense ultimately. But, as soon as their minds had grasped the idea, it became clear that this was a rebirth of Pythagorean intuition of the unity of Nature and that it solved many of the unnoticed absurdities of the traditional conception.

That traditional conception, to be sure, made persuasive and

Bibliothèque Nationale, Paris

GALILEO, AGED SIXTY

This portrait, by Ottavio Leoni, was made in 1624 and probably during the stay in Rome in which Galileo obtained permission from the Pope to write the *Dialogue*.

Bibliothèque Nationale, Paris

PAUL V BORGHESE IN 1614

Clichè Alinari

BENEDETTO CASTELLI, GALILEO'S DISCIPLE AND CORRESPONDENT

Bibliothèque Nationale, Paris

ROBERTO BELLARMINO IN 1604, AGED SIXTY-TWO

The view is from his palace near Santa Maria in Via; in the background, the Antonine Column.

comfortable sense as far as the Earth was concerned; but, as for the things of heaven, it had to consider them some sort of decorative adjunct to the earthly setting. It had never developed any real physics for them. It insisted, in fact, on heaven being "different." The thought of Aristotle, always absorbed in the concrete, had dwelt on describing separate behaviors. For him, it was proper of the stone to strive downward as of fire to strive upward, and each living being in turn had a different kind of motion; as to the motion of the stars in heaven, it could not but be infinitely different in quality from anything here on earth. So the astronomers and mathematical specialists had been left, with barely disguised condescension, to devise diagrams which might "save the appearances" but were understood to explain nothing. The assignment was to devise as many circular and uniform motions as, combined, could be said to describe the apparent path of the planets on the vault of heaven. The astronomers, and chief among them Ptolemy, had proceeded in this modest spirit to devise a dodge which was called the "theory of epicycles." If one circle was not enough to describe the motion of a planet, another smaller circle was added, fastened onto its circumference like a roller bearing, and, going around on that the planet, it could perform all the curlicues that its apparent path in heaven suggested (Fig. 3). By adjusting speeds and dimensions in this kind of diagram, the positions could be predicted with a fair amount of precision, including conjunctions, eclipses, and all that was needed. But it was well understood that this was not a *physical* description and was not meant to be.

Still, there it was, and it was the only one available. Since the philosophers, who had retained legislative authority in physics, had nothing of their own to offer as a mechanism, the irresistible tendency was to materialize the device of the astronomers into crystal spheres and hope no one would inquire as to how it made sense. The result, through the Middle Ages, had been a visualized Chinese-box system of spheres within spheres, each of them thick enough to carry its own little epicyclic sphere, just as a ball bearing carries its steel balls. Such a system bore a merely coincidental analogy to anything physical or mechanical; but again there it was, and it looked miraculous enough to discourage people from asking further. With it went a corresponding fancy of what the bodies of the

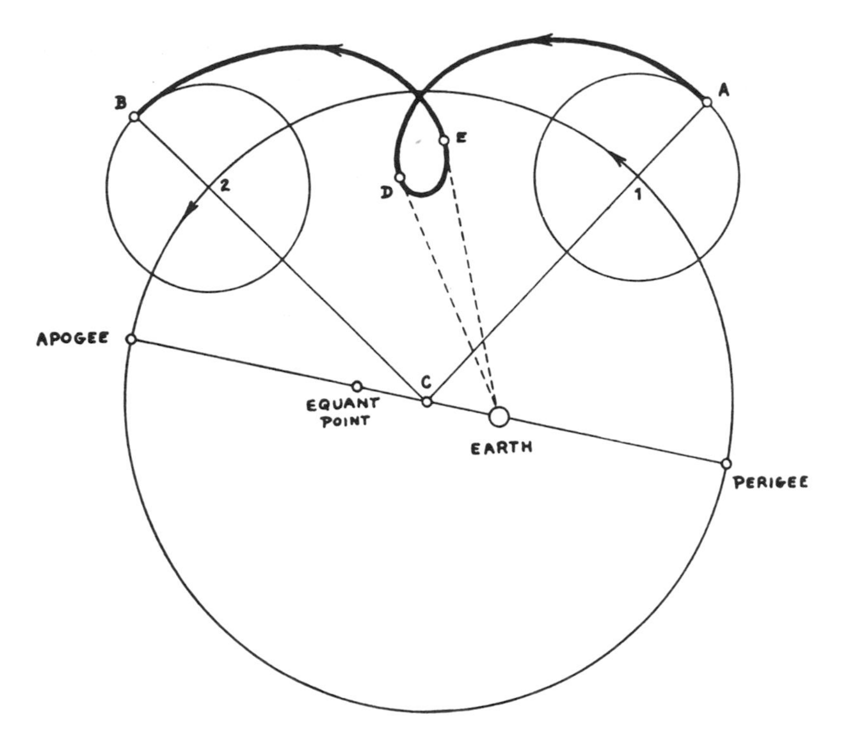

FIG. 3.—FUNCTION OF AN EPICYCLE

Since the planets travel around the Sun at different speeds, their motions relative to an observer on the moving Earth are complex. One phenomenon in particular was puzzling to those who thought the Earth motionless in the center of the universe. This was known as "retrogradation" and is easily explained in the heliocentric Copernican system. In the case of the outer planets, since the Earth travels faster than they, it periodically overtakes them and "laps the field," so to speak. When this happens, an observer on Earth sees the phenomenon in question. The planet being overtaken appears to slow down in its normal easterly course, stop, reverse directions and travel west for some weeks, then stop and reverse directions once more and continue on in its regular orbit. This strange appearance is neatly handled in the Ptolemaic system by one of the several uses of epicycles. (The other use, that of accounting for the actual ellipticity of the orbit, is dealt with by use of extra epicycles, which are those that Galileo thought he had to retain.) In Figure 3 imagine the planet to be located at point *A* of the *epicycle* with center at *1*. The epicycle in turn is on the *deferent* circle whose center is *C*. The stationary Earth is located within the deferent. Now (1) the planet at *A* begins traveling around its epicycle in a counterclockwise direction and (2) the epicycle itself is carried around the deferent from *1* to *2*. The combination of these two motions is the supposed motion of the planet and is represented by the heavy line between *A* and *B*. In the loop the motion appears retrograde.

planets themselves might be like: obviously hard matter, more dense and luminous than the crystal sphere bearing them, since we can see it, but at least as durable—certainly at least as good as diamond and more exalted. It was all a coherent chain of images (Fig. 4). The official prerogative of heaven being its eternity and immutability, any attempt at forming a physical idea, however honorific, e.g., of the Moon, made it out as an exquisitely polished sphere of some jewel-like substance. This was felt on all sides as the proper thing for the Moon to be. But there are certain minds which have a different sense of values. A revealing passage of Frank Lloyd Wright's autobiography shows a mind of this singular type:

> Grandfather preached as Isaiah preached: "The flower fadeth, the grass withereth, but the word of the Lord thy God endureth forever." The boy, his grandson, grew to distrust Isaiah. Was the flower any less desirable because it seemed to have been condemned to die that it might live more abundantly? As they all went to work in the fields, the grass seemed always necessary to life in the valley, most of all when it withered and was hay to keep the stock alive in winter so the preacher himself might live.

Galileo would never have thought of challenging the eternity of the Word of God, but it appeared to him very clearly that these other worldly symbols of eternity, understood by the pious to represent the virtues of heaven, were by way of becoming very shabby literary clichés, out of place in any philosophy mindful of the majesty of the Cosmos:

> I cannot without great wonder, nay more, disbelief, hear it being attributed to natural bodies as a great honour and perfection that they are impassible, immutable, inalterable, etc.: as, conversely, I hear it esteemed a great imperfection to be alterable, generable, and mutable. It is my opinion that the Earth is very noble and admirable by reason of the many and different alterations, mutations, and generations which incessantly occur in it. And if, without being subject to any alteration, it had been all one vast heap of sand, or a mass of jade, or if, since the time of the deluge, the waters freezing which covered it, it had continued an immense globe of crystal, wherein nothing had ever grown, altered, or changed, I should have esteemed it a wretched lump of no benefit to the Universe, a mass of idleness, and in a word superfluous, exactly as if it had never been in Nature. The difference for me would

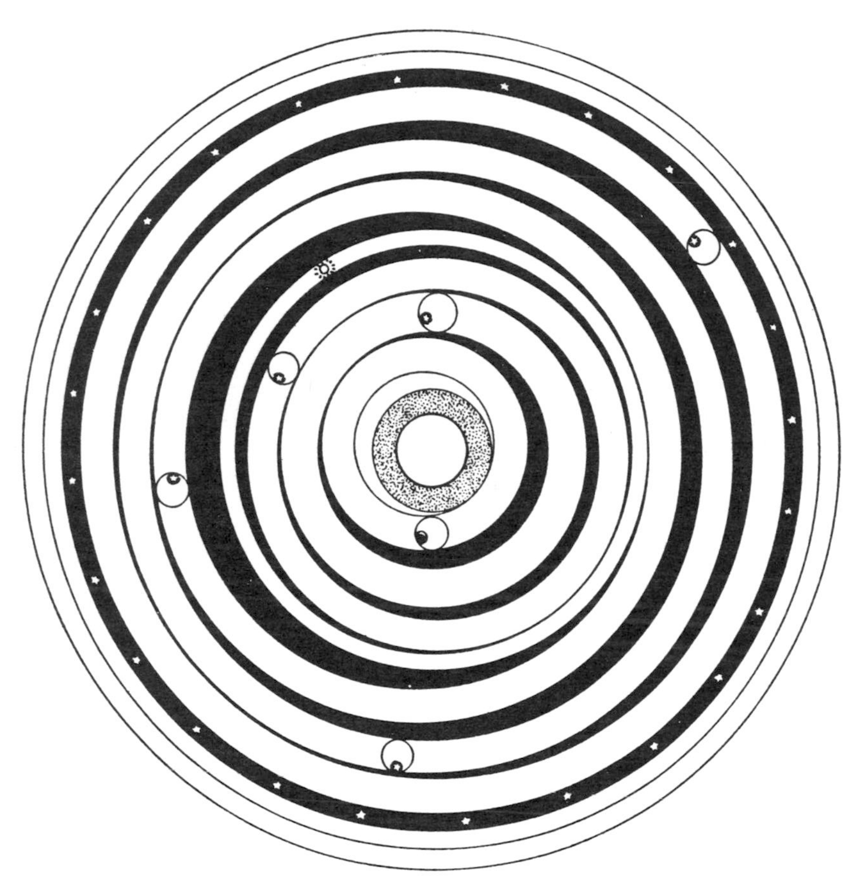

FIG. 4.—RECONSTRUCTION OF A FIFTEENTH-CENTURY COSMOLOGICAL SCHEME UTILIZING SOLID SPHERES

The notion of the planets—the "wandering stars"—being attached to spheres and spheres within spheres which carry them around the stationary Earth has a long history, developing with the Arabs into something that looks like modern ball bearings. By the fifteenth century this idea was being seriously questioned, and by Copernicus' time it had completely lost favor. The drawing is by courtesy of Dr. W. D. Stahlman.

be the same as between a living and a dead creature. I say the same concerning the Moon, Jupiter, and all the other globes of the Universe. The more I delve into the consideration of the vanity of popular discourses, the more empty and simple I find them. What greater folly can be imagined than to call gems, silver, and gold noble, and earth and dirt base? For do not these persons consider that, if there were as great a scarcity of earth as there is of jewels and precious metals, there would be no king who would not gladly give a heap of diamonds and rubies and many ingots of gold to purchase only so much earth as would suffice to plant a jessamine in a little pot or to set a tangerine in it, that he might see it sprout, grow up, and bring forth such goodly leaves, fragrant flowers, and delicate fruit?

It is scarcity and plenty that makes things esteemed and despised by the vulgar, who will say that here is a most beautiful diamond, for it resembles a clear water, and yet would not part with it for ten tons of water. These men who so extol incorruptibility, inalterability, and so on, speak thus, I believe, out of the great desire they have to live long and for fear of death, not considering that, if men had been immortal, they would not have had to come into the world. These people deserve to meet with a Medusa's head that would transform them into statues of diamond and jade, that so they might become more perfect than they are.[2]

Here we see a profoundly new idea of the universe taking shape, ancient and powerful in its roots, incalculable in its expansion, and as different from the Aristotelian caricature taught in the schools as it is from the scant and angular mechanistic dogmatism that Descartes was to introduce a few years later and Newton was reluctantly to adopt as a basis for his theories. Not quite biological, for Galileo is essentially a physicist; not mechanical, surely, for the underlying reality is imagined to be a flow of transforming and vivifying energy which is in essence, as will be revealed eventually, light itself. It is what Galileo does not shy from calling by its proper name, the "Pythagorean philosophy."

The later mystical and contemplative overtones which had been transmitted as part of that philosophy are originally reinterpreted in a way not very different from what ancient Philolaus himself

---

2. *Dialogue*, pp. 68–69.

would have meant,[3] and we see Galileo finding expressive symbols of the unifying power of reason in the creative force of life: "It seems to me that, if the celestial bodies concur to the generation and alteration of the Earth, they themselves are also of necessity alterable; for otherwise I cannot understand how the application of the Sun and Moon to the Earth to effect production should be any other than to lay a marble statue in the chamber of the bride and from that conjunction to expect children."

In such words Galileo shows himself truly as a figure of that Renaissance which had been struggling to transfer the full dimensions of the ancient and medieval heritage into a new world. Born in the same year as Shakespeare, he had worked his way through the echoing wilderness of the sixteenth century, full of hints, vast possibilities, half-understood realizations, great words from the past, panic emotions, and limitless outlooks. He had proceeded amid a multitude of problems and answers, which his responsive and experimental mind had "weighed" (the so-oft-repeated word) and sifted in every direction, turning down answers that were merely verbal and searching for the real "clues." A couple of ideas in dioptrics, and the vision of analytical geometry, were enough for Descartes in his Dutch hermitage to project a complete explanation of the universe; whereas the powerful auxiliary of the telescope was used by Galileo to show some new physical characters of the planets, but from those could be deduced conclusions more valid and far-reaching than Descartes's cosmology. Another "clue," that of accelerated motion, had extended Galileo's thinking. Then, others had come—hydrostatics, the novae, virtual velocities, magnetism, tidal motion. Always in the midst of arguments, events, and "effects," Galileo conceived of science as an endeavor without end,

---

3. Philolaus was a Pythagorean of the "second generation" (fifth century B.C.) who suggested for the first time that the Earth may be a planet revolving around the center of the universe, which he imagined to be a Central Fire. He also taught the plurality of inhabited worlds. Modern critics have doubted the authenticity of the few fragments that have been transmitted of his writings, but their reasons are not convincing (cf. G. de Santillana and W. Pitts, "Philolaus in Limbo," *Isis*, Vol. XLII, n. 128 [June, 1951]).

reaching down toward the principles even as it reached out forever to an impossible completion.

More fortunate than Leonardo, Bruno, Campanella, and a great many predecessors, he had formed the opinion that the real clues were to be found in the "demonstrations of mathematical science," which, whenever they could be applied to Nature, provided reasons not merely plausible but necessary and, as such, indistinguishable from truth itself. But all his life he had had to wage a long uphill fight to establish it against the obtaining system of values. It was next to impossible to prove to a well-conditioned scholar that mathematics was not merely a sport for the curious mind or an auxiliary to the menial and mechanical arts but an integral part of philosophy and, indeed, the proper language of science which ought to replace the disputation about purposes and attributes. As he said once, physical science told him nothing about a *why* that anyone could dig up to please his sense of fitnesses, but it gave him at times a *how* that was certainly true.

As he found that these truths tied up into a system of natural philosophy extending in all directions, he fortified himself in the conclusion that here was a glimpse of the groundwork, or at least of *a* groundwork, of Nature. But it was not before his sixtieth year that he dared to write that "the book of Nature is written in mathematical characters." Thirty-five years of search stood in back of that, which showed, not only on earth, but throughout the universe, the "Pythagorean supposition" to be no supposition at all but corresponding to a state of fact. It was his work in dynamics which had provided the chief clue. In creating "a very new science on a very ancient subject," he had given as early as 1604 the correct law for the path of missiles and had shown that it was composed of an inertial horizontal trajectory and a vertical uniformly accelerated one. The horizontal path he imagined as being really a vast circle described around the Earth, as he was, after all, entitled to do at that stage of the game; and this in turn had become a hint of how planets keep to their circular orbits, "the path that neither rises nor descends" with respect to the Sun. A fragile supposition, but it was like the rope bridge that the climber throws across a crevasse. After all, was there any mechanism, real or conceivable, in his opponents' image of the heavenly spheres? Surely not, and yet it had found acceptance. Why should he not venture ahead, then, at least in his own thoughts? For, as he wrote to Kepler, he did not dare come forward yet with such ideas. But then, suddenly, the telescope had come to turn what had been for him an intellectual wager into a shining certainty. "Oh, Nicolaus Copernicus," he must have thought as he makes Sagredo say in the *Dialogue*, "what would have been thy joy in seeing thy system confirmed by such manifest experiences!" The Great Project seemed at last possible, where mathematics, physics, and astronomy would converge into a wholly new theory of the world system.

That it would ultimately prove acceptable he never doubted, for he could not imagine that it could be contrary to revealed truth. Like Newton, he felt he had been gathering some new and beautiful shells on the shore of the vast unknown, whose nature remained inaccessible to man except through faith. He merely intended to suggest that official philosophy bring up to date its "argument from design." The new design, as he gained a first glimpse of it, he could not but find infinitely more worthy of God's majesty and hence, in all senses from the metaphysical to the common, more intrinsically *true:*

I think we arrogate too much to ourselves when we take it for granted that only the care of us is the adequate reason and limit, beyond which Divine Wisdom and Power does or disposes nothing. I will not consent that we should so much shorten its hand, but desire that we may content ourselves with an assurance that God and Nature are so employed in the governing of human affairs that they could not apply themselves more thereto if they truly had no other care than only that of mankind. And this, I think, I am able to make out by a most pertinent and most noble example, taken from the operation of the Sun's light, which, while it attracts these vapours, or heats that plant, attracts and heats them as if it had no more to do; yea, in ripening that bunch of grapes, nay, that one single grape, it does apply itself so that it could not be more intense, if the sum of all its business had been the maturation of that one grape. Now if this grape receives all that it is possible for it to receive from the Sun, not suffering the least injury by the Sun's production of a thousand other effects at the same time, well might we accuse that grape of envy or folly if it should think or wish that the Sun would appropriate all of its rays to its advantage. I am confident that nothing is omitted by the Divine Providence of what concerns the government of human affairs; but that there may not be other things in the Universe that depend upon the same infinite wisdom, I cannot, of myself, by what my reason holds forth to me, bring myself to believe. Surely, I should not forbear to believe any reasons to the contrary laid before me by some higher intellect. But, as I stand, if one should tell me that an immense space interposed between the orbs of the planets and the starry sphere, deprived of stars and idle, would be vain and useless, as likewise that so great an immensity for receipt of the fixed stars as exceeds our utmost comprehension would be superfluous, I would reply that it is rashness to go about to make our shallow reason judge of the works of God, and to call vain and superfluous whatever thing in the Universe is not of use to us.[4]

This was beautifully said. But it was subversive of traditional cosmology and of all its motives, from the higher eschatological ones to the less avowable. Resistance against it did not even have to be rationalized in order to be immediate and clamorous. It came from the depths. The course of his thought could not but remain impenetrable to the doctors and divines of his time, had they even taken pains to understand it, which they did not. To them, notwithstanding his discoveries, and even while they flatteringly called him to his face "a second Archimedes," he remained a presumptuous and froward technician who was trying to go beyond the limits of his art and to draw the attention of the curious by means of some novel subtilities and paradoxical conclusions.

4. *Dialogue*, pp. 378–79.

IV

SAINT ROBERT BELLARMINE

Most Holy Father, you say that the question [de auxiliis] *appertains to the faith, but if that be so it is everybody's concern, according to the dictum of Pope Nicholas. Therefore it should be discussed in the full light of day, and not secretly, with a mere handful of advisers.*

BELLARMINE TO CLEMENT VIII, 1601

I

ITH his theological letters of 1615, Galileo had appealed to the hierarchies of the Church against the troublemakers of the lower echelons. Throughout this crisis it is Cardinal Bellarmine much more than Pope Paul V who is in command. The nature of the man therefore becomes important.

Roberto Bellarmino was by then in his seventy-fourth year. His (rather inadequate) portraits reveal an Etruscan prow-nosed face, heavy in the lower part, eyes slightly too close together, suggesting ready peasant wit, but brooding and tense in expression, the face of a dedicated man. His had never been a speculative metaphysical temperament; he was a Jesuit, a soldier of the Church, and a specialist in applied theology. The Catholic catechism in its present form is his. He had fought the Venetian Senate, the Neapolitan Primatists, the Gallicans, the Lutherans, the Anglicans, the Calvinists, the physical premotionists, and all other deviationists and "innovators" in the name of orthodoxy and papal supremacy. His enemies paid him the compliment of stealing his arguments whenever they could,[1] for he had brought to the fight all that consummate apologetic skill and vast patristic scholarship could produce in the way of weapons. His leading activity, in fact, had been mostly as "Master of Controversial Questions" in the Collegio Romano, where he supplied armament for the Jesuits on all fronts.

His name is now almost forgotten in our countries, but it was once a name to conjure with. Madison and Jefferson are known to have consulted his texts. As the chief advocate of the papal position, he had become to the loyal English of his time a byword and a bugaboo; they did not refrain from calling him responsible for the Gunpowder Plot. Doctors organized refutation colleges against him; preachers belabored him with epithets: a "petulant railer," "the head of the popish kennel of Monks and Mendicants," "a furious and devilish Jebusite." Doggerels pursued him:

> First to breakfast, then to dine,
> Is to conquer Bellarmine.

The common people had found their own way of copious refutation, if not of liquidation, by giving the name of "bellarmines" to certain paunchy jugs used for liquor, whose neck was in the grotesque effigy of a bearded man.

As to the reasons for this animosity, we may take them from Dr. Johnson's own summary of Bellarmine's contention, which minces no words: "That the Pope is invested with all the authority on heaven and earth. That all princes are his vassals, and that he may annul their laws at his pleasure. That he may depose kings if the good of the Church requires it. . . . That the Pope is God upon earth . . . and that to call his power in question is to call in question the power of God: maxims equally shocking, weak, pernicious and absurd; which did not require the abilities and learning of Father Paul [Sarpi] to demonstrate their falsehoods and destructive tendencies." We have deleted certain clauses in his text to keep it within the bounds of fairness, for Dr. Johnson was apt to resort to the

1. "But of our priests and doctors how many have been corrupted by studying the comments of Jesuits and Sorbonists, and how fast they could transfuse that corruption into the people, our experience is both late and sad" (Milton, *Areopagitica*).

"scurrility of expression" with which he taxes his late learned opponent. But, then, Johnson as a loyal subject of the king felt good reason to be exercised, for Bellarmine had been a not imaginary threat to the English state.

The Oath of Allegiance of 1605, with the following Act against the Recusants, had been itself England's answer to the Jesuit challenge contained in Bellarmine's theory of the Pope's indirect power, and it marks a turning point in the history of modern politics.[2]

Englishmen were ordered to "abhorre, detest and abjure as impious and hereticall, this damnable doctrine and position that Princes which be excommunicated or deprived by the Pope may be deposed by their subjects," and this was the essential point of the oath, which had been drafted long before the Gunpowder Plot. Small wonder, then, that the controversialist who pursued the Cardinal in choicest language, and with prodigious expenditure of learned labor, should have been no less than King James I himself, "Professor, Maintainer and Defender of the True, Christian, Catholic and Apostolique Faith." Bellarmine had reminded him coldly that this very title had been bestowed by the Pope upon Henry VIII only "for his fight against Luther and the other innovators" and had gone on taking Queen Elizabeth herself to task:

> Indeed Our Lord might very aptly have addressed her as he once addressed the woman of Samaria: "Thou hast well said, I have no husband, for thou hast five husbands, and he whom thou now hast is no husband." However, though Her Majesty's life was not chaste, it was cautious . . . and she showed her great prudence too, by skilfully fostering wars and seditions in her neighbors' kingdoms, that she might enjoy peace in her own . . . and yet further evidence of the same virtue was provided by her treatment of your Majesty's mother. . . . But she freely followed her fancies in everything, and proclaimed herself the first *Sacerdos magna* or rather *Pontifex maxima* since the world began, although not only human and divine law but even grammar itself protested.

There was bitter point enough here to cause James to forget the treatment of Mary Stuart. "Christ is no more contrary to Belial,"

2. This is C. H. McIlwain's own summing-up in his Introduction to *The Political Works of James I* (Cambridge, Mass., 1928), pp. xlix and lvi.

he thundered, "light to darkness, and heaven to hell, than Bellarmine's estimation of Kings is to God's." But he was launched, and there was nothing to do but go on: *Apologia, Responsio, Premonitio,* went back and forth in wearisome succession, with the contestants heaving ton-loads of quotations at each other. "I was never the man, I confesse," remarks the King haughtily, "that could think a Cardinall a meete match for a King; especially having many hundred thousands of my subjects of as good birth as he." But he is not going to leave that task to his doctors, however impatient they may be to serve him:

> No desire of vaine glory by matching wits with so learned a man, maketh mee to undertake this taske; but onely the care and conscience I have, that such smooth Circes charm and guilded pilles, as full of exterior eloquence as of inward untrueths, may not have that publique passage through the world without an answere.

Soon, however, James I perceives that he has an incalculable bear by the tail, and his tone grows peevish:

> My booke being first written in English and translated into Latine, it commeth home unto me now answered in both the languages. And, I thinke, if it had been set forth in all the tongues that were at the confusion of Babel, it would have returned answered in them all again. Thus may a man see how busie a Bishop the Devil is. . . .

A modern Alexander *in partibus,* the King was moved to bring out a book entitled *Triplici nodo triplex cuneus,* or "A Threefold Wedge for a Triple Knot." The most serviceable wedge, of course, still was the Gunpowder Plot itself, that early version of the Reichstag fire. A pioneer in the techniques of the cold war and a man of uncommon intelligence, James used it in order to prove that the Catholic religion was really not a religion but a conspiracy. But, for all his understandable grievances against "caitiffe monsters, traitours and pestilent papists," it was not easy for him to extricate himself from the knot of his own actions. The Cardinal could retort with stringent logic:

> Even though it were true, which it is not, that no one suffered death for conscience' sake in England who had not first openly transgressed the law, yet since the law forbids anyone to receive a priest into his house under grievous penalties, to be reconciled to the Church, and to

hear Mass, one who dies for transgressing such a law may rightly be said to have died for his religion. It is an old pagan device to make a law and then murder men, not intolerantly for religion's sake, of course, but with wise statesmanship, because they offended against the majesty of the constitution.[3] . . . As for the gracious proclamation whereby all priests who are not actually in chains might go out of the country by such a day, what wonderful kindness it was to allow men to go into exile whom His Majesty could not catch, try he ever so hard! And if exile seems a mercy to the royal author, one may wonder what sweet names he has for the rack and rope.

Truly, as the King said, "if the Devil had studied a thousand yeeres," he could not have made more mischief than those men in Rome:

For some of such Priests and Jesuits who were the greatest Traitours and fomenters of the greatest conspiracies against the late Queene, gave up Bellarmine for one of their greatest authorities and oracles. And therefore I doe not envie the great honour he can win by his vaunt of his inward familiaritie with another Princes' traitours and fugitives; whom if he teach no better manners than hitherto he hath done, I think his fellowship are little beholding unto him.

Of the two contestants, the King was clearly the more painful casuist, if by far the greater writer. But his case was resting on a couple of very solid realities, namely, that the British were disinclined to be ruled by the Pope, even symbolically, and that they did not want their Parliament to be blown up; hence he had won out even before starting.[4] In his later years the King seems to have

3. When the trial of Father Ogilvie began, in 1613, the books of Bellarmine and Suárez were on his judge's table. He was asked whether he believed the doctrines taught in them, and, answering that indeed he did, he was condemned to death. This is one of the many instances in which James I did act undeniably as a Roman emperor.

4. The battle of the books went on for a long time, with learned doctors on both sides plunging into the fray. Mountains labored to bring forth more mountains; it was *Bellarminus Destructus*, *B. Enervatus*, *B. Defensus*, *B. Vindicatus*. Divines told each other violently and vainly to shut up in several languages; it went from the *Confutation of Certaine Absurdities, Falsities and Follies, etc., etc., by F. T.*, to *Collins' Epphata to F. T.*, then to *The Obmutesce of F. T. to the*

felt secure enough to relent, for "he constantly carried about his person" a copy of Bellarmine's little devotional book, *The Lament of the Dove,* and spoke of it as a wondrous aid to spiritual comfort. It is hard to imagine today the President of the United States carrying about his person a copy of Lenin's *What Is To Be Done?* for spiritual consolation, or Mr. Malenkov taking an occasional look at the homiletics of Dale Carnegie.

We have dwelt at some length with the Anglican controversy for reasons of familiarity and also for the amusement that could be afforded by the prancing periods of the King. But it represents a too simple issue and should not distract the attention from the vast and complex crisis in which Bellarmine was playing the leading role. His fight was no less against the Venetian Senate and the parliamentary faction in France, all of them solid Catholics, than against the avowed schismatics of England. The bitterest words are from orthodox Catholic politicians. Take a passage from the anonymous *Tocsin to the King,* printed in Paris in 1610, when young Louis XIII was under the regency of Marie de Medici:

> This precious Cardinal, this sophistical dunderhead, this blood-sucker of princes, this reptile with hooked teeth, would cram his pontiffs with ambition to possess the whole world and reduce every nation to their sway. The pages of his book are as dangerous as the drooling slime of a mad dog. O drowsy France, open thy eyes. . . .

This is no more than a pamphleteer's violence, coming a few months after the assassination of Henry IV. But the Catholic polemic was carried on also on a level of strong juridical argument by such men as Barclay and Widdrington. The names are enough to show how the quarrel cut across frontiers, for here are Scottish and English Catholics defending the sovereign rights not only of France, which was harboring them, but of England, which had sent them into banishment, and even writing an apology for the Oath of Allegiance.

Bellarmine personally had never hidden his partiality for mon-

---

Epphata of Dr. Collins, and so on. We need not dwell upon the "revelations" of Dr. Titus Oates. They had their effect, which was more tragically serious. Two centuries later old men were still declaiming against "Rum, Romanism, and Rebellion."

archy against all other forms of government, but to the French *politiques* he was the worst of monarchomachs, because he pitted his authority against the absolute monarchic principle. The "divine right of kings" was a term which hid the most modern development of the times, namely, the birth of the present national and secular state. Against that, Bellarmine and Suárez at the head of the Jesuit legions were not simply reaffirming, as they believed they were, the proud age-old doctrine of Boniface's *Unam Sanctam*. For they, too, who wanted only to maintain eternal verities, were men of their own time. In them and around them were those new things, Jesuit spirit and Jesuit discipline; against the theorists of the national state, they were, in a way they would never have dreamed of, the early theorists of the modern superstate.

II

As such Bellarmine stands today, enshrined forever in sainthood by his Church, his figure so completely identified with his function that the name has become as much of a cipher as Caesar's Tenth Legion. Yet, if we probe beneath the layers of conventional panegyric and vituperation, we find a very interesting personality indeed.

A nobleman from Montepulciano in Tuscany, and a distant nephew of Machiavelli on the distaff side, he had of his own the vivid and powerful nature which might have made him, three centuries earlier, into a great political leader in the turbulent affairs of the free communes, a figure not unworthy of Dante's Farinata or Provenzano Salvani. One can still discern from scattered bits of testimonial the original man, immensely ambitious, direct, prompt to flashing anger, as passionate for Virgil since his childhood as his own fellow-townsman Poliziano; musical and artistic, conceited about his intellectual and rhetorical gifts, as he reveals candidly in his scant autobiographical notes. That original man is in more than one way a fitting counterpart to Galileo. He was quite sure, on the other hand—while modestly discounting it—that he had the gift of prophecy; and one wonders whither this would have led him in a Protestant environment.

But, once the man has been plowed up and remolded by the discipline of Loyola, all these qualities are transmuted into dedication, as Galileo's were tempered by the discipline of science. We have the Bellarmine of history, an indefatigable self-denying laborer consumed in prayer and penance, ascetic in his vows of poverty, patient, humble in obedience, prone to copious tears. The original man flowers then unexpectedly in the other side of his Tuscan nature, easygoing, light, and unassuming, with nothing in it of the *romana grandezza* so much in evidence in the Vatican of those times. He comes, then, to resemble in more than one way his older fellow-townsman, St. Philip Neri. The profound security and trust of his inner life allowed Bellarmine to preserve to the end a childlike quality that was noted by all who came in contact with him, and which was nowhere more in evidence than in his streaks of subdued but undeniably impish merriment and in his addiction to lighthearted punning. It was at times his escape. His heart must have been set against Paul V's policy of pompous monumental display, which he felt deprived the Church of the money she owed to the poor; for, on hearing the Pope criticized for it, he winked slyly and said: "At least you cannot deny that he is a man of great edification." It was as much irony as he could allow himself toward the master who was for him God on earth. Had he found himself face to face with the grimness of New England divines, he would have remarked that it was clearly the mark of the Evil One that these people had no gaiety in them.

We are trying here to liberate something that was present and authentic in him from the testimonial of his own expressions, for the effusions of humility, tenderness, and holy joy have become such a cloying cliché of Counter-Reformation writing that the reader who delved through the actual Jesuit prose might be tempted to find them as unconvincing as his famous syllogisms. The man's whole life was the living of an impenetrable convention, yet the seal of his nature is on it, a Tuscan simplicity as genuine as Loyola's Spanish fire.

The reports of realistic ambassadors are a very revealing source, as we shall also see presently in the case of Galileo. The Count of Olivares was writing to the King of Spain after the death of Pope Sixtus: "Bellarmine is beloved for his great goodness, but he is a scholar who lives only among books and not of much practical ability [*de poca sustancia in agibilibus*]. . . . He would not do for a Pope, for he is mindful only of the interests of the Church and is unresponsive to the reasons of princes. . . . He would scruple to accept gifts. . . . I suggest that we exert no action in his favor." The King annotated curtly: "To be left to run his chance."

There remains the intellectual side of the man to be considered. If Galileo was laying considerable hope in his benevolence, he had reasons which were obvious to any person of his time. In his anomalous position as a Jesuit in the Curia, Bellarmine was sure not to have his judgment swayed by any excessive sympathy for the Brothers of St. Dominic. The controversy *de auxiliis* was not far behind him, with its fantastic battle of the books which had plunged Rome in a cloud of theological dust; and from that battle the Jesuits had not come out well. Bellarmine himself, in his role of papal theologian, had tried to reconcile the contestants, while not letting down his brethren of the Company, and had gotten himself diplomatically exiled for his pains to the archbishopric of Capua.

What had happened was this. Certain Dominicans of Spain, succumbing to one of those recurrent attacks of the Puritan genie which comes out of the pages of St. Augustine to take hold of the indiscreet logician, had developed a theory of divine grace which ran perilously close to Calvinism. The Jesuit Luis Molina had tried to resist with a closely reasoned argument and had been subjected to an implacable barrage of refutation on the part of the Dominicans, led by Domingo Bañes, who were reasserting the position of theological paramountcy held by their Order. The Jesuits had come to the help of their brother, and it had become a pitched battle. The gradually multiplying subtilities of the Jesuit position have been pitilessly exposed and preserved by Pascal for literature two generations later; but, if it is sure that the controversy brought forth some of the strangest specimens of quibbling that the world has ever seen, this still should not cause us to forget that the issue was as clear and fundamental as could be: Do all men stand a chance of saving their souls with the help of divine grace, or is their fate irresistibly predetermined?[5]

5. Once Augustine had firmly established the need of God's grace for salvation, any theory of ethical decision developed on the basis of

In this quarrel Bellarmine interposed himself with a good sense that was to gain him later the unexpected sympathy of Bayle.[6] The efficacy of divine grace had to be defended against Pelagians old

---

God's omniscience and omnipotence was bound to get itself into a maelstrom of logical difficulties. One way to keep out of it was to do as Calvin had done and to follow the logical line inflexibly to the conclusion of predestination irrespective of faith and of merit—and also of infant damnation. A Scots Dominie might find it all very simple, but a truly Evangelic soul would have balked at following the logic to its bitter end, or, maybe, we should say, starting from the gloomy assumption of mankind's utter indigence and vileness, as expressed in Jonathan Edwards' famous simile of the "loathsome spider." Even the Dominicans of Bañes had avoided doing so; they had discovered an entity called "physical premotion" which was not quite predestination. But the formal terrain remained very slippery, as Molina had pointed out.

The technical point (all too briefly) is this. God is the First Cause, and no secondary cause can act efficaciously unless predetermined by Him. Moreover, since secondary causes cannot act until moved by the First Cause, God's concurrence with His creatures must be conceived as antecedent and not merely simultaneous. It is not a motion but a "premotion," and, since He is an omnipotent being whose decrees are irresistible, this premotion is a "force of Nature" in this sense; it is a "physical premotion." Now God has determined men's wills freely to determine themselves. This is a case of physical premotion. But corresponding to it in the supernatural sphere is efficacious (not merely sufficient) grace, and corresponding to both in the mind of God is the predetermination whereby from all eternity He decreed to influence His creatures in such and such ways, using premotions and efficacious graces of infinite variety, but all infallibly certain of their effect. God foresees everything that men will do in the decrees of His divine will, because it is only in virtue of these decrees that men can act at all. Against this, Molina (and Bellarmine) had created for God's foreknowledge of the conditioned future the term *scientia media*, or "middle knowledge," because it embraces all objects that are found neither in the realm of pure possibility nor, strictly speaking, in the realm of actuality. They are actual in the sense that they would exist, were certain conditions granted. In the light of this knowledge God foresees from all eternity what attitude the will of man would adopt under any conceivable combination of circumstances, and then only, though the relation is not temporal but ontological, does He decree to share out His graces according to His

and new,[7] and the freedom of the will had to be defended against Lutherans, Calvinists, and Catholic deviationists. The Cardinal works back to the strict orthodoxy of the Thomist line, even if it involves being accused of the "abomination of semi-Pelagianism." As the Dominicans, indeed, have recourse to Caccini-like practices, he recalls them brusquely to correct behavior:

> As the matter is still *sub judice,* the authors of the *Memorial* show a great deal of impudence by talking as if it had been decided, and as if the Fathers of the Society, whom they invariably style innovators, had already been condemned.

No doubt, in order to restore a difficult philosophical balance, the Cardinal is compelled at times to use many an "*argumentum stramineum* framed upon strawes," as King James would call it; but there is no mistaking the firm line of the whole, as also the humanistic spirit in which he undertakes to defend the essential freedom of man.

Throughout the *Controversies* there is such evidence of an ample, organic, and orderly mind, with an immense storage capacity for texts of the Fathers, and a unifying vision that supports its effort unerringly, even to the disregard of any conflict among the actual authorities so carefully quoted. Bellarmine does not stand out as a rigorous logician; he does not have the steel-trap mind of a Suárez. But, then, his preoccupation is to keep away from any "original" development, and he takes infinite pains to show that he is rediscovering or reaffirming only the "common sentence" of the Fathers and doctors. His mind is a smoothly running organization aimed at restoring the intellectual status quo.

---

pleasure. Sufficient grace in this scheme does not differ really from efficacious, or irresistible. It is perfectly adequate in itself for the purposes of salvation, but God foresees that such and such ones to whom it is offered will infallibly refuse it.

6 (*on preceding page*). See Pierre Bayle, *Dictionnaire historique et critique* (1697), art. "Bellarmin."

7. Pelagius, a monk of the third century A.D. (his original name was Morgan), had practically denied the effect of original sin by maintaining that man is naturally good and does not need the help of divine grace to attain salvation. His doctrine was condemned by the Council of Ephesus in 431.

In his capacity to incorporate new facts and new techniques in the structure, Bellarmine the Jesuit is a modern personality; and, as such, he could arouse hopes in Galileo. But his modern thought, as we have said, really tends to the creation of the frame of a theological superstate, which means that, as far as his time went, he was working in a kind of historic vacuum. It is only on the formal plane that his work takes on the solidity of a Baroque monument. Like the architecture of the time, it is based upon unerring craftsmanship which can hold together incredible voids and apparently conflicting elements in a strong and subtle design.

In this over-all design the scientific component is far from negligible. But, if we try to take it by itself, it will show no consistency of its own.

As sometimes occurs with men immersed in the affairs of state, Bellarmine liked to play with the ideas of astronomy. It stimulated his sense of wonderment. We might think, for instance, that his appeal to the words of the Psalm, "He rejoiceth like a giant in running his course," is nothing but reference to a normative text; but it is not. He liked to dwell upon the grandeur of the thing, even to do a bit of reckoning on it, as we can see from some thoughts he was writing for a devotional treatise, in those very same months in which Galileo was hoping he would give some thoughts to his problems:

> I myself being once desirous to know in what space of time the Sun set at sea, at the beginning thereof I began to recite the Psalm *Miserere*, and scarce had read it twice over before the Sun was wholly set. It must needs be, therefore, that the Sun in that short time did run much more than the space of 7,000 miles. Who would believe this unless certain reason did demonstrate it?[8]

He finds it natural here to rely on "certain reason." At other times he is apt to get a little impatient with it, if it wants to legislate too much. Thus, in a sermon preached in 1571 on the text "There shall be signs in the Sun and in the Moon and in the stars," he speculates as follows:

> It is a matter of the very greatest difficulty to decide what ought to be understood by the expression, the "falling of the stars." Should

8. *De ascensione mentis in Deum.*

we wish to interpret the word "stars" as meaning those igneous appearances which are commonly called falling stars . . . we ought to be careful lest we find ourselves in contradiction with the Gospel, for if the Gospel speaks of the real Sun and the real Moon, does it not follow that it also means real stars? On the other hand, if, swayed by the authority of the Gospel, we dare to affirm that the stars will really fall from heaven at the Last Day, we are immediately confronted by a mighty mob of mathematicians, out of whose hands there is no means of escape. They will vociferate and clamor in our ears, just as if they themselves had measured the size of the stars, that it is impossible for the stars to fall upon the Earth, for even the least of the fixed stars is so much bigger than the Earth, that the Earth could not possibly receive it if it were to fall.

To these asseverations of the mathematicians we might oppose the opinion of St. Basil the Great, St. John Chrysostom, St. Ambrose, the most learned St. Augustine, and very many others, who hold that, with the single exception of the Sun, the Moon is bigger than any of the stars, from which it follows that the Earth must be much bigger than any of them, for even the mathematicians admit that the Moon is much smaller than the Earth.

Still, such an argument would not keep the mathematicians quiet, and, as we have no wish to be drawn into a dispute with them, we give as our opinion . . . that the problem cannot be solved until the signs actually appear. In this way the confession of our ignorance would be our answer to the difficulty. All that Our Lord said about the judgment to come, the end of the world, and the signs that would precede it, was said in prophecy, and it is a characteristic of the sayings of the Prophets that, until what they have foretold comes to pass, their speech remains almost completely enigmatic to us. . . .

This is rather revealing. Bellarmine was not going to deny the claims of mathematicians, but he thought of them as we in our time tend to think of statisticians and pollsters: wizards in their own way, but simple-minded and heavy-fingered gents who are apt to go wrong with great assurance.

Yet he did not lack a knowledge of the subject. He had even taught it in his young years, out of a romantic interest which had sprung from an early study of Macrobius' solemn and mystical speculations on the *Somnium Scipionis*. In 1564 he had lectured in Florence on "the doctrine of the spheres and the fixed stars." However much he may have dwelt on such subjects as "the number and places of the elements, whether each of the stars is a separate species, and the ultimate boundaries of the world,"[9] it did not go without a minimum of geometry. This was actually at about the same time as Galileo was being born. . . .

The following year, lecturing at the College of Mondovi in Piedmont, he had taught again about the theory of the heavens, "philosophically and astrologically." We remarked already how astrologically minded scholars were inclined to be cold to Copernicus, whom they considered to have deluded their expectations. This may be one reason why Bellarmine never examined the Copernican ideas. Much more solid reasons, no doubt, were that the stability of the Earth was for him a truism, Aristotle's the only sensible way of dealing with physics, and astronomers a curious kind of people who wasted a lot of time making up unrealistic suppositions. We have a record of his opinions from his encounter with Vimercati, an elderly pedagogue of the Duke of Savoy:

> Many years ago I had a discussion with Vimercati, the celebrated philosopher, about the number of the celestial spheres. Personally I was convinced that there were eight of them and no more, but I found it impossible to win over any of these astronomers to my opinions, because they all persisted in clinging to the observations of Hipparchus and Ptolemy, as if they were articles of faith.

These few lines are a dead giveaway. His own simple and uncorrected observations on the speed of the Sun he is willing to take for reason itself, but the precision of the astronomers is irritating. It spoils the physical system of the philosophers. In this Bellarmine is more Thomist than Thomas himself, for the Angelic Doctor had never gone so far in his distrust of mathematics. In his commentary on the books *On Heaven* Thomas had made it clear that the Ptolemaic hypotheses had to be taken as the best description of appearances, although "we must not say that they are thereby proved to be facts, because perhaps it would be possible to explain the apparent movements of the stars by some other method which men have not yet thought out." In other words, as a serious thinker would, Aquinas held that this split between mathematics and phys-

---

9. J. Fuligatti, *Vita del Cardinale Bellarmino* (Rome, 1624), p. 32.

ics was only a temporary makeshift and that with time a way would be found to incorporate both into a cogent system. But Galileo would never have dared quote this as a hint in his favor, for it was clear that Aquinas was expecting it would be done out of Aristotle as the only acceptable physics: he was looking one way in time while Galileo was working the other way.

With all this, however, Aquinas was adequately comprehensive.[10] He was waiting for a third solution. But Bellarmine is quite satisfied with the Aristotelian idea of reality *en gros*, an attitude which goes on par with his belief in astrological forces and which is out of sympathy with precisionism and the "paradoxical conclusions sought after by curious minds." No doubt, too, he shared a feeling common to many thinkers interested mainly in human affairs, which has been expressed for them by Montesquieu: "I have come to be deeply suspicious of the tyranny of geometry." Bellarmine's very humanism is typically that of a Jesuit, in that it tends to stress the practical side:

> The soul of man is endowed with another kind of science, whose object is more practical than speculative. Out of it were born so many books of philosophers about vices and virtues, so many laws of princes, so many opinions of jurists, so many institutions and treatises which teach the art of right living.[11]

In a more homely vein this attitude reappears in his sermons: "Men are so like frogs. They go open-mouthed for the lure of things which do not concern them, and that wily angler the Devil knows how to capture multitudes of them."

Such, then, was the personal thought of the Cardinal on the delicate subject. It is to his wisdom that Galileo is now commending his cause as he writes his desperate letters to Monsignor Dini[12]

---

10. Aquinas did hope for a real mathematical system which should be closer to the homocentric diagram of Eudoxus than to the unnatural epicycles of Hipparchus; on the other hand, he did not believe much in the crystal spheres that Aristotle had tried to construct out of Eudoxus. But he thought, rightly, that any physical system ought to be homocentric.

11. *De ascensione mentis in Deum* viii. 4.

12. See p. 53.

(dispatched posthaste as soon as he had heard that the sinister Caccini was on his way to Rome), which are really meant for Bellarmine. He realizes what is the Cardinal's main concern, as he protests humbly, in the words of Scripture: "I would tear out my own eye, rather than have it give scandal." What he offers is meant not as an argument but as a submissive request, to be further developed if given a hint of encouragement. Prudently, he concludes his last letter to Dini thus:

"What you have here is but a poor and rough offspring, which would need to be patiently and lovingly licked into shape; I hope to bring it some time to better symmetry; meanwhile, I beg of you that you let it not come into the hands of any who, using on it, in lieu of the softness of the motherly tongue, the cutting sharpness of the novercal tooth, might rend and tear instead of shaping it. With this I respectfully kiss your hand, together with Messrs. Buonarroti,[13] Guiducci, Soldani, and Giraldi, who are present at the closing of this letter."

III

The "stepmotherly tooth" was so vigorously at work already that Dini delayed showing the letter to the Cardinal. A few weeks later he writes: "You see how right I was. The inclosed document will show you the humor of these Lords." (The document was Bellarmine's answer to Father Foscarini, of which more later.) To Dini's personal entreaties, however, the Cardinal had answered that "he did not think the work of Copernicus would be prohibited, at most some saving addition [*postilla*] might be made to the effect that it was only meant to explain appearances, or some such phrase, and with this reservation Signor Galileo would be able to discuss the subject without further impediment."

Bellarmine may have added "with a countenance not very grave" (so a biographer describes him): What if Copernicus *did* get suspended pending correction? Such things happened all the time. He

---

13. This is the younger Buonarroti, a distinguished poet, the nephew of Michelangelo. He was to prove a constant friend in adversity. Mario Guiducci was the secretary of the Florentine Academy and was later to write, together with Galileo, the *Discourse on the Comets.*

need not remind Dini that he himself, Bellarmine, had had his great text of *Controversies* put on the Index "pending correction" in 1590 by the irascible Sixtus V for not going far enough in his championship of papal absolutism and that, had Sixtus not died, he might have stayed on the Index for a good long time. As a matter of fact, the Jesuit general Acquaviva had written to him, twenty-five years earlier, in exactly the same vein: "The most that could be asked of you would be the change of a few words in a new edition, as, for instance, where you speak of *errors*, that you should say instead *errors or opinions of certain writers*."[14]

Cardinals Barberini and del Monte sent similarly soothing reports through Dini and Ciàmpoli.[15] The latter added on his own (March 21, 1615): "Of these roaring waters of which allusion has been made to you, one does not hear anything here, and yet I am not deaf, and I go around in many places where I ought to detect the noise." Father Maraffi, the friendly Preacher-General,[16] had tried to sound out influential members of his Order, but the Domini-

14. It had been the hope of a moment. Sixtus was bent on prohibiting. Wrote the Spanish ambassador, Olivares: "The cardinals of the Congregation of the Index did not dare tell His Holiness that the teaching of the book is drawn from the works of the saints for fear he might give them a bit of his brusque temper and perhaps put the saints themselves on the Index." Even beyond the time of Sixtus, the "consecrated whirlwind," the feeling seems to have been current in Rome that the Index was a kind of administrative misadventure that occurred sooner or later to anyone writing on serious subjects and that it was a matter of waiting until the official line changed again. Of the three theologians of the Inquisition who were the experts at Galileo's trial, two subsequently incurred prohibition—and one of them a cardinal, Oregius.

15. Monsignor Giovanni Ciàmpoli (the accent is on the *a*) was a recent recruit to the circle of Galileists. A brilliant young Latinist, he was marked for a great career. "It seems impossible to me," he had written to Galileo, "that one should frequent you and not love you. There is no greater magic than the beauty of virtue and the power of eloquence; to hear you is to be convinced by your truth, and whatever I can do will always be at your service." He kept faith only too well, as we shall see.

16. See p. 45.

cans had heard of nothing; they knew nothing. Caccini, it was said, had come to Rome for a certain baccalaureate of his.

Ciàmpoli's suggestions, however, end up in the same note of uncertainty as Cesi's and Dini's. Yes, it would be a good idea if Galileo came to Rome. He hears that there are Jesuits who are holding back but who are secretly of the Copernican persuasion. On the other hand, it is essential to give no chance for provocation, to go on working, let the fuss die down; then the road will be clear again. In these men's minds there is no conflict. Like Galileo, they are good Christians unafraid. Whoever heard of the Church opposing true science, since she is the guardian of all truth? But it is hard going "in these matters in which the monks are not wont to concede defeat." High quarters have let it be understood that it is well to soft-pedal the issue for a while, and they have their good reasons. Avoid new occasions for scandal-makers. Do not ruffle high quarters while they are pondering high policy. Send us your briefs. "We shall get them into the hands of honest people when the occasion arises; for, as to the others, we had rather leave them out of it." You have more friends than you would think; etc.

To see duplicity, on the other hand, in the evasive statements of the prelates of the Tuscan clan,[17] as so many historians have done, is unfair. They themselves are in the dark. Their advice, on the whole, is sound: The less noise the better. As to Bellarmine, himself, who is the only one to know, he does not try to deceive. His forecast corresponds to the decision he has already taken. He is not thinking or pondering much. He is waiting for the Commissary of the Inquisition to tell him when the thing will be ready to go on the docket. (Caccini's denunciation had come in on March 21, 1615, but the interrogatories lasted, as we have seen, until the end of November.) There is occasional consultation with the friendly cardinals—even Grienberger is called in—but it all amounts to periodic *tours d'horizon,* as they are called in the trade. The scientific issue itself obviously is not touched upon; no one gives it a

17. The Cardinals Bellarmine, Bonsi, Barberini, and del Monte were Tuscans and under the allegiance of the Grand Duke, and so were Dini and Ciàmpoli.

thought. Even Grienberger has obediently made up his mind that it is irrelevant.

It is difficult to generalize on this occasion. Church education did not prevent the rise of first-rate mathematical talent, as in Castelli and Cavalieri. Churchmen like Dini, Ciàmpoli, Foscarini, Stunica, Piccolomini, Maraffi, and, not least, Sarpi were among the most fervid promoters of the Copernican cause; but they were at most in the position of executive assistants. Where responsibility began, perception ceased; and the top echelons, as we can see now, seem to have thought of intellectual issues purely as a matter of administration. The trouble with these leaders' minds, so subtly logical on points of law, was that they stopped functioning as soon as they dealt with a diagram or with this kind of "new stuff, paradox to the philosophical vulgar," as Ciàmpoli called it.[18]

They had a high regard for all sciences, but as lawyers they would always come back with the question: Is there not another way to present this case? Could you reverse a finding on that? It was not a good sign that Cardinal Joyeuse found Colombe's *Discorso* (which is a mass of errant nonsense) quite plausible and said that he would like to have Galileo's opinion on it.[19]

Brought up to mental compromise, the clerical mind shied away even from what it had learned in its own schools. Nothing is more revealing than a little speech of Cardinal Federigo Borromeo, as good a scholar as any and the founder of the great Ambrosian Library, to the Jesuits embarking for the South Seas. While exhorting them to contribute to the knowledge of Nature in those far places, he added the hope that, since they were going to the antipodes, they would find out about "the foundations of the deep."

---

18. Ingoli, a much-esteemed lawyer and polymath in the employ of Propaganda Fide, submitted a counterbrief which was considered excellent by the authorities (cf. Ed. Naz., VI, 510). His level of geometrical reasoning can be inferred from this one remark: "The point in the center will have a greater distance from the surface of the sphere than any other inside the sphere, and a parallax correspondingly greater; but the Moon has a greater parallax than the Sun; therefore the Sun cannot be in the center."

19. Letter of Gallanzoni, June 26, 1611 (Ed. Naz., XI, 131).

Now he might have known from Aquinas, over whom he had labored for so many years, that there was no such thing, since the Earth was no longer in official doctrine a pillar "founded on the deep," as the Old Testament suggests, but a sphere symmetrically suspended at the center of the universe. But even the orthodox diagram had not registered on his mind.

Such men could not react favorably to Galileo's attempt at showing inherent deficiencies in the official interpretation of Scripture. Granted, Joshua's story was not so easy to account for in Ptolemaic theory. Granted, even Aristotle and Ptolemy did not get along any too well together. But, once the layers, so laboriously joined, of Greek, Hellenistic, and Hebrew tradition were pried apart, a swarm of most indiscreet doubts would assail the mind. We know from Ciàmpoli's gossip the kind of alarmed questions that were raised among a certain public about the new ideas: Did it mean that there were men in the Moon? What then of Adam and of Noah's Ark? What of the Devil that is supposed to be at the center of the world? Where is the angel that moves the Earth? For it is clear from Aquinas that planets do not move by themselves.[20]

---

20. Aquinas states that the heavens are said to move naturally because they have no repugnance to circular motion but still have no inclination to it (i.e., have no active potency toward motion but only passive), and they are moved supernaturally because the motor, which is an angel, is a voluntary motor.

As to the previous point, viz., the location of hell, it also remains a serious difficulty today if we consider "grave opinion." The present stand of the question may be gathered from the learned pen of Father J. Hontheim, in the *Catholic Encyclopedia* (New York: Appleton, 1910). We can see better from it how the mind of the Qualifiers of the Holy Office was bound to work: "Holy Writ seems to indicate that hell is within the earth, for it describes hell as an abyss to which the wicked descend. We even read of the earth opening and of the wicked sinking down into hell (Num., xvi, 31 sqq./ Ps., liv, 16; Is., v, 14; Ez., xxvi, 20; Phil., ii, 10, etc.). Is this merely a metaphor to illustrate the state of separation from God? Although God is omnipresent, He is said to dwell in heaven, because the light and grandeur of the stars and the firmament are the brightest manifestations of His infinite splendour. But the damned are utterly estranged from God; hence their abode is said to be as remote as possible from His

Ciàmpoli and Dini went on, like loyal servants of a great administration, thinking of inscrutable long-range designs; they would have been astonished to know how great a place those same "simple-minded" alarms that they had derided took in Bellarmine's mind. He knew how much had been conceded through the centuries; still, he knew best what an incredibly disparate assemblage of notions,

---

dwelling, far from heaven above and its light, and consequently hidden away in the dark abysses of the earth. However, no cogent reason has been advanced for accepting a metaphorical interpretation in preference to the most natural meaning of the words of Scripture. Hence theologians generally accept the opinion that hell is really within the earth."

The author then sets forth tentatively his own personal opinion, which is that we know that there is a hell but that we do not know exactly where it is. Then he goes on: "Beyond the possibility of doubt, the Church expressly teaches the eternity of the pains of hell as a truth of faith which no one can deny or call in question without manifest heresy. But what is the attitude of mere reason towards this doctrine? Just as God must appoint some fixed term for the time of trial, after which the just will enter into the secure possession of a happiness that can never again be lost in all eternity, so it is likewise appropriate that after the expiration of that term the wicked will be cut off from all hope of conversion and happiness. For the malice of men cannot compel God to prolong the appointed time of probation and to grant them again and again, without end, the power of deciding their lot for eternity. Any obligation to act in this manner would be unworthy of God, because it would make Him dependent on the caprice of human malice, would rob His threats in great part of their efficacy, and would offer the amplest scope and the strongest incentives to human presumption. . . . According to the greater number of theologians the term *fire* denotes a material fire, and so a real fire. We hold to this teaching as absolutely true and correct. However, we must not forget two things: from Catharinus (d. 1553) to our times there have never been wanting theologians who interpret the Scriptural term *fire* metaphorically, as denoting an incorporeal fire; and secondly, thus far the Church has not censured their opinion. Some few of the Fathers also thought of a metaphorical explanation. Nevertheless, Scripture and tradition speak again and again of the fire of hell, and there is no sufficient reason for taking the term as a mere metaphor. It is urged: How can a material fire torment demons, or human souls before the resurrection of the body? But, if our soul is so joined to the body as to be keenly sensitive to the pain

principles, beliefs, and sentiments he had kept together in a lifetime of heroic struggle. As a Jesuit, too, he seems to have been concerned with hints from Germany that certain of his confreres favored secretly the Copernican idea but dared not discuss it with their superiors. Now that he thought of it, had not Grienberger himself looked a little lost? There was a beginning of confusion in the ranks. Once he allowed ideas to start moving, he could feel no longer responsible for the outcome. *Sint ut sunt, aut non sint.*[21]

The modern reader may feel that we are more intelligent about these things, but it is largely an optical illusion. Our statesmen are legal minds, too, if not so well trained as Bellarmine's, and they too would be somewhat baffled, even today, by Galileo's proofs. If it had not been indoctrinated into them that the irresistible black magic that stems from those ancient proofs has been able to deliver the conveniences of modern life and one-hundred-billion-dollar budgets, they would not stand in awe whenever the word "science" is spoken. In those times even such a sensitive and adventurous mind as John Donne, in *Ignatius His Conclave,* had wanted Copernicus haled before the Judge of Hell, with Machiavelli and Paracelsus, as one of those "innovators" who had upset the world. Church statesmen like Bellarmine, to whom science was still an ornament

---

of fire, why should the omnipotent God be unable to bind even pure spirits to some material substance in such a manner that they may suffer a torment more or less similar to the pain of fire which the soul can feel on earth? This reply indicates, as far as possible, how we may form an idea of the pain of fire which the demons suffer. Theologians have elaborated various theories on this subject, which, however we do not wish to detail here (cf. the very minute study by Franz Schmid, 'Quaestiones selectae ex theol. dogm.,' Paderborn, 1891, q. iii; also Gutberlet, 'Die poena sensus' in 'Katholik,' II, 1901, 305 sqq., 385 sqq.)."

21. Among the arguments against Galileo that are quoted by Campanella in his *Defense of Galileo* (1622), there is this: "Holy Scripture counsels us to seek 'nothing higher, nor attempt to know,' that we 'leap not over the bounds which the Fathers set'; and that 'the diligent searcher of majesty is overcome by vainglory.' Galileo disregards this counsel, subjects the heavens to his invention, and constructs the whole fabric of the world according to his pleasure."

of the mind, may be excused for wondering whether these novelties about the heavens would be all to the good of the spiritual order that it was their duty to uphold.

IV

Galileo himself was not at all reassured. In the confident letters from Rome he could see only the tragic gap that separated him from his best friends there; for they insisted that all would be well, as Bellarmine had said, and that Copernicanism would at most be restricted to the geometrical field. They themselves saw nothing very serious in this; they were not physicists or, even less, independent metaphysicians, although in some of them there was a romantic overtone of Platonism. They were "open minds," disliking the crabbed Aristotelian pedantry, and they wanted their friend to have a free hand in his "new and marvelous demonstrations." Most of all, they wanted to have him vindicated as a good Christian against the monks.[22]

Galileo instead was in deadly earnest. He saw the irrevocable taking place before he had time to convince anybody. On the repeated urging of Monsignor Dini, he set out to complete his great apologetic letter to Madama Cristina, the Grand Duchess Dowager.[23] So long as the guillotine of mandatory interpretation had not fallen, there was still hope.

The *Letter to the Grand Duchess* is a powerful solemn plea, worthy to stand beside Milton's *Areopagitica,* though less secular in tone and less polemical. There is only expressed, in the beginning, a measured grievance against those who insist on distorting his thought and against such as slandered it from the pulpit "with hardly charitable and still less considerate indictment of all of mathematics and of mathematicians also." It is prefaced by a grave reminder from

---

22. They did not dare pronounce themselves in the delicate matter of metaphysics; but they would have nothing to do with compromisers. When the cowardly Luca Valerio, who was the only mathematician among them, tried to dissociate himself from their defense of Galileo after the decree, they expelled him from the Lincei for unworthiness.

23. See above, p. 39.

St. Augustine: "We should not hold rashly an opinion in a scientific matter, so that we may not come to hate later whatever truth may reveal to us, out of love for our own error." After vindicating the memory of Copernicus, Galileo claims to be the one who has the interests of religion at heart, "insomuch as I am proposing not that this book be not condemned, but *that it be not condemned, as they would, without understanding it, without hearing it, without even having seen it.*" Scripture often speaks figuratively, as is well recognized, whereas Nature is inexorable and immutable and never goes beyond the terms of the laws imposed on her, does not care whether her recondite reasons and ways of working are accessible to the capacity of men; but it is hardly reverent toward the Spirit of God to suppose that it may have laid pitfalls for man by establishing contradictory truths.

Galileo then quotes again from St. Augustine (being apparently unaware, like the Jansenists a few years later, that Augustine had become a "controversial" authority to be quoted at one's own risk): "The inspired writers knew what the truth was about the heavens, but the Spirit of God that spoke through them did not choose to teach it to men, as it was of no use for salvation." God expressly has left His works to our disputations, and it has been found good that the wise men of antiquity should have speculated profoundly about them. Are we then to leave the vulgar, whom any rabble-rouser can inflame with base passions and prejudices, to grab any passage of Scripture they please and swing it as a club to crush the endeavor of science?

There are, on the other hand, he goes on, theologians (very saintly no doubt) who claim supreme authority in all matters simply because theology is supreme. "It is as if an absolute ruler should demand, without being either a physician or an architect, that people should treat themselves, or erect buildings, according to his directions, to the great jeopardy of the poor patients and the manifest ruination of edifices."

As far as new discoveries are concerned, the Church could have suppressed astronomy altogether, or suppressed Copernicus' book as it came out. But to permit the book and condemn the doctrine, while so much evidence is publicly accumulating in its favor, *would be the most pernicious possible way for the souls of men, as it would allow them the opportunity of convincing themselves of the truth of an opinion which it was a sin to believe.* "Do not hope to find among the Fathers, or in the wisdom of Him who cannot err, those hasty conclusions to which you might be led by some passion or particular interest; beware of moving the Church to flash her sword in your cause; for in all these propositions which are not directly *de fide,* the Supreme Pontiff no doubt retains absolute power to admit or condemn; but it is in the power of no creature whatever to make them true or false, otherwise than they are *de facto.*"

The views concerning the interpretation of Scripture contained in Galileo's theological letters have become the official doctrine of the Church since Leo XIII's encyclical *Providentissimus Deus* of 1893. But in 1615, when the *Letter to the Grand Duchess* was forwarded to Rome, it sank out of sight as softly as a penny in a snowbank. Dini did not dare any longer discuss it with his superiors. Father Foscarini's tract, which had recently come out, had been raising fresh and most unfortunate trouble.

V

Paolo Antonio Foscarini was a Carmelite monk from Naples, of excellent reputation, a Provincial of his Order, and the work he had published showed real understanding of the Copernican system. It was in the form of a letter addressed to his General. After mentioning Galileo's pioneer work, he suggested that it was time heliocentrism be considered as a physical reality and embarked with theological zeal on a reconciliation of the system with the relevant passages of Scripture. As he wanted to be an obedient monk above all, Foscarini had submitted his text to Cardinal Bellarmine for criticism.

Bellarmine's answer was courteous and earnest, and it gives us the full measure of his thought on the subject:

My Very Reverend Father,

It has been a pleasure to me to read the Italian letter and the Latin paper you sent me. I thank you for both the one and the other, and I may tell you that I found them replete with skill and learning. As you ask for my opinion, I will give it as briefly as possible because, at the moment, you have very little time for reading and I have very little time for writing.

1. It seems to me that your Reverence and Signor Galileo act prudently when you content yourselves with speaking hypothetically and not absolutely, as I have always understood that Copernicus spoke. To say that on the supposition of the Earth's movement and the Sun's quiescence all the celestial appearances are explained better than by the theory of eccentrics and epicycles is to speak with excellent good sense and to run no risk whatever. Such a manner of speaking is enough for a mathematician. But to want to affirm that the Sun, in very truth, is at the center of the universe and only rotates on its axis without going from east to west, is a very dangerous attitude and one calculated not only to arouse all Scholastic philosophers and theologians but also to injure our holy faith by contradicting the Scriptures. Your Reverence has clearly shown that there are several ways of interpreting the Word of God, but you have not applied these methods to any particular passage; and, had you wished to expound by the method of your choice all the texts which you have cited, I feel certain that you would have met with the very greatest difficulties.

2. As you are aware, the Council of Trent forbids the interpretation of the Scriptures in a way contrary to the common opinion of the holy Fathers. Now if your Reverence will read, not merely the Fathers, but modern commentators on Genesis, the Psalms, Ecclesiastes, and Joshua, you will discover that all agree in interpreting them literally as teaching that the Sun is in the heavens and revolves round the Earth with immense speed and that the Earth is very distant from the heavens, at the center of the universe, and motionless. Consider, then, in your prudence, whether the Church can tolerate that the Scriptures should be interpreted in a manner contrary to that of the holy Fathers and of all modern commentators, both Latin and Greek. It will not do to say that this is not a matter of faith, because though it may not be a matter of faith *ex parte objecti* or as regards the subject treated, yet it is a matter of faith *ex parte dicentis*, or as regards him who enounces it. Thus he who should deny that Abraham had two sons and Jacob twelve would be just as much a heretic as a man who should deny the Virgin Birth of Christ, because it is the Holy Spirit who makes known both truths by the mouth of the Prophets and Apostles.

3. If there were a real proof that the Sun is in the center of the universe, that the Earth is in the third heaven, and that the Sun does not go round the Earth but the Earth round the Sun, then we should have to proceed with great circumspection in explaining passages of Scripture which appear to teach the contrary, and rather admit that we did not understand them than declare an opinion to be false which is proved

to be true. But, as for myself, I shall not believe that there are such proofs until they are shown to me. Nor is it a proof that, if the Sun be supposed at the center of the universe and the Earth in the third heaven, everything works out the same as if it were the other way around. In case of doubt we ought not to abandon the interpretation of the sacred text as given by the holy Fathers.

I may add that the man who wrote: *The Earth abideth for ever; the Sun also riseth, and the Sun goeth down, and hasteth to his place whence he arose,* was Solomon, who not only spoke by divine inspiration but was wise and learned, above all others, in human sciences and in the knowledge of created things. As he had all this wisdom from God Himself, it is not likely that he would have made a statement contrary to a truth, either proven or capable of proof. If you tell me that Solomon speaks according to appearances, inasmuch as though the Sun seems to us to revolve, it is really the Earth that does so, just as when the poet says: "The shore is now receding from us," I answer that, though it may appear to a voyager as if the shore were receding from the vessel on which he stands rather than the vessel from the shore, yet he knows this to be an illusion and is able to correct it because he understands clearly that it is the ship that is in movement. But as to the Sun and the Earth, a wise man has no need to correct his judgment, for his experience tells him plainly that the Earth is standing still and that his eyes are not deceived when they report that the Sun, Moon, and stars are in motion.

With this I salute your Paternity affectionately and pray God to grant you all happiness.

From my house, 12 April 1615.

Your very Reverend Paternity's brother,

R. CAR. BELLARMINO[24]

The modern reader may well be bewildered by the type of reasoning evinced in this letter. It must be admitted that Bellarmine's dismissal of Copernicus is not bred of any notable familiarity with his work. But then very few people had read Copernicus, or even Rheticus' summary, and what they had come across would have been much more a repetitive amount of windy refutation. It is all the more deserving on the part of the Cardinal not to dismiss Copernicus summarily as "that fool" in the way Martin Luther had done; on the

24. Ed. Naz., XII, 159–60.

other hand—and this is a point often forgotten—what Bellarmine *had* read, or at least heard of, was a very distinctive part of Copernicus' book as it stood, namely, the famous Introduction. In that introduction it is expressly stated that the theory is purely a mathematical supposition, which has no bearing on the reality of the heavens, whatever it may be. Thus, Bellarmine was entitled to think that Copernicus himself was philosophically on his side. This impression would have promptly been dispelled by a perusal of the book itself, but that was beyond anyone but a specialist; and no one knew then that the unsigned Introduction was not the work of Copernicus at all but had been added by Osiander, a Lutheran pastor who was trying in this way to make it acceptable to fundamentalist prejudice. It was, as Kepler said, "written by a jackass for the use of other jackasses," but the difference could not be detected by the casual observer; and Bellarmine was only too glad to have there a confirmation of his views.

Had he looked a little further, in the dedication to Paul III, he might have found Copernicus' very own remarks about the danger of mixing Scripture with science: "Did not Lactantius say childish things about the shape of the Earth?" He might have heeded Copernicus' grave warning: "*Illos nihil moror. . . .*" But it would have been too much to ask of a man who had never re-examined anything in a spirit of doubt, who instead had trained himself to re-establishing, reasserting, and reconfirming an acknowledged truth throughout his life. Thus, Bellarmine did not go back to studying Copernicus before he wrote his letter, nor did he spend the midnight oil in perpending the profound modern ratiocinations that later apologists have construed into his text.[25] He had, as he stated candidly, very little time; he was an old man, plagued with ill-health, harassed with work, who found escape from it only in prayer and in sighing for the consolations of the other world. At this very same time he

---

25. "It is a curious and paradoxical circumstance . . . that as a piece of Scriptural exegesis Galileo's theological letters are much superior to Bellarmine's, while as an essay on scientific method Bellarmine's letter is far sounder and more modern in its views than Galileo's" (J. Brodrick, *The Life and Work of Blessed Robert Francis, Cardinal Bellarmine, S.J.* [1928], II, 360).

was using the watches of the night not at all on natural philosophy but in composing a little treatise to be called *The Lament of the Dove, or Of the Value of Tears.* It was a comment on the text: "Who will give me wings like a dove, and I will fly and be at rest." In it he showed the necessity of penance, compunction, and holy tears from passages in Scripture and in the Fathers and then went on to describe twelve sources of sorrow for the Christian heart in as many chapters, namely, the consideration of sin, of hell, of the Passion of Christ, of the persecutions of the Church, of laxity among priests, of the decline of fervor in religious Orders, of the careless lives of worldlings, of the miseries of mankind, of Purgatory, of the love of God, of the uncertainty of salvation, and of the temptations of the Devil.[26]

This was indeed what Bellarmine cared about. Even his great controversialist work was now far behind him, as he meditated his *nunc dimittis.* It was only an iron sense of duty which led him to answer at length on the wearisome question to a good friar who was asking for advice.

On the other side, Galileo, when he got to read the letter to Foscarini, felt the noose tightening. He had been trying to say, as clearly and as dangerously as he could, what the point was; and all that he was getting back was the considerate reply: "I trust I have not heard you."

---

26. The book came out in 1617, was reprinted times without number, and was translated into many languages. St. Francis of Sales praised it beyond measure. It became, as we said earlier, the favorite devotional reading of Bellarmine's archenemy, James I of England. But it did also arouse anger among certain religious who had found their order criticized, though ever so mildly. In 1625 a Dominican named Gravina published—in Naples of all places—a book called *Vox turturis, or The Voice of the Turtle-Dove, a Declaration concerning the Flourishing Condition Up to Our Times of the Benedictine, Dominican, Franciscan and Other Religious Orders.* He was answered by a French Jesuit with a counterblast: *A Cage for the Turtle-Dove That Crows over Bellarmine's Mourning Dove.* Gravina's counter-counterreply was called *The Doubly Powerful Voice of the Turtle-Dove Reiterating the Flourishing Condition, etc., after the Collapse of a Certain Anonymous Person's Cage.* We do not know what followed next.

Surely, he wrote back to Dini, it had never been his desire to enter the scriptural field, "that no astronomer, or natural philosopher, has ever had to deal with, who stayed within his limits." He had never wanted to do anything but insure freedom for a physical theory. There would be the sure and direct way—he adds with despair—to show that it is not against Scripture, without going out of his province, "and it would be to show by a thousand proofs that it is true, and the contrary one can in no way subsist. But how am I to do this, and how is all effort not going to be in vain, if my mouth is locked, if these Peripatetics, who ought to be persuaded, show themselves incapable of understanding even the simplest and most easy reasons?"

This was a veiled indictment of Bellarmine himself, and it was the inescapable truth. (Dini certainly did not allow it at the time to escape his drawer.) As a theologian you tell a man to restrict himself to natural philosophy and not to meddle with Scripture; then you invade his own scientific field with your Peripatetic prejudice without troubling to understand his reasons, and you shut him up with the theological taboo. This is the way that cannot but lead to the "subversion of commonwealths," as Galileo was to write later.

This instinctive confidence shared by his friends, that it was he, Galileo, after all, who stood for the traditions of Christendom, and that it was Bellarmine who was failing, is not what good Catholics are supposed to feel; but, as a matter of fact, they often do, and they consider it no crime.[27] It must have been actually queer to these men to see the leaders of the Roman Church committed to a fundamentalist position which has always belonged to Protestant sects. In a hierarchy which in its long experience had seen the denial of the antipodes come and go, and many more important things besides, this must have seemed moon-struck obstinacy; and it was becoming clear that it was not Bellarmine's religious convictions that stood in the way but simply his Aristotelian condition-

---

27. As we have said, it is Galileo's views which have become official Church doctrine since the encyclical *Providentissimus Deus* of 1893, and Bellarmine's have been in fact rejected, although their author has since been canonized.

ing and his fear of "scandal." Copernicus in his quiet dedication to the Pope is more exactly the Catholic than Bellarmine was at this moment.

Such reactions find an interesting echo on the other side of the fence. The brothers of Tommaso Caccini were very far from any intellectual interest. They were of that conformist small gentry which was forever busy wangling pensions or preferments from the favor of the mighty. When Matteo Caccini, who lived in Rome and in the employ of the Vatican, heard of Tommaso's oratorical venture, he wrote him forthwith, stumbling over his own sentences from rage and haste:

I hear of such greatly extravagant antics on your part that I am amazed and disgusted beyond measure. It may yet come to such a pass that you'll regret ever having learned to read. You could have done nothing more annoying to the high authorities here, up to the very highest. God grant you may not have to learn it the bitter way.

It is no use your draping yourself with the mantle of zeal and religion, because here [in Rome] everybody knows how you friars use such cover currently to indulge your ugly drives, and far from believing you they are able to see you all the better as you are.

Truly it is a great impertinence, in matters that have to be judged by men far above you, and where there are men of such authority and wisdom, and they don't speak, that the impertinence of a friar should come prancing in thus. What idiocy is this of being set abellowing at the prompting of those nasty pigeons or whatever they are [*da piccione, da coglione, o da certi colombi*, referring to Lodovico delle Colombe and his Academic League].

Yet you got into trouble enough in the past, and will you never learn?

Brother Thomas, take it from me, reputation rules the world, and those who make such *coglionerie* as you do lose their good name. Just as we were trying to open up a career for you through high protections. . . . What will the Order and the world think of you? This performance of yours makes no sense in heaven or earth, and no one cares for it, and the proof is that it is very poorly appreciated here, let me tell you, because I know for sure. Now don't let people hoist you on your high horse again for running such a ridiculous race. I ask that you stop preaching, and, if you won't do this for me, I know a way to make you do it. You have been warned.

Try to think where you would like to go, because I don't like it where you are, and here even less; and, if you don't find a way to move out,

I shall find one for you. I who am no theologian can tell you what I am telling you, that you have behaved like a dreadful fool. With this you have my good wishes.[28]

Matteo dispatched this letter with orders to show it to Fra Tommaso but not to let him retain it in his hands. One could not be too careful in that vicious political struggle, where everything might change overnight through an upset or the death of the reigning Pontiff, and it explains why no one dared write what he knew. Matteo's words are thus doubly valuable, because they reflect an assurance derived from his master, Cardinal Arrigoni, and from the latter's friends in the Curia with whom Matteo was in daily contact; we see whence came the confidence expressed by Ciàmpoli. It is sound conservatism itself. The perpetual encroachments and aggressiveness of those monks at Santa Maria sopra Minerva raised undisguised annoyance in the Vatican. Top-level decisions were not reserved for them. The Church has always been wiser than her children.

Galileo himself, in fact, did not indulge in his despairing mood. "Go again and knock at the door of the Jesuits," he wrote to Dini. "I still think that, if I came down and explained my reasons in person, I would get some result."

The correspondence from the next few months is lost, probably destroyed by Galileo in order not to compromise his friends who had taken to writing him in more and more covered terms. But it was already clear from what Ciàmpoli had written that there was not much to hope for in the direction of the Collegio Romano.

Galileo did not have too many illusions on that score. He had been told that he was being fenced in, oh, so lightly, for his own good; but he saw the disastrous reactionary attempt in its true nature: a deadly consolidation that was imperceptibly closing in to freeze him like a fly in amber, or, rather, in Dante's image, which corresponded much more to those men's minds, a lost soul imbedded forever in eternal ice. Nineteen centuries of organized thought were piling up to smother him, which had started with the "loss of nerve" of Greek science after Aristarchus. The astronomers, still groping toward a physical system dimly seen, had been told off then by the

28. Cf. A. Ricci-Riccardi, *Galileo e Fra Tommaso Caccini: Una corrispondenza inedita* (1902). The letter is dated January 2, 1615.

philosophers, who had what they considered a satisfactory cosmology; they had accepted not without some plaintive protest the subordinate role of "saving phenomena" by means of abstract models and fictions. The minds of men had been molded through ages on the tenets of solid Scholastic logic and experience. The statesmen of thought could not but smile at the pathetic attempt of a few astronomers, repeated over the centuries, to erect a house on sand. The smile was now turning to impatience. A ruling seemed in order, as Colombe suggested, to prevent rash people from building again on the unsafe spots.

To such men Galileo could not explain what only he and Kepler saw: the three forces of mathematics, physics, and astronomy converging rapidly toward a junction which would make them irresistible. He was not bringing any facts that the Jesuits did not know.[29] He was pleading for time, but he was pleading also for much more: for the rights of scientific imagination to build its own world, to follow its quest for the secrets of the universe wherever it led; and this meant inevitably invading the reserved field of metaphysics. "With what right did he expect them," writes a modern apologist, "to believe him on his word?" There is a grim unintended irony in these words. For any aggressive lawyer. indeed, his case would have

---

29. This would have been the time indeed to produce Kepler's laws, at least the two first ones, which had been published. But the ignorance (or ignoring) of those laws pursues Galileo through they years like an irony of fate. He probably had the *Astronomia nova* of 1609 right on his shelf, for there is evidence that Kepler had sent it to him and waited in vain for his comments (Letter, *Opera omnia*, ed. Ch. Frisch [Frankfurt, 1858–71], II, 489). But he invincibly distrusted Kepler's cosmological fantasies, and it would have taken much faith and much labor to find the discoveries about the orbit of Mars, deeply buried as they are in that strange book. Kepler admitted later that he himself had difficulty with it: "My brain gets tired," he says, "when I try to understand what I wrote, and I find it hard to rediscover the connexion between the figures and the text, that I established myself" (III, 146). Galileo seems to have heard from someone (Cesi or Cavalieri) a casual mention of the elliptical orbits, but it must have set in motion a protective mechanism in his own mind, for his theory needed circles as a physical reality.

been less than airtight. What scientific speculation is made of is volatile stuff to a blinkered and sophistic mind.

One can watch this kind of sophistry going on even in our own time. Thus Pierre Duhem, a distinguished French physicist who has also gained a great and deserved renown in history of science, could write in 1908: "Logic was on the side of Osiander and Bellarmine and not on that of Kepler and Galileo; the former had grasped the exact significance of the experimental method, while the latter had been mistaken. . . . Suppose the hypotheses of Copernicus were able to explain all known appearances. What can be concluded is that they may be true, not that they are necessarily true, for in order to legitimate this last conclusion, it would have to be proved that no other system of hypotheses could possibly be imagined which could explain the appearances just as well."[30]

The last statement is of course, as far as it goes, scientifically quite correct. To take it with modern connotation and project it backward into the historical picture of the seventeenth century turns it into worse than a paradox, an intellectual solecism which would be enough to reveal in its author the unscrupulous apologist *ex parte*. If those prelates knew exactly, in advance of everybody, what true scientific method was, it is permissible to ask why they never made use of it.

Duhem was perfectly well in a position to know that Bellarmine's alleged "positivism" was only a position of indifference in a limited area of knowledge (viz., the theory of heaven) completely contained by a physical and metaphysical realism of the Scholastic kind. In no admissible way could it be presented as the permanent starting point (as if there were such a thing) for an organized natural philosophy and an "experimental method." So far from being that, the conventional theory of heaven defined for Bellarmine, as well as for Aquinas himself, an area of ignorance or "soft spot" that ought to be reabsorbed eventually into the surrounding Aristotelian coherency. The idea of that area expanding instead to cover

30. *Essai sur la notion de théorie physique de Platon à Galilée* (1908). Translated in English under the title, *The Theory of Physical Reality* (New York, 1952).

the field of natural knowledge with its empty "hypotheses" would have been received by Bellarmine with a shudder, for it would have looked to him as an intellectual cancer. It would have shocked Galileo no less, who would have refused to accept Duhem's costive dogmatic formalism as the refined version of his procedure and would have asked indignantly whether the greater cosmos that he had started out to discover was bound to turn out again an unendingly pointless paper universe scribbled o'er with intellectual epicycles and excentrics;[31] whereas it is fair to surmise that the actual universe of Maxwell, Einstein, and Heisenberg would have made fascinating if difficult sense to his mind.

Socrates had remarked already that unnatural reasoning has a way of turning against its author. To disperse it artfully over the landscape of history affords only momentary protection, for it will appear even more clearly, in the end, whether a contention does make sense in actual time. Minerva's bird is supposed to fly in the dusk, not in the murk of smoke-pots.

If the good faith of the modern nonscientific reader can still be led astray by such painful quibbling, it is no wonder that three centuries ago it should have been difficult to get minds much more prejudiced to see what Kepler had seen, "the telescope as a ladder to scale the highest walls of the visible world, and from there to look down on our hovels, I mean the planets, comparing the outmost with the inmost, the highest with the lowest"; nor to make them understand that such an intuitive certainty could be legitimate even while there remained problems to be solved.[32] Galileo could only demonstrate past absurdity, flash impressive "natural effects" before the eyes of his judges, make what he had found "make do" for what he had not found yet. He must dissociate himself from the dreaded memory of Bruno, reassure suspicious officials about their

---

31. "We are concerned with the real universe, not with a paper one," remarks Salviati impatiently in the *Dialogue*, and it turns out an effective jab at Duhem's early dogmatic form of positivism. It goes far to explain why Duhem's great work in thermodynamics has been so rapidly forgotten.

32. Cf. Kepler's *Astronomia nova* (*Opera omnia*, ed. Frisch, VI, 450).

metaphysics, and yet make them feel that its physical foundations were coming apart. And he must do so in, of all places, Rome.

We do not know under what circumstances the final decision was taken. Young Attavanti, after his hearing on November 14, may have warned him, breaking his oath of silence, that he was accused of more sins that he dreamed of. Armed with strong recommendations from the Grand Duke, Galileo set off for Rome on December 3, 1615. He must save those men in spite of themselves from the disastrous consequences that he could foresee for their obduracy.

V

THE DECREE

Mi vien serrata la bocca ...

GALILEO

Auf Teufel reimt der Zweifel nur
Da bin ich recht am Platze.

MEPHISTOPHELES

I

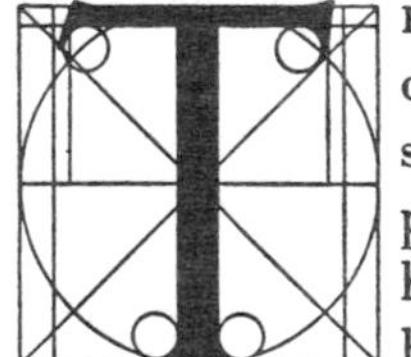

HE Florentine ambassador in Rome, Piero Guicciardini, had been informed by the secretary of state of Galileo's impending arrival. He felt that pointless trouble was coming his way and wished him somewhere else. "I do not know," he wrote back on December 5, "whether he has changed his theories or his disposition, but this I know, that certain brothers of St. Dominic, who are in the Holy Office, and others are ill disposed toward him, and this is no fit place to argue about the Moon or, especially in these times, to try and bring in new ideas." But his instructions were explicit. Galileo was lodged at the "Gardens of the Embassy," which was the Villa Medici at Trinità de'Monti (today the Academy of France), "with board for himself, a secretary, a valet, and a small mule."

He found himself but a small item of interest in the turmoil of the capital, now that the excitement about the telescope had worn off. Rome was being born anew in those years. The vast architectural transformation undertaken by Sixtus V and carried on by his power-minded successors was tearing down the old medieval city and replacing it with the modern design of monumental squares and thoroughfares, with the harmony of palaces, statues, ever green gardens, and splashing fountains intended to proclaim to the world the restored magnificence of Catholicity, triumphant over the disorganized forces of life and the hapless confusion of history.

As for the role of science in all this, the ambassador's dim-viewed diagnosis was correct. Paul V Borghese was not an open mind, nor much of any kind of mind. He was a strong and somber executive, a canonist by training, by temperament doctrinaire and inflexible. As he once said, he preferred new jobs for workmen to new ideas from scholars.

Galileo for his part, no doubt stung to action by the ambassador's cold skepticism, was not to be discouraged. On January 8, 1616, he wrote to Curzio Picchena, who was Vinta's successor as secretary of state: "From day to day I am discovering what a good inspiration it was for me to come here, for such snares had been laid against me that I could not have hoped to save myself later." From Caccini's denunciation we have an idea of what those "snares" were—part of an organized campaign to make the astronomers look like blasphemous enemies of Christianity in all its most sacred tenets.

The reception that Galileo found in official quarters was flattering. His detractors, who had spread the news that he had fallen into disgrace at Florence, were discomfited to see him arrive with the full favor of his sovereign. But his letters back home describe what he had to cope with:

My business is far more difficult, and takes much longer owing to outward circumstances, than the nature of it would require; because I cannot communicate directly with those persons with whom I have to negotiate, partly to avoid doing injury to any of my friends, partly because they cannot communicate anything to me without running the risk of grave censure. And so I am compelled, with much pains and caution, to seek out third persons, who, without even knowing my object, may serve as mediators with the principals, so that I may have the opportunity of setting forth, incidentally as it were, and at their request, the particulars of my interests. I have also to set down some points in writing, and to cause that they should come privately into the hands of those whom I wish should see them; for I find in many quarters that people are more ready to yield to dead writing than to living speech, for the former permits them to agree or dissent without blushing, and then finally to yield to the arguments used—since in such discussions we have no witnesses but ourselves, whereas people do not so readily change their opinions if it has to be done publicly.

On February 6, 1616, he felt he could write confidently:

I have terminated the business as far as my own person is concerned; but there is a decision which affects all those who in the last eighty years have written about a certain doctrine not unknown to Your Excellency; and I owe it to my conscience to provide what information I can, deriving from the sciences that I profess.[1] I reserve for your ear alone an account of the truly incredible deeds that could be perpetrated by those three most powerful operators, ignorance, malice, and impiety. Be it enough to say that my enemies, once defeated and disgruntled in their enterprise against my person as I have been freely assured by these Lords, have now turned their batteries against the ideas I stand for.

This difficult lobbying (as we would call it now) Galileo implemented with a social activity which would keep him, he hoped, in the limelight of the gossipy Roman world as an orthodox and unchallenged scientist. He loved discussion and seems to have had an inexhaustible faith in man's capacity to understand. Writes a typical man about town, Monsignor Querengo:

We have here Sig. Galileo, who, often, in gatherings of men of curious mind, bemuses many concerning the opinion of Copernicus that he holds for true. . . . He discourses often amid fifteen or twenty guests who make hot assaults upon him, now in one house, now in another. But he is so well buttressed that he laughs them off; and although the novelty of his opinion leaves people unpersuaded, yet he convicts of vanity the greater part of the arguments with which his opponents try to overthrow him. Monday in particular, in the house of Federico Ghisilieri, he achieved wonderful feats; and what I liked most was

1. We have a few of those memoranda for the authorities (Ed. Naz., V, 351–66). They are first drafts of the arguments that are developed in the Third Day of the *Dialogue*. They are impersonal and dispassionate to the point that we no longer recognize the author behind them. It is as though the emotional tension of those days had resolved itself into a higher objective clarity. We have also the names of "those persons" to whom they were addressed from Galileo's later deposition in 1633. They were the Cardinals Bellarmine, Bonsi, d'Ascoli, S. Eusebio, and Aracoeli. Not one of them did anything.

that, before answering the opposing reasons, he amplified them and fortified them himself with new grounds which appeared invincible, so that, in demolishing them subsequently, he made his opponents look all the more ridiculous.

Visitors also came to him, one of whom startled him considerably. It was Tommaso Caccini. "The person who started the trouble," he writes guardedly to Picchena, "was with me for over four hours, trying to draw me out about the controversy; in the first half-hour he tried with many demonstrations of humility to make excuses for what he preached in Florence; then tried to persuade me that he had not been the mover [*motore*] for the other mover here. . . . But in all his discourses I discovered a very great ignorance, no less than a mind full of venom and devoid of charity. What he and some others have done since shows me again how dangerous it is to have to deal with such people and how inevitable to have them arrayed against me."

Of what those people had been actually doing we may be afforded a glimpse through the letters of Matteo Caccini. Matteo was a discreet man of the world; he had grown up to respect Galileo, were it only because his elder brother Alessandro had made his early career in the banking interests controlled by Filippo Salviati, Galileo's close friend and sponsor. He had settled in Rome and found solace from the intrigues of the Court in the pursuit of horticulture (it may interest the modern reader to know that he had an important part in the shaping of the admirable Villa Borghese, which is now the public park of the city).

As a matter of family interest, Matteo Caccini was trying to get lucrative preferments for his Dominican brother, but he was also greatly concerned with getting him away from Florence and from his scandalous involvement with those "nasty pigeons." A gentleman-in-waiting to Cardinal Arrigoni, and friend of several members of the Curia, he was very much *au courant* of Roman affairs. He strove now with might and main, mobilizing all sorts of Court influences, to get Tommaso the title of Resident Bachelor of Arts at the Minerva so as to have him under control in Rome. His early concern is seen from what he writes Alessandro on January 9, 1615: "If F. T. looks like more trouble, let me know. I have ways to have him removed out of Italy if necessary." But F. T. seems willing to calm down, and on February 6 Matteo writes triumphantly that he has been able by moving heaven and earth to secure the post over a dangerous competitor; let Tommaso come to Rome immediately: "But for heaven's sake let him try to keep his trap shut; he might ruin all our plans. His confreres in the Order seem to think well of his capacities, but, as I know him, he is lighter than a leaf and emptier than a pumpkin. I shall not feel comfortable until the deal is closed."

Tommaso, as we know, did come down to Rome on February 20, but without showing much interest in the prospects opened to him by his brother. He had other and greater plans in mind. His arrival had been timed to coincide with that of Lorini's letter. While Ciampoli was writing Galileo (February 28) that "the Friars don't seem to talk or think about that business any more," Tommaso Caccini was busily conferring with his fellow-Dominicans, and on March 13 he was introduced to Cardinal Aracoeli, who was to sponsor his secret denunciation.

It was only on April 30 that Matteo realized what had been going on.

"As to F. T.," he writes, "I am so angry that I could not be more, but I don't care to discuss it. He opened up with me in private the other day, and he came out with such dreadful plans that I could control myself only with difficulty. In any case, I wash my hands of him forever and ever."

What Tommaso had revealed, obviously, was that he was out to "get" Galileo by fair means or foul; that he had found powerful associates; and that, if the Holy Office could be moved to action, he had ahead of him a career of honors and preferments far greater than the one his brother had planned for him. He was suggesting now that the latter give up his previous efforts (they had come to nothing anyway) and follow his lead.

Matteo was as good as his word and refused to see the friar again. In November, 1615, he followed his Cardinal to Naples (this was while Galileo was still in Florence), and from then on he could only relay indirect information. But a new note of aloofness has crept into his writing. Obviously, he had been told that the Galileo affair had indeed become an Inquisition matter and that it was wise to have strictly nothing to do with it. On February 19, 1616, he writes:

"I understand Sig. Gl. went to the Holy Office." The dealings that Galileo alludes to confidently and even cheerfully in his letter of February 6 to Picchena have become here the object of a frightened whisper. The worldly Matteo has concluded that his brother did make the right bet after all. "He seems to stand high with the Order. Well, let us hope that this will recoup his fortunes."[2]

Galileo knew only too well that the town was alive with informers and *agents provocateurs* in many official and unofficial capacities. That was why he diplomatically understated his real errand and insisted that he had come only to vindicate his good name. His diplomacy found approval. But he went on waiting for an audience that never came.

II

He was moving in a haze of equivocation. Whenever he tried to persuade, he found listeners who were merely amused. Amusement, even cruel, was at a premium in that atmosphere of weary conformism. But the originality had to be that of "conceits."

It remained Galileo's fate through life to create an excitement and consensus around him which had little to do with real understanding. His was the tragedy of an excess of gifts; for, while the telescope was his key to success, his real social strength lay in his extraordinary literary capacity, his brilliant repartee, his eloquence and charm, which gave him rank in a culture founded exclusively on belles-lettres and humanistic accomplishments. "You have a way of bewitching people," Ciàmpoli had said. His writing is, indeed, the one achievement of Italian Baroque prose that has survived the centuries. In that, his contemporaries could easily recognize a master; but what remained with them of his "incomparable demon-

---

2. As it turned out, Tommaso Caccini never attained the reward that he considered adequate to his merits. After taking up and dropping a couple of small preferments he had been granted, he got himself embarrassingly involved in a feud between Duchess Sforza and Cardinal Borghese. A compromising letter of his to the Duchess came into the hands of the all-powerful Cardinal, and he had to leave Rome. Although he tried again and again to attach himself to the powerful, he never rose in the hierarchy, and he was to end his days in 1648 as Prior of S. Marco in Florence.

strations" was as dim as the memory of a symphony to the untrained ear. This Galileo could never bring himself to realize. As he talked reason to his hearers, he believed, he forever wanted to believe, that they were following the course of his thought, and he spent himself unsparingly in explaining and persuading. They applauded; but, when the time came, this success showed again and again as fool's gold in his hands.

The younger men who could understand the full scope of his thought, like Castelli and Cavalieri, were but a handful (of them, Filippo Salviati remains the symbol enshrined in the *Dialogue*). Of men at the age of responsibility and influence, there was almost no one in Rome. His noble friends of the Lyncean Academy were willing souls, but they were romantic Platonists and naturalists who did not really understand his physics. His high-placed sponsors and "protectors" were very much like that United States senator who, when physicists from Los Alamos came to him with pressing pleas about dangers and moral responsibilities, cut them short reassuringly: "Believe me, gentlemen, I have always been a great friend of atomic energy." Galileo thought he was submitting briefs as a consultant and "friend of the court." To the court itself he was simply a patient under observation.

What it must have looked like to a cynical man of the world, we can infer from the letters of the Florentine ambassador, Guicciardini, full of undisguised annoyance:

> He is all afire on his opinions, and puts great passion in them, and not enough strength and prudence in controlling it; so that the Roman climate is getting very dangerous for him, and especially in this century; for the present Pope, who abhors the liberal arts and his kind of mind, cannot stand these novelties and subtleties; and everyone here tries to adjust his mind and his nature to that of the ruler. Even those who understand something, and are of curious mind, if they are wise, try to show themselves quite to the contrary, in order not to fall under suspicion and get into trouble themselves. Galileo has monks and others who hate him and persecute him, and, as I said, he is not at all in a good position for a place like this, and he might get himself and others into serious trouble. . . . This gives me grave concern toward the announced coming of the Most Serene Cardinal [de' Medici]. . . . To involve the Grand Ducal House in these embarrassments and risks,

without serious motive, is an affair from which there can come no profit but only great damage. I do not see why it should be done, the more so when this happens only to satisfy Galileo. He is passionately involved in this quarrel, as if it were his own business, and he does not see and sense what it would comport; so that he will be snared in it, and will get himself into danger, together with anyone who seconds him. . . . For he is vehement and is all fixed and impassioned in this affair, so that it is impossible, if you have him around, to escape from his hands. And this is a business which is not a joke but may become of great consequence, and this man is here under our protection and responsibility. . . .

Vox clamantis in deserto. We should try to think of the Rome of those times, where much saintly work was being done for the poor and the pilgrims from all parts of the world, where true saints could be found, to be sure, but which otherwise was the most corrupt of administrative capitals, and still and forever such as Du Bellay had found it a century earlier and as Belli was to portray it two centuries later: packed with fanatical and petulant monks, shrewd intriguers, postulants, paid and unpaid observers, diplomats, cynical secretaries, fulsome literati and inane versifiers living off the bounty of some prelate; lazy insolent nobles, curialist lawyers, stony-faced publicans rack-renting for the princes and the convents; spies, informers, go-betweens, men about town, unctuous priests and officials, careful hypocrites, suspicious hard old men, meeching young men on their way to preferments through oily conformism; all the parasitical, torpid, cunning, and malevolent society that vegetated like a pestilent mushroom growth on the fringes of an imperial world bureaucracy and for whom the stability and prestige of that bureaucracy in matters spiritual meant their career and their income. Around it all, the stones and the sky and the people of the Eternal City, expressing its spirit as it endures through time: a rocklike tolerant indifference to ideas, a quick estimate of men's motives, a weary certainty that all has been thought and said already, the eye on what pays. Truly, as Guicciardini said, no place to come and argue about the Moon.

Galileo was writing home in a spirit of unquenched hope. But he knew that he was a marked man and that the door was slowly closing in his face. The audience had never come. Cesi, Ciàmpoli, and Dini found growing reserve against their patient inquiries. The Jesuits, who had given hopes of support, were quietly withdrawing. Father Grienberger had said that it would have been better if he had produced more convincing proofs of his theory before trying to adjust Scripture to it. This was technically correct; but, for a man in Grienberger's position, it was, as Dini admitted, a lamentable out. The worst was that he said it after having been called in by Bellarmine for consultation. He was a broken reed. It was known that the Jesuits had a strict directive, issued to them by their General, to keep away from anything that might weaken the Aristotelian position.[3] Galileo had been hoping against hope from such as he. After three months of pleading, begging, and demonstrating, he realized at last that he stood alone.

There was still his Grand Duke in Florence, who had never let him down, although Lorini was known to be working hard in the ducal household. He got himself a pressing letter of commendation, in which Cosimo II made the cause his own personal concern.

It was addressed to Cardinal Alessandro Orsini, a nice youth of twenty-two, who felt flattered by such an important request. To him, as he had previously to Maffeo Barberini, Galileo disclosed the "conclusive physical proof" of the Copernican system, which he had not yet published, and begged him to use his influence with the Pope, so that he might at least suspend judgment. The proof, alas, was the theory of the tides, which is given in the Fourth Day of the *Dialogue*. It has turned out not to be valid, but it was impressive enough for anyone who could follow its close reasoning. Galileo could not yet produce Foucault's pendulum, and he must needs make shift with what he had.

---

3. Letter of Giovanni Bardi, June 14, 1614. Of this we have independent proof. Father Grienberger had written also in 1614 to a friend of Galileo apropos the controversy on floating bodies that, were it not for the deference which by the direction of his superiors he was obliged to show toward Aristotle, he would have spoken his mind clearly on the matter, in which Galileo was perfectly right. This was not the only instance, he added, in which the Stagyrite could be proved to have been wrong.

III

Here is the ambassador's unsympathetic version of what followed:

> Galileo has relied more on his own counsel than on that of his friends. The Lord Cardinal del Monte and myself, and also several cardinals from the Holy Office, had tried to persuade him to be quiet and not to go on irritating this issue. If he wanted to hold this Copernican opinion, he was told, let him hold it quietly and not spend so much effort in trying to have others share it. Everyone fears that his coming here may be very prejudicial and that, instead of justifying himself and succeeding, he may end up with an affront.
>
> As he felt people cold toward his intention, after having pestered and wearied several cardinals, he threw himself on the favor of Cardinal Orsini and extracted to that purpose a warm recommendation from Your Highness. The Cardinal, then, last Wednesday in Consistory, I do not know with what circumspection and prudence, spoke to the Pope on behalf of said Galileo. The Pope told him it would be well if he persuaded him to give up that opinion. Thereupon Orsini replied something, urging the cause, and the Pope cut him short and told him he would refer the business to the Holy Office. As soon as Orsini had left, His Holiness summoned Bellarmine; and, after brief discussion, they decided that the opinion was erroneous and heretical; and day before yesterday, I hear, they had a Congregation on the matter to have it declared such. Copernicus, and the other authors who wrote on this, shall be amended or corrected or prohibited; I believe that Galileo personally is not going to suffer, because he is prudent, and he will feel and desire as Holy Church does. [March 4.]

This report has been discounted as unreliable by historians because of Guicciardini's manifest ill will and because the dates are clearly manipulated in order to accredit his version. The decision was not taken two days before the decree but on the nineteenth of February; therefore, any pressure that Cardinal Orsini may have tried to exert in the Consistory of March 2 (or even February 24) could not have decided the course of events. But it seems to us the account is all the more important because of this misstatement.

Governments have never been averse to feeding the curiosity of ambassadors with timely indiscretions and confidential material colored to suit their purposes. The Vatican knew that Guicciardini was well informed of all that happened in the palace through the

Tuscan prelates and officials in every department. Only the doings of the Holy Office were shrouded in secrecy. It was easy for the well-exercised curial skill, after having spread for many weeks dark rumors that Galileo was asking for trouble, to let a couple of known facts (the intervention of Orsini and then the audience of Bellarmine on the second) appear by a calculated "leak" as the decisive events, whereas the decision had already been taken in secret session many days before. In this way, the informers were shielded; things were made to look as though only Galileo's impatience and indiscretion had goaded the long-suffering authorities to action; and, with Guicciardini's co-operation, the best way had been found to discredit Galileo with the Grand Duke. This version has gone on being far from useless to certain modern writers *ex parte.*

What actually happened, as we know now from the archives, was this: On the nineteenth of February of that year 1616 (it may or may not be a coincidence, but Caccini's peculiar visit to Galileo came three days later),[4] the Qualifiers, or experts of the Holy Office, had been summoned by decree to give their opinion. This summons was decided on at a meeting of the General Congregation of the eighteenth, of which all trace is lost. From the general style of the *Decreta* we may infer, however, that this one said no more than strict procedure required: "*Relata causa Galilaei mathematici* by the Most Reverend Commissary-General, Sanctissimus decided to submit for censure two propositions held by defendant."

Historians have always considered the course of events in the Holy Office as hidden behind inquisitional mystery, and yet this one would seem to be a fairly run-of-the-mill affair. For eight months, we should remember, nothing had happened while Father Ximenes was being located. In February less than three months had elapsed since Attavanti's deposition, which concluded the inquiry, and since the last annotation by the Assessor in the file. The case had been allowed to rest while Galileo produced his justifications (we see why his protectors told him it was lucky he had come), for he had been formally denounced, if only by hearsay, for grievous heresy and blasphemy concerning the nature of God. It took him almost two months, as we know from his letter of

4. See above, p. 113.

February 6, to dispel these charges against his person, and it was the way of the Inquisition not to move until some definite opinion had been reached by informal investigation. The suspicion had not been very strong from the start; he had been, as it were, cleared in quarantine of infectious diseases, and he was even told so. But he was still under observation for his scientific opinions, and those were obviously no good; it was time now to act on that part of the imputation, which had been proved.[5] This last decision was a matter of days, and it does not go beyond the ordinary judicial delays. In early February the Commissary reported that the case could be put on the docket for the next Congregation.

The propositions submitted to the censure of the Qualifiers were the following:

I. The Sun is the center of the world and hence immovable of local motion.

II. The Earth is not the center of the world, nor immovable, but moves according to the whole of itself, also with a diurnal motion [*ma si move secondo sè tutta, etiam di moto diurno*].

The theologians met four days later, on February 23, and announced the result of their deliberations on the following day. The first proposition was unanimously declared to be "foolish and absurd [*stultam et absurdam*], philosophically and formally heretical, inasmuch as it expressly contradicts the doctrine of the Holy Scripture in many passages, both in their literal meaning and according to the general interpretation of the Fathers and Doctors." The second proposition was declared unanimously "to receive the same censure in philosophy and, as regards theological truth, to be at least erroneous in faith."[6]

---

5. It seems plausible, then, to suppose that Caccini was quietly told to go and apologize to Galileo for the first imputation and to report whether or not the accused stood firm on the second and in what spirit. It is hard to see his visit on the fifth as a coincidence.

6. The wording of the "propositions" is not of the most felicitous. We shall see later where it came from. But at least it has afforded wonderful material for the casuist. In 1840 Father M. B. Olivieri, Deputy of the Dominicans (see also p. 141), set out to prove that Galileo's condemnation had been "according to reason and religion." He is willing to admit (against some other apologists who call this a slander)

The distinction between *heretical* and *erroneous* may sound subtle indeed. It is based on the weight of accredited opinion behind the two statements, quite independently of each other. The reasons may be found in Cardinal Conti's letter.[7]

This censure was submitted to the General Congregation of the Inquisition on February 25 and came back with the executive sanction of the Pope, as we have it in the Inquisition file:

Thursday, 25 February 1616. The Lord Cardinal Mellini notified the Reverend Fathers, the Assessor, and the Commissary of the Holy Office that the censure passed by the theologians upon the propositions of Galileo—to the effect that the Sun is the center of the world and immovable from its place, and that the Earth moves, and also with a diurnal motion—had been reported; and His Holiness has directed the Lord Cardinal Bellarmine to summon before him the said Galileo and admonish him to abandon the said opinion; and, in case of his refusal to obey, that the Commissary is to enjoin on him, before a notary and witnesses, a command to abstain altogether from teaching or defending this opinion and doctrine and even from discussing it; and, if he do not acquiesce therein, that he is to be imprisoned.

---

that Galileo remained a Copernican—an obstinate and "premature" one—while he abjured Copernicanism in 1633. His point is rather that the wording of the condemned propositions must have been inspired by profound wisdom, for it afforded Galileo an opportunity to recant without changing his mind. Galileo could swear in 1633 without perjuring himself that he never believed that (1) "the Sun is the center of the world," because, if "world" means universe, the Sun is not at the center of the universe, and, if it means Earth, the Sun is not at the center of the Earth; that (2) "the Sun is immovable," because he himself had demonstrated its rotation. Further, he could swear with a good conscience that he had never believed that (3) "the Earth is not immovable," because it is immovable with respect to the things moving on it; that (4) "it moves according to the whole of itself, also with a diurnal motion," because the first part of the statement explicitly does not refer to the diurnal motion, and in the case of the yearly revolution the Earth cannot be said with any sense to revolve according to the whole of itself (too true); and therefore it is only motion through the air (?) which is excluded. We are not sure we have done justice to this last point, which takes extensive elaboration in the original.

7. See p. 27.

On March 3, at the next meeting of the General Congregation, Bellarmine reported that Galileo had submitted (*acquievit*), and the decree of the Congregation of the Index was issued, with the order to publish it immediately:

. . . And whereas it has also come to the knowledge of the said Congregation that the Pythagorean doctrine—which is false and altogether opposed to the Holy Scripture—of the motion of the Earth, and the immobility of the Sun, which is also taught by Nicolaus Copernicus in *De revolutionibus orbium coelestium*, and by Diego de Zuñiga (in his book) on Job, is now being spread abroad and accepted by many—as may be seen from a certain letter of a Carmelite Father, entitled *Letter of the Rev. Father Paolo Antonio Foscarini, Carmelite, on the Opinion of the Pythagoreans and of Copernicus concerning the Motion of the Earth, and the Stability of the Sun, and the New Pythagorean System of the World, at Naples, Printed by Lazzaro Scorriggio, 1615:* wherein the said Father attempts to show that the aforesaid doctrine of the immobility of the Sun in the center of the world, and of the Earth's motion, is consonant with truth and is not opposed to Holy Scripture. Therefore, in order that this opinion may not insinuate itself any further to the prejudice of Catholic truth, the Holy Congregation has decreed that the said Nicolaus Copernicus, *De revolutionibus orbium*, and Diego de Zuñiga, *On Job*, be suspended until they be corrected; but that the book of the Carmelite Father, Paolo Antonio Foscarini, be altogether prohibited and condemned, and that all other works likewise, in which the same is taught, be prohibited, as by this present decree it prohibits, condemns, and suspends them all respectively. In witness wherof the present decree has been signed and sealed with the hands and with the seal of the most eminent and Reverend Lord Cardinal of St. Cecilia, Bishop of Albano, on the fifth day of March, 1616.[8]

---

8. The decree makes a distinction between scientific hypothesis and theological interpretation, which is not in the findings of the Qualifiers. That distinction is to be seen in the suspension of Copernicus against the suppression of Foscarini. "Paul V was of opinion to declare Copernicus contrary to the faith; but the Cardinals Caetani and Maffeo Barberini withstood the Pope openly and checked him with the good reasons they gave" (from the diary of G. F. Buonamici [Ed. Naz., XV, 111]). This is confirmed by Barberini's own words sixteen years later to Niccolini: "These difficulties of which we relieved Galileo when we were Cardinal." In addition to the above distinction, there is also the fact that the prohibition is issued by the secondary Con-

On the fourth, as we have seen, the Tuscan ambassador was informed "confidentially" that the Pope had taken an adverse decision the previous day. On the fifth the decree was published and forwarded to the Inquisitors in all parts of the world with orders to enforce it rigorously. It was read from the pulpits and announced in the universities; books were confiscated in shops and libraries. The Inquisitor of Naples reported that Foscarini's printer, Scorriggio, had not been able to produce the license and had been cast into jail. The Congregation took time out to confirm that it was "well done."

Roma locuta, causa finita. The affair which had started with Lorini's denunciation was finally settled, and an incipient scandal had been quashed. The Curia could go back to the serious affairs of the Church. Writes the same Querengo who had been so enchanted with Galileo's dialectic:

> The disputes of Signor Galileo have dissolved into alchemical smoke, since the Holy Office has declared that to maintain this opinion is to dissent manifestly from the infallible dogmas of the Church. So here we are at last, safely back on a solid Earth, and we do not have to fly with it as so many ants crawling around a balloon. . . .

The Roman world has gone back to "normalcy" with a shrug.

---

gregation of the Index and *in forma communi* without higher indorsement. All this was profound strategy born of reflexes of prudence—so profound, indeed, that it remained hidden to most contemporaries, who considered that anything declared in Rome to be false and altogether opposed to Scripture is as good as dogmatically prohibited. But of this later. The official texts are, most of them, from the English edition of Gebler. They have been checked against the originals.

VI

BELLARMINE'S AUDIENCE

MARFORIUS: *Quid agunt dominicani?*

PASQUINUS: *In tympano et choro, in chordis et organo, laetati sunt quia Deus deduxit eos in portum voluntatis eorum.*

I

HAT had happened actually to Galileo himself? This is what Guicciardini indicates only briefly in his report. He trusts (in other words, he was told in confidence) that he has nothing to fear personally. And, in fact, the *Solar Letters* were not prohibited in the decree, although the "scandal" and the decree itself had been occasioned by Galileo's teaching and writings.

The source for the ambassador's informant is the decree of February 25, 1616, already quoted. We do not have it in the original of the *Decreta* but from the Inquisition file where it was transcribed:

> His Holiness has directed the Lord Cardinal Bellarmine to summon before him the said Galileo and admonish him to abandon the said opinion; and, in case of his refusal to obey, that the Commissary of the Holy Office[1] is to enjoin on him, before a notary and witnesses, a com-

1. The Roman Inquisition was not like the Spanish Inquisition, with its "Council of the Supreme" and its Grand Inquisitor. It was really a committee of the Curia and had been devised mainly to keep the bishops in check. Hence there were a number of Cardinal-Inquisitors (usually six) who functioned as a board of directors but could in-

mand to abstain altogether from teaching or defending this opinion and doctrine and even from discussing it [Vat. MS, fol. 378v].

There follows in the same page the procès-verbal which has become the crucial piece in the drama:

Friday, the twenty-sixth. At the palace, the usual residence of the Lord Cardinal Bellarmino, the said Galileo, having been summoned and being present before the said Lord Cardinal, was, in presence of the Most Reverend Michelangelo Segizi of Lodi, of the Order of Preachers, Commissary-General of the Holy Office, by the said Cardinal, warned of the error of the aforesaid opinion and admonished to abandon it; and immediately thereafter, before me and before witnesses, the Lord Cardinal being still present, the said Galileo was by the said Commissary commanded and enjoined, in the name of His Holiness the Pope and the whole Congregation of the Holy Office, to relinquish altogether the said opinion that the Sun is the center of the world and immovable and that the Earth moves; nor further to hold, teach, or defend it in any way whatsoever, verbally or in writing; otherwise proceedings would be taken against him by the Holy Office; which injunction the said Galileo acquiesced in and promised to obey. Done at Rome, in the place aforesaid, in the presence of R. Badino Nores, of Nicosia in the kingdom of Cyprus, and Agostino Mongardo, from a place in the Abbey of Rose in the diocese of Montepulciano, members of the household of said Cardinal, witnesses.

The document is startling even on first inspection, for we have a very different procedure being followed from that prescribed. The instructions had said: "in case of his refusal to obey"; but there is no indication here that Galileo objected or demurred. What we have instead is: "immediately thereafter" (*successive ac incontinenti*) the Commissary-General read to him the formal injunction to cease and desist "in any way whatsoever."

Now this makes no sense as to substance, for the notification by the Cardinal himself was an act of juridical and social consideration.

---

tervene personally. The highest permanent post was that of the Assessor, who seems to have functioned mainly as liaison with the Curia. There was at times, above him, a Cardinal-Secretary. The real executive responsibilities rested on the *Commissarius Generalis,* who had to be a Dominican, and on his staff (composed of a Vice-Commissary, two associates, and a number of assistants). See also n. 2, p. 29.

To have called in Galileo a week before the public release was not only intended to spare him embarrassment; it was also, in etiquette, an acknowledgment of his status as a consultant—an empty cloture gesture, since he had never been allowed to act like one, but still a recognition of his official position stemming from the Grand Ducal Court. The Congregation decree instructing Bellarmine to inform him cannot be construed otherwise. And, in fact, Foscarini was granted no official advance notice of the condemnation, because he was an ecclesiastic under obedience and considered to have spoken at his own risk. If the plan had been to spring the news on Galileo so as to trap him into an unwary reaction, someone else would have been detailed to it than a Prince of the Church and certainly not by Congregation decree. Bellarmine himself would not have lent his person to it, or his own house. We know from his biographers the scrupulous consideration he insisted on in all circumstances. "If any of his own personnel came to his room to speak to him, he would not let them begin until they had taken a chair. When they had concluded their business, he would remove his cap and accompany them to the stair with as much ceremony as if they were distinguished strangers." There is no doubt that, in the mind of Bellarmine, the whole transaction was conceived on a formal and dignified plane. It was, indeed, *the* audience that Galileo had been expecting all along, granted at last when it could no longer serve his purpose. It was to be followed by the inquisitorial injunction (which was a stigma of social dishonor), *only in case* the subject proved recalcitrant; in which case, then, if necessary, incarceration became the next step.

But Galileo simply submitted himself (*acquievit*). We can well imagine that he did not find it a time to protest.[2] Faced with Bellar-

2. Galileo knew better than to argue with princes of the Church when they were not consulting him but stating their considered opinion, even in a private way. In those weeks Maffeo Barberini, who was his friend and protector, had given, in the course of a conversation, his answer about the theory of the tides, which was later to become famous (see p. 165). "When Galileo heard these words," writes Cardinal Oregius, who was a witness, "he remained silent with all his science and thus showed that no less praiseworthy than the greatness of his mind was his pious disposition." We need not doubt Oregius' word,

mine addressing him in his throne room, surrounded by his retinue of "black and white hounds of the Lord," he must have kept a stunned silence. But, then, why should the Commissary have sprung forward with a threatening injunction?

The document makes little sense as to form either. The instructions said "before a notary and witnesses," but the notary has not signed; nor are any officials mentioned as witnesses, as was the strict custom. Whenever the Inquisition served this type of injunction, it required the accused to sign with his own hand and then had the signature authenticated by the notary and the whole countersigned by its officials.[3]

Here we have only what amounts to an administrative minute, unsigned, casually transcribed. It was a very Catholic historian, but a distinguished one, Professor Franz Reusch, who in the 1870's drew attention to this fact. Something else is strange about it. Not only are official witnesses left unmentioned but in their place a couple of the Cardinal's servants have been brought in, who certainly were not qualified to understand or bear witness to Inquisition procedure. The location of the document in the file, as we shall now see, is no less out of order.

The dossier of the investigation of Galileo may look incomplete to those who expect to find there the story of the instigations, intrigues, pressures, and counterpressures that made up the famous affair. But it is not. It is simply the legal file of the material that

---

since he was one of the three experts chosen in 1633 to decide about the *Dialogue* who found it damnable.

3. See fol. 398 of the Acts, where Galileo in 1632 acknowledges receipt of the summons to come to Rome (cf. p. 269) with a declaration written in his hand and signed. This is authenticated by five ecclesiastics of the Inquisition; then the whole is notarized by the Chancellor of the Holy Office in Florence. Even this was a substitute for a full-dress injunction, as we shall see. The attempts at getting an injunction served in due form in the trial of Vergerio in 1545–47, in the face of a defendant who refused to accept it, gave rise to all sorts of ludicrous incidents and substitute procedures. In the case of an interrogation the notary and witnesses did not have to sign, but the document had to be authenticated by the principal himself in due form: "Io N. N. ho deposto come sopra."

had to go into the making of a legal decision, and as such it is fairly complete. It is the report of investigations carried out and measures taken by regular authorities. The pagination, at least the first one, was demonstrably carried out quite early, at the same time as the documents came in, and it is continuous. Hence we know that nothing is missing.[4]

The way it is built up is also quite definite and natural. Every single legal act, or official letter, was written (or started) on the first verso of a new double sheet and then incorporated and stitched into the file according to date. This, of course, left a large number of blank second pages in the context. These, too, are numbered. Some of them were used for administrative comment, forwarding notes and follow-up instructions, all in the proper time order. But in this as in any other administration of the times, there is no single letter, report, legal act, or certified copy which does not start on the first page of a new sheet. That is, with one apparent exception: the Bellarmine injunction. This most essential piece is written on space that was only accidentally available, being provided by the back pages of two other documents. Its place as well as its form emphasizes that it is only a minute.[5]

---

4. Or, rather, very little is missing, and that unconcealedly. Thus, two contiguous folios, belonging to the same double sheet, have been neatly cut out, before the first pagination, but leaving large margins to remind us of their existence. They come right after Lorini's falsified copy of the *Letter to Castelli* (fol. 346). There is another half-sheet, the first half, cut out in the same manner, to face p. 376, which contains the *propositio censuranda*. The same with pp. 431, 455, and 495.

5. These pages (fols. 378^{v} and 379^{r}), facing each other, are the verso of the blank second page of the Qualifiers' report (fol. 377) and the blank recto of what is the second half of p. 357, which belongs to Caccini's deposition. This is the way other transcriptions are set down too; cf. those referring also to papal commands, 352^{v}, and the one on an unnumbered sheet following 534. The procedure followed is quite regular as far as the first part is concerned (the Pope's order to Bellarmine on the twenty-fifth), for the original of that was supposed to be in the *Decreta* and here only reproduced for information. But then it slips on with deceptive casualness into the second part, dated February 26, which is the injunction itself and should have been preserved in the original.

Thus, the text that we have is not, and does not purport to be, an original but a mere transcription of relevant material, unsigned like all the similar ones.[6] But, then—where is the original? It clearly belongs at this place, on a separate sheet; it should be here, like all the other originals, but it is not in the file and never has been, as the continuous pagination proves. The only evidence that something happened that day is not a legal document, whether genuine or not; it is an administrative minute. It is strange that so many acute historians should have overlooked this as a starting point for their inferences. Did they suppose that the Inquisition file had been lugged around to Bellarmine's residence like a register in order to write the protocol on its back pages? The file never went out of the office; protocols made out somewhere else were incorporated into it.

That the original should have existed there is no doubt, for Bellarmine's instructions were explicit, and it was to be signed by the notary and countersigned by the recording secretary of the Holy Office and eventually by Galileo, too.[7] But that document was suppressed before reaching the file, or maybe even before being written, and the transcription substituted which purported only to be a copy. It purported that, too, with becoming modesty. The scribe

---

6. It does not even pretend to be an exact copy but only a paraphrase, as seen from the unusual abbreviations "said opinion" and also "said Galileo," which refer directly to the Congregation decree quoted immediately above but which would be out of place in an independent protocol.

7. This is not to say that all commands of the Inquisition had to be acknowledged. There are plenty of examples to the contrary. But they are on immediate matters (e.g., not to leave town until further orders). Even so, they are countersigned by qualified officials. When the Inquisitor gave them away from his headquarters, he was accompanied by his assistants as witnesses. But here, if the higher instructions were followed, we have an injunction on matters of intention to be given only in case of resistance. Hence we expect to find: "Io G. G. ho ricevuto precetto come sopra e prometto di obbedire." To say that the acknowledgment was not necessary is to say that the injunction was served without the demurring which motivated it, and then it would become a grave irregularity, to be challenged on these grounds alone.

remained able to state in confession or under oath that he had never falsified a document but had written down a minute that was judicially meaningless, since it lacked all the signatures.[8]

Even so, the good Father who did the job with such prudence had overreached himself. Following routine dutifully, he had first transcribed the text of the papal decree of the twenty-fifth; but had he known that the original of the decree was to be lost, as it is, to future historians, he would have cut off his hand rather than preserve the text in this place, where it was not strictly needed; for nothing can hide now the glaring contradiction between the orders and their purported execution.

If Galileo did not, explicitly, resist, there was no legitimate ground for the absolute personal prohibition of the Commissary to teach and discuss "in any manner," which goes beyond the wording of the decree and is of the type reserved for persons whose intentions were vehemently suspect. (In this case, submission became technically an abjuration.) The decree, as made out for all good believers, formally allowed the discussion of Copernicanism as a mathematical hypothesis, since Copernicus was only to be "corrected"; it forbade simply its presentation as a philosophical truth. It mentioned Galileo not at all, and great pains had been taken to keep him out of any injurious implication.

This is how Galileo himself understood it, for, two months later, he decided to counteract just such rumors as that he had been faced by the Inquisitor. Sagredo, among others, had been writing from Venice: "Those friends of ours confederated with Messer Rocco Berlinzone have done a foul job on you, spreading the rumor that you had been called to account by the Inquisition and had to go around like a whipped dog. I believe those thieves do their work

---

8. We have said earlier, and we must emphasize it here, that the first Catholic historian, to our knowledge, to have found that there is something strange about the document is Professor Reusch. He remarks that there is no regular record at all of an injunction. What was taken for it, he adds, is a "Registratur," i.e., a note made by the notary of the Inquisition and incorporated in the Acts, as if referring to a document that is not there. Sherwood Taylor, a Catholic historian also, accepts this definition.

against us in many parts, but God will confound their evil counsels."[9] Hence, to safeguard his personal honor, Galileo requested of Bellarmine a certificate of the proceedings and promptly received it in the following form:

We, Roberto Cardinal Bellarmino, having heard that it is calumniously reported that Signor Galileo Galilei has in our hand abjured and has also been punished with salutary penance, and being requested to state the truth as to this, declare that the said Signor Galileo has not abjured, either in our hand, or the hand of any other person here in Rome, or anywhere else, so far as we know, any opinion or doctrine held by him; neither has any salutary penance been imposed on him; but that only the declaration made by the Holy Father and published by the Sacred Congregation of the Index has been notified to him, wherein it is set forth that the doctrine attributed to Copernicus, that the Earth moves around the Sun and that the Sun is stationary in the center of the world and does not move from east to west, is contrary to the Holy Scriptures and therefore cannot be defended or held. In witness whereof we have written and subscribed these presents with our hand this twenty-sixth day of May, 1616.[10]

There is certainly no mention here of any injunction; in fact, what would have followed on it (i.e., an apology or retraction) is formally denied.

---

9. Of what was currently said we have also a document in a letter from Naples of Matteo Caccini (June 11): "The Congregation of the Index published a decree against the opinion of Galileo, after a consultation had taken place in the Congregation of the Holy Office in the presence of the Pope, and in this meeting Sig. Galilei made his abjuration." This misleadingly precise account is part of a letter relaying direct news from Rome; we know his contacts were excellent ("My very dear friend the Secretary of the Holy Office," he says elsewhere). Thus, it is not an idle rumor but a strongly accredited indiscretion coming straight from Dominican or allied circles. It caused Matteo Caccini to withdraw from Galileo as from a marked man, and quite a number of people to do the same.

10. The original draft of this certificate has been found in the Bellarmine file of the Secret Archive and published by Favaro (Ed. Naz., XIX, 348). It shows that the Cardinal had written originally in the middle line "but that" (*sì bene che*) and then, realizing this might not be explicit enough, had erased it and replaced it with "but that only" (*ma solo che*).

Historians *ex parte* have maintained that this is the merciful way of the Church: she wanted to protect Galileo from any public slur, out of respect for him and for the Grand Duke, and therefore released only an honorable certificate; but she knew very well he was a dangerous and obstinate character and tried to keep him on the straight path by a secret injunction. This sounds reasonable enough, and knowledgeable, and experienced. It impressed even historians from the other side, like Th. Henri Martin, so much that they forgot to ask for the exact context of the injunction. But in 1870 out came another piece of evidence, not from the yet undisclosed dossier, but from the collection of papal decrees, which had been searched by Gherardi during the few hectic weeks of the Roman Republic of 1849, when, the Pope having fled, the archives became suddenly, if too briefly, open to inspection.

This is what Gherardi discovered among the *Decreta* of the Congregation of the Holy Office:

> The Lord Cardinal Bellarmine having reported that Galileo Galilei, mathematician, had in terms of the order of the Holy Congregation been admonished to abandon [*deserendam* (*disserendam*, "discuss," was the word originally written)] the opinion he has hitherto held, that the Sun is the center of the spheres and immovable and that the Earth moves, and had acquiesced therein; and the decree of the Congregation of the Index having been presented, prohibiting and suspending, respectively, the writings of Nicolaus Copernicus, of Diego de Zuñiga *On Job*, and of Paolo Antonio Foscarini, Carmelite friar—His Holiness ordered this edict of prohibition and suspension, respectively, to be published by the Master of the Palace.

This is the context. It is a document for the authorities only, a regular report on business transacted. It corresponds exactly to the instructions of February 25. Those instructions had envisaged three successive steps to be taken in the three several cases: acquiescence, objection, or obstinacy on the part of Galileo. The steps were: admonition, injunction, and prison. The report now says that admonition was met with acquiescence and goes on to other matters. If there had been an injunction, it would contain at least a mention of it. Otherwise, there should be attached a separate report by the Commissary-General. But there is none. On the strength of this one report, the authorities could have no idea that an injunction ever was needed or had been served; and, indeed, as we shall see later, for several years, they apparently did not have the slightest idea.[11]

Nor did Galileo himself seem to be aware of it, judging from this. He would not have dared to ask Bellarmine for a certificate if he had not expected that certificate to come out absolutely favorable. We have his request, which has been found among Bellarmine's papers. It is simple and straightforward and does not demand or suggest any leniency. In his first letter to his secretary of state, a few days after the decree, he notes with satisfaction that his person has been left out of it, that Copernicanism has not been condemned as heretical but only interpretations of it, and that Copernicus has been suspended only for correction. He says (Bellarmine or Cardinal Caetani must have told him) that the corrections will cover only ten lines of the Introduction (about the agreement with Scripture) "and here and there a word, as where Copernicus calls the Earth a star." He adds: "I have, as will be seen from the nature of the case, no involvement in the matter and should not have troubled myself about it had not my enemies drawn me into it."

This is simple and explicit. It corresponds to the letter of February 6. He has learned that he must write no more theological letters; but then he would not have written them if he had not been dragged into it; and now that the thing is decided, he does not have to pursue the matter further. His personal philosophical endeavor, which he always kept in the background, has now to be abandoned.

---

11. A frequent way of burying the issue is to say, or imply, that laymen have raised much ado about some ordinary short cuts in procedure and that Galileo, himself a layman, may not have understood very well what was taking place. But the judge who wrote the sentence in 1633 was certainly no layman, and we shall see him walking on eggs in the matter of that injunction. In fact, the irregularity would appear more shocking to the trained eye than it would to us. Nor did the Vatican authorities of the nineteenth century feel more comfortable about it, for (notwithstanding the promise they had given the French government when the abducted archives were brought back from Paris) they released only a few selected documents, woven into an ingenious apologia by Monsignor Marini, in 1850; and it was only much later that they decided there was more to be gained from publication than from concealment. Hence they encouraged M. de l'Epinois to publish an integral reproduction in 1877.

For the rest, he holds himself free, like anyone, to discuss heliocentrism as a mathematical hypothesis and is awaiting the new edition of Copernicus as an approved textbook. He then goes on: "It may be seen from my writings and my doings here in what spirit I have always acted, and shall always continue to act, so as to shut the mouth of malice; my conduct in this business has been such that no saint could have shown more reverence for the Church or greater zeal."

This may have been said largely to appease the Grand Duke; it may be whistling in the dark; but it is certainly not the language of a man terrified by the Inquisition, told that he is under special surveillance, and enjoined never to discuss or mention the system in any way. It corresponds exactly to what the ambassador learned confidentially and in covert language from the authorities. The feeling of pride is, in fact, more genuine than one might suspect, for Galileo knew by then that his *Letter to the Grand Duchess* had been a strong, if unacknowledged, factor in the last-minute compromise.[12] Nor do his later acts belie this attitude in the least.

To this cool attitude of the scientist there come also official sanctions. Cardinal del Monte wrote an explicit letter of indorsement.[13] The Pope received Galileo on March 11 and gave him an audience which lasted three-quarters of an hour. As Galileo mentioned the persecution of his enemies, the Pope assured him that he need not fear, for he was held in such esteem by himself and the whole Congregation that they would not listen to these calumnies. He also repeatedly expressed his readiness to show his favor with deeds.

Now Bellarmine was, in his own way, a saintly and benevolent

---

12. This we know from the Buonamici diary (see p. 289 below).

13. It should have been the Cardinal's concern, as a relative and as a Florentine, to warn the Grand Duke unofficially that, however decorous the proceedings, Galileo had not come out very well and should *not* be encouraged and shown too much favor. He wrote instead: "I can assure your Highness that Galileo has come out of this in excellent position . . . and I wanted you to know it, for it is to be expected that his enemies will not desist from their machinations, as they have not reached their intentions in this way." The same tone is in Cesi's letter: "Let them bark in vain."

scholar. He was also the man who could retain a personal friendship with Sarpi even across the havoc of war and anathema and warn him of the danger to his life. But Paul V Borghese, according to all contemporary reports, was an authoritarian martinet, a literal, rigid mind, and a man "so averse to anything intellectual," as Guicciardini says, "that everyone has to play dense and ignorant to be in his favor." Such a Pope would not have shown signal benevolence to a suspect under inquisitorial reprimand, not even to please the Grand Duke. This means that Bellarmine had stated exactly what the report of March 3 says, and no more. We would have to imagine, although it would seem rather fantastic, that Bellarmine and Father Segizi had arranged to keep the injunction a secret from the Pontiff himself.

We have thus the gravest reasons to doubt the authenticity of the minute of February 26, and this is a point to be established toward later developments. As for Galileo, to all appearances he never doubted his position then or later. As he stood, he felt unhappy but clear. His fighting temper had not left him. "He is of a fixed humor," writes Guicciardini with alarm on May 13, "to tackle the friars head on [*di scaponire i frati*] and to fight where he cannot but lose. Sooner or later you will hear that he has fallen over some unsuspected precipice. I hope that the season, at least, will drive him from hence."

But Galileo stayed on. He would not have it look as though he had been driven away by base gossip and intrigue. He even indulged in a little matchmaking between Prince Cesi and Isabella, the sister of his late friend, Filippo Salviati (". . . the splendor of such names and, on the side of the Prince, a grave wisdom surpassed only by a truly angelical virtue . . ."). The Grand Duke reassured him of support and, over the ambassador's protests, sent him funds. But at last the secretary of state wrote him: "Your Honor, who has had to deal with monkish persecutions, knows what is the taste of them, and their Highnesses fear that a further stay in Rome might bring you into trouble. You have got out of this honorably; you can let the sleeping dog lie and return here. There are rumors going around that we do not like, and the monks are all-powerful; and I who am your friend and servant ought to warn you."

This was an order. Galileo left Rome on June 30, still unenlightened and unreconstructed. "Of all hatreds," he wrote, "there is none greater that that of ignorance against knowledge."

II

Many things could be said in extenuation of the mistake of the authorities which have been rarely said, while most of the defensive position takes its stand on legal quibbling. One may well say—we have stated it ourselves in the opening chapters—that this was a vast conflict of world views of whose implications the principals themselves could not be fully aware.

The opposing reasons were of majestic dimensions, stemming from the night of ages; the new developments both compelling and dangerous; the consequences still not to be grasped by us who live three centuries later. Hence an ecumenic council would appear as the proper instance before which to present the issue, either for decision or for postponement of decision. Of this, Galileo was aware. He could not suggest it under penalty of excommunication, but we know that he often said or implied as much in private. It is very true that the world situation, and the Church's own Counter-Reformation policy, made the idea of a council look exceedingly implausible. We do not presume to pass judgment on the subject. We are simply saying that, if a decision had to be taken, a council was in order. To deal with the question on an administrative level was not only an arbitrary procedure; it was an inexcusable mistake, which is the necessary premise to the graver mistake of the trial sixteen years later. Technically, it was not the eleven Qualifiers who can be accused of being wrong (they could hardly have answered anything else under the circumstances, as we shall explain later); it was the authority who put the question up to them. Yet, even so, granting the lines of procedure set down by the immovable machinery of the times, it should be said withal that a spark of understanding and leadership, the informal intervention of a higher mind inside the hierarchy, might well have saved the situation.

The drama is really more poignant in this first phase, when all is still fluid, than in the later crisis, when positions had hardened and the juridical machinery had taken over.

All was still possible in that fatal year 1616, the year that saw the deaths of Shakespeare and Cervantes and spelled the end of the

Renaissance. What Galileo was begging for was pitifully small: that the authorities should keep judgment suspended for another generation—for another few years at least. He was made to look as though the decision were the fault of his own nagging indiscretion. He was asking that the Word of God be not taken in vain, and he was maneuvered and driven and cornered, as if he were Satan himself, into tangling with Scripture to his own undoing and to that of his cause. The man who has been so persistently (and sometimes rightly) accused of vanity and conceit plays a role in this phase which appears to justify fully his words to the Grand Duke: "No saint could have shown more reverence for the Church or greater zeal."

For he certainly had come in simplicity of heart and as a true son of the Church, as the Pope could not deny. He had come not to make a scandal but to avoid it; not to raise a danger but to make one plain; not to oppose a truth but to offer it. What was taken to be his pride of mind was the urgent warning that such things would come to pass as would make pride of mind inevitable. Like the prophets of old, he had spoken of a shadow over the land, and the priests had cast him out.

He was pleading for an understanding from the highest minds, and what he met with was invincible ignorance, gilded with flattery for his "inimitable conceits"; he was begging for a hearing, and what he got was Caccini.

III

Because, if we must leave the philosophy of history and go back to facts, here are the cold facts as shown in the 1616 sentence itself. The eleven Qualifiers of the Holy Office had been requested to give a ruling on the following opinions:

I. The Sun is the center of world and hence immovable of local motion.

II. The Earth is not the center of the world, nor immovable, but moves according to the whole of itself, also with a diurnal motion.

These last words sound obscure, to say the least. They are in Italian, which caused some historians like Domenico Berti and Karl von Gebler to believe carelessly that they were taken out of the

Solar Letters. Of course they are not. No Copernican would express himself thus.[14] Galileo might have said, with the reflexive as was done in his time (it occurs once or twice in the *Dialogue*), that the Earth moves *in* itself of a daily motion, not *according* to itself. We would have no clues to these phrases if we did not have from the secret archives the original Italian which is in Caccini's denunciation: "La terra secondo sè tutta si move, etiam di moto diurno." It makes no sense in any language, but there it stands. It is a decomposition into pseudo-Thomistic double talk (*secundum se*) of the simple statement: "The Earth turns around itself in a day"—which is, incidentally, how Aristotle himself refers to the theory.[15] But it is obviously a garbled version of the way Colombe had described it to Caccini as he tried to translate Copernicus into "philosophically sound" language.[16] The *et etiam* left over allows us to reconstruct the original wording: "The Earth moves as a whole around the Sun, *et etiam secundum se* of a daily motion." As for Caccini, a low-comedy character and a turbulent ignoramus,

---

14. The origin of this mistake is the summary from an unknown hand that precedes the Acts in the official file and was apparently prepared as a brief for the meeting of the Congregation of June 16, 1633, that was to take a decision about the trial. It is said there actually: "having seen the two propositions from the book on the *Solar Spots*, etc." The author of the summary had been led astray by the contiguity in the file of two different documents. One of them, as we have seen (fol. 375^{v}), was an instruction to look up the *Letters on the Solar Spots*. It follows immediately Attavanti's deposition. The next one (fol. 376^{r}) is the circular of convocation about the *propositio censuranda*, as it was sent out to the RR. PP. DD. Theologis on February 19, assigning them for the fourteenth hour ½ of Tuesday, February 23. The slip is natural in one who hastily summarizes an incomplete collection. If the file had been kept properly, the mistake would not have occurred. What is missing between the two items are the minutes of the Congregation of March 18, which started the whole proceedings. But of this important document no copy has been found anywhere.

15. Cf. *De coelo* 293 *b* 30, 296 *a* 26–29, *b* 2–3.

16. Cf. Colombe's *Discorso:* "se noi consideriamo ciascun cielo secondo sè tutto," etc. At another point Colombe ridicules the theory "which compels the Earth to go around the center according to accident and never to the center according to itself."

he cared less about meaning than about the man in the moon. He simply repeated the words, mixing them up, as he mixed up many other things of a less innocent nature.

The eleven consultants of the Congregation, among whom we are told were several deeply versed in the natural sciences,[17] met on February 23. They had been convoked, as appears from the act of February 25, "concerning the propositions of Galileo." The *Letters on the Solar Spots* had been procured. They had available, at their wish, the book of Copernicus to which the propositions implicitly referred; they had Foscarini's pamphlet; they had, informally submitted, the memoranda and briefs that Galileo had forwarded to their superiors; they had his letters to Castelli and Dini; they had at their beck and call Father Grienberger at the Collegio Romano, who was their consulting astronomer. To all this they gave no thought, nor, actually, were they supposed to. They probably had not even been informed about the issue. They looked up their schoolbooks, compared Caccini's denunciation with the texts, and came

---

17. Hartmann Grisar, *Galileistudien*, p. 38. The names of these distinguished experts (some of them had indeed attained considerable fame in the theological controversies of previous years) are signed as follows on the protocol:

Petrus Lombardus, Archiepiscopus Armacanus.
Fr. Hyacintus Petronius, Sacri Apostolici Palatii Magister.
Fr. Raphael Riphoz, Theologiae Magister et Vicarius generalis ordinis Praedicatorum.
Fr. Michael Angelus Seg.s, Sacrae Theologiae Magister et Com.s S.ti Officii.
Fr. Hieronimus de Casalimaiori, Consultor S.ti Officii.
Fr. Thomas de Lemos.
Fr. Gregorius Nunnius Coronel.
Benedictus Jus.nus, Societatis Iesu.
D. Raphael Rastellius, Clericus Regularis, Doctor theologus.
D. Michael a Neapoli, ex Congregatione Cassinensi.
Fr. Iacobus Tintus, socius R.mi Patris Commissarii S. Officii.

"Seg." stands for Segizi, the Commissary-General of the Inquisition; "Jus." for Giustiniani, the only Jesuit on the committee, which contained a majority of Dominicans, as was the custom in matters of theology.

back with the answer. They did not trouble to remove the illiterate *etiam* or to try to restore a meaning.[18] To them, as to their superiors, this was something that did not sound well because it spoke of the Earth moving and the Sun standing still, and it had to be condemned as philosophically foolish and absurd.

The ship of state had sailed past the issue. It was only the backwash which hit Copernicus, causing him to be suspended *donec corrigeretur*. Foscarini, who had been an acceptable author a year earlier, was now wholly forbidden, because such discussions "gave occasion to scandal" or, as we would say today, were bad for public relations. As for Galileo, he was left untouched, his *Letters* uncensored, and his theological epistles never mentioned, although Caccini's denunciation had been specifically aimed at him and the procedure as well. The protection had worked. But the Copernican movement had been stopped dead in its tracks, with what consequences for Italian culture the next hundred years would show.

There is a logic to it all, even a considerate logic. The state hath its own reasons that reason knoweth not. Galileo's ideas and his person had been carefully left out of the issue, as we noticed above. The question submitted to the consultants was one of public order: Certain opinions are circulating, as related by an informer, and are stirring a scandal. A ruling is requested, so that the correct directives may be imparted to the thought police. Only the consequences of the theories mattered on the level of public relations; that is why the only material submitted is a third-hand denunciation by an informer. The incipient scandal had to be dealt with on its own level.

As it happened, the scandal had been created by the informer

---

18. That the meaning is inscrutable is comically granted by Father Olivieri (see p. 121). They even went worse than their superiors on one point. The proposition submitted had been: the Sun is in the center and *hence* immovable; they erased the *hence* and replaced it with *wholly*, as if to give formal assurance that they were totally unacquainted with the content of Galileo's discoveries, theories, and theological letters, in which the rotation of the Sun was given outstanding significance.

himself. Deprived of guidance, the police apparatus had become the tool of its own *agents provocateurs.*

This fatal short circuit between the judiciary and the executive seems to be a constant feature of the streamlined state—or of the state which feels itself compelled to go pragmatic under the stress of emergency. The case is not unknown in our time, and even in free countries, of a politician who serves at one and the same time as disturber of the peace, prosecuting attorney, judge, jury, and detective agency. The serious trouble begins when the higher authorities find themselves in his tow.

In the Rome of 1616 the legislative decisions had come from the Council of Trent: "Petulant minds must be restrained from interpreting Scripture against the authority of tradition in matters that pertain to faith and morals." This was aimed essentially at the fundamentalist reformers who were forever protesting the word of Scripture against the Roman authorities. The book of Copernicus had come out by then, and yet no specific clause is directed against that kind of interpretation. (It must be admitted that the prelates of the Council, lawyers, literati, preachers, and executives all, who had found it difficult even to follow the arguments of their own Scholastic consultants, had never thought that "mathematics" might give them trouble.)

Thus the judiciary might well have felt some doubts. It was a "conciliar affair," as Descartes was to write with cold Gallican sense, to reconsider the whole issue. In his anomalous position as chief theologian as well as chief executive, Bellarmine made up his mind that it was a mere matter of "petulance." He had the question framed, on behalf of the General Congregation, leaving out the main issue. This question he submitted on February 19 to the Qualifiers, and he received in answer, on February 24, the echo of his own words. On the twenty-fifth, as chief executive, he drew up the decree of the General Congregation, had it passed on to the Congregation of the Index, and intrusted its execution to the Commissary of the Inquisition.

The historic responsibility, then, falls on Bellarmine alone. He was a great Jesuit, tempered in thought, dedicated mind and soul to the welfare of the Church. If his intellect had been able to grasp the issue, there is no doubt that he would have put it on the agenda of a future Council, and the new science would have had a chance to enter the circle of orthodoxy. All that was really needed in the meantime was a damper on theological excursions, and that would have been the part of discretion. But fear and suspicion were much closer to the heart of the matter, and, besides, Bellarmine did not even like to think of the next Council. He was of the anticonciliar persuasion. He felt that all had been settled and that what was needed henceforth was administrative resource. We are led back, then, to the incredible passiveness of Bellarmine's brothers in the Order, the mathematicians of the Collegio Romano, who apparently took their vow of obedience *perinde ac si cadaver* to dispense them from any intellectual responsibility, perhaps also of intellect *tout court,* according to the instructions of their General, Acquaviva; for of their personal good disposition toward Galileo there is no doubt. But they accepted the function of mere technicians of the transit instrument. Obedience and preoccupation with "scandal" had been bred into the bones of the Order, from Bellarmine down, to such an extent that the intellectual reflexes were dead.[19]

The leader who fails in leadership has only himself to blame if he falls prey to a conspiracy of his subordinates. The explanations of Bellarmine's conduct in terms of scientific prudence and mature consideration turn out to be whitewash. Dini and Ciàmpoli had been mistaken in their trust; it was Caccini, the "subversive," in his minklike cunning, who had made the right bet. Bellarmine was semiconsciously frightened by a problem he had never faced: What if the Aristotelian substructure were to prove unreliable? The problem went beyond his training and his mental capacities. He decided it was no problem at all and fell back on the police for an

---

19. See Father Grienberger's remark quoted on p. 118. We shall return to this subject on p. 290. Monsignor Majocchi wrote in 1919: "The authorities simply gave Galileo a lesson in positivism." This is only too true. They virtually did—in the Comtian sense of the words. To stick to historical fact, however, it should be noted that in the arguments that Campanella had heard used against Galileo's theory, eleven of them, there is no mention at all of that which is brought up by modern Church historians, namely, that the theory was not sufficiently proved. As far as we know, only Father Grienberger used it to motivate his abstention.

estimate of the situation. They gave him Caccini's stuff, under the name of Galileo's propositions; it went in, was processed, qualified, came out—still with the same label—was condemned, stamped, and expedited by the General Congregation. No one had ever bothered to look at it.

VII

THE YEARS OF SILENCE

I will keep my mouth as it were with a bridle: while the ungodly is in my sight. I held my tongue and spake nothing: I kept silence, yea, even from good words; but it was pain and grief to me.

PSALM 39

I

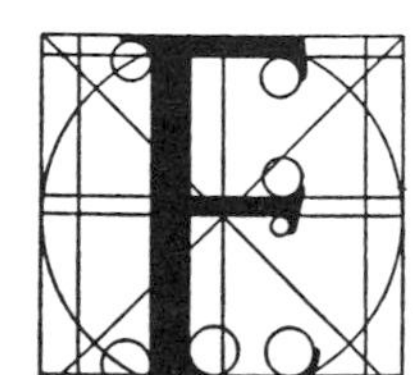

IGHT years followed in which "life went on." The old commonplace is still apt to describe an activity which has lost its clear goal while the nature of the protagonist remains unchanged. The great work in progress had been sidetracked, perhaps forever; the road was blocked ahead. "Those three most powerful operators," as he wrote, "ignorance, malice, and impiety," had won the day. But, after the first weeks of disgust and dejection, Galileo was again in harness.

There was frequent illness in those years, a painful rheumatic condition, with complications, which had plagued him recurrently. There was much thinking also on the foundations of mechanics and on profound infinitesimal questions, which carried his attention far afield to reaches he had never considered before. There were also the consolations of country life in his villa of Bellosguardo, overlooking Florence and the sweep of the Arno: the care of the olive crop and the cutting and grafting of vines, at which Galileo was enormously proud of being a renowned expert. And there was the pleasant company of his literary friends.

"His conversation," says Viviani, although he knew him only in his last years, "was full of wit and conceits, rich in grave wisdom and penetrating sentences. His subjects were not only the exact and speculative sciences but also music, letters, and poetry. He had a wonderfully retentive memory and knew most of Virgil, Ovid, Horace, and Seneca; among the Tuscans, Petrarch almost whole, the rhymes of Berni, and all of the poem of Ariosto, who was his favorite author."

There was also, by now, Sister Maria Celeste, turned seventeen, who was going to become a major presence in the old man's life. In her passionate love for her father, the girl was able to draw from his visits and his letters and from the small world of her rustic convent in Arcetri the subjects for a correspondence of such bubbling freshness and grace as might have made her, had she lived under different conditions, an Italian Sévigné.[1]

In her penurious and menial surroundings Suor Maria Celeste had created an intense life all of her own.

"I cannot rest any longer without news," she writes, "both for the infinite love I bear you, and also for fear lest this sudden cold, which in general disagrees so much with you, should have caused a return of your usual pains and other complaints. I therefore send the man who takes this letter purposely to hear how you are, and also when you expect to set out on your journey. I have been extremely busy at the dinner-napkins. They are nearly finished, but but now I come to putting on the fringe, I find that of the sort I send as a pattern, a piece is wanting for two dinner-napkins: that will be four ells. I should be glad if you could let me have it immediately, so that I may send you the napkins before you go; as it was for this that I have been making such haste to get them finished.

"As I have no cell to sleep in of my own, Sister Diamanta kindly allows me to share hers, depriving herself of the company of her own sister for my sake. But the room is so bitterly cold, that with my head in the state in which it is at present, I do not know how I shall remain, unless you can help me by lending me a set of those

---

1. Some of it has been collected in an anonymous English translation (by Mary Allen Olney): *The Private Life of Galileo through the Letters of Sister Maria Celeste* (London, 1870). But much of the quality of the original is bound to be lost in any translation.

white bed-hangings which you will not want now. I should be glad to know if you could do me this service. Moreover, I beg you to be so kind as to send me that book of yours which has just been published, so that I may read it, for I have a great desire to see it.

"These few cakes I send are some I made a few days ago, intending to give them to you when you came to bid us adieu. As your departure is not so near as we feared, I send them lest they should get dry. Sister Arcangela is still under medical treatment, and is much tried by the remedies. I am not well myself, but being so accustomed to ill health, I do not make much of it, seeing, too, that it is the Lord's will to send me continually some such little trial as this. I thank Him for everything, and pray that He will give you the highest and best felicity.

"P.S. You can send us any collars that want getting up."[2]

To be nearer to her, Galileo eventually moved to the little villa in Arcetri which was to be his final dwelling; and promptly she started reweaving around him the threads of his broken family life. The loss of the father's letters is an irreparable literary loss, for he told her everything, but even through the mirrored reflection in her writing we know more about his life in that period than about any other. "I keep and put aside all the letters that Your Honour writes me every day, and with much delight read and re-read them, so I leave it to you to judge whether I should not like to read also those that are written to you by such virtuous and loving persons."

Her own letters give us back the ways and sounds of Tuscan country life as scarcely any others. We see her instructing the maid, taking care of the house and the stable, keeping check on the farm. She prepares delicate dishes and sends them up to him by special courier; she makes for him preserves, sweets, canel water and rosmarine; mends his linen; picks for him the last December rose she found in a corner of her garden. "Spending my time in the service of Your Honour," she writes, "I do enjoy immensely, and I hardly notice the limitations of a nun's life, except when I hear that Your Honour is sick, for then I wish I could come and live in the house." From her we learn of his visits, of his gifts and attentions, of the time he glazed the windows of her cell with his

2. Sister Maria Celeste to Galileo, November 21, 1623 (*ibid.*).

own hands, so that she and her friends could have some daylight to work by in the winter months. "Truly this is work more befitting a carpenter than a philosopher." She comes back to ask him more serious favors, for what she resents deeply in the convent is not their poverty but the neglect of the authorities in providing spiritual assistance to such uncertain or forced vocations as she sees around her, and she asks her father to use his influence at Court in order that they may be given some better confessors than those they have, "more used to hunting hares than to caring for souls."

The epistolary activity of Galileo in those years was immense, for he kept in constant touch with his disciples, whose fame was growing, and he was never weary of assisting their thought in a vast range of subjects. Young Father Cavalieri had taken up from him the study of infinitesimals, from which was to come his *Geometry of Indivisibles.* As for Castelli, he had published his pioneer treatise on *The Motion of Water* and had been appointed chief consultant for hydraulic projects. But consulting engineers did not command high fees then. Pushed from pillar to post, ever faithful, ever cheerful, he would write from Rome: "I am eating cucumbers as the day is long, since my purse is not enough for melons, drink cold wine like a millrace, pass the dog days as I can, and the Masters preserve me in their favor." Another time he wrote: "This project of Lake Trasimeno is getting bigger as time goes on. I am in water up to my chin, but we'll let it stay there, '*exclusive*,' and the wine inside, '*inclusive*.' "

A project Galileo had long postponed offered a merciful opportunity for dull time-consuming labor. It was that of working out the tables of the satellites of Jupiter and of using them as a celestial chronometer for the measurement of longitude, which entailed much observation, much repetitive computation, and an interminable exchange of letters through embassies with the representatives of Spanish sea power, who had suddenly evinced interest in this possible new aid to navigation.

Through all this he was collecting himself. As the diver descending into the dark depths feels his strength rise from the burning of his oxygen under pressure, so the scientist's mind, as it receded into isolation, burned brighter to itself. The past compromises and loose adjustments of thought discarded, Galileo seems to be facing more decisively the full implications of his theory.

It is an inhuman wrench for the mind to tear itself loose from the instinctive world of the senses around us, so "full of a number of things," peopled with familiar substances which reassuringly go about subsisting in their own several ways as if they knew how—and to uncover instead everywhere the mysterious realization of abstract laws; to conceive of mathematical function determining each point of being in a dizzying tension between the infinite and the infinitesimal, where the lonely intellect has to feel its way with new instruments of rigorous analysis. It implies a dedication; a new feeling not only of nature but also of the divine. When the time for expression comes again, the quiet prose of the physicist will rise of itself to compelling heights, spark and crackle with contained metaphysical power. But, for many years yet, silence was in order.

Slowly and painfully, Galileo was learning to adjust to a world of absurdity, to create for himself a language of ambiguous and unseizable irony, to believe what he did not believe while thinking what he thought. "I wear a mask, but of necessity," as Sarpi had written ten years before, "because without it no one can live in Italy." Sarpi had still been able to defend Venetian sovereignty against the Curia and had been knifed for his pains in a dark alley in Venice. "I recognize the stylus of the Holy Office," he had said with a wry pun and had taken to moving about only in a gondola, well escorted. Galileo, too, now wore a mask, and it was not that of worldly expediency. It was that of the man who has to combine an ingrained respect for a holy and legitimate institution with disrespect for its judgment and with bitter sorrow for the consequences of its action. He knew—none better than he—the damage that had been wrought by the decree of 1616. The slow growth of public interest in astronomy, which, following the era of geographic discoveries, had spread in the preceding generation from high to low, tying up with the new idea the Italians had been forming of the importance of natural science, had just reached the point where it was ready to burst into flower. The heliocentric theory, under its ancient name of Pythagorean philosophy, had become common cultural property and common interest, an uncertain but exciting expectation voiced from many sides; it was awaiting the very type of richly endowed leader that Galileo happened to be in order to develop into a great scientific movement. The decree of the Inquisition had put a stop to all that. The "Galileist" brush fire had died out; people had turned quietly to other more conventional interests. The old man felt like a survivor, surrounded by useless and sterile respect.

He had not lost the last hope, however. Prohibitions come and go, and he knew this one to be such a departure from established practice and common sense that it could not long survive.

Prohibition in itself was an old and reasonable thing. It was the guardian of dogma. It applied to actions, to a personal "choice" on tenets (*hairesis*), and, beyond those, to instrumental arguments, to matters of policy—in brief, to all expressions which covered an intention. Supposing that Father Olivieri had been ordered to abandon the quibbles that we have painfully reproduced on page 121, he could not have protested even in his conscience. He had concocted a sophistry; it had been found no good as an instrument; let him invent another.

There was here a semantic difficulty between the old and the new. To men of the old persuasion, like Galileo, the new-fangled Jesuit word of "blind obedience" meant nothing that was orthodox, and the feeling was shared by many in the regular and secular clergy. The idea of transferring obedience to the intellectual field was quite new indeed; for it was understood that dogma was of faith, first and last, and that otherwise the intellect was bound by its own laws. Who had ever heard that one's mind, created free, must submit itself passively to the decisions of a committee of incompetents? "These," wrote Galileo later, and he must have said it many times among friends in these years, "these are the innovations which are bound to lead to the ruin of states and to the subversion of commonwealths."

Out of this certainty grew his invincible hope. Two years had not elapsed when Galileo was cautiously probing the ground. In 1618, having been requested by the Archduke Leopold of Austria for some work from his pen, he ventured to send him his most risky piece of writing (it was the memorandum he had prepared in 1616 for young Cardinal Orsini), accompanied by the following letter:

With this I send you a treatise on the causes of the tides which I wrote at the time when the theologians were thinking of prohibiting Copernicus' book and the doctrine enounced therein, which I then held to be true, until it pleased those gentlemen to prohibit the work and to declare the opinion to be false and contrary to Scripture. Now, knowing as I do that it behooves us to obey the decisions of the authorities and to believe them, since they are guided by a higher insight than any to which my humble mind can of itself attain, I consider this treatise which I send you to be merely a poetical conceit, or a dream, and desire that your Highness may take it as such, inasmuch as it is based on the double motion of the Earth and, indeed, contains one of the arguments which I brought in confirmation of it.

But even poets sometimes attach a value to one or other of their fantasies, and I likewise attach some value to this fancy of mine. . . . I have also let a few exalted personages have copies, in order that in case anyone not belonging to our Church should try to appropriate my curious fancy, as has happened to me with many of my discoveries, these personages, being above all suspicion, may be able to bear witness that it was I who first dreamed of this chimera. What I now send is but a fugitive performance; it was written in haste and in the expectation that the work of Copernicus would not be condemned as erroneous eighty years after its publication. . . . But a voice from heaven aroused me and dissolved all my confused and tangled fantasies in mist. May therefore your Highness graciously accept it, ill arranged as it is. And if divine mercy ever grants that I may be in a position to exert myself a little, your Highness may expect something more solid and real from me.

There is no mistaking the scornful irony in those words. The true meaning becomes explicit when we find again the same terms of "fantasy," "paradox," and "vain chimera" ten years later as a saving clause at the end of the *Dialogue*, but this time with the full impact of the Copernican proof behind them.

II

The skies themselves seemed not to leave the issue in peace, for soon the attention of the world was shaken by the comets of 1618, of which one has remained the most impressive in the memory of man. Coming, as it did, at the outset of the Thirty Years' War, it could appear only too justifiably a portent of God's wrath. Princes were frightened, the public was in a turmoil, and apocalyptic specialists computed anew the end of the world. Of the innumerable writings that it prompted, Pierre Bayle's *Pensées sur la comète* (which was really written about this one, although it was published on the occasion of the comet of 1680) is the only one that has survived. Much more modest, and indeed unimportant, was a discourse delivered in the Collegio Romano amid great concourse of public by a learned Jesuit, Father Horatio Grassi. But Galileo read it, and his temper began to rise. There is no misplaced gentleness in the marginal jottings on his copy. The expletives alone would make a vocabulary of good Tuscan abuse: *pezzo d'asinaccio, elefantissimo, bufolaccio, villan poltrone, balordone, barattiere, poveraccio, ingratissimo villano, ridicoloso, sfacciato, inurbano.* So these trained seals who had kept to their holes in time of crisis were now gloating about him and oraculating again. One had only to glance through Grassi's *Discourse* to realize that the good man did not even understand the working of the telescope while displaying its use so complacently. But, even before looking at the text, Galileo knew very well that the author had not come on stage amid applause to bring new ideas but simply to drive another nail, as he thought, in the coffin of Copernicanism, well assured that by this time the Man of Florence ("quello di Firenze," as they called him) was in no condition to answer back.

Moved by the helpless anger of his friend, Mario Guiducci, "consul" of the Florentine Academy, offered to write an answer himself.

Comets and new stars have always fascinated the mind which believes in a magic and miraculous order of things. It is the regularities, rather, that have been taken for granted, until the advent of scientific speculation. It seems natural enough for heaven to go round and for the Sun to rise every morning, but a comet in the skies becomes a portent of vast significance. Conversely, for the scientific mind as it had been at work since the Greeks, eternal harmony and periodicity are the true awesome portent of a higher design, and irregular events become a disturbing problem. The accepted explanation for the wise since Aristotle had been that comets are exhalations of earth vapors rising above the sphere of fire. This keeps their freakish behavior away from the harmony of the spheres. But Tycho by his measurements on the comet of 1577 had shown that they must be higher than the Moon and also that they have an orbit of some strange sort. Kepler, then, had thought he could show that the path was rectilinear. What Father Grassi was now suggesting was a compromise. He agreed that the comet was in heaven, but, following the Aristotelian distinction between earthly and heavenly matter, he insisted that its path must be circular.

As for Galileo, he found himself against almost everybody, for he held that comets are only optical effects born of earthly vapors. This was no doubt wrong, but there were serious reasons for his choice. In the matter of novae he had gone all out in favor of Tycho's and Kepler's findings, which placed the new stars in the firmament, for that was to him, as it was for Kepler, an excellent way of proving that the heavens were not fixed and unalterable. But new stars were obliging enough to stay put, as flares in the sky, whereas the comets had been shown by Tycho to have paths which were utterly aberrant from a Copernican point of view. Some were even retrograde. Newton would be able eventually to turn Halley's comet into the triumph of the new system. But Newton had not yet come; and Galileo, who had his own reasons to believe that circular paths were the only ones physically possible in outer space, thought it best to try to prove that the comets did not belong to heaven at all but were optical effects in the atmosphere. It came surely *ex parte*, but it still was a sensible effort in the manner of the Presocratics to extend physics to the heavens, and well worth a try. In fact, the connection that he inferred between comets' tails and the Sun's beams turned out to be substantially right. The real trouble with his position is that it broke the old alliance with Kepler, who was the better astronomer of the two, and brought Galileo the wrong kind of backing in astronomy.

Grassi's opinion, by contrast, may appear closer to the truth, but it was such only in appearance. It was a compromise position, and it was a purely political one. We have seen how Tycho's system had been pressed into the service of the Vatican as providing the most opportune deviation from the Copernican issue; what Grassi was doing was only mixing Tycho and Aristotle, half and half, to provide a more fashionable version of the same old brew. As for the scientific reasons, they remained so far behind that Grassi used the telescope, the means now made available for reaching new conclusions, in a way that made no sense. He assumed that telescopic magnification was in inverse ratio to distance and hence that he could prove the great distance of the comet by the small difference he found between the telescopic and the visual image.

Galileo was only too well aware of what Grassi was trying to do. But, as we follow his marginal notes, we see his anger gradually turning into a chuckle. These gentlemen apparently still labored under the impression that physical problems could be solved with a school exercise in rhetoric, adorned with the proper quotations. Well, he could ask them a few questions about their physics.

The *Discourse on the Comets* came out in June, 1619. It was signed by Guiducci, but there was no mistaking the hand behind it. Much applause and favorable comment greeted it in Rome, for the *Discourse* showed a Galileo disposed to carry on with his contributions to science while exercising his ingenuity on acceptable subjects. His old friend Cardinal Maffeo Barberini, as if to ask him to forget the old bitterness connected with the prohibition decree, sent him a Latin poem in his honor entitled "Adulatio perniciosa" ("Dangerous Adulation"). But Ciàmpoli wrote that the Jesuits "were much offended and were preparing to strike back." In fact, the year had not elapsed when Grassi came out with a Latin dissertation, *The Libra* ("Balance"), under the anagram "Lothario Sarsi Sigensano." Since he had not been attacked personally, he would not answer in person. But there was no misunderstanding his intention either. Guiducci, who had maintained a vertical rising path of the comet as born from earthy vapors, had admitted discreetly that "a further cause" might have to be found in order to explain the deflection toward the north. "Sarsi," after more than one slighting remark, comes to a halt before this admission:

> What is this sudden fear in an open and not timid spirit which prevents him from uttering the word that he has in mind? I cannot guess it. Is this other motion which could explain everything and which he does not dare to discuss—is it of the comet or of something else? It cannot be the motion of the circles, since for Galileo there are no Ptolemaic circles. I fancy I hear a small voice whispering discreetly in my ear: the motion of the Earth. Get thee behind me thou evil word, offensive to truth and to pious ears! It was surely prudence to speak it with bated breath. For, if it were really thus, there would be nothing

left of an opinion which can rest on no other ground except this false one. . . . But then certainly Galileo had no such idea, for I have never known him otherwise than pious and religious.

On reading these ugly provocations, Galileo must have wondered whether he had not been a fool to get himself involved in such quarrels. He might have known his motive, had he cared to ask himself. The long-pent-up bitterness had found a way out. But, if *they* were considering him as dead and buried already, he would show them. There was no decree that forbade showing up an ass. Besides, now, "Sarsi" had him on the spot. Even his most anxious friends admitted that he must step forward in person to cover Guiducci and to vindicate the honor of science. Cesi and Ciàmpoli advised the form of an open letter. Cesarini, who was intimate with the Jesuits, was willing to be the recipient. But Stelluti, another Lycean friend, wrote from Rome: "To take on the Fathers would mean never to see the end of it, for they are so many that they could face the whole world, and, even if they are in the wrong, they will never admit to defeat." Right, agreed Galileo, the Jesuits would be left out of it. But here was a straw figure, this "Lothario Sarsi" of unknown address; he was going to pelt the scarecrow with rotten eggs and tomatoes.

Yet those were times of trouble. His friend and patron, Cosimo II, had just died (1620). The protection of a strong-minded prince who had helped him unswervingly was replaced by the more uncertain favor of the widowed Grand Duchess, a very pious lady, who had assumed the regency until young Ferdinand II should come of age. There was also the trend of things in Rome. The College of Propaganda Fide was being organized for the conquest to the faith of far continents which would offset the losses to Protestantism in Europe; and with it the word "propaganda" had entered on its career. The Jesuits were gaining ascendancy even though Bellarmine had died in 1621; Loyola and Xavier were being enrolled among the saints.

Gagged and tethered, watched by malevolent suspicion in every move (Tommaso Caccini had come back and started afresh on his persecutions), beset by sickness, pressed by the hopes and angers of Florence, Galileo had to proceed with great care and deliberation.

It was only two years later that he could tell his friends that the answer was on its way to the press.

III

Suddenly, in August, 1623, the news burst like a star shell over the bleak landscape: Maffeo Barberini had been elected Pope. There was rejoicing in Florence. After Paul V, a dull and savage-tempered old man, the brief reign of Gregory XV had brought only slight improvement. But Maffeo Barberini, or rather Urban VIII, as he was now, was a friend of the arts and a Lycean academic himself. It was in everybody's memory that, only three years before, following the *Discourse on the Comets,* he had written his "Adulatio perniciosa" in honor of Galileo—as if to remind him that, even through the crisis of 1616, he had always defended the new science.[3] Now that he had no longer to play a covered political game in the

---

3. Those lines, again, are rarely quoted; yet, quite apart from their classical distinction, they have an interest because of their unwittingly prophetic import. Galileo's discoveries of new things in the skies, and even of spots in the Sun, are brought in as an example of how greatness and glory deemed to be above the changes of fortune will eventually show their weakness and come to grief—how even hundred-eyed Argus let something escape him. "Truth is unwelcome to the mighty: The enemy is often more useful":

Cum Luna caelo fulget, et auream
Pompam sereno pandit in ambitu
  Ignes coruscantes, voluptas
    Mira trahit, retinetque visus.

Hic emicantem suspicit Hesperum,
Dirumque Martis sidus, et orbitam
  Lactis coloratam nitore;
    Ille tuam, Cynosura, lucem.

Seu Scorpii cor, sive Canis faciem
Miratur alter, vel Jovis asseclas,
  Patrisve Saturni, repertos
    Docte tuo Galilaee vitro.

At prima Solis cum reserat diem
Lux orta, puro Gangis ab aequore
  Se sola diffundit, micansque
    Intuitus radiis moratur.

. . . .

Nil esse regum sorte beatius,
Mens et cor aeque concipit omnium,
  Quos larva rerum, quos inani
    Blanda rapit specie cupido.

Non semper, extra quod radiat jubar,
Splendescit intra: respicimus nigras
  In Sole (quis credat?) retectas
    Arte tua, Galilaee, labes.

Sceptri coruscat gloria regii
Ornata gemmis; turba satellitum
  Hinc inde procedit, colentes
    Officiis comites sequuntur.

. . . .

Fugit potentum limina Veritas,
Quamquam salutis nuntia: nauseam
  Invisa proritat, vel iram:
    Saepe magis juvat hostis hostem.

Curia, it was surmised, his true inclinations could not fail to come out. Happy omens confirmed it: Cesarini was made Master of the Chamber, and Ciàmpoli was confirmed in his newly won position as Secretary of the Briefs, which was equivalent to a private secretaryship in the British system. "I am fully confident," announces Rinuccini, "that this is going to be the papacy of the *virtuosi*."

Ciàmpoli was writing to Galileo: "Here there is felt a great desire for some further production of your thought; if you would resolve to commit to print those ideas that you still have in mind, I am quite sure that they would be most acceptable to His Holiness, who never ceases from admiring your eminence in all things and preserves intact his attachment for you. You should not deprive the world of your productions while there is time to work them out, and please remember that I am yours as ever."

When Prince Cesi came to congratulate him on his accession, Urban interrupted him eagerly: "Is Galileo coming? When is he coming?"

"He is dying to come, your Holiness," was the answer.

The scientist, on his side, wrote Cesi: "I am revolving in my mind plans of some moment for the republic of letters, and perhaps can never hope for so wonderful a combination of circumstances to insure their success."

But he took his time, for he wanted to effect his *rentrée* in style.

By the end of October the long-awaited answer to Grassi came out in Rome. It was the *Saggiatore* ("Assayer"), and it was promptly and unanimously recognized for what it was—the masterpiece of Italian polemic prose. Galileo had written his *Provinciales*. As in Pascal's case, the argument was not always meticulously fair, but it nailed the enemy to the post. Sparkling wit and destructive irony took the place of the weapons that had been forbidden. In a seemingly leisurely and impersonal excursion over the wide—too wide—field of "Sarsi's" utterances and references, Galileo went to work on learned nonsense and academic prejudice and brought forth what has remained in history as a breviary of the scientific method.

What was left of "Lothario Sarsi's" arguments was not much. We shall give here a brief passage from that polemic. It has been often quoted, but it loses nothing from repetition:

I cannot refrain from marveling that Sarsi will persist in proving to me, by authorities, that which at any moment I can bring to the test of experiment. . . . If discussing a difficult problem were like carrying a weight, since several horses will carry more sacks of corn than one alone will, I would agree that many reasoners avail more than one; but discoursing is like coursing, and not like carrying, and one hunter by himself will run farther than a hundred drayhorses. When Sarsi brings up such a multitude of authors, it does not seem to me that he in the least degree strengthens his own conclusions, but he ennobles the cause of Signor Mario and myself, by showing that we reason better than many men of established reputation. If Sarsi insists that I must believe, on Suidas' credit,[4] that the Babylonians cooked eggs by swiftly whirling them in a sling, I will believe it; but I must say that the cause of such an effect is very remote from that to which it is attributed, and to find the true cause I shall reason thus. If an effect does not follow with us which followed with others at another time, it is because, in our experiment, something is wanting which was the cause of the former success; and if only one thing is wanting to us, that one thing is the true cause. Now we have eggs, and slings, and strong men to whirl them, and yet they will not become cooked; nay, if they were hot at first, they more quickly become cold; and, since nothing is wanting to us but to be Babylonians, it follows that being Babylonians is the true cause why the eggs became cooked, and not the friction of the air, which is what I wish to prove.[5] Is it possible that in traveling post, Sarsi has never noticed that coolness is occasioned on the face by the continual change of air? And if he has felt it, will he rather trust the relation by others of what was done two thousand years ago at Babylon than what he can at this moment verify in his own person? I, at least, will not be so wilfully wrong, and so ungrateful to Nature and to God, that, having been gifted with sense and logic, I should voluntarily set less value on such great endowments than on the fallacies of a fellow-man and blindly and blunderingly believe whatever I hear and barter the freedom of my intellect for slavery to one as liable to error as myself.

As for Grassi-"Sarsi's" astronomical theories, they fare no better than the physical:

---

4. Suidas was a late Alexandrine commentator who wrote a dictionary of philological and other curiosities.

5. Someone has remarked that Suidas and Sarsi were the prophets of guided missiles. They were not. They were talking about eggs.

And so here we have, both Sarsi and I, expended a great amount of words in searching whether the solid concavity of the lunar orb (which does not exist), by moving in a circle (whilst it never did), drags along with it the element of fire (if perchance there be such an one) and, by way of it, the exhalations which in turn ignite the matter of the comet, which we do not know whether it is really in that place but do well know that it is not the kind of stuff that burns. . . .

Grassi was pulverized in the public eye and went off to nurse his grudge. The Jesuits ordered him to lie low henceforth and not try to answer. This did not go without some very bitter feelings, for Grassi had only voiced the acceptable and accepted opinion of Jesuit astronomers. He himself was no discredit to the Order. He had drawn the plans for the Church of Sant'Ignazio in Rome and had even proposed, after Leonardo, the construction of a submarine boat of his own designing. His faults were only those of his confreres. They had learned their geometry from geometricians, their engineering from engineers—and their physics from rhetoricians. They imagined the combination could stand forever, because they had been taught to use normal intelligence in human affairs, and in the problems of Nature that of circus performers; for that was what their eloquence amounted to in the face of a nonpersuadable reality. But this time defeat had to be conceded. Galileo had effected his comeback and was again firmly established in the center of the literary scene.

VIII

URBAN VIII

Habituees of the mirror, famous readers, they fall in love with historical characters, with the unfortunate queen, or the engaging young assistant or a great detective, even with voice, of the announcer, maybe, from some foreign station they can never identify. . . . Why not go out together next Sunday; say, casually, in a wood: "I suppose you realize you are fingering the levers that control eternity!"

W. H. AUDEN, "THE ORATORS"

I

AT THE end of April, 1624, after a leisurely voyage and a stay of two weeks with Cesi at his castle in Acquasparta, Galileo arrived in Rome. He was bringing with him a delightful novelty, the first microscope (he called it simply "occhialino"), with which one could see all sorts of "horrendous things" moving about in a drop of water. He was received by the Pope with "infinite demonstrations of love" and in the course of six weeks had as many long conversations with him. Very soon, however, he realized that he was not going to get very far. He was talking no longer to Maffeo Barberini, but to Urban VIII.

Urban felt himself, with some reason, to be of the stuff of which the great Popes of the Renaissance had been made. In that critical period early in the Thirty Years' War, when the fate of the Reformation hung in the balance, he was planning a great political campaign which would change the balance of Europe. Splendor and power were going to be his insignia. On being shown the marble monuments of his predecessors, he said that "he would erect iron ones to himself." The fortresses on the northern borders, the new breastwork of Castel Sant'Angelo, the new manufacture of arms at Tivoli, the Vatican Armory taking up the rooms of the old library (where imported technicians cast guns for the fortress out of the old Roman bronze ceilings of the Pantheon), finally, the costly harbor of Civitavecchia—all were meant as manifest symbols of the desire of Urban VIII to establish pontifical power again as the vice-regency of Christ with the two-edged sword of the world.

Urban VIII was not of the old feudal nobility and did not share their medieval dreams. He came of a family of Florentine merchant princes who, like the Chigis and the Medicis, had entered the aristocracy only a few generations before. A Florentine himself, talented, bright, sharp, and realistic, he had cloaked his ambition while still a prelate in the dignified forms of conventional literary achievement, legal competence, and careful demeanor. Once in power, his latent pride and vanity were to break forth without restraint, and with them his natural temper, quick to anger and suspicion.[1]

He never lacked an adequate feeling of his own capacities. He ignored ancient constitutions, because "the sentence of one live Pope was worth more than all the decrees of a hundred dead ones." On being informed that the notables wished to erect a monument to him, which was usually done for Popes only after their deaths, he said: "Let them. I am not an ordinary Pope either."

He liked the theatrical side of Baroque production, the bustle of engineering projects, and his own ornate contributions to Latin poetry in hexameter and Sapphic verse. We have seen that he had written an ode to Galileo, the "Dangerous Adulation." But for the real ideas of science he had as little understanding as for the real forces stirring in war-torn Europe around him. His whole political conception and his master-plan were quite conventional: how to

---

1. In this, too, he appears an epigone in the line of Sixtus V, for the latter, as Felice Peretti, had given an English visitor the impression of being "the most crooching, humble Cardinal that was ever lodged in an oven" but, once crowned with the triregnum, had broken forth as a "consecrated whirlwind" and the terror of the Curia.

attach the powers to his chariot while at the same time increasing his own domains. In these very days of April, 1624, Cardinal Richelieu, still an obscure political figure, was preparing to enter the King's Council. By September, Urban would meet his full challenge with the ultimatum to raze the papal forts in the Valtelline. It was a new departure in that struggle between modern nations, rising and formidable contestants that were to play the destructive game of the Thirty Years' War to the utter frustration of theocratic power.

But in those days Urban was still dreaming of spectacular successes. It was the morning of his reign, a morning full of magnificence and confidence. Amid the turmoil of the affairs of state he found time for long audiences with Galileo.

What took place in those audiences will forever remain a matter for speculation. But from scattered data we may infer that the conversation went something like this. On being copiously complimented on the *Saggiatore* and being told by the Pope that he had had it read aloud at table, Galileo deprecated the poor merit of these feeble excursions on a perforce limited subject, whereupon the Pontiff exclaimed his wish that more such incomparable creations should flow from his magical pen. Thereupon Galileo tactfully alluded to the malice of his many enemies and to the many disadvantages under which he labored, and the Pope reassured him that, if he remained such a dutiful son of the Holy Church as he had shown himself hitherto, his enemies would bark in vain. The System of the Schools, in intelligent hands, ought to fear nothing from the new science, for it was established on natural evidence itself; and he, the Pope, could show it quite easily. He expanded on that subject.[2] The campaign against Galileo was really alarm born of the incompetence of certain people who usurped the privileges of the scholar, and it would be kept in check.

Frustrated, thus, in his first approach, the scientist bethought himself of indirect pressure. Some time later Cardinal Hohenzollern, on his leave-taking audience, was moved to represent to the Pope what difficulties he had in converting German noblemen who had been shocked by the prohibition of 1616. The Holy Father was

---

2. Cf. the dispatch of Niccolini, June 12, 1642.

sympathetic. But he remarked that the Church neither had condemned nor would condemn the doctrine of Copernicus as heretical, but only as rash (*temeraria*), and that there was no chance that it would ever be proved wrong, for a convincing proof was impossible.[3] The statement of fact, we may observe, was less than accurate, for, in the first place, the Congregation of the Index is not "the Church," and, in the second place, it had declared the opinion *false,* not *rash;* in the third place, its Qualifiers had specified reservedly that it was "foolish and absurd philosophically and formally heretical."

Be that as it may, the Pope could, even without pronouncing himself *ex cathedra* for the first time on the subject, have had the findings corrected or reversed. He did neither. He somewhat attenuated the content and at the same time confirmed it as a juridical precedent. The main objective was lost. But those remarks left a slight opening.

Galileo in his contacts had "begun to discover new land," as he wrote. This appears to mean, from other allusions, that the prelates he consulted (Cobelluzzi, Barberini, Borghese) agreed that there had been entirely too much fuss about this affair, that it was a purely juridical matter, and that the decree could not be revised for reasons of prestige but that anyone could go and be as Copernican as

3. This is from the letter to Cesi, January 8, 1624. We have, moreover, the following in G. F. Buonamici's memorandum of 1633: "Cardinal Zollern encouraged Galileo, telling him that the Pope had reminded him of having defended Copernicus at the time of Paul V and assured him that, were it only owing to the respect justly due the memory of Copernicus, he would never allow this opinion to be declared heretical in his time." As Buonamici's paper is inaccurate on several factual details concerning the events of 1633, this reference remains in doubt. On the other hand, the paper contains confidential statements that cannot have been communicated by any except Galileo himself (such as his conditions for going through with the abjuration); this about Cardinal Zollern ought to be one of them. The compliments to Copernicus reserved for a German audience agree with Urban's diplomacy at the time. They also dovetail with the other part of the statement above. On the Buonamici memorandum see n. 4, p. 286.

he pleased, provided he gave no scandal and played the game.[4] The Roman hierarchy knew itself too well not to countenance a skeptical worldly conformism in others.

Fortified by these opinions, Galileo in the next audiences again approached the subject. He steered through many mutual deplorations on the decline of good writing toward the remark that a number of very wonderful conceits and effects of Nature were still waiting to be written about, were it only for the delight of the mind—if he understood the decree rightly to read that a free discussion of natural hypotheses was still allowed. He was assured that this was the very spirit of the decree, as everyone should know: not to restrain the mind in its ingenious conjectures but to prevent the wrong philosophical conclusions from being drawn. We Ourselves, said the Pope, have validly defended Copernicus in 1616, and he pointed out that it would expose the Church to the ridicule of the heretics if the very man who gave such a valid contribution to the reform of the calendar carried through by Pope Gregory were declared heretical in his thoughts.[5] So long as he reigned, insisted the Pontiff, the memory of Copernicus had nothing to fear. The Church knew very well how much prudence is required in this delicate matter of the interpretation of Scripture. Surely, it was not her intention to clip the wings of Signor Galileo's subtle speculations and

---

4. Cardinal Antonio Barberini, Sr., had cautioned against one difficulty, namely, that Copernicus had made the Earth a star. Galileo and Castelli had assured him that it could be handled. It is difficult for a modern to realize how rigid conservatism in official places could coexist with a seemingly free ferment of ideas. In 1624 the theological faculty of Paris, which held in France most of the functions of the Inquisition, condemned the anti-Aristotelian theses of three candidates, and the Parliament in consequence ordered the theses destroyed and the candidates expelled. But apart from doctoral theses, all sorts of ideas found expression. From the administrative vantage point of the authorities, "novelties" could look like a very limited local disturbance in the orderly flow of approved scholarship. On Wolynski's count, there were 2,330 works published on astronomy between 1543 and 1687 (which brings us to the time of Newton's *Principia*); of those, only 180 were Copernican (see *Archivio storico italiano*, 1873, p. 12).

5. Buonamici's memorandum (see n. 4, p. 286).

admirable discoveries, which were an adornment of the true faith and might also lead to remarkable improvements in engineering, as long as he was quite sure he intended to leave theology alone.

But, then, suggested Galileo hastily before the Pope could revert to discoursing of absent friends, the decree must have been misunderstood by many, for there was ill-informed muttering at home and sneering abroad that it had been the work of uninformed consultors.[6]—Nonsense, said the Pope, We Ourselves were part in it. There were then high reasons. But it was certainly a regrettable necessity, most regrettable. And, then, urged Galileo, would it not be to the benefit of the true faith if the many natural reasons for and against could be probed carefully and dispassionately so as to show that the issue, maturely examined, needed a higher decision? That, agreed the Pope, would be a good idea. To prove that all the ingenuity of man could devise in the matter of the heavens could lead to no conclusive statement was all to the benefit of obedience. Let the Signor Galileo assay theories with that exquisite balance of scruples wherewith he was wont to test the truth, and show again that "we are not to find out the work of His hands."

Better still, suggested Galileo, supposing that one took the following line, which had occurred to him while writing a poetic conceit which perhaps His Beatitude remembered from years back, a curious fantasy on the ebb and flow of the sea to which he was attached and which had been possibly too much appreciated by certain foreigners who had taken it for their own: supposing that one could produce proofs of the Pythagorean theory that imposed themselves as physically necessary, if not metaphysically. . . .

Urban VIII cut him short with a little lecture:[7] "Let Us remind

---

6. The source for this and the following is in the *Letter to Ingoli* and in the Preface to the *Dialogue on the Great World Systems.* There are also Riccardi's instructions to the licenser and Oregius' text, of which later. Needless to say, there is no record of the conversation, and we have only stitched together indirect references in the way that seemed the most plausible.

7. Historians usually date this idea from the conversation of 1630. But we have seen (p. 127) that it is mentioned in Oregius' *Praeludium,* whence we have paraphrased the statement quoted below. The passage

you of something that We had occasion to tell you many years ago, speaking as one philosopher to another; and, if We remember, you were not willing then to offer Us any definite refutation.

"Let Us grant you that all of your demonstrations are sound and that it is entirely possible for things to stand as you say. But now tell Us, do you really maintain that God could not have wished or known how to move the heavens and the stars in some other way? We suppose you will say 'Yes,' because We do not see how you could answer otherwise. Very well then, if you still want to save your contention, you would have to prove to Us that, if the heavenly movements took place in another manner than the one you suggest, it would imply a logical contradiction at some point, since God in His infinite power can do anything that does not imply a contradiction. Are you prepared to prove as much? No? Then you will have to concede to Us that God can, conceivably, have arranged things in an entirely different manner, while yet bringing about the effects that we see. And if this possibility exists, which might still preserve in their literal truth the sayings of Scripture, it is not for us mortals to try to force those holy words to mean what to us, from here, may appear to be the situation.

"Have you got anything to object? We are glad to see that you are of Our opinion. Indeed, as a good Catholic, how could you hold any other? To speak otherwise than hypothetically on the subject would be tantamount to constraining the infinite power and wisdom of God within the limits of your personal ideas [*fantasie particolari*]. You cannot say that this is the only way God could have brought it about, because there may be many, and perchance infinite, ways that He could have thought of and which are inaccessible to our limited minds.[8] We trust you see now what We meant by telling you to leave theology alone."

It was only then, probably, that Galileo was able to measure the

---

in question, according to Berti, occurs also in the first edition of 1629. Hence the argument dates back at least to 1624 and probably, as Oregius implies, was used for the first time in 1616.

8. The last two sentences are those Galileo quotes as a conclusion to the *Dialogue* as coming from "a very high authority," and we must assume the quotation to be faithful.

chasm which separated his thought from that of the Pontiff; for the latter's words, taken seriously, would have implied that all investigation of Nature was bound to lead to nothing. He might have objected as he does in the *Dialogue:* "Surely, God could have caused birds to fly with their bones made of solid gold, with their veins full of quicksilver, with their flesh heavier than lead, and with wings exceeding small. He did not, and that ought to show something. It is only in order to shield your ignorance that you put the Lord at every turn to the refuge of a miracle."[9]

But this was no time to argue. He kept his peace. He must have been familiar already with that type of argument and known how difficult it was to cope with. From the point of view of Church philosophy, it was sound and orthodox doctrine. Robert Grosseteste had provided the epistemological part of it back in the thirteenth century. Taken on the pragmatic level, it did not make much sense, for it permitted, while not permitting, science to proceed, with the proviso that it would not be getting anywhere. For all his literary sympathies, the Pope was utterly unable to grasp the implications of the new thought. A humanist of the sixteenth century, schooled by the Jesuits in Peripatetic principles, Urban lived in a world of significant forms and sensuous substances, varied and multiple, with many wonderful names and qualities apt for the learned discourse; the paradox of mathematical physics, the bridge thrown directly from the extreme abstraction of geometry to basic monotone matter defined only by mass and measure, remained beyond his conceiving. The new "natural conclusions," he felt, had their proper place in enriching the world, not in reducing it to geometric space.

This is where his thinking was backed by the great schemes of the Renaissance and its hope in unknown harmonies. "There is nothing that is incredible," Marsilio Ficino had said. "For to God all things are possible, and nothing is impossible. There are numberless possibilities that we deny because we do not happen to know them." This was also what Pico della Mirandola had maintained, hinting at reaches of "natural magic" beyond our dreams; and

---

9. This remark and others to the same effect are tucked away in the text so as not to appear a direct answer to the Pope's argument.

Campanella, too, was supporting Galileo in the hope of results such as no scientist could ever produce. It was "Platonic theology" itself, urging man to extend his imagination beyond what he could see and test; it was Leonardo's belief in the creative power of artistic "fantasy." And this is clearly, even more than subtle Scholastic theories, the idea behind Urban's words: We cannot suppose that Nature has to be contained within the limits of our "particular fantasy," for she is all the possible as well. Moreover, in good Christian religion, no creature can "necessitate" its maker, were it even by true knowledge; and the transcendence of God makes it impossible that from this world we should ever know His ways. It was known that we are not allowed, for example, to think of space as infinite by nature, for then it would become a necessary part of the nature of God and thus lose its creatureliness.

Surely, it is written: *Dominus scientiarum Deus,* "God is the Lord of sciences." But this does not allow us to try to impose the seeming "necessities" of one science upon all the other ones, and it does not go without a certain arbitral role assigned to His vicar on earth.

All these things Sanctissimus had learned in his time. Therefore, he concluded, the Church is not doing any damage to science if she precludes a serious treatment of such ideas which would give scandal to the faithful. They cannot be really true and should be labeled "fantasy." As such, they may have their charm; and the Pope could show that he was able to appreciate it, for it was he who had restored Campanella, the incorrigible maverick Dominican, to freedom and literary activity.

Urban's thought was a late version, even as he himself was a late copy of the Renaissance Popes. No one could explain to him that, under his very reign, the Church was going to face things that his philosophy had never dreamed of. As a humanist, he felt he had given an adequately ample answer. As a lawyer, he decided the case was settled and turned to more urgent business.

II

Would he still have been able to answer thus if Galileo had produced one fresh proof, viz., Kepler's laws? He probably would have; still, doubt is allowable. But Galileo had never read Kepler's work on Mars that was in his library; it was as though he had not heard of it, although it would appear that Cavalieri was teaching it in Bologna. The irony of this incomprehensible blindness seems like a cruel sport of the gods; the more so as Kepler had come out in 1619 with his third law, the most impressive of the three to a mathematical mind. Even while Galileo was sitting there with the Pope, Kepler was publishing his *Gleanings from the Saggiatore*, in which he defended Tycho Brahe from reproaches of inaccuracy,[10] for he could not appreciate from his distant perspective the causes of Galileo's disdain of Tycho. To him the Tychonic system remained valuable, because it provided nothing but a natural transition to the truth of Copernicus; and he did not realize how effectively others were deliberately using it as a diversion to shunt astronomy into a dead end. But then, remarks Kepler, in a soothing way, it is said that, when Orpheus was deprived of Eurydice by the inexorable decrees of Orcus, he turned in his sorrow with unconsidered words against Eurydice herself. What Kepler understands even less, living far from the Inquisition, is the explicit way in which both contestants dissociate themselves from any Copernican implication. "Could it be," he asks in gentle mockery, "that Aegle has become afraid of Silenus' forehead, after having herself daubed it with red?"

The trouble with Kepler was that truly angelic nature of his, incapable of any self-seeking thought or even of resentment. The persecutions of Tycho's kin over twenty years (Tengnagl had only recently died, in 1622) had moved him not in the least to deviate from his filial preoccupation with the honor of his master. As for his own discoveries, they could wait until someone brought them

10. Kepler had entered the lists as the defender of Tycho's memory against Scipione Chiaramonti and his *Antitycho*. By defending Tycho's observations in the matter of the nova, he was playing unwittingly into the hands of the Jesuits, who needed Tycho for very different reasons. This was the beginning of a regrettable difference between the two scientists which damaged their friendship. Galileo backed Chiaramonti (on the comets if not on the nova), at least indirectly, for tactical reasons and was later knifed in the back by the latter for his pains. It was a case of what Galileo himself had warned against: "In order to defend a mistake, one is compelled to make a hundred more and in the end is left with nothing to show."

to light. "Has not God waited six thousand years to have His works explained?"[11]

In his defense of Tycho, Kepler goes over the data of the orbit of Mars from which his research started; and yet, there is not a word to remind Galileo of the book he had sent him fifteen years before, or of his laws, or of their importance. There is, indeed, not a word of reproach about his having neglected those discoveries—no appeal, no pressing reminder to the friend who was drifting away from him and who might have been called back to his sense of scientific solidarity. Thus the discoveries go unmentioned again. The two men go on as ships that pass in the night.

Left to his own devices, Galileo at this point of his Roman solicitations felt that he had a pullet in the hand which might well be worth a fat hen in the bush. To Cesi, who wrote that time and patience would help, he replied that life is short, that to play the courtier one must be young and strong, and that he could not sit around forever waiting for officials pressed by business to lend him an ear. He discussed the situation with Father Niccolò Riccardi, the new Master of the Holy Palace (Urban had surrounded himself with Florentines). The Padre Maestro, also called familiarly "Padre Mostro" because of his immense girth and erudition, was an old friend of his. As the chief authority in charge of licensing, he had written an enthusiastic appraisal of the *Saggiatore*. He was now giving much hope and encouragement. All these difficulties about the heavens, he averred, had been trumped up by those hard-shelled Roman curialists—speaking strictly in confidence. The truth about the heavens was that stars are moved by angels, and that was that. But many wonderful discourses could still be excogitated thereupon. In so far as he understood the words of His Holiness, they represented an explicit directive to Galileo not to deprive the world of the miracles of his discoveries and to continue adorning Italy with the splendor of his mind.

---

11. The history of Kepler's laws during the seventeenth century remains most obscure. Descartes had still never heard of them when he died; nor had Mersenne, who read everything and knew everybody. Horrocks knew but did not publish anything about them in his brief life. Bullialdus was the first to announce them in France, without arousing much notice, in 1639; then Wallis discussed them; and this takes us to a time very close to Newton's adoption of them in 1666.

As he departed, loaded with favors, holy medals, "Agnus Dei," and pensions for his family, escorted by an orotund papal parchment of commendation for His Most Serene Highness the Grand Duke (". . . We embrace with paternal love this great man whose fame shines in the heavens and goes on earth far and wide . . ."), Galileo felt that he had not been wholly unsuccessful. He was sixty years old by now, and he had learned what one could expect from the world. Eight years of prudence had taught him the way of devious implication. If he had pulled through with the *Saggiatore*, he could hope, this time with papal favor, to mention his subject in a more explicit manner and let it quietly sink in.[12] He had confidence in the force of the truth, once it is intrusted to the pen, which, as he used to say, "is the touchstone of the mind." Copernicanism was not heretical. It was not even so wild as all that. So far so good. He now had permission to present his brief to the public. From what he understood of the authorities, they were interested only in formal clauses of submission that would safeguard their prestige and punctilio. "If we cannot get past *that* outfit, call me Grassi," he must have said to Ciàmpoli, or the Florentine equivalent of it, for that certainly was the way he felt.[13] The *Dialogue on the Great World Systems* had been decided upon.[14]

---

12. The *Saggiatore* was denounced to the Inquisition in 1625, and a motion was made in the Congregation to have it prohibited. But Father Guevara, General of the Theatines, gave it a favorable report, in which he explained that even the opinion of the Earth's motion, maintained with due submission, would not have appeared to him a reason for condemning it (see Guiducci's letter from Rome, April 18, 1625).

13. What he and his friends really thought of the above-mentioned outfit of consultants comes out only rarely in the letters. But the good Guiducci, who was even then being fooled by Grassi's "magnanimous" behavior, wrote, in approving the *Letter to Ingoli* (see below): "I like your idea of getting rid of such people, who are glad murderers of courtesy and charity. You ought to show them up without mercy." The Italian phrase, "che la cortesia e pietà ascrivono a lor trofei," says even more in its terseness: "who count courtesy and charity among their trophies," which implies not only killing those virtues but setting them up stuffed.

14. See letter to Cesare Marsili, December 7, 1624; to Cesi, December 24, 1624.

III

He decided to try out the ground. He wrote a long-overdue reply to Francesco Ingoli's brief of 1616,[15] in which, after correcting his opponent's naïve mistakes in geometry in a good-natured and leisurely way, he took a resolutely Copernican stand: "I maintain further," he concluded after giving several cogent reasons, "that I know other facts of experience which have been hitherto observed by no one, from which, within the limits of natural and human considerations, the rightness of the Copernican system appears incontrovertible." He had prefaced the letter, however, with a careful diplomatic statement of submission: he would never say the doctrine was true—far from it—but he wished to prove to the heretics of Germany that, if in Catholic Italy the views of their great countryman had been rejected, it was not from ignorance of their great probability "but from reverence for Holy Scripture and the Fathers and from zeal for our religion and holy faith." The more valid the proofs, he added, "the clearer the beneficent conclusion that there is no trusting purely human reasoning and that we must rely implicitly on the higher knowledge which alone can bring light to the darkness of our mind." The chuckle is almost audible. The well-worked-out submission clause hides it impeccably.

There was no question of printing the letter, but it circulated widely, was read by Ciàmpoli to the Pope, and raised no objections. Galileo had boldly tested his own interpretation of the papal directive; he was going to discuss heliocentrism not as a mere mathematical supposition but as a physical conclusion which ought to be accepted if only supernatural wisdom did not deny it. The trial balloon, from all indications, had worked well.

He was hoping now to bring the *Dialogue* to a conclusion in a couple of years, the more so as several parts of the argument had been worked out previously and needed only a recasting. But many circumstances, not the least of them illness, delayed him year after year. There seems to have been a complete intermission to the almost-finished work between 1626 and 1629. This interruption,

---

15. See p. 92. Kepler had also written a reply from a copy that had reached him.

which changed the whole timing probably to Galileo's disadvantage, was due, he implied, to his many occupations, mainly engineering consulting work. But there seems to have been also a certain amount of hesitation and discouragement. Cesi and Ciàmpoli kept pressing him. "We hear," writes the latter in 1628, "that your *Dialogue* is coming along very slowly, and we bewail the loss of such rare treasures. We cannot wait to read at least some small part. Your friends beg of you to disregard the counsels of repose and to follow the urge to glory and our exhortations.... Do not defraud the expectations of the world."

But Galileo knew how carefully he must organize his forces before striking. He was no Bruno or Campanella, to rush into print with generous certainties and uncertain reasons. The "immense design" was proving even more appalling as he faced it at long last, and more difficult to encompass. As the physicist's thought was grappling with its difficulties, it had to mature at the same time the foundations of that theory of motion which was to be the subject of his later *Discourses on Two New Sciences.* They were taking shape in his own mind even as he labored at his cosmological exposition. All could not but go together. It is characteristic of Galileo that from this time on in his sixties, which is when most men conclude and crystallize their thought, his intellect was most fully mobilized down almost to the last hours of his life, reshaping, reinterpreting, reorganizing without cease the vast array of his ideas, even through the tragic times that he was to traverse, in invincibly resurging creativeness.

On October 29, 1629, he wrote to Elia Diodati, his Paris correspondent, a Tuscan *émigré* and Protestant statesman who had had a great part in the French translation of the Bible: "I have taken up work again on the Dialogue of the Ebb and Flow of the Sea, which was left aside for three years, and with God's grace I have found the right line, which ought to allow me to terminate it within the winter; it will provide, I trust, a most ample confirmation of the Copernican system."

On December 24 he was able to announce to his friends in Rome that the *Dialogue on the Great World Systems* was completed.

IX

THE *DIALOGUE*

When shall I cease to wonder?
SAGREDO

I

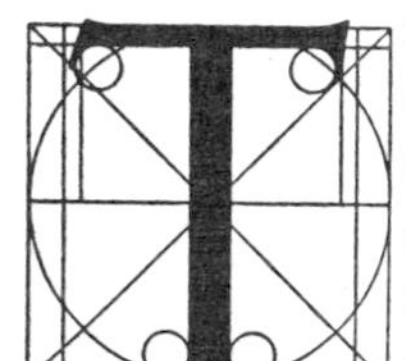

HE *Dialogue,* this fateful work which was to become such a "captain piece" in Western history, meanders at ease across the whole cultural landscape of the time, carrying in its broad sweep much strange material of various origin. As a composition, it looks unfinished, unpolished, at times inconsistent. This is partly nature, partly art. It has no unity except that of life itself. It is, in fact, "the story of the mind of Signor Galileo." But it is the mind of a man who knew very well where he was going. In the work there is all of him: the physicist, the astronomer, the man of the world, the littérateur, the polemicist, even at times the sophist; there is, above all, the totally expressive and expressed Renaissance man.

Galileo, like Newton, had been brought up on Archimedes and Euclid; but, unlike Newton, he was far from making an idol of the style of the pure geometricians "who utter not a single word not imposed by absolute necessity." For he holds that "the nobility, greatness, and magnificence which make our actions and enterprises marvelous and excellent do not consist only in what is necessary but also in the unnecessary; I would consider base and plebeian that banquet in which food and drink were lacking; yet it is not the presence of them which can make it noble and magnificent, for much more grandeur is brought to it by the beauty of the sumptuous apparel, the splendor of the furnishings, the sheen of silver and gold which delight the eye, the harmony of songs, the performances on the scene, the pleasurable drolleries."[1] The heroic poems with their episodes, the flights of Pindar's fantasy, are his avowed models. There is a price to be paid for this—the sacrifice of straight scientific language. A modern may miss the intellectual tension of abstract developments, the tightness of the formula which brings the theory its shape. But Galileo is willing to pay that price in order to remain a man among men, a person and a force within his own culture. What is characteristic of the prose is certainly not economy; it is expression, the warmth and passion throughout, the ever returning wonder. The motto of the work might well be Sagredo's word: "When shall I cease from wondering?"

Micanzio remarked on reading it: "And who before now had guessed what the Copernican issue was all about?" He was substantially right. Adventurous notions like Digges's, wild visionary pronouncements like Bruno's, which frightened people off with their avowed heresy, technical pamphlets like the *Sidereal Message* and the *Letters on the Solar Spots,* had allowed readers to guess or piece together some important new ideas; but they had left things on the level of an emotional difference between people who had a taste for the new and those who stuck to the old. Copernicus, even had he not been prohibited, remained a book for specialists; Kepler was unreadable. Of men who had disliked the System of the Schools and had struck out at it with brilliant but inconclusive remarks, there had been many even before Copernicus. But the real movement of thought had never come to a head, and the prohibition of 1616 had swooped down at the strategic moment to check it and disperse the efforts. The cognoscenti could still applaud the high-class fencing of the *Discourse on Floating Things* or of the *Assayer,* but it remained good spectator fun; and they went home without being able to piece together the great puzzle that stayed disassembled by superior orders.

---

1. "Lettera sopra il candore della luna." It should be said that these words are written by way of ribbing Fortunio Liceti's intolerable diffuseness. But Galileo is amiably willing to admit to the same weakness.

The *Dialogue* did exactly that: it assembled the puzzle and, for the first time, showed the picture. It did not go into technical developments; it left all sorts of loose ends and hazardous suggestions showing to the technical critic. But it was exactly on the level of educated public opinion, and it was able to carry it irresistibly. It was a charge of dynamite planted by an expert engineer.

It is Socratic in a novel way. The argument starts with a frontal attack on the science of the professors but soon is deep in the physical realities shown to us by the surface of the Moon. It follows thus the very sequence of the discussions of the early years. It moves on in a leisurely manner from one question into another, taking pot shots at casual objectives until we are far off the track, picks up with a "Where were we?" and comes back for a while to playing cat-and-mouse with Simplicio as a butt, but soon is off again in another direction, in full cry after some luckless lay figure who has brought up the needed asininity. Meanwhile the web of proof is being woven unobtrusively, until after a while the reader asks himself what kind of people could be blind to the evidence; what other opinion could be held except the Copernican?

In form as in substance, the work is a break with the academic tradition; it goes back through the dialogue form of the Renaissance to the true Platonic vein. The names of the characters are not Hylas, Philonous, or Philalethes. They address each other as "Sig. Salviati," "Sig. Simplicio mio"; they quarrel and make up; they move with their feet solidly planted on the marble floors of a Venetian palace on the Canal Grande. Their forms of address are those of Italian society of the period; the scenes and interludes of action are managed by Galileo as a man of the theater who had tried his hand successfully at comedy. Salusbury, in his translation, by Latinizing the names and using the English forms of address, has removed them to a slightly imaginary space as "Three Gentlemen of Venice"; but the life still comes through.[2]

---

2. The Salusbury translation, on which we have based our English text of the *Dialogue* (Chicago: University of Chicago Press, 1953), remains, with all its faults, better, once corrected, than any modern one could be. Although we had to modernize it and shorten the sentences, the text preserves a measure of the original spirit. It has in it the

Of the three characters, Filippo Salviati is obviously the one closest to Galileo's soul. He speaks for the author himself. Of the temper of the man and his intellectual personality, we have almost no traits in the few letters left by him. Nor does the author help us much when he says that "in him the lesser splendor was distinction of lineage and magnificence of wealth; a sublime intellect, which set no delight higher than exquisite speculation."

The known facts of his life are equally scanty. Born of Averardo Salviati in 1582, Filippo inherited, when still young, his father's senatorial rank in the Florentine nobility. He had also inherited his father's banking interests, for the Salviatis were and remained bankers and merchants, like the Medicis, like most of the great houses which had risen to power in the Republic after the checkmating of the feudal nobility and the razing of their towers in the thirteenth century. Filippo Salviati seems to have studied with Galileo in Padua and to have stayed with him in Venice, but the *Dialogue* is our only evidence for this. In 1611, as soon as he settled

---

leisurely unrolling of seventeenth-century thought, with that peculiar ingenuous quality that would be lost in any imitation. Unfortunately, Salusbury is no Thomas Browne. It is a far cry from his efforts at achieving the elegance of Jacobean prose to the style of the Italian original, a masterpiece of Baroque production. The Galilean harmony is the full equal of Monteverdi and Palestrina, while Salusbury is at best a village organist. What is worse, his translating is miserably unreliable. Yet he, too, is an artist of sorts. Of facts about him we have next to nothing, yet he makes himself known to us in his Introduction more vividly than any biographer could do. Even the text shows more of his personality than should be allowable. He loves to show off his erudition, which is fair, and his exactness, which is more doubtful. He takes sternly to task Bernegger's Latin translation for each trifling mistake, thus demonstrating to his sponsors the necessity of his work; at the same time, every few pages, he takes off on flights of inaccuracy that would make one doubt of his sanity. A familiar casualness with the original was common to all seventeenth-century translators: witness Florio and Adlington; it must also be admitted that the Italian original, with its tricky adverbs and anacoluthons, might lead better men astray. But when, as here, it is a matter of a carefully reasoned argument, one wonders what the translator must have thought on rereading the nonsense that he had written down. There is a suspicion that he never did.

down in Florence, Galileo visited Filippo in his magnificent Villa delle Selve, which is still to be seen on the hillside above Signa, with its ample façade and terraces overlooking the valley of the Arno and its view reaching out as far as the mountains of Carrara. He came back at frequent intervals as much for the "salubrious air which was balm to his afflicting ailments" as for the company of his friend Salviati, with whom he shared an enthusiasm for burlesque poetry and low comedy, and who writes him that no one can read Ruzzante more delightfully than he and that he is being awaited impatiently by the whole company. But there is also record of long work on the satellites of Jupiter at the villa's observatory.

In 1612 they carried out the series of observations and inferences on the sunspots which are described in the Third Day of the *Dialogue*. In the same year Sagredo came to visit in his turn; later Castelli drove up to discuss hydraulics. Still in 1612, Salviati was made, on Galileo's sponsoring, a member of the Accademia dei Lincei, and he in turn sponsored the admission of Ridolfi and Castelli. In 1613 he introduced to his master a new disciple, G. B. Baliani, a Genoese patrician who seemed to be interested in problems of hydrostatics and was to become one of the most important of Galileo's correspondents. A last letter of Salviati from Genoa of January, 1614, still concerns Baliani.

But, as Salviati is leaving the scene, we are vouchsafed a brief revealing glimpse of his personality. He had left Florence in a fit of pique, after losing out in a quarrel of precedence about entering church with Bernardetto de' Medici. There is more to this than the "quaint mores" of aristocracy. The Salviatis, like the Bardis and the Pazzis, had once been contestants for primacy in Florence. Piero Salviati had been Savonarola's chief supporter against the Medici faction, as anyone who has read *Romola* knows. The shrewd and ruthless policy of old Cosimo I had put his competitors out of the running by undercutting them financially at the crucial time. There had been reconciliation and intermarriage, but the old grudge was bound to flare up, as it did in the desperate attempt of the Pazzis. Filippo Salviati set out on a long voyage which was to lead him we know not whither, for in March, 1614, death put an end to it in Barcelona. He was then thirty-two years of age.

We have no elements to appraise his personal contribution. But

Salviati has been fortunate above many greater than he in that his intellectual personality comes to us through the pages of the *Dialogue* with the evidence of a poetic creation. We see him as a light, quick, serious mind, impatient of pedantry and minutiae, relying on his own razor-sharp logic and sound scientific instinct more than on an academic education, with an unfailing eye for essentials, a great respect for reason, and a laughing wit. He is the man with the gift of the gods. Galileo was no modest man himself (indeed, who was in his time?), and what he expects from others when writing about him is apt to shock our sense of understatement. But, as he puts his gifts under the invocation of a beloved shade, he forgets himself in his creation, and we face a delicately drawn silverpoint, the Portrait of the Scientist as a Young Man.

Sagredo is the Man of the World in the *Dialogue*. He has been set up as the standing portrait of a Venetian nobleman, endowed with the traditional statesmanship of his castè, attentive to new developments in science, open to argument but careful not to commit himself on theoretical issues.[3] The man who signed himself familiarly "Il Sagredo" or "Il Sag" did indeed appraise his own position thus: "I am a Venetian gentleman, nor did I ever pass myself off as a man of letters; I have had literary friendships, and I spent my protection on writers, but I do not intend to advance my fortunes or to acquire praise and reputation through my interest, however sincere, in philosophy and mathematics; I have rather identified my position with the integrity of the magistrates and the good government of the Republic, to which I bent my efforts in my young years, following the custom of my fathers, who gave to it all they had of life and strength." But there was also in him a waywardness and instability which prevented him from going too deeply into anything. One is reminded at times, in the elaborate care he gives to pleasurable trifles, of Voltaire's Senator Pococurante. He was, in fact, a *bon vivant,* and this was not the least of the characteristics which endeared him to Galileo.

Born of Niccolò Sagredo and Cecilia Tiepolo in 1571, Giovanfrancesco Sagredo was made a member of the Supreme Council of

3. Micanzio wrote in 1632: "How beautifully you have given life to our dear Sagredo. God help me, it is as if I heard him speak again."

the Republic at the age of twenty-five as befitted his name and rank; but his varied interests, as also his love of pleasure, made him take as little as he could, after his "young years," of the heavy responsibilities of business and state which were the accepted lot of the Venetian aristocracy. His quick intelligence and good judgment made him the very listener that Galileo had always desired, the *honnête homme,* as it was later called; and his independence of mind asserted itself often, at times successfully, against his master. We know him better than Salviati from his letters. He is the faithful and resourceful friend, always ready with ideas and counsel, whether it be about a pleasure trip, a business settlement, or an experimental difficulty. He enjoys life and wants his friends to enjoy it; he is very much of a gentleman but is an outspoken, practical, and acute gentleman.

He wrote over many years on the making of telescope lenses and thermometers (he had artisans from the glassworks of Murano trying out new formulas for him); on magnetism; on the theory of light, arguing with Galileo, who maintained the idea of an agitation of the medium against that of a transmission of substance; and on sundry scientific novelties. Once in a while a melancholy feeling came over him that he had wasted his life, and he wrote in a lofty Stoic vein about the blessings of philosophy and the pleasures of moderation. But soon his bubbling nature would reassert itself, and he would write about life in Venice, "that city of all delights," wild parties in his country estate on the Brenta, and the unending difficulties in finding reliable servants. He would send delicacies or would request Galileo's good services in finding new breeds of dogs or works of art for his collection, especially a Bronzino "at any price." He died in 1620, at the age of forty-nine. His brother Zaccaria, the hard businessman, wrote coldly that he had been carried away by a bronchitis, which was "also brought about by his infinite disorders."

As to Simplicio, it is reasonable that he should remain under an ancient pseudonym, for his name is legion. He is the average obstinate and literal-minded Aristotelian professor of the universities. Yet he is not what he might so well have been—a satire on the shrill and cantankerous opponents that had made Galileo's life miserable with their intrigues. He is the literary creation of a sunny temperament. There is a rather charming good nature in his bookishness that allows him to survive defeat after defeat and emerge patient, pleasant, willing and eager for more. He does not mind submitting himself to merciless cross-examination and having truths extracted out of him that go against all his convictions. He can get stuffy when driven into a corner and at times can lose his head. Then he will start clamoring: "This manner of thinking tends to the subversion of all natural philosophy and to the disorder and upsetting of heaven and earth and the whole universe!" But he regains his composure easily and goes on arguing. One feels that, if he had not been indoctrinated beyond repair in his earlier years, here would be a good mind.

Toward the end he loses himself quietly and unprotestingly in the thickening fog of incomprehensible novelties, only to emerge in the very last minute, summoned by his creator, to emit the Pope's opinion about the impossibility of true knowledge; his conclusion, it must be said, is lame, unprepared, and out of character. The last lines spoken on his own a few pages earlier had been only to explain his silence:

> I believe, verily, Sagredus, that you are put to a stand; and I believe that I know the cause of your confusion, which, if I mistake not, rises from your understanding part, and only part, of Salviatus' argument. It is true, as you suspect, that I find myself free from the like confusion; but not for that cause which you think, to wit, because I understand the whole. No, it happens quite the contrary, namely, from my not understanding anything; and confusion is in the plurality of things and not in nothing.[4]

This is said not without grace, but it does not build up Simplicio's intellectual stature for the decisive pronouncement with which he is to conclude the discussion. Worse, it is with a repeated admission of incompetence that he prefaces his final saying:

> As for the past discourses, and particularly this last, of the reason of the ebbing and flowing of the sea, I do not, to speak the truth, very well comprehend it. But by that slight idea, whatever it be, that I have formed thereof to myself, I confess that your hypothesis seems to me far more ingenious than any of all those that I ever heard besides; still,

4. *Dialogue*, p. 456.

I esteem it neither true nor conclusive, but, keeping always before the eyes of my mind a solid doctrine that I once received from a most learned and eminent person, and to which there can be no answer, I know that both of you, being asked whether God, by His infinite power and wisdom, might confer upon the element of water the reciprocal motion in any other way than by making the containing vessel to move, I know, I say, that you will answer that He could, and also knew how to bring it about in many ways, and some of them above the reach of our intellect. Upon which I forthwith conclude that, this being granted, it would be an extravagant boldness for anyone to go about to limit and confine the Divine power and wisdom to some one particular conjecture of his own.

SALV.: An admirable and truly angelical doctrine, which is answered with perfect agreement by the other one, in like manner divine, which gives us leave to dispute touching the constitution of the Universe, but adds, withal (perhaps to the end that the exercise of the minds of men might not cease or become remiss), that we are not to find out the works made by His hands. Let, therefore, the disquisition permitted and ordained us by God assist us in the knowing, and so much more admiring, His greatness by how much less we find ourselves capable of penetrating the profound abysses of His infinite wisdom.

SAGR.: And this may serve for a final close of our four days' disputations, after which, if it seem good to Salviatus to take some time to rest himself, our curiosity must, of necessity, grant it to him. . . . In the meantime, we may, according to our custom, spend an hour in taking the air in the gondola that waits for us.[5]

After five hundred pages of argument in which words have not been spared on either side, one might have expected something less perfunctory. Nor was Simplicio the man to say it. It was in the character of the obstinate logician to go down fighting and not to save himself with some theological weasel words. It would have been better, artistically and philosophically, if Galileo had followed a line that he obviously considered at a certain point[6] and had Salviati throw aside his Copernican "mask," unveiling himself in a *coup de scène* as a skeptical mystic who resigns all his science to God. We can imagine several possible reasons for the switch, all interesting, but they have to remain pure guesswork.

---

5. *Ibid.*, pp. 471–72.
6. *Ibid.*, p. 146.

II

When Galileo announced to his friends in Rome that the *Dialogue* was ready, he got nothing but cheerful messages. Castelli wrote that the road was clear and that Padre Riccardi, who, as Master of the Holy Apostolic Palace, was the chief licenser, promised his ready assistance and asserted that theological difficulties could be circumvented. In another letter Castelli brought the exciting news that the Pope had admitted to Campanella in an audience that the prohibition of 1616 was a nuisance and had added: "It was never Our intention; if it had depended upon Us, that decree would not have been passed." These are not quite the empty words that historians have declared them to be, for we know that he had exerted a restraining influence at the time; but they were certainly such as to encourage the fondest hopes.[7] Ciàmpoli wrote: "You are awaited here more than any most beloved damsel."

Galileo arrived in Rome on May 3, 1630, and on the eighteenth he was writing: "His Holiness has begun to treat of my affairs in a spirit which allows me to hope for a favorable result." Urban VIII had again indorsed the idea of an astronomical dialogue, provided the treatment were strictly hypothetical, and had left the rest to the licensers. The diplomatic way in which Galileo presented the intention of his work to the Pontiff may be gathered from his "Preface to the Judicious Reader," which opens the *Dialogue*. Urban made only one specific restriction, namely, that the title should not be "On the Flux and Reflux of the Sea" but "On the Two Chief World Systems," for he did not want the book organized around a "necessitating" proof such as that through the tides.

After that, it was time for Father Riccardi to go to work. The bustling "Padre Mostro" went hastily over the manuscript and was not entirely reassured. He did not understand much about astronomy, but the stuff did not look to him as hypothetical as he had been told. He delegated his assistant Father Raffaello Visconti to examine it and make such alterations as were needed. Father Visconti,

---

7. Especially as they were said to Campanella, whom the Pope knew very well to be a passionate anti-Aristotelian, an unreconstructed Copernican, and the author of a *Defense of Galileo* which had been printed in Germany in 1622.

who was supposed to be versed in mathematics, went over the text, changed a few words here and there, and gave his approval. He had obviously understood insufficiently either the text or the papal instructions. But now the imprimatur for Rome was as good as granted.

Father Riccardi was still not reassured. The hostility of certain circles told him that this was going to mean trouble. But he could not ask the author to rewrite the book, and, besides, he could not imagine exactly how it should be rewritten. To Galileo and the ambassador Niccolini, Riccardi's cousin-in-law, who fed him pleasant Chianti and many assurances, he did not know what to say. He decided he was going to look at the text himself. As this entailed further loss of time, he agreed to pass on to the printer each sheet as soon as revised. But, in order to start, the printer needed a license, so the license was granted, while the text remained in Riccardi's hands. He insisted meanwhile that the Preface and the conclusion be rewritten so as to correspond more exactly to papal intentions. Since the license had been given for Rome only, and the text was going to be printed under the supervision of Prince Cesi and the Lyncean Academy, he was obviously relying much more on Cesi's assistance than on his own acumen in arranging things.

By the end of June, Galileo, fearing the heat and the "unhealthy air" of Rome (there really was some malaria in the city at the time), left for Florence, with the understanding that he would be back in the autumn with a new version of the Preface and the conclusion. He knew that nothing much would be done during the summer, and he expected to be present while most of the correcting took place.

All looked well; but a few weeks after his return to Florence the grievous news came to Galileo of the death of Prince Cesi. This was an irreparable blow, for no one else could fulfil Cesi's double function of executive and mediator in the difficult enterprise. The situation soon became obscure. On August 24, Castelli, usually a temperament not given to evil suspicions, wrote Galileo urgently, "for many most weighty reasons which he did not wish to commit to paper, to have the work printed at Florence, and as soon as possible." While Galileo was wondering what this might mean, a new factor came to force his decision: the plague of 1630, which had been making fearful ravages in the north (it was the one later classically described in Manzoni's *Promessi Sposi*), showed up sporadically in central Italy, quarantine stations were set up everywhere, and communications became difficult.

Galileo had to rely now on the good offices of the Florentine ambassador. Luckily, it was no longer Guicciardini who had the post but Francesco Niccolini, a faithful friend. He and his wife (she was Riccardi's cousin) had the "Father Monster," as they called him affectionately, as a habitual guest, and now they bent their efforts on extracting a permission from him. Riccardi at first refused; then, yielding to the subtle pressure of Caterina Niccolini, he relented and sent permission to have the final revision done in Florence. The Preface and the conclusion, however, he retained in his hands, "to arrange them according to the wishes of His Holiness."

The Florentine Inquisitor, Father Giacinto Stefani, read the book, changed a few words, but found nothing wrong with it. Indeed, he was "moved to tears at many passages by the humility and reverent obedience displayed by the author." But, still, nothing could come out without the Preface and the conclusion, and Father Riccardi would not let go of them. What follows is a pitiful comedy that it would be useless to detail. From Castelli's dark allusions it is easy to infer that the Jesuits, advised by Grassi and Scheiner, had swung into action. The new opposition was far more dangerous than that of Caccini and his Dominicans. The unfortunate Father Monster, fully aware by now of the delicate situation and of the dangers to his career, was on the rack. He could not very well refuse an imprimatur he had already given, and he did not know how to withhold it. Caught between the Niccolinis on one side and Ciàmpoli on the other, squirming under summons from the Grand Duke, who was, after all, the liege lord of his family, he twisted and turned in despair, delaying, raising new problems, imposing new clauses, pretending he did not have the papers, invoking the reserved intentions of the Holy Father. He asked that still another theologian revise the text in Florence and sent pressing instructions to make sure of the hypothetical treatment.[8] Another revision by the Inquisitor himself, Father Clemente Egidii, and still another imprimatur for the text; but a year had gone by, and still the Preface

8. The text of his instructions is reproduced on p. 317.

and concluding statement were lacking.[9] Galileo was in despair. He could show any commission appointed by the Grand Duke, he insisted, that "I have never entertained any other views or opinions than those held by the most venerable Fathers of the Church"; he was willing to describe again and again, if needed, his own theories as "dreams, nullities, paralogisms, and chimeras"; but there was nothing to do against this kind of sabotage. "The months and the years pass," he exclaimed, "my life wastes away, and my work is condemned to rot."

Riccardi obviously did not dare come again before the Pope with his problem and ask for help concerning his wretched revision. He hung himself like an albatross around Ciàmpoli's neck and asked for a direct order. He got his clearance. Even so, he tarried. It was only on July 19, 1631, "dragged by the hair," as Niccolini puts it, that he surrendered the packet to the embassy.

In February, 1632, Galileo was able at last to present to the Grand Duke the first printed copy of the *Dialogue*.

---

9. It remains a profoundly puzzling question why Riccardi, with all his fears, did nothing about the conclusion, which he retained admittedly in order to "arrange" it. There was a stylistic fault in the text that he could perceive as well as anyone. It would have been easy for him to give the conclusive argument a more adequate formal dressing, such as we have sketched out ourselves on p. 166, following Oregius' paraphrase. Later, he was to say to Magalotti (see p. 188) that there had been in the manuscript "two or three arguments invented by our Lord's Holiness himself" which had been omitted in print. This was obviously not so, for the Preliminary Commission did not sustain the charge. Riccardi was only seeking an excuse for the mental paralysis that had seized him in the face of the text. One explanation might be this: that Galileo had told him that this was exactly how the Pope had wanted it; and it is indeed very possible that Urban, who disliked pedantry, may have given him once the gist of the argument in those few words that we find in the text. Moreover, Galileo may have thought it clever flattery to couple that "admirable and truly angelical doctrine" with another, "in like manner divine," taken directly from Scripture, and may have insisted on conciseness as part of the rhetorical effect. Riccardi, patently, realized that the effect had not been obtained; but it was then up to him to submit the text to the Pope and ask for a revision, and this he never did.

X

THE SUMMONS

Flectere si nequeo superos, Acheronta movebo
VIRGIL

I

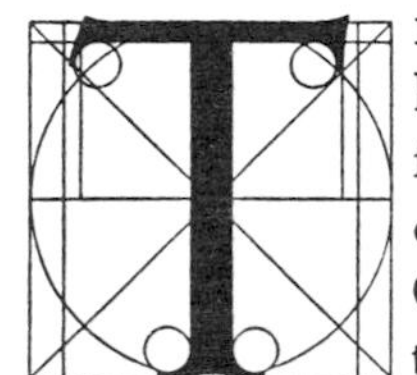

HE book was greeted with rapturous praise by the literary public. The edition sold out as it came from the press. Owing to persistent difficulties of quarantine, it went on sale in Rome only in June. Campanella wrote in great emotion: "These novelties of ancient truths, of new world, new systems, new nations, are the beginning of a new era. Let God make haste, and let us for our small part help all we can. Amen." Father Scheiner had known for a long while that the forthcoming *Dialogue* would not spare him.[1] He was in a bookshop when a friar from Siena wandered in, singing its praises. He turned pale, was seized with a fit of trembling, and said to the bookseller: "Ten scudi if you can get me a copy right away." Father Riccardi felt his heart sink. "The Jesuits," he said to Magalotti, "will persecute this with the utmost bitterness."

1. Father Christopher Scheiner, a German Jesuit from Ingolstadt, had considerable standing as an astronomer and had been once a friend and correspondent of Galileo. But an embittered and rather pointless priority rivalry about the discovery of the sunspots had driven them apart since Scheiner's letters to Mark Welser, published in 1612 under the nom de plume of Apelles, and Galileo's answering *Letters on the Solar Spots* of 1613. Galileo, while writing the *Dialogue*, knew that

The letter of Magalotti (August 7) which contains this important item of information is interesting also in other more human respects:

"On Monday morning," he writes, "I was in the Church of S. Giovanni, when the most reverend Father [Riccardi], having heard that I was there, came to seek me. He signified to me that it would be agreeable to him were I to give up the whole of the copies of Signor Galileo's book of *Dialogues* which I had brought from Florence, promising to return them in ten days at the farthest. I answered that I regretted infinitely not being able to comply with his wish, for, of the six copies which I had brought, five were for presentation, and his Reverence knew that they had already been presented. . . . He must know that in this particular it was impossible for me to satisfy him. At the very utmost I could only have given him my own and Monsignor Serristori's copy. He appeared sensible of the difficulty but assured me that it was only for the sake of the book and its author that he had wished to have the said copies. Then I took occasion to ask why such diligent perquisition should be made to have the books, since I was sure that if the author

---

Scheiner was preparing to revive the twenty-year-old polemic with a frontal attack on the Copernicans in a forthcoming treatise entitled *Rosa Ursina.* The treatise was intended to pay back Galileo not only for Scheiner's personal grudge but also for the defeat of Scheiner's fellow-Jesuit, Horatio Grassi, in the *Saggiatore.* Galileo therefore did not refrain from tackling Scheiner's theories in advance as he was writing the *Dialogue.* This he did—apart from some pointed remarks about the Apelles letters—by singling out a little anti-Copernican treatise of Locher, a favorite pupil of Scheiner, and using it as chief target for his destructive refutation. The device was polemically effective and quite legitimate; it even turned out to be a riposte instead of a preventive counterattack, because Scheiner's book came out earlier than the *Dialogue.* It was Scheiner, rather, who was able to launch his preventive counterattack by campaigning against the *Dialogue* two years in advance of its publication and with an adequate idea of its contents. What made the situation worse was that, as Father Athanasius Kircher admitted later (see p. 290), Scheiner was a Copernican at heart and sacrificed throughout his scientific conscience to the political convenience of his superiors. His enmity was not only that of the rival but that of the man who had "sold out" on his beliefs.

were written to, and given to understand the feeling of the Superiors, he would have divined that it was a case for obedience; and that, having received the permission of our Lord's Holiness and of the Sacred Congregation to publish the work, as anyone might see by the imprimatur in the beginning of it, it was not to be believed that he would fail to give every possible satisfaction. I also hinted that he had already been written to on the subject. To this he answered in the affirmative but without any specification. This, as you know well, was because the dealings of the Holy Office cannot be revealed, even the very smallest particle, under pain of the severest censures. He just added that what had been written and ordered was in a spirit of kindness and leniency and with no object but the glory of God and the tranquillity of Holy Church and that no damage should accrue to the reputation of the author, whom he looked upon as one of his best friends.

"Then he proceeded to disclose another reason for wishing to have these copies of the *Dialogue*. I should be ashamed to repeat it to you, for the sake of his reputation and for the inventor's, only that I know I can speak to you in confidence. It is this. Under the seal of secrecy he told me that great offense had been taken at the emblem which was on the frontispiece, if I recollect aright (I say this because I paid no great attention to the frontispiece and have not the book by me just now). This emblem, unless I am mistaken, consists of three dolphins holding each other's tails in their mouths, with I know not what motto. On hearing this, I burst out laughing and showed him plainly how astonished I was and said I thought I could assure him that Signor Galileo was not the man to hide great mysteries under such puerilities and that he had said what he meant clearly enough. I declared that I believed I could affirm that the emblem was the printer's own. On hearing this, he appeared greatly relieved and told me that, if I indeed could assure him that such was the case (now see what trifles rule our actions in this world), the result would be most happy for the author. I thought I had by me a small book written by a Portuguese doctor about a preventive for the plague which would convince him of the truth of what I was saying. He said my word as a gentleman was quite enough. But I answered that, in case this book had not the emblem on its title-page (which indeed it has not, though it is printed by Landino), I would sent to Florence for what would convince him clearly enough, and he was extremely glad to accept my offer.

"So the matter stands. Other motive for censure I do not think there is, except that already mentioned by the Master of the Sacred Palace; namely, that the book has not been printed precisely according to the original manuscript and that, among other things, two or three arguments have been omitted at the end which were invented by our Lord's Holiness himself and with which, he says, he convinced Signor Galileo of the falsity of the Copernican theory. The book having fallen into His Holiness's hands, and these arguments having been found wanting, it was necessary to remedy the oversight. This is the pretext; but the real fact is that the Jesuit Fathers are working most valiantly in an underhanded way to get the work prohibited. The reverend Father's own words to me were: 'The Jesuits will persecute him most bitterly.' This good Father, being mixed up in the matter himself, fears every stumbling block and wishes naturally to avoid bringing trouble on himself for having given the license. Besides which, we cannot deny that our Lord's Holiness holds an opinion directly contrary to this [of Galileo's].

"Now, if it is true that the original manuscript was altered, I know not what to say; but, if not, it will be easy to convince the authorities, and, once convinced, they can go no further, I should think. . . .

"But if some omission has been made through inadvertence, particularly the omissions I have mentioned, I would advise that the utmost readiness be shown to add, take away, or change, so as to save appearances. Meanwhile do not fail to send me as soon as possible some publication of Landino's, were it but an almanac, that I may be able to show it to the reverend Father, and if possible get me one which was published before the publication of the *Dialogue*."

On receiving this, Galileo must have been staggered by the monstrous hypocrisy of it all, for the suspension was already official, and it had struck him like a bolt out of the blue. On the first of the month the Inquisitor of Florence had presented himself at Landini's bookshop with orders to suspend the publication of the book and to deliver all the copies he had in stock. To this Landini was able to answer blithely that he had not one copy left. Father Riccardi had obviously been unaware that the scandal was in the open while he was trying to worm and writhe his way out of the predicament.

While letters of congratulation were still pouring in, Galileo was furiously denouncing the miserable intrigues of his enemies and warning that an unheard-of abuse of authority must have taken place somewhere. But on August 21 he received a fighting letter from Father Campanella which confirmed the bad news:

I have heard that they are having a commission of irate theologians to prohibit your *Dialogue;* and there is no one on it who understands mathematics or recondite things.

Please note that you may hold that the opinion of the moving Earth was properly forbidden, without having also to believe that the reasons alleged are good. This is a theological rule, and it can be proved, for in the Nicene Council it was decreed that "the angels may be portrayed because they are truly corporeal." The decree is valid but not the motivation, for all Scholastics say, in our time, that angels are incorporeal. There are many more grounds.

I fear the violence of people who do not know. The Father Monster makes fearful noises against; and, says he, *ex ore Pontificis.* But His Holiness is not informed, nor can he think this way. My advice is, have the Grand Duke write that, as they have put Dominicans, Jesuits, Theatines, and secular priests on this commission, they should admit also Father Castelli and myself, and if they win, *succumbemus,* etc., even in the proposition, let alone the reasons. But I am not supposed to know about it, *quia,* etc. Or you may ask for us as lawyer and attorney in the case; and, if we do not win it, hold me for an ass. I know the Pope is of great mind and when he will be informed, etc. God keep you.

Galileo must had read it with a variety of feelings, for the grand old friar was known to be an adept at getting himself into trouble. Nothing daunted by the news, however, he wrote the draft of a stiff diplomatic note, which the Grand Duke, who shared his concern, ordered promptly signed by his secretary of state and dispatched. It requested of the Pope the appointment of a mixed commission in Florence to investigate the matter. But when Niccolini, on September 5, called at the Vatican with the protest, he was met with a blast from Urban that checked his prepared statement. "Your Galileo," the Pope fairly shouted at him, "has ventured to meddle with things that he ought not and with the most grave and dangerous subjects that can be stirred up in these days."

I replied [Niccolini goes on] that Signor Galileo had not printed his work without the approval of the Vatican. He [the Pope] replied with the same fury that he and Ciàmpoli had circumvented him, especially Ciàmpoli, who had dared tell him that Galileo would be entirely guided by the papal commands and that all was well; and it was all he had known without ever having seen or read the book. He made bitter complaints against Ciàmpoli and Father Riccardi, although he said the latter had been circumvented too, for with fair words had been extracted from him first the license, and then again a permission to print in Florence without following the instructions given to the Inquisitor, and then also putting on it Riccardi's name, which has nothing to do with licenses outside of Rome. Here I came back, saying that I knew a special commission had been appointed, and since it might happen (as is the case) that there might be persons in it evilly disposed toward Galileo, I respectfully begged him to give him a chance to justify himself. Then His Holiness replied that, in these affairs of the Holy Office, nothing is ever done but to pronounce judgment and then to summon to retract. I answered: "Does it not then appear to your Holiness that Galileo should be informed beforehand of the difficulties, oppositions, and censures that are made to his work and what it is that annoys the Holy Office?" He answered violently: "The Holy Office, We are telling you, sir, does not proceed in that way and does not take that course, nor does it ever give information beforehand. It is not the custom. *Besides, he knows well enough what the difficulties are, if he wants to know them; for We have discussed them with him, and he knew them all from Ourselves.*" And as I represented that the book had been dedicated to the Most Serene Master, that it was a matter of one of his servants, and that I humbly hoped that some consideration would be shown, he said that in these things which might bring religion very great prejudice, of the worst that has ever been invented, His Highness must concur in punishing them, as he is a Christian prince, and that therefore I must write him not to become involved in this if he wants to come out of it with honor.

Niccolini was no fool, and he had realized by now that the Pope was blustering. There had been an unavowed tension in those last months between the Holy See and Tuscany, for the Grand Duke could not but side with the Hapsburgs at that turn in the Thirty Years' War which had brought the Pope to the side of France. The Pope was now scoring an unexpected advantage by threatening with the spiritual weapon that he alone could wield. But the flimsy complaints brought up were nothing that could be made to look like heresy. Niccolini took occasion from those last words to counter on his own initiative with a clear diplomatic threat:

> I answered it was certain I would get orders to have to weary him still further, as I was doing, but that still I could not believe that His Beatitude would go so far as to countenance the prohibition of a book that had been already approved, without first hearing Signor Galilei.

This meant: "We stand on good ground. If you want to bring about an international incident, please go ahead and suit yourself." The Pope was aware that he had ventured on thin ice and that he was being politely told now to mind his own business—which was confusion and insubordination in his own house. But it was not easy for him to retreat. He unmasked his batteries.

> He said prohibition was the least that could happen to him [Galileo], and *he had better take care he was not summoned before the Holy Office;* that he had decreed a commission of theologians and of other persons versed in different sciences, all grave men and of holy mind, who would weigh every particular, word for word, for it was a question of the most perverse business that could ever be handled. And he went on with grievances against him and Ciàmpoli. Then he charged me to inform our Master that the doctrine was perverse in the extreme; everything would be maturely considered; let his Highness not commit himself and proceed softly. . . . He added he had acted with great consideration for Galileo, by having impressed upon him what he knows and by not having referred his affairs, as he ought to have done, to the Holy Office but to a specially appointed commission. Which was something. He concluded: "I have used him better than he used me, for he deceived me."

The Pope had used the threat of the Inquisition in order to browbeat the Grand Duke, but it was clear he did not see very well as yet how it could be carried through. It was to this end, and not out of any consideration, that a special commission had been appointed.[2] If it did not discover sufficient grounds, and if the Grand

2. The Pope said again a few days later that "the commission had been formed out of the ordinary to see whether it would be possible not to bring the matter before the Holy Office" (dispatch of September 18). Now, as we shall see from the report of the commission, the several enumerated counts of Galileo's transgression do not contain

Duke stood firm, the Pope might find himself in a very difficult position indeed. But the dreadful specter of heresy had been raised, and with that he had won his first round.

Niccolini's report came as a bombshell in Florence, knocking out a whole set of patient political combinations, and sent the ministers scurrying for cover. "The Grand Duke," quavers Cioli, the new secretary of state, "has read your dispatches and has come into such a violent upset of anger that I do not know what will happen next. What I know is that his Holiness will never have to blame the ministers here for giving bad advice."

II

Galileo was aghast and utterly at a loss to understand what was the matter from the roundabout messages of his friends in Rome. The secretary of state was reticent, for Niccolini's dispatches were under the seal of strictest secrecy.

What had actually happened began gradually to transpire. Certain Jesuits, apparently the only ones in the administration who could read the book and understand it, had shown the Pope that under the rhetorical mask the whole argument was a compelling plea for the Copernican system. While Grienberger and the old hands were looking on with mixed feelings,[3] Grassi, Scheiner, and their group had sparked the vast forces of the Society of Jesus into a purely political campaign against these novelties which threatened its hold on education, the whole carefully controlled and contained "humanistic" program on which they brought up the ruling classes —and beyond those the principle of authority itself. As Stelluti had once warned Galileo, once the Society had come in, he was never going to see the end of this business.[4] The personal vanity of the

---

any reference to the Inquisition. In fact, it is admitted that they might involve merely corrections in the text. It is only because of a new document discovered by the Holy Office that the possibility of prosecution comes up. This goes far to deny the Pope's contention.

3. Torricelli's letter, September 11, 1632. See p. 201.

4. "It would be a business of which you would never see the end if you picked a quarrel with those Fathers, for they are so many that they could take on the whole world, and, even if they are wrong, they

Pope had been cleverly roused when it was represented to him that his argument against the tides had been put into the mouth of Simplicio the simple, obviously to ridicule him. Nothing could have been further from the author's mind. He had simply obeyed his instructions literally by letting the Aristotelian have the last word; but he had understood this as a purely formal clause, not to be carried through artistically. Riccardi seems to have concurred in this view, since he did not request any addition to that section which he pondered over for months, searching for new ways to make it "safe."

There is no fury like a philosopher scorned. Urban VIII, as Cardinal Bentivoglio said of him, liked to lay down the law in all fields of human knowledge. Amid the chorus of respectful indorsement, this one single voice had aroused in him the sharp feeling that perhaps he was not taken very seriously as an intellectual, for indeed he could realize that Galileo, for all the proper compliments, had made his "medicine of the end" look pretty silly. "There is one argument that *they* will never answer," the Pope was to complain to Niccolini, like so many frustrated authors before and since; and, as he mentioned it, says the ambassador, his fury rose again in most unpastoral fashion. Even after Galileo's death, ten years later, his rancor was unabated. Niccolini describes him then as a very old man, his head sunk so low that it was on a level with his shoulders. But when the talk came around to Galileo, and he intimated that he would not countenance a monument over his enemy's grave, he was impelled to recount all that he had explained to him once, and what the other had tried to answer, "and before he was through with it a long time had gone by."

It is, however, somewhat unfair of historians to expand upon this Simplicio incident as the single motivation of the Pope's actions. The business was unpleasant enough without it. It looked as though he had been fooled successfully and in a legally airtight way. As a matter of simple truth, of course, it was he who had fooled himself by reserving decision for himself and then not having an expert advise him, by handing down instructions through Riccardi in a

---

would never concede it . . . the more so as they are no friends of the new opinions" (January 27, 1620).

matter that neither of them understood, by telling Ciàmpoli several contradictory things in his changing moods, and by leaving Ciàmpoli to take a flying chance on one of his remarks. But this he could not bring himself to admit. He decided that the real cause was a conspiracy involving his closest collaborators. It was tantamount to disaffection; it was as though his own staff had silently manifested their lack of confidence in his own superior judgment. A ruler in that predicament is apt to lose his head; many horrid doubts may have come to him in the watches of the night. He had been a Pope now for nine years, his autocratic grand policy must begin to be judged by its fruits, and there was not much to show.

The Emperor of Austria himself, the mainstay of the Church, the author of the Edict of Restitution, was no longer in such a good position, and, what is worse, he was no longer a friend. The initiative in the great game had passed to his main opponent, Richelieu, who had won his most far-reaching victory, namely, the launching of Gustavus Adolphus of Sweden. He had pried apart the Austro-Spanish coalition, forcing the Italian powers into his system, so that the Pope had found himself bound in covert alliance with him—and the Swedish heretic—against the House of Austria. And right now the newly risen power in the north was beginning to frighten Rome. Even as Niccolini came in for his audience, the Pope must have received the news that the Swedish king had neutralized Brandenburg and been joined by the Saxons. In another three weeks he was to hear that the only Catholic army in the field, that of Tilly, had been destroyed at Breitenfeld. But worse than the alarming advance of the heretic must have been the galling awareness for Urban that all this upset was the carrying-out of the plans of Richelieu and that infernal Père Joseph, the men who had financed Gustavus Adolphus with five tubfuls of gold and were now on their way to establishing the paramountcy of France in Catholic Europe. Urban's great combinations and diplomatic maneuvers had been in vain, as had been his attempts to carve out a domain in Italy at the expense of his associates, and his own underhanded dealings with the Swedes. He had quarreled with the Emperor, had been threatened and humiliated by Spain, was checkmated in Italy itself by the Venetian Republic. And now this.

Urban VIII must have felt the issuing of the *Dialogue* at this juncture as a churlishly planned aggravation of Fate. Although harassed by politics, he was intelligent enough to perceive that the argument about the heavens threatened the very bases of the educational system established since Trent; he could appreciate the reasons of incensed Jesuits who told him that this kind of thing was potentially more disastrous than Luther or Calvin.[5] And he himself in Maecenian vanity had encouraged the author. He was in a cleft stick.

The judgment of political observers in Rome reflects his quandary. The ambassador from Modena wrote home in November shortly after the news of the death of Gustavus Adolphus at Lützen and of the uncovering of the Pope's secret alliance with the Swede: "Instead of bringing him back to his senses, these events moved him only to fury. He has lost his head to the point that he will act without the least judgment."

Precluded from satisfactory action, Urban's anger vented itself

---

5. See p. 216. The other considerations are inferred from the Pope's own words. There is also a desperate letter of Campanella, October 22: "If I were to write to you the reasons and interests that move them against you while they should nót, you would be staggered. *Ex arcanis eorum sacris et politicis.* But I was not admitted. . . ." They are the reasons that were set forth later in Inchofer's *Tractatus syllepticus,* where it is said indeed that it is more criminal to disbelieve the mobility of the Sun than the immortality of the soul. How far did those reasons weigh in the actual inception of the scandal? There is hardly a hint of them in the contemporary documents. Even outside observers like Buonamici, Peiresc, Gassendi, and their informants saw nothing in the crisis but the work of personal hatreds. "Le Père Scheiner luy a joué ce tour, *ut creditur.*" This opinion is echoed on all sides. But, instead of subsiding after the trial, the antiscientific movement gained momentum steadily in the next decades, and this shows that political decisions had taken place, at least immediately after 1632. In 1693, sixty-one years after these events, Viviani, by then a very old man, asked for permission to issue a corrected edition of the *Dialogue.* Newton's *Principia* had already come out. But this is what his friend Father Baldigiani had to tell him: "There is a general movement here in Rome against the physicists. Extraordinary meetings of the cardinals and of the Holy Office are taking place, and there is talk of a general prohibition against all authors of the new physics, including Gassendi, Galileo, and Descartes."

on his hapless subordinates. Riccardi was called on the carpet and anxiously protested his innocence. He was able to show that he had delivered the papers only on receipt of a clearance from Ciàmpoli. As for Ciàmpoli himself, he had nothing to show, for he had boldly used whatever words the Pope had let fall upon some undefined occasion.[6]

Riccardi managed to retain his post, but Ciàmpoli was finished. The prelate who but a few weeks before had been rated for elevation to cardinal in the next Consistory was exiled as governor to the small town of Montalto della Marca, later transferred several times to obscure posts. He was never allowed to return to Rome. His letters to Galileo in 1633 are those of a man who has made his peace with the world. "Come to see me, my persecuted Socrates," he wrote, "we shall take good care of your health here. . . . As for myself, I have found my consolation in study, and I still hope to write something whereby I may be remembered." He died in Iesi ten years later, at the age of fifty-four. When Urban VIII heard of the passing of the man in whom he had once placed so much trust, he was moved to say: "Another great person is gone."

III

If the Pope felt that he had been successfully fooled, he had considerable reasons which Galileo might have perceived well in advance. Yet Galileo seems to have refused even to consider them. He was obviously dismayed at the turn of events, but he did not cower as the man who has been found out, nor did he evince the helpless resignation of Ciàmpoli, who knew himself beyond appeal. He, like the Pope, was genuinely angry, and his anger may be

---

6. From what the Pope said to Niccolini, we can infer that Ciàmpoli had simply vouched for Galileo's argument being strictly orthodox and had begged the Pope to relieve the censors of their fears about a text that they could not understand, much less arrange to suit their scruples. The Pope must have accepted his assurances and his promises as a way out rather than have to spend his own time on the question. Ciàmpoli's play had obviously been to make the Pope feel that only those two great minds, his and Galileo's, could understand each other and that he could count on Galileo's following the spirit of his instructions.

clearly perceived in his letter under the words of submissive protestation. From the very genuineness of his anger we may infer that the Pope had given him something fairly substantial in the way of authorization. If these people now—and he still thought of the palace executives—did not know how to play the game according to the rules, or were swayed by puny intrigues, he would give them his mind. He had been authorized to write on Copernicanism; he had not been asked to lie but only to profess obedience; his text had been approved.[7] He had not spoken in the first person; he had let a literary character defend a position, which much more godless fictionary characters had been allowed to do. As to the thesis itself, long ago tried out in the *Letter to Ingoli,* it had had the ample written indorsement of Riccardi to the Florence Inquisitor, sent just before the printing. The text had been revised and rerevised, licensed and relicensed, and then licensed again, in two cities; it had been prefaced and provided with a proper ending and even with a title by the highest authority. There they were, the five imprimaturs, "together, dialogue-wise, in the piazza of the title-page, complimenting and ducking each other with their shaven reverences."[8] What more could the strictest discipline require? His strongly rooted juridical sense made him conclude that someone here was getting out of hand; and, as it could not be the licensing authorities themselves, it must be an informal conspiracy that had momentarily captured the Pope's judgment, and he should expose it.

It cannot be maintained, as Wohlwill does, that this was simply the old man's self-delusion, for we have the same opinion reflected more or less strongly by his Roman correspondents, who were not simpletons. Old Filippo Magalotti, who had taken the place left vacant by Cesi, is explicit:

---

7. Campanella had called Aristotle and the Scholastics all sorts of names, had come out boldly for the Copernican system, and had propounded new and arbitrary interpretations of Scripture, but it had been enough to protect him that he should have written at the end of his *Defense of Galileo:* "In the above discussion, I at all times submit myself to the correction and better judgment of our Holy Mother the Apostolic Roman Church."

8. Milton, *Areopagitica.*

You need not fear that the commission can ask the authorities to declare the Copernican opinion damnable and heretical; even if they decided that the opinion is false, I do not believe that it would be requested to be declared such by the supreme authority; I tell you this because I am told so by the members of the Congregation of the Holy Office, which handles dogmatic matters. They say that there are in the Church controversial matters wherein the authority of the Fathers is divided, such as, e.g., the Immaculate Conception; and they all say definitely that without a most urgent necessity, or without the declaration of a General Council, such issues can never come to a head. Now this is certainly not the way things are tending, and the Padre Maestro too is of opinion that it will come to a slight arrangement of your *Dialogue* by adding or removing a few things.

Niccolini, an experienced diplomat, who should have felt uneasy about his own involvement, says the same. And yet he had faced the Pope in his anger. The archbishop of Siena, Ascanio Piccolomini, an experienced churchman, wrote on September 29:

It seems exceeding strange to me that such a recent and precise approbation should be opposed by the passions of some people who might find fault only in what they conceive of the book, for the work itself ought to appease the most timid conscience. On the other hand, I will say you deserve this and worse, for you have been disarming by steps those who have control of the sciences, and they have nothing left but to run back to holy ground.

As for Castelli, he wrote: "This is the time to stand up to them and answer with the words of Copernicus to Paul III: *Illos nihil moror. . . .*" And later: "I have said openly that if the Inquisition were really called in, and if this holy and supreme tribunal did not proceed in the manner that is due, it would work damage to the reputation and reverence owed to it, and that, if they prosecuted a man who had written so modestly, reverently, and reservedly, it would mean that others would henceforth write brutally and resolutely."

The consensus of the correspondents is: "There is nothing they can do to you. But things are out of hand for a while, because the Pope has made an impulsive move. Sit tight, do not yield more than you have to, but do not irritate them." We have from more than one source the same colloquial expression: "*They* have gone off half-cocked, and now they feel they have to run the tilt; when they come back, it will be time to talk." But there was also nervousness around, because it was realized that they had to deal with a spoiled amateur of absolute power who was playing by ear.

As most of those who have the responsibility of advice feel themselves constrained to "pussyfooting," it is like a breath of fresh air to have the uninhibited opinion of the good friar of Venice, Fra Fulgenzio Micanzio:

> But what miserable sect can that be to which anything that is good and founded in Nature by necessity appears contrary and odious? The world is not limited to a single corner; you shall see your work printed in many places and languages.[9] . . . My worry is that I may see myself deprived of the thing I hoped for most, your other dialogues that were coming [i.e., the *Two New Sciences*]; if they are stopped because of this, I shall send to a hundred thousand devils these hypocrites without Nature and without God.

In Rome itself there were many who were not at all impressed by all this talk of heresy. A still obscure young scientist by name of Torricelli (a discovery of Ciàmpoli) turned to Galileo right in the turmoil of those September days. He wrote, shyly introducing himself as "Copernican by conviction, by profession and sect Galileist." He had defended the thesis of the book with Father Grienberger, who was his friend, he said, and who expressed only mild disapproval.

IV

The sane people, the "cautious optimists," turned out to be wrong. They had not yet realized that the authorities had gone off the deep end. But there was one man at least who should have entertained fewer illusions, and that was Galileo himself. He knew best what the book meant, and what the Pope had meant on his side, and what an abyss divided the two conceptions. Once the Pope's eyes had been opened, Galileo had everything to fear. Yet, strangely enough, he is the "fightingest" of them all. He is sure he can convince the authorities if they but give him a chance; he pri-

---

9. This reassurance is repeated in several letters: "Il suo dialogo andrà in molte lingue, e sbattasi chi vuole" (August 5, 1631).

vately asks, as Campanella had suggested, for a discussion *in concilio Patrum.* He wants to go over the book point by point with any committee which may be appointed. Yet "unworldliness" is not the word that describes him; and he knew the value of discretion. Even his enemy Piero Guicciardini had granted him that.

To expatiate on hybris as has so often been done is no explanation. Galileo thought his personal position juridically sound, but he knew it to be politically weak. The infinite deliberation he displayed in bringing out the *Saggiatore* is the best proof. Then why, in an old man of worldly experience, this venture, this—as it turned out—truly insensate gamble? If he had only wanted to publish his ideas, he could easily have played safe. The man who had composed the *Saggiatore* knew he could write rings around the censors (even the judges at the trial were unable to find fault with the pamphlet). There was one obvious and quite easy way that he was, in fact, compelled to consider later—but it was then too late. He could have concluded the *Dialogue* by having Simplicio, or perhaps better Sagredo, produce triumphantly out of a hat the Tychonic system, which had never been discussed, and have Salviati, tongue in cheek, admit himself vanquished; this would have allowed him to conclude more convincingly with the Pope's wisdom. The Church would have indorsed this, for it was as good as the hard-working Jesuit Riccioli could invent in 1657 to refute Galileo officially in his *Almagestum novum.*

Moreover, if he had wanted to look utterly innocent, Galileo could have sacrificed what he knew perfectly well to be an untenable, if enticing, theory on circular fall[10] and himself produced Riccioli's "crushing physicomathematical argument," which would have confused the trail completely. Riccioli made a fool of himself with it, as Borelli did not scruple to show in 1668, notwithstanding the still rigid prohibitions; yet he was universally applauded as a champion of the faith. All the more easily could Galileo have clowned with such devices, since the rest of the *Dialogue* left no doubt as to where reason lay. His vanity, which was great, would have found its profits therein, for he would have been complimented by all and

10. *Dialogue,* p. 178.

sundry, including the hypocrites, while the scientific-minded would have read between the lines. He and his friends might have sat back to enjoy the joke on the authorities. The book would have penetrated freely and quietly to destroy gradually the established teachings of Church philosophy, while Galileo's position remained secure for his lifetime.

He might have done this; he might have done even less, viz., had Salviati step forth to offer himself the "medicine of the end"—and yet he had refused to do it and still did. He gambled everything on speaking the truth unequivocally. It was a reckless gamble, but it was a generous one. Galileo knew very well that he was working a surprise coup. He had been sufficiently warned on his theory of the tides, as the Pope said to Niccolini, and the Pope was right. But he expected the argument to be so irresistible as to checkmate his enemies, bring even the authorities to a grudging acceptance, and so to save Catholic science in this perilous crisis. After all, they had scrutinized it; they could not very well admit they had not understood a word of it. No sane man will run his head into the stone wall of logic once he has been shown the wall. The old illusion of 1615 took long to die in the scientist's mind. And this time, too, he did have written permission. He knew, beyond doubt, that he had disregarded the Pope's explicit intentions. But he was strong in his certainty that he had not disobeyed the edicts of the Church. He obviously thought—as Ciàmpoli did, for that matter—that he had to contend with the fancies of a vain and headstrong but brilliant personality who was still, for all his pontifical robes, the old Maffeo Barberini whom he had known and loved. There is scarcely an intelligent man who will not believe that people in power cannot take themselves seriously all of the time and who will not naïvely extend to them his sympathy in the hope of a shade of refreshing complicity in return, of a trace of humor.

Galileo had far more positive grounds than these wistful ones, however, for his hope; these should be spelled out, since no one seems to have noticed them. In 1616, at least so Buonamici says, it was the *Letter to the Grand Duchess* which had provided Maffeo Barberini with the grounds he needed to withstand a proclamation of heresy.[11] No one had acknowledged it openly; discreet silence had prevailed among the parties. But Galileo knew by this that Barberini's bark was worse than his bite. He was in a way entitled to hope for a second stage of the same coy performance. He was even more entitled to expect it, in that Barberini, as Pope Urban VIII, had shown himself not ungenerous intellectually or a narrow-minded fanatic. He had, two years previously, saved Campanella, notwithstanding the old communist's infinite philosophical indiscretions (which included avowed Copernicanism), and gotten him out of the jail of the Spanish Inquisition in Naples, where he had rotted for years as the result of a truly devilish persecution plot.

Galileo had, thus, grounds to think that he could force Urban's hand ever so little, while appealing to Barberini's judgment; and, beyond the first moment of spite, he expected understanding and magnanimity. It was reasonable of him to hope, if only to hope, that the Pontiff, under the impression of the *Dialogue*, would become his secret ally and, while pretending aloofness, would quietly move to extricate the Church from her scientific impasse. Even if that were too much to expect, he had certainly the right to expect a measure of intelligence or, at least, discretion in these men who were intrusted with steering the Christian Republic—or, at the very least, diplomacy.

Shall we call this self-begotten blindness, conceit born of applause and flattery? Shall we call it deluded trust in one's fellow-men, a trust certainly strengthened by their liberal compliments but shown at its best in Galileo's patient and unremitting attempts at reasoning with them? These and similar psychological motives have been presented to satiety. What should be considered more seriously are the political factors.

As we stated at the outset, Urban VIII and his court may be considered much less the oppressors of science than the first bewildered casualties of the scientific age. They did not have the least idea of the momentum of the new type of thinking. Only one group of men could, or should, at least have guessed: and those were the Jesuit astronomers. They were more than half-convinced that Galileo was

---

11. Or at least Galileo was sure it was so, which amounts to the same thing in this case. It is his version of the story that has been preserved in Buonamici's diary, of which more on p. 286.

right—we would know this from Father Kircher even if we did not have any other sources. Galileo had plenty of information about their thought, and he kept expecting that, whatever their personal feelings, their duty to the Faith would cause them to interpose a word of advice. It was they, and no one else, whose obligation it was to prevent the Pope from making a fool of himself. But the vast apparatus of indoctrination and constriction that their Order had devised was now working to its own undoing. Following "like unto corpses" the corporate political will of their Society, they shut their eyes, their ears, and their minds. The power of discipline fed back into the complex steering machinery in a circuit of self-destruction.

Thus, beyond the failure of the evaluating mechanism, we are led back to that "political will" of which the Jesuits had become the spearhead but which was shared in various measure by all the hierarchy; and here the pattern becomes visible at last. Galileo had once thrown down the challenge, and now he was going to pay for it. The original challenge went far back in time. He had become a danger when he started writing in Italian and when he decided to bypass the universities and vested intellectual authority and reveal his mind to enlightened public opinion. This was traditional enough as a move. Had not Dante had recourse to vernacular for reasons not very dissimilar from his own? But, then, Dante had remained in the eyes of the authorities a very suspicious character, and so, clearly, was he.

In short, this man was a troublemaker. The scientist as an isolated specialist had not been understood as a social danger, which he might well be considered to be, even to the present day. It was Galileo, the Renaissance figure who wanted the scientific awareness spread to the whole advancing front of his civilization, from its expressive and technological capacities and its critical activity to its philosophical reflection, who appeared as a dangerous novelty-monger.

"If," writes Joseph de Maistre patronizingly, "if he had not written, as he had promised not to; if he had not tried to prove Copernicus by way of Scripture; if he had only written in Latin. . . ." Three untruths and one unhelpful suggestion. The proper balanced formula. We may still pick up gingerly the one suggestion. There is that typical "prudence" in it. If he had written in Latin, he would have left it to someone else like Foscarini or Bruno to tell the facts in the vernacular and take the consequences, for such things were not to be kept under a bushel. As to himself, true enough, he would have risked at most being put on the Index, for, in sum, what could it matter? Of the writing of unreadable tomes there is no end.

Let us try, standing under the correction of better-informed authorities, to put some substantive content into the frivolous Maistrian *if*'s.

If he had waited another century or so for his superiors to understand; *if* he had not inevitably collided with the monopoly of the most powerful organization within the Church, self-charged with controlling the flow of new ideas; *if* he had not felt he had to go over their heads, urgently, to the responsible minds in what still remained the fundamental entity, the *Ecclesia*, the Community. . . . Why, surely.

He had laid himself wide open instead. Those who still refer to the Preface of the *Dialogue* as a miserably ineffectual piece of hypocrisy seem to be overlooking that he was saying specifically what had to be said both ways, and so carefully said, that even the inadvertent italicizing of it could become explosive, as Magalotti reported wryly:

"*There is no want of such as inadvisedly affirm that the decree was not the production of sober scrutiny but of an ill-informed passion, and one may hear some mutter that consultors altogether ignorant of astronomical observations ought not to clip the wings of speculative minds with rash prohibition. My zeal cannot keep silence when I hear these inconsiderate complaints. . . . I was at that time in Rome and had not only the audience but applauds of the most eminent prelates of that court; nor was the decree published without previous information given me thereof. Therefore, it is my resolution in the present case to give foreign nations to see that of this matter as much is understood in Italy, and particularly in Rome, as transalpine diligence could imagine. . . . I hope that by these considerations the world will come to know that, if other nations have navigated more than we, we have not studied less than they; and that our returning to assert the Earth's stability and to take the contrary for a mathematical fantasy proceeds not from lack of acquaintance with others' ideas thereof but* (*had we no other inducements*) *from those reasons that piety, religion, the knowledge of the Divine Omnipotence, and a consciousness of the incapacity of man's understanding dictate to us.*"

This is the formal cover that was needed in order to write the book at all. It had to pretend to be like so many authorized books, an empty and noncommittal exercise in philosophical rhetoric, an arrangement of Japanese flowers—in brief, some kind of work of art. The Master of the Holy Palace had found the presentation "just right" and insisted that it be not altered further.

A mere cover it was, though, a flimsy veil of convention which stood by tacit agreement. As is the rule in such matters, whoever touched it made a fool of himself. In the clear, for the "Judicious Reader" (*Discreto Lettore*) to whom those words were addressed, it made excellent sense: "Since the authorities have chosen to get themselves into a jam, and refuse to realize it, it is for us, the Italian believers, to extricate them quickly and inconspicuously so as to save their face, before our faith suffers humiliation at the hands of its enemies." (Once the veil of convention was torn, once the book was malevolently scrutinized, it became impossible to construe the Preface otherwise, as was to be ragingly pointed out by the experts for prosecution.)

The audience with Bellarmine is underlined in that text, challengingly, with the quiet pride that becomes the acknowledged consultant. At the hour of what he knows to be scientific victory, Galileo is generously throwing the mantle of his intellectual prestige around the authorities so as to cover their past incompetence and obduracy. And this, more than anything else, more than what was said about his theological "meddling," his derogatory tongue, his infernal telescope—this was what could not be forgiven.

V

The fourth act of the tragedy had started. On the first of October the Inquisitor of Florence appeared at Galileo's house and served him with a formal summons, on the part of the Holy Office, to present himself in Rome within thirty days. Galileo realized at last with terror the full gravity of the situation; he took to his bed in unfeigned sickness. In a letter to Cardinal Francesco Barberini, Urban's nephew, he begged to be spared the winter voyage, fearing that, in his condition, he would not terminate it alive. "I curse the time devoted to these studies in which I strove and hoped to move away somewhat from the beaten path. I repent having given the world a portion of my writings; I feel inclined to consign what is left to the flames and thus placate at last the inextinguishable hatred of my enemies."

He still suggested, however, that a revision of his book might appease the authorities, and he asked that a commission be appointed in Florence to supervise it. But, he concluded, "if neither my great age, nor my many bodily infirmities, nor the depth of my grief, nor the hazards of a journey in such a condition are considered sufficient reasons, by this high and sacred tribunal, for granting a dispensation, or at least a delay, I will undertake the journey, esteeming obedience to be worth more than life."

With this Galileo was not only trying for a last intercession; he was also giving notice to his protectors that he would not try to escape, as he might well have done, for he had received among others, it seems, a message from Francesco Morosini. Magnanimously forgetting the break that had occurred between them twenty years before, when Galileo left Padua, the old statesman had offered him the inviolable sanctuary of Venetian territory. We know that several of his friends were urging him to do just that, and it would appear that even Niccolini—very privately—inclined to the same advice. But at that juncture the fight seemed to have gone out of the old man. He was no Sarpi, to organize his defiance within great and recognized issues of power policy. He had held up to then in his own mind, not much caring, two incompatible frames of reference which had grown out of the contradiction of the times—for he was deeply a man of his times. Now the precarious security had been shattered, and he found himself suddenly a helpless displaced person, an old man, broken and sick, "struck from the book of the living," in need of some kind of protection and comfort. The pallid specter of fear, a craving for acceptance and forgiveness, and the humiliation of begging were besieging the man who had hitherto been a joyous and whimsical warrior.

What had happened in Rome, unfortunately, made the last attempt at a compromise worse than futile. In fact, the Pope was given the letter by Cardinal Barberini, and he annotated curtly:

"Business settled in last Congregation. No further answer needed. See from Assessor whether orders have been carried out." But Galileo was still in the dark concerning the latest events. If he had known, he might have reconsidered his decision to deliver himself up.[12]

On September 11 Niccolini had received a very agitated Padre Riccardi, who had again advised prudence and submissiveness, for the *Dialogue*, it appeared now, had really been a signal piece of disobedience. He had tried, he said, to get Campanella and Castelli on the Preliminary Commission but had failed; he would still do all he could. "But, above all, he told me, under the seal of absolute confidence and secrecy, that there had been found in the books of the Holy Office that, sixteen years ago, it having been heard that Galileo entertained this opinion and spread it in Florence, *he had been summoned to Rome and forbidden by Cardinal Bellarmine in the name of the Pope and the Holy Office to discuss this opinion, and that this alone is enough to ruin him utterly.*"

The situation had changed, and obviously in a sense that no one had foreseen; for, when Urban made his scene before Niccolini on the fifth, he had shouted that "Galileo should take care not to be summoned by the Holy Office." Expatiating on Galileo's crimes, he had accused him of coaxing a permission out of the licensers and of sundry minor transgressions which really implied only laxness on the part of the censors and administrative short cuts on the part of the author; but it was clear that, if he thought of referring the case to the Inquisition, he did not yet see exactly how it could be done.

It was with that end in mind that the Preliminary Commission had gone to work, and the results had been gratifying. What they had found in the acts of the Inquisition was the injunction of February 26, 1616, on the part of the Commissary-General (p. 126) with the clause "not to teach in whatsoever manner" that no one had

12. Cf. Buonamici's memorandum: "He obeyed against the opinion and advice of his truest friends, who would have had him go abroad, write an apology, and not expose himself to the impertinent and ambitious passion of a monk [i.e., the Commissary-General of the Inquisition]."

suspected before and least of all the Pope himself, who had told Galileo to go ahead and write about Copernicus.

This was what Riccardi, in great agitation, confided to Niccolini on September 11. Something new had been added which made the prosecution possible. It was also—but this he did not say—what saved his head and deflected the storm on Galileo. Fright turned him henceforth into a man of perfidious counsel.

The Preliminary Commission had just then, after five sessions, which took about a month, submitted to the Pope a three-page memorandum on the Galileo affair.[13] The three following indictments were outlined against the author: (1) Galileo has transgressed orders in deviating from the hypothetical treatment by decidedly maintaining that the Earth moves and that the Sun is stationary; (2) he has erroneously ascribed the phenomena of the tides to the stability of the Sun and the motion of the Earth, which do not exist; and (3) he has further been deceitfully (*fraudolentemente*) silent about the command laid upon him by the Holy Office, in the year 1616, which was as follows: "*To relinquish altogether the said opinion that the Sun is the center of the world and immovable and that the Earth moves; nor henceforth to hold, teach, or defend it in any way whatsoever, verbally or in writing, otherwise proceedings would be taken against him by the Holy Office, which injunction the said Galileo acquiesced in and promised to obey.*"

Then follows the remark: "It must now be considered what proceedings are to be taken, both against the person of the author and against the printed book." Yet the nature of these proceedings is

13. Ed. Naz., XIX, 324. It is amusing to note that the scribe had written "Campanella" and then erased it to replace it with "Galileo." This *lapsus* ought to show that the great utopian had caused considerable comment in the Commission with his request to be consulted. No one had forgotten his *Defense of Galileo,* published in Germany in 1622. In fact, he had been threatened. He wrote to Galileo on October 22: "They had their committee, with many invectives against the new philosophers, etc. And I was named too." It did nothing to improve the atmosphere. What with Sarpi and Campanella and the "German mathematicians," it was plain in Rome that Galileo did not have the right kind of friends.

not in any way discussed in the document, but it now refers "as to fact" in five counts to the historical events, from the time when the *Dialogue* was submitted in Rome in 1630 to its publication in Florence in 1632. A sixth count considers that the following points in the *Dialogue* itself must be laid to the author's account:

a. That, without orders and without making any communication about it, he put the imprimatur of Rome on the title-page.

b. That he had printed the Preface in different type and rendered it useless by its separation from the rest of the work; further, that he had put the "medicine of the end" in the mouth of a simpleton and in a place where it is hard to find; that it is but coolly received by the other interlocutor, so that it is only cursorily touched upon and not fully discussed.

c. That he had very often in the work deviated from the hypothesis, either by absolutely asserting that the Earth moves and that the Sun is stationary, or by representing the arguments upon which these views rest as convincing and necessarily true, or by making the contrary appear impossible.

d. That he has treated the subject as undecided and as if it were waiting for explanation, while he has really given it.

e. That he contemns and maltreats authors who are of a contrary opinion and those whom the Holy Church chiefly employs.

f. That he perniciously asserts and sets forth that, in the apprehension of geometrical matters, there is some equality between the divine and the human mind.

g. That he had represented it to be an argument for the truth that the Ptolemaics go over to the Copernicans but not vice versa.

h. That he had erroneously ascribed the tides in the ocean to the stability of the Sun and the motion of the Earth, which do not exist.

The two first points are miserably revealing of the search for any kind of motive. The Special Commission, however, by no means draws the conclusion, from all these errors and failings, that the *Dialogue* should be prohibited but says: "All these things could be corrected, if it is decided that the book to which such favor should be shown is of any value."

Immediately after, there follows the seventh count, stating again ("as to fact") that "the author has transgressed the mandate of the

Holy Office of 1616, 'that he should relinquish altogether the said opinion,' etc., down to 'and promised to obey.' "

Even as an exploratory report, the paper is strangely inconclusive. After listing the author's several transgressions, it suggests that a corrected edition of the book might be enough of a sanction, as though the violation of the injunction of 1616, if true, were not in itself a damnable enough crime. Since the majority of the members were bitterly opposed to Galileo, it is clear that the juridical situation must have looked to them extraordinarily embarrassing.

There were undoubtedly two major stumbling blocks: one was that the book had been licensed; and the other, as Magalotti had said, that there was no way of declaring the Copernican doctrine formally heretical. (This was also how Father Guevara had understood the rules when he declared in 1625, after the publication of the *Saggiatore*, that the Earth's suggested motion is by itself not blameworthy.)[14] The case was admitted to be very far from clear, but—said rather doubtfully—there was enough to have the Holy Office look into it, if this was what was desired.

It was not much, but it was enough for the Pope's needs. On September 15 he informed the ambassador that he could do no less than hand over the affair to the Inquisition.[15] At the same time the strictest secrecy as to this information was enjoined on both ambassador and sovereign, with a threat that otherwise they would be proceeded against according to the statutes of the Holy Office. He should not have spoken, he stressed, but he was doing it out of regard for his Highness. What he meant, of course, was that he wanted to offer the Grand Duke a chance to disassociate himself from the scabby sheep before he was struck by the dishonoring summons.

---

14. Cf. Ed. Naz., XIII, 265.

15. In fact, one wonders why the authorities did not insist on this point: that as soon as the injunction was discovered, it being clear that Galileo had infringed it by writing the book, he was liable to immediate arrest. This is very far, however, from what Francesco Barberini implies in his letter to the Nuncio of September 25 (see p. 268) or from what was said to Niccolini. Much more consideration is shown in this phase in which feelings are high than in the later one. It is as though the authorities felt that they were venturing onto unsafe ground and that Galileo might rebel and move to safe territory.

The insistent requests of Niccolini for reconsideration His Beatitude evaded with what he was pleased to consider a humorous anecdote.

On September 23 the General Congregation pronounced that Galileo had transgressed the injunction of 1616, and on October 1, as we have seen, the official summons was served on him at Arcetri.

Niccolini soon received the news of the event and of Galileo's despair and set out again indefatigably to help. He pleaded with the prelates of the Holy Office the ailments of the old man and the difficulties of a two-hundred-mile journey in the worst season. They "only heard what he had to say and answered nothing." He went to the Pope himself. "Your Holiness incurs the danger," he said, "of his being tried neither in Rome nor in Florence, for I am assured that he may die on the way."

"He must come," was the Pope's reply. "He can come by very easy stages, in a litter, with every comfort, but he really must be tried here in person. May God forgive him for having been so deluded as to involve himself in these difficulties, from which We had relieved him when We were a cardinal."

Niccolini then made bold to remark that, if there was any fault, it was with the licensers, whereupon Urban went off again into a tirade against Riccardi and Ciàmpoli. "But he should have known better," he concluded, "than to get himself into such a tangle [*ginepreto*] of questions which are of the most delicate and pernicious kind there is. Now he must come." He added, "between his teeth," says the Ambassador, something to the effect that there might be, among the judges of the Holy Office, some who had already been in the Preliminary Commission. This referred, as came out later, to the three consultors who had been asked to report on the book.

Niccolini had not even obtained a delay. On the nineteenth of November Galileo received a second summons. This time he sent in a certificate signed by three doctors:

. . . We find that his pulse intermits every three or four beats. . . . The patient has frequent attacks of giddiness, hypochondriacal melancholy, weakness of stomach, insomnia, and flying pains about the body. We have also observed a serious hernia with rupture of the peritoneum. All these symptoms, with the least aggravation, might become dangerous to life.

The Holy Office answered with a papal mandate which said that such evasions were not going to be tolerated and that in case of further delay a commissioner escorted by a physician would set out to bring Galileo back as a prisoner in irons (*carceratum et ligatum cum ferris*). If danger to life made a postponement advisable, he must be brought back as soon as he could travel, but still as a prisoner and in irons.[16]

This time the Grand Duke himself advised Galileo to go. History has branded him a weak-kneed ruler who handed over his protégé to persecution. Yet he should be granted considerable extenuation. He was not the king of France or the Venetian Senate; he was himself a protégé—a princeling caught between the House of Austria, his suzerain, and the Papal States, his neighbor. He could not expect protection from the Emperor in such matters concerning orthodoxy, as Cosimo I had had in the contest concerning his coronation (it had nearly come to a war with Pius V). Tuscany was in an exposed position on the southern border of the Empire and might have to take on the Papal States alone. In his own house the young man of twenty-two had to contend with the pious alarm of his dowager mother; as a ruler, he had to consider the possible repercussions of a conflict with the monks among the superstitious populace. He found no help in his ministers, who were furious at this sudden upset of their delicately calculated moves and countermoves on the diplomatic chessboard and were all for washing their hands of the ill-omened astronomer.[17] He did not. He offered Galileo his own litter for the voyage and his own embassy in Rome for a residence and, against the advice of his secretary of state, gave orders to Niccolini to go all out in his defense.

---

16. All statutes and laws impeding the free action of the Inquisition, directly or indirectly, were null and void *ipso jure* (see Farinacci, *De haeresi quaestiones 182*, No. 76).

17. Objectively, it no doubt looked bad, even at the time. Grotius, writing to Vossius in 1635, speaks of the Grand Duke surrendering "in craven fear" (*socordi metu*) and suggests that a way should be found to remove Galileo to Holland. (His own experience in escaping from well-guarded fortresses made him confident on this point.) Galileo himself thought he should have been better protected. His later work he pointedly dedicated to the French ambassador, Noailles, as a patron.

Galileo, on his side, after the first shock, had fully recovered his fighting spirits. He was for "having it out" with the ecclesiastical authorities on the whole issue, including the dangerous theological subjects that he had obediently left alone for so many years and that were now again brought out against him.

In a strong letter to Elia Diodati in Paris, written on January 15, after the final summons of the Inquisition and shortly before leaving for Rome—a letter probably intended as a kind of intellectual testament intrusted to the Protestants in case he were to be silenced forever—he comes back squarely to his position of 1615 as outlined in the *Letter to Castelli.* The pretext is given by some recent anti-Copernican tracts of Froidmont and Morin on which Diodati had asked his opinion, but what he is expressing in no uncertain terms is what he thinks of the Pope himself:

As to Froidmont, I could have wished not to see him fall into, in my opinion, a grave though widespread error; namely, in order to refute the opinions of Copernicus, he first hurls scornful jests at his followers, and then (which seems to me still more unsuitable) fortifies himself by the authority of the Holy Scripture, and at length goes so far as to call those views on these grounds nothing less than heretical. That such a proceeding is not praiseworthy seems to me to admit of very easy proof. For if I were to ask Froidmont, who it is that made the Sun, the Moon, the Earth, and the stars, and ordained their order and motions, I believe he would answer, "They are the creations of God." If asked who inspired Holy Scripture, I know he would answer, "The Holy Spirit," which means God likewise. The world is therefore the work and the Scriptures are the word of the same God. . . . Nothing ever changes in Nature to accommodate itself to the comprehension or notions of men. But if it be so, why, in our search for knowledge of the various parts of the universe, should we begin rather with the words than with the works of God? Is the work less noble or less excellent than the word? If Froidmont or anyone else had settled that the opinion that the Earth moves is a heresy, and if afterward demonstration, observation, and necessary concatenation would prove that it does move, into what embarrassment he would have brought himself and the holy Church.[18]

---

18. The rest of the letter is important:

"Many years ago, when the stir about Copernicus was beginning, I wrote a letter of some length in which, supported by the authorities

The one who had lost his head was, rather, Urban VIII. He felt around him a chill little wind of criticism. It had been said of him for a long time that he had sacrificed the interests of the Church to his personal ambition, to his vanity, to the cupidity of his relatives, and to the interests of the House of Barberini. The ambassador of Modena in Rome was writing in those very days to his prince: "These rulers want to aggrandize their family; they love wealth; they lust for power; but, when a decision is at hand, they do not have the guts to go out and take serious risks. They look arrogant enough, but then they cut a pitiful figure." Urban was in truth not unaware of his predicament; he knew his people were murmuring, and those months had brought nothing that could spell hope for the future on the chessboard of international politics. Early in the game, in his sanguine debuts, he had felt, not without reason, modern and farsighted in staking the newly rising French nation against the traditional power of Spain and Austria; as he surveyed the situation, he could hardly feel that it had been a successful gambit. He had been used by Richelieu instead of using him; he had alienated Austria for no profit and had given scandal by his undercover

---

of numerous Fathers of the Church, I showed what an abuse it was to appeal so much to Holy Scripture in questions of natural science, and I proposed that in future it should not be brought into them. As soon as I am in less trouble, I will send you a copy. I say 'in less trouble,' because I am just now going to Rome, whither I have been summoned by the Holy Office, which has already prohibited the circulation of my *Dialogue*. I hear from well-informed parties that the Jesuit Fathers have insinuated in the highest quarters that my book is more execrable and injurious to the Church than the writings of Luther and Calvin. And all this although, in order to obtain the imprimatur, I went in person to Rome and submitted the manuscript to the Master of the Palace, who looked through it most carefully, altering, adding, and omitting, and, even after he had given it the imprimatur, ordered that it should be examined again at Florence. The reviser here, finding nothing else to alter, in order to show that he gone through it carefully, contented himself with substituting some words for others, as, for instance, in several places, 'Universe' for 'Nature,' 'quality' for 'attribute,' 'sublime spirit' for 'divine spirit,' excusing himself to me for it by saying that he foresaw that I should have to do with fierce foes and bitter persecutors, as has indeed come to pass."

alliance with the Swede. The King of Spain in his anger had gone so far as to challenge him in Consistory, through Cardinal Borgia, to be reminded of "his more pious and more glorious predecessors" and to stop these unseeming collusions with heretical power; he had had to move swiftly to crush a political plot in his own Curia. He had begun to see enemies everywhere.

"The Pope lives in fear of poison," writes a diplomatic correspondent. "He has gone up to Castel Gandolfo and shut himself in; no one is admitted without being searched. The ten miles of road are heavily patrolled. He is in great suspicion that the preparations made in Naples might be aimed at him, that the fleet of the Grand Duke of Tuscany may any day set sail against Ostia and Civitavecchia. The garrisons and lookouts on the coast have been reinforced." This nervous apprehension corresponded less to actual dangers than to a deep sense of failure. With the eclipse of French power following the death of the Swedish king, the illness of Richelieu, and the alignment of England against the Netherlands, he realized that his elaborate game was up and that it was only a matter of time until he would be forced back into the Hapsburg orbit, which was indeed to happen three years hence. And if he had only known, just at a time when France was again to be decisively on its way to victory. Bad luck without a break, all mistimed and mischanced.

And if he brought down his gaze from grave world perspectives to this annoying learned fuss about the planets, he could discern in a small version the same story all over again. He had tried to play the big-hearted Renaissance prince and to take science under his mantle, and here he stood outwitted by Galileo as he had been by Richelieu. Galileo, while offering himself as an ally, had mobilized lay thought against the intellectual authority of the Church and created a scandal. But at least he, Urban, could do something there. He could break his back and humiliate that gang for all to see. He was going to make a terrific intervention. Here was an occasion to recoup his prestige and reaffirm his position as head of the Faith. He was going to show those Florentines that there were limits to their impertinence. He had banged his fist publicly upon the table and ordered the *ad hoc* Commission to produce a case against that man on the double-quick. The Commission doubled up and produced a case, or at least what could look like one. But there was uneasiness all around.[19]

VI

Absolutely elsewhere, in a Hyperborean corner of the New World that no one in Rome had even heard of, in those very days, an unknown and faintly absurd young cleric named Roger Williams, sitting in the wigwam of Chief Massasoit, was preparing his case against another—minuscule and preposterous—theocratic state: "The STATE RELIGION of the World," he wrote, "is a POLITIC invention of men to maintain the CIVIL STATE . . . GOD requireth not an UNIFORMITY of RELIGION to be INACTED and INFORCED in any CIVIL STATE; which inforced UNIFORMITY sooner or later is the greatest occasion of CIVILL WARE, RAVISHING of CONSCIENCE, PERSECUTION of CHRIST JESUS in his servants, and of the HYPOCRISIE and destruction of millions of souls. . . . It is the will and command of GOD, that a PERMISSION of the most PAGANISH, JEWISH, TURKISH, or ANTICHRISTIAN CONSCIENCES and WORSHIPS, bee granted to ALL men in all NATIONS and COUNTRIES; and they are onely to bee FOUGHT against with that SWORD which is onely (in SOULE MATTERS) ABLE to CONQUER, to wit, the SWORD of GODS SPIRIT, the WORD of GOD. . . ."

Half the world away from there, and also from Rome, in Marco Polo's fabulous city of Cambaluc, which had been discovered only lately to be the same as Peking, Father Adam Schall von Bell, S.J., known in China as T'ang Jo-wang, on whom the Emperor had con-

---

19. Notwithstanding the unexpected boon of the injunction of 1616 that the Commission had dug up, which provided a legal handle for the prosecution, the Pope toned down his language considerably after the report. In the first interview with Niccolini on September 5 he had spoken of "la più perversa materia che si potesse mai avere alle mani," "dottrina perversa in estremo grado," which terms would apply only to grave heresy. Later it becomes "un gran ginepreto, del quale poteva far di meno, perche son materie fastidiose e pericolose" (September 18); "materia gelosa e fastidiosa, cattiva dottrina.... fu mal consigliato.... era stata una certa Ciampolata cosi fatta" (February 27, 1633). Apparently, as Magalotti had foretold, the Holy Office had raised difficulties about a prosecution on dogmatic grounds, and he had fallen back on the political.

ferred the titles of "Most Profound Doctor [*tung kwan hsiao*], Superintendent of the Imperial Stud, High Honorable Bearer of the Imperial Banquet, and Exploring Teacher of the Mysteries of Heaven," was having to struggle not only against the intrigues of court officials but with his own authorities in the Vatican. Sharp letters from Rome had reminded him that, as director of the Imperial Bureau of Astronomy in charge of the calendar, he was indorsing with his authority all sorts of "superstitious excrescences" connected with alleged miraculous events in the heavens.

The imperious Jesuit, more used by then to rebuking the Emperor than to begging permission from his superiors, had to plead patiently that his own position remained undeviatingly scientific but that it was wise to give some leeway to ancient superstitions. Miracles in the sky, he said, could come in very useful, in so far as it was he who had the authority to interpret them. And, after all, he suggested, if we are to believe in the miracle of Joshua, why should we not let the Chinese believe in the significance of comets, the more so if we can turn their credulity to good political use?[20]

VII

Galileo was coming in to Rome to meet his fate. After twenty-three days on the road, which included a painful quarantine, on the thirteenth of February he reached the embassy, where a warm bed was ready for him, and he was cared for by the ambassador's wife, Caterina Niccolini, "queen of all kindness." He was allowed to stay there undisturbed for several weeks, visited by one or another prelate of the Inquisition in a noncommittal way. Monsignor Bocca-

---

20. This plea found acceptance eventually, but the rest of Schall's policy did not fare so well. Matteo Ricci, Schall, and Verbiest, the founders of the Chinese mission, as well as their French successors, had been so deeply impressed by Confucianism that they considered it a part of the Old Dispensation. They worked out a theological compromise which accepted both names and rites from Chinese worship. This line ran at last into categoric condemnation from the Holy Office: "Falsa est, temeraria, scandalosa, impia, Verbo Dei contraria, haeretica, Christianae Fidei et Religionis eversiva, virtutem Passionis Christi et Crucis ejus evacuans." The Dominicans had paid back their old rivals, as Father Navarrete's book on Jesuit excesses admits not without satisfaction. What was lost in the scuffle was only the Chinese Empire.

bella, the former Assessor, was very friendly; Monsignor Serristori, helpful. The Commissary-General was not to be seen, but Galileo paid his respects at the Holy Office and was introduced to the new Assessor, Monsignor Febei. Otherwise, he waited. "We find a wonderful pleasure," wrote Niccolini, "in the gentle conversation of the good old man." And on the nineteenth: "I think we have cheered up the old gentleman by showing him all that is being done for his cause; yet at times he comes back to finding this persecution very strange. I told him to show a will to obey and to go very softly."

Through these engaging words we can see a Galileo not at all cowed but vigorously annoyed, still amazed, and willing to remonstrate with the authorities high and low. This is confirmed by a letter of Galileo himself to his brother-in-law: "We [Niccolini and Galileo] hear at last that the many and serious accusations are reduced to one and the rest have been dropped. Of this one I shall have no difficulty in getting rid, once the grounds of my defense have been heard."

A dispatch of Niccolini five days later is more explicit:

> As far as I can learn, the main difficulty consists in this—that these gentlemen here maintain that in 1616 he was ordered neither to discuss the question nor to converse about it. He says, on the contrary, that those were not the terms of the *precetto*, which were that that doctrine was not to be held or defended.

So the secret communicated in dread secrecy to the Grand Duke alone on January 15 was out, and Galileo was scoffing at it. If it was Bellarmine's notification that made the trouble, they might not know that he had a copy of it in Bellarmine's own hand, which allowed him to call their bluff at any time; for the rest, he felt he had the law on his side so positively that he was for challenging the authorities on all this fuss, if Niccolini had not restrained him. This is, in itself, enough to prove conclusively, if further proof were needed, that Galileo was utterly unaware of any action taken on that day of February, seventeen years before, except the statement on the part of Bellarmine.[21]

---

21. All the allusions, by the Pope as well as by the officials, referred to "an injunction by Bellarmine." There was certainly intentional in-

We have said "if further proof were needed," because all Galileo's behavior since 1616 is proof enough in itself. He could not possibly have "forgotten," as early as 1618, a command *nec quovis modo docere* coming from the Inquisitor in person, when he wrote the letter on tidal motion to the Archduke Leopold; and no one but an utter fool could have written what he did, including the *Letter to Ingoli,* up to the *Dialogue* in 1630, with such a Damocles' sword over his head; nor is it conceivable that a man of his sense would not have asked in his papal audiences to have the injunction lifted as a preliminary to any encouragement to write.

Thus, it was a completely clear and reassuring picture that was in the minds of the two friends as they discussed the issue at the embassy in those early days of March, 1633. The signs were encouraging. The grim Senior Inquisitor himself, Cardinal Desiderio Scaglia, had read the *Dialogue* with the help of Castelli and had the points cleared up one by one for him; the monsignors of the Holy Office dropped comforting hints. Both friends expected that, now "the tilt had been run" and obedience shown, the case would be gradually allowed to drop. The Grand Duke was already putting pressure on the Pope to have Galileo sent back home.

It was, therefore, a very dismayed Niccolini who heard from the Pope on March 13 that Galileo was going to be summoned to the Holy Office as soon as the trial came around on the agenda. To Niccolini's expostulations, the Pope answered that there was no way out. "May God forgive Galileo," he said, "for having intruded into these matters concerning new doctrines and Holy Scripture, where the best is to go along with common opinion; and may God help Ciàmpoli too concerning these new notions, because he has a leaning toward them and is inclined toward new philosophies."

He added that Signor Galileo had been his friend, that often they had dined familiarly at the same table, and that he was sorry to subject him to these annoyances, but that it was a matter of faith and religion. I think I remarked that when he was heard he would be able, without difficulty, to give all explanations requested. He answered me that he

---

accuracy here, as otherwise the surprise scene prepared for April 12 (see p. 239) could never have taken place. But it would seem that the Pope himself was taken in by this version (see p. 281 below).

will be examined in due time but that there is an argument to which they have never yet given an answer, and that is that God is all-powerful, and, if He is, why should we try to necessitate Him? I said that I did not know how to speak on those matters, but that I thought I had heard Galileo saying that he was willing not to believe in the motion of the Earth, but that as God could make the world in a thousand ways, so it could not be denied that He could have made it in this way too. He grew angry and replied that we should not impose necessity upon the Lord Almighty; and, as I saw him working himself up to a fury, I avoided saying more that might have hurt Galileo. I just added that anyway he was here to obey, to cancel or retract whatever he would be told in the interest of religion, and that I did not know enough of this science and did not want to get myself into some heresy by talking about it. And so handling it lightly, for I was taking good care to steer wide of the Holy Office, I went on to other business.

This last passage is revealing. One has to appreciate the fine blend of caution, cool contempt, and intellectual freedom that those men brought to their dealings with the super state. It has not proved easy to duplicate in our times. In a dangerously close play, acting with familiar ease, Niccolini had conveyed to the person on the sacred throne how little he thought of him, while preserving intact the formalities owed to his position. The Pope had winced, and Niccolini knew the Grand Duke would like to hear about it. The Grand Duke let him know in return that he was "thrilled." The tone of the correspondence in those times remained diplomatic throughout. What those men really thought was something else again. It has been vividly expressed for them by their senior, Francesco Guicciardini, in his autobiographical notes—but this is part of another story.

As for the memories of past friendship, they were polite conversation. The Pope's feelings had really changed into an enduring rancor. We can see it if we take a brief glimpse at what was to come. A year later, after the sentence, when Galileo petitioned from Arcetri that he be allowed to move into Florence for medical treatment, the answer was: "Sanctissimus refused to grant the request and ordered that said Galileo should be warned to desist from handing in supplications, or he will be taken back to the jails of the Holy Office." This time the Grand Ducal Court gasped: "Incredible"; "Unheard of." "But, then," as one of them writes, "anything that comes from the Inquisition is bound to be most new and unprecedented." Old Nemesis, however, was to catch up with Urban VIII, the lover of novelties; for what posterity remembers of the incident is Galileo's letter to Diodati, July 25 of that year 1634: "This period has been further darkened for me by great loss. During my absence, which my daughter considered most perilous for me, she fell into a profound melancholy which undermined her health, and it came at last (two months after my return) to a crisis of which she died after an illness of six days, just thirty-three years of age, leaving me in desperate grief. And by a sinister coincidence, on returning home from the convent, in company with the doctor who had just told me her condition was hopeless and she would not survive the next day, as indeed came to pass, I found the Inquisitor's Vicar here, who informed me of a mandate of the Holy Office at Rome that I must desist from asking for grace or they would take me back to the actual prison of the Holy Office. From which I can infer that my present confinement is to be terminated only by that other one which is common to all, most narrow, and enduring forever."[22]

VIII

What Niccolini extracted from the Pope that day of March 13 was a promise that the accused would be assigned comfortable rooms, with the assistance of a servant who could come and go instead of being isolated in a cell or *secreta* as was the procedure.

He did not tell Galileo about the impending trial. There would be time enough for that. But he set out to visit the prospective judges one by one, spending the name of the Grand Duke freely. To Cardinal Barberini he represented "the poor state of health of the good old man, who for two nights continuous had cried and moaned in sciatic pain; and his advancing age and his sorrow." All he received were assurances of the greatest possible consideration.

22. See also his letter to his brother-in-law, April 27, 1635: "I suffer much more from the rupture than has been the case before; I have no sleep, my pulse intermits, the most profound melancholy has come over me. I loathe myself, and I hear my little daughter perpetually calling me. . . ."

Even in his prudent seclusion, however, Galileo could feel that the going had become hard. The fair-weather friendships, the facile admiration, and the ornate compliments had evaporated; influential people were turning a cold shoulder. No one of his acquaintances dared approach the authorities in his favor, except old Buonarroti, whose letter has been preserved; and his supplication did not weigh much. Even the ministers in Florence were trying to get rid in some inconspicuous way of the luckless mathematician. Cioli wrote the ambassador that he should not commit himself too deeply and that, anyway, the administration could not be financially responsible for Galileo beyond the first month of his stay. The ambassador wrote back with cold scorn that it made no difficulty, that henceforth he, Niccolini, would be glad to meet the expenses out of his own pocket.

When Galileo was told on April 8 what was awaiting him, he took it with astonishing spirit. Here at last were ten cardinals on a bench who would have to listen and stand reason. This was going to be a "showdown"; he announced that he would tackle the whole issue, from theology to physics. The so-oft-told tale of intimidation and surrender has obliterated in history this very real struggle unto the last. The legendary "Eppur si muove" that Galileo is supposed to have murmured after the sentence would have been a mere emotional escape; whereas there is true and tragic grandeur in this invincible hope, at the very gates of the Inquisition from which so many had not returned, of moving men whom he had always known to be "unmovable and unpersuadable."

It was Niccolini who had to tell him that this was not the way things were going to be. The merit of his case was being decided without a hearing, and he had better not try to maintain anything at all "but to submit to whatever he may see they want in that business of the motion of the Earth."

This was the final blow for the old man. "He fell into the deepest dejection and since yesterday has sunk so low that I am greatly concerned for his life. We are all trying to ease him and comfort him, and to work for him through our connections, because truly he deserves everything good; and all this house of ours, which loves him extremely, is stricken with great sorrow."

Fogg Museum

URBAN VIII IN THE YEAR OF HIS ACCESSION
TO THE PONTIFICAL THRONE

Photo Alinari

CARDINAL FRANCESCO BARBERINI

As nephew to Urban VIII, and his closest collaborator, he held the position currently called of "Cardinal-Master," which was replaced after him by the post of Secretary of State. He tried to save Galileo from recanting.

Bibliothèque Nationale, Paris

ASCANIO PICCOLOMINI, ARCHBISHOP OF SIENA

He was Galileo's friend, who harbored him for five months after the trial.

Bibliothèque Nationale, Paris

GIOVANNI CIAMPOLI

This portrait, by Ottavio Leoni, was made in 1627, at the height of Ciampoli's career, when he was Secretary to Urban VIII, and five years before his downfall.

XI

THE INQUISITORS' PLIGHT

Hora novissima
Tempora pessima
Sunt: Vigilemus.

I

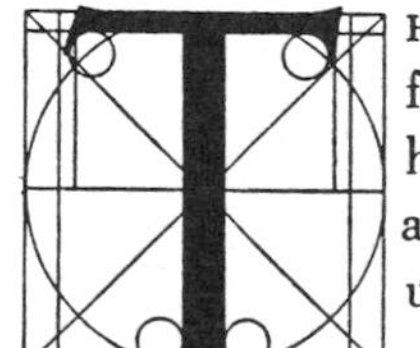
HE problem confronting the Inquisition was far from simple. With the personal injunction that had been discovered in the file, they had enough, as the poor Father Monster said, to "ruin Galileo utterly" if they wanted to. This was clearly the original idea of the procedure as seen by the Preliminary Commission and suggested vividly in Riccardi's indiscretions. The injunction provided a legal handle for the Holy Office. Otherwise the charges were vague and difficult to substantiate. This seems to have remained the feeling during the early phase of Galileo's stay in Rome. "The charges," he wrote, as we remember, "have gradually been allowed to drop, except one." So much he had gathered from his informal conversations with Monsignor Serristori and other officials.

Was this only a trap, laid in order to encourage him to pronounce himself more freely on scientific subjects? It could not but work poorly. It is a custom to credit the Inquisition with all sorts of hypocritical ways, but then also one can suppose anything. We have run into this kind of supposition already in the case of the first trial. Historians have descanted upon the duplicity of the Curia which allowed Galileo to carry on his efforts until the end of February,

1616, while the decision had fallen several months before. We have found that it was not so and that Bellarmine himself had never tried to deceive.

It might be better to start with a concrete question: Why did those officials give away so informally a secret which had been previously guarded with jealous care—with such care, indeed, that the Pope had not even allowed Niccolini to transmit it to the Grand Duke in a dictated report but exacted from him the promise that he write the dispatch in his own hand? The secret had a purpose, and the damage and risk of this informal disclosure could not be ignored. Most of all, the surprise effect on the defendant was lost for the interrogator; and, in case it were decided to sentence Galileo to prison on the injunction alone, there were now witnesses, Niccolini and his friends, ready to divulge that he had been sentenced on the strength of a command which he asserted had never taken place and which could not be shown to bear his acknowledgment.

Once the question is raised, there seems to be only one reasonable answer: The authorities were genuinely worried about the injunction, which certainly did not look very good, and those weeks of pause were spent in trying to get Galileo in an unguarded mood to confirm it. He could guess that they were probing the ground; a whole month passed in these perplexities.

The decision reached apparently, as we shall see from the course of the proceedings, was that, since the Pope had requested a sentence, the injunction would be considered valid, although they had managed to extract no confirmation of it from Galileo. It was needed for getting around the licenses, in order to have a case at all. But it was to be retained only in the capacity of a "*b* factor," as engineers impolitely call it, of undefined weight. The case itself should rest on the question of merit. Otherwise the sentence would not achieve its aim as a deterrent on public opinion.

But here the difficulties began. To raise the question of merit meant to bring into the foreground again the responsibility of the licensers, who had given in so many words permission to present the Copernican opinion and even to maintain it on purely physical grounds. The embarrassment is clearly to be perceived in the indecisive report of the Commission, which tries to find safe grounds in such ridiculous charges as that the Preface had been printed in different type; that the Roman license was abusively mentioned, since the book had been transferred to the Florence licensers; etc.

Nothing really would do except the theological crime. But how to prove it? It might be said that this, in principle, need not embarrass the Inquisition, which, like all secret state police, was entitled to do exactly anything. It was the image of absolute power whence it sprang. Its action was in principle *extra ordinem,* for it was an emergency tribunal which had created its own administrative law and could change it at will. Moreover, it was the guardian of "revealed truth" as a whole, that is, not only Scripture and dogma but the whole "deposit of the Faith" as it has come down to us through tradition and belief. Like all living things, the Church will not admit an outside definition of her contents. Thus, in principle, the powers of the Holy Office were discretionary. This principle was fearfully abused by the Spanish Inquisition. But there was a rationale behind it, with inherent limits that we should see.

II

And, first of all, there is the fact that the Church is not an impersonal power like the Roman praetor but the mother of the faithful.[1] The irreconcilable apostate, the social virus, she has to eliminate. All the others she does not punish; she "penitences." Willingness is assumed, the correction is supposed to be welcome, and indeed the penitential life that is offered to the culprit is the very same that the judging monks have elected for themselves in free vocation. He must be made to see himself as the Church sees him. What counts is the union of wills. With the evolution of the Church into a state, the metaphysical requirement of a union of wills remains; but it gets admittedly a bit strained at times. In a theological state, man is not innocent until proved guilty. Much the reverse,

1. It may be illuminating to note how specifically, except for this, the Roman Church continued the Roman Empire. It had inherited from it on one side the science and rigor of Justinian's *Institutions,* on the other the figure of the Emperor, ruling directly through a group of freedmen of undefined responsibility. The cardinals had, of course, a status that put them far above the freedmen, but they too might have to run for their lives, as the Barberinis did after the death of Urban VIII.

he is presumed guilty, and God or the authorities alone can know how much. This was the assumption not only in Rome but also, about the year 1630, in Boston. Today, it is the Russian condition. We must, if anything, admire the cautiousness and legal scruples of the Roman authorities in that civilized period.

What the individual does on his own, so runs the logic, can lead him only to disaster, and indeed this has been proved again and again. That is why guidance is needed. Man, the "timid, staring animal" man, is the least able to know what he is doing or why or whither it may lead him. What he should have ready in his soul is a willingness to childlike submission. In front of the Tribunal of the Inquisition a person was not supposed to *prove* his innocence; at best he could find himself innocent after scrutiny. It would have been bad form to expect it, for sin is man's condition, and to be called to account meant that one's noxiousness had already been long and carefully weighed. It was only awaiting exact evaluation. The best that one could expect, as an equivalent of acquittal, was a warning. The very fact of being called before the court was social disgrace.[2]

We have tribunals of orthodoxy in our own time, and the state of mind with respect to them has been well described by a Russian historian who went through the Yezhov purge: "I could not claim to be an orthodox Marxist, because the continual alterations in the party line made a consistent attitude of orthodoxy incompatible with scientifically founded convictions. But in my historical work I always tried to remain within the bounds of official instructions, to use the 'classical heritage' of Marxism to the full, and to conform with the intentions of Soviet policy. I had been regarded as a loyal Soviet scholar. Nevertheless, I was prepared for arrest. Why? Because, like all other Soviet citizens, I carried about with me a consciousness of guilt, an inexplicable sense of sin, a vague and indefinable feeling of having transgressed, combined with an ineradicable expectation of inevitable punishment."[3]

---

2. "Être cité a ce tribunal n'est pas une recommandation, et en sortir, même par la porte d'un acquittement, ne sera jamais un titre de gloire" (Grimaldi).

3. F. Beck and W. Godin, *The Russian Purge and the Extraction of Confession* (1951).

This goes to show how much less fearsome the Inquisition really was than its modern counterpart. In an age of social stability, which had not yet codified the dynamics of dialectical change, one knew at least what the general line was; it had never changed for generations, and people had learned to know where essentials lay. If we go through the list of fifty-one questions that was set up by the Italian Inquisition in the sixteenth century to test orthodoxy, we can see that they all bore on pretty fundamental aspects of faith or morals. In fact, the best testimonial in favor of the Inquisition is the resolute confidence of Galileo and his friends that there was no case at all against him.

On the part of the Holy Office itself, we have corresponding scruples which kept it hunting over the scale for a correct definition of Galileo's transgression, in the zone that goes between "error" and "heresy." This element of uncertainty rests on a subtle but very real distinction. Something that is not essential to the faith may not be a heresy *ex parte objecti,* as Bellarmine had said, but it may become a heresy *ex parte dicentis* when maintained in such a way that he who utters it has set his will against that of the Church. This becomes a matter of intention, however, and what happens in the secret of a man's soul is not easy to determine.

At that very time the Puritans of Boston were quite sure that they could know whether a man was of the elect and so worthy to be a citizen of the Republic of Regenerate Saints. In the mind of the Roman authorities, with many centuries of experience behind them, holiness was less easy to identify. A man had to have run his mortal course, and very concrete miracles had to come from his intercession above, before he was recognized as one of the elect. On earth all was very uncertain. What counted was behavior. The rest had to be left to God and the secret of the confessional.

The Holy Office knew it best of all. The very amplitude of its powers, which set it apart from the other Congregations (for it was not merely administrative as they were, but it was supreme court, judge, jury, and law-enforcer all in one), compelled it to be careful. Heresiology is no more of an exact science today than it was at the time of Athanasius. But, since a definition there has to be, it can come only operationally through form, procedure, and precedent. Heresy admits of no degree; but in practice propositions are of many kinds. They can be heretical, close to heresy, erroneous, temerarious, or simply offensive to the pious soul. To determine the exact degree is a juridical problem, based strictly on the consensus of the texts and on the weight of "grave opinion" in their interpretation.[4] In so far as there is no direct and proclaimed heresy involved, a qualification is always subject to revision and hence to reasonable (if submissive) question.

III

The present-day apologetic version, then, which settles the Galileo incident by charging the censors of 1616 with a "grave and deplorable error in using an altogether false principle as to the proper interpretation of Scripture"[5] is at best an evasion of the problem. The eleven wretched men, who have to bear a blame that should properly fall on the judges of 1632 and on certain others, were average officials who looked up their books and condensed in two paragraphs the "grave opinion" of established teaching. They had been asked categorically, and this was the answer. In the lack of any new weighting which should have been supplied by Grienberger and Bellarmine, it is difficult to see what else they could have done.

We have seen, for instance (on p. 93), from the learned pen of Father Hontheim: "Scripture and tradition speak again and again of the fire of hell, and there is no sufficient reason to take the statement metaphorically." This, then, is the consistent criterion of interpretation as of today, and the Qualifiers did not deviate from it. If he had not been allowed by the Pope in 1757 to understand the motion of the Sun allegorically, Father Hontheim would still today be in duty bound to believe the Ptolemaic position.

---

4. See Aquinas *Quaestiones quodlibetales* ix. 16, about the rule of faith: "It is certain that the judgment of the universal Church cannot possibly err in matters pertaining to the Faith; hence we must stand rather on the decisions the Pope judicially pronounces than by the opinions of men, however learned they may be in Holy Scripture." This, we may notice, applies specifically to dogmatic questions or to traditions which are no longer historically verifiable—in general, to things which cannot be discussed *de facto*.

5. J. Wilhelm, in *Catholic Encyclopedia* (New York: Appleton, 1910), art. "Galileo."

In fact, his colleagues still do believe what amounts to almost the same. Father Agostino Gemelli, a well-known physiologist in his own right and late Rector of the Gregorian University, stated in the press in 1953 that the increased belief in the occurrence of conscious life in other planets or galaxies that is noticed in present-day cosmological speculation can come only of an ignorance of theology; for theology, while leaving a completely open field to scientific speculation, is able to affirm categorically in advance of facts that there are not and cannot be any beings endowed with soul anywhere in the universe except on the Earth. This type of qualification, however individual, has considerable theological grounds to support it, of a more stringent nature indeed than those concerning the mobility of the Earth. It would probably be ratified if necessary, as the exclusion of evolutionary theories has been, and hang like a Damocles' sword over the heads of such astrophysicists as are willing to abide by Church rulings. A sacramental and dogmatic institution like the Church does not surrender its basic cosmological tenets at the behest of public opinion, or it would become an ethical culture society. At best it will decide to wait until its own mind is made up.

In other words, from the point of view of interpretation, the findings of 1616 were no mistake at all. They only became a mistake once they were declared to be such. But mistakes come and go, and this is not the point that hurt. It was the rash and unprecedented tampering with the underlying mechanism of change that created the crisis.

The issue becomes clearer if we take, not a present-day author, but the Vatican astronomer Settele, on whose repeated request Galileo's work was removed from the Index in 1822. Up to that date he had had to believe "with a true assent, internal and sincere," if not absolute, that the immobility of the Sun was tolerable since 1757, while Galileo was still wrong for suggesting it. The day after, he was allowed to change his mind. Well, of course, this is a caricature. Of course, the Church accepted perfectly well that he should have been a "Galileist"; in fact, she was herself persuaded by his reasons. She indorsed, in other words—as she had always indorsed—the idea that a man is entitled to entertain opinions that have been declared false and even to prove them right, so long as it is with the proper external submission. But that was exactly Galileo's position in his letters to Castelli and to Dini, in his *Letter to the Grand Duchess,* and in his behavior in 1632. He himself had inherited it from the doctors of the thirteenth century who had opposed the decision denying the existence of the antipodes.[6] The legal situation never had changed by one jot.

There are in the Church controversial matters in which the authority of the Fathers is divided or insufficiently expressed. There are, in fact, any number of them. On such issues, as Magalotti had learned in the Holy Office, the policy was that "without the declaration of a General Council, or without the most urgent necessity, they can never come to a head." That the cosmological question was of this kind was not only admitted tacitly (as Descartes remarked, Copernicanism was taught without objection); it had been proved by the *Letter to the Grand Duchess.* The forty pages of that letter, bristling with venerable texts, present an impressive counterbattery of opinions of the Fathers on the subject. No one had acknowledged it openly, but it had given pause to Caetani and to Barberini himself, as Galileo knew, and had caused them to have the decree of 1616 proclaim heliocentrism only "false" and to proclaim it so only *in forma communi.* It had been put into a kind of limbo from which it would have taken "some extravagant resolution," as Magalotti said, to move it to the formal status of heresy, for dogmatic truth is not manufactured overnight; it takes a vast and gradual convergence of opinion throughout Catholicity on the subject, and the Pope only makes it irrevocable by his pronouncement. It had been the wisdom of the Church to commit her word through the ages only on supernatural subjects which could not be challenged by any new discovery.

As for what concerned Nature or society, any slow change of opinion would eventually register. The trouble was that no legitimate change had ever been imagined that would not be slow. As we said in an earlier chapter, the Earth had already been half-

---

6. It is remarkable that throughout his pleadings this precedent never comes up. Even Copernicus, who referred to the point, ascribed the opinion to Lactantius, an individual. They knew that great administrations, like pretty women, will never admit to a mistake.

allowed to move "imperceptibly" after Cusanus; if it gained only a mile of speed a day, in less than two centuries it would be revolving inconspicuously and comfortably on its orbit, with no one to object. The world was a static affair, and knowledge even more so.

IV

Thus, when Bellarmine told Galileo that he must give up the opinion, he was not expecting an "absolute assent" but only obedience. "Galileo acquiesced and promised to obey." He pledged, in other words, not to commit his personal affirmation. He was not forbidden to entertain it in his mind as "mathematical" or "probable" or to discuss it quietly with his peers.[7] With time that brings all things, respectful pressure of educated minds might cause a change which would eventually register in official decisions. (It actually did in 1757.) The Jesuit mathematicians themselves, if left far in the background, were willing to be parties to the invisible conspiracy. It was Father Grienberger himself who stated that, if Galileo had not incurred the displeasure of the Company, he could have gone on writing freely about the motion of the Earth to the end of his days. Grienberger's judgment can hardly be suspected of heresy.

Galileo's crime lay in having perceived that change in the "new things" of science could not be so slow as expected. Catholicity did not have world enough and time to make up its mind at leisure, as was the case concerning papal infallibility. He saw "prematurely" (a term which in our fast-shifting times has forced its way even into police language) what ordinary minds like the Vatican astronomers could realize and communicate only a century too late. But his formal position was as correct as theirs. He had with great

7. We have the jurisprudence on it. In 1651 Father Caramuel Lobkowitz asked the Congregation for directives concerning cases of conscience submitted to him by people who were disturbed by Galileo's sentence. The answer was: "The Congregation did not deal with doctrine, but by order of the Pope prohibited [certain] actions by positive law." The authorities had nothing to object to the Father's own summing-up: "'When an opinion is thus forbidden, it is stated not that it is improbable but that it is not probable." This seems to have clarified the situation entirely.

care established his intention as strictly pious and submissive and had surrounded himself with the legal guaranties required. It was his bad luck and nothing else to run into a coalition of forces which decided that he must be liquidated.

But how to make him out as a heretic? Readers of American history may find an interesting parallel here with Governor Winthrop's problem in the case of Anne Hutchinson. In both cases there was only one way—to prove a criminal intention—and it was less easy to do in Rome than in the somewhat highhanded Bay State Republic. To go after men's minds was an unrewarding job, and not recommended, for who would 'scape whipping? The Commissary-General had to proceed gingerly. There was actually no such thing as a "thought crime" in his book, although heresy is theoretically defined as such. There was only identifiable acts of the will—what was currently called the "sowing of tares." Whatever evil intention there was had to be proved.

Now, Galileo, as we have seen, had taken great care to submit and check the intention with the Pope himself and then have it repeated back by the Master of the Holy Palace. He had been explicitly allowed to prove, if he could, that "it is impossible to get away from the Pythagorean doctrine, except for the reasons of Divine omnipotence dictated to him by our Lord's Holiness." He had been given by the Pope the proper title for the book which involved a comparison between the "Great World Systems." He had had his text prefaced, concluded, revised, and licensed. The simple fact, and the Commissary knew it, was that His Beatitude had changed his mind about the instructions after the book had come out. Even dogmatic almightiness could hardly turn that into an incrimination of the author. All he was entitled to do was suspend the book. Acute frustration was bound to result. Wrote Campanella desolately in his last letter to Galileo: "It seems fate that, the more we strive to serve our Masters, the more harshly they turn against us and maltreat us. God's will be done."

Such, then, was the predicament. If the trial could be based only on the injunction, they had a case. If the trial had to be based on the book, they had only the beginning of a case and must trust luck to bring it to a conclusion.

The heart of the matter was that the Pope had thought he could use Galileo for his purposes. He had found himself outwitted and serving Galileo's purposes instead. It was a very imponderable business—a situation which did not involve a demonstrable act of the will. But, still, intention is part of a contract. This contract had turned out to be a deal with one man's wits matched against the other's; and he needs a flameproof suit who plays a lone hand of poker with theocracy. Dissimulation of aim could become criminal, and there certainly had been dissimulation of a kind. It was a delicate matter, however, to make the charge stick unless the defendant committed mistakes during the interrogation. Once the trial was on, there would always be the risk that it would turn against the Master of the Holy Palace. We have seen these hesitations reflected in the report of the Preliminary Commission and in the long weeks of probing. The text appeared too well protected; charges against it could not be substantiated, as Niccolini writes.

Finally, there was only one thing to do. And that was to break precedent. Three experts for the prosecution had been chosen from among the members of the Preliminary Commission, as the Pope announced to the ambassador "between his teeth." Two at least were enemies of Galileo—Inchofer and Pasqualigo. And they were not of the Holy Office. It was their assignment to tear the veil of established convention and prove that the defendant had really "held" the doctrine he claimed only to discuss.[8]

It can hardly be maintained that this was not a breaking of precedent. Dozens of publications were held up or condemned every year for holding the most grievously erroneous views. But, in so far as their authors had submitted in advance to the judgment of their superiors, no question was made of their intention, and they were not even troubled in their careers. We have seen the case of Campanella and that of Bellarmine himself. Galileo was exactly in the same position, and he had been discussing a doctrine considered

8. A report from experts was in order. All that ought to have been needed for a regular prosecution was to establish that Galileo had violated the injunction "not to teach or discuss, in whatsoever way." It was easy to establish that. But, as we shall see, the Consultors went further and showed that Galileo "held" the opinion, so as to bring him into collision with Bellarmine's instructions.

simply "false." It was only after the success of the *Dialogue* that it suddenly became "the most perverse and pernicious matter that could be thought of." For that reason, a "novelty" indeed was needed in order to trap him. Once his evil intention was established a priori, it was a matter of maneuver to get him off the safe track and make him fall into either an admission or an untruth. In his eagerness to shy away from admission, there was a good chance that he might slip into the deeper chasm. This device does not bear a pretty name in the practice of the courts, but nothing better had been found to serve the intentions of His Beatitude.

To conclude, then—and this may help us over several strange features that will follow—the trial was conceived from the first as dictated by Reason of State, and as such above law and custom. All the outward show of regularity did not deceive anyone. Reason of State was held to justify many things; it led James I to sentence Balmerino, his innocent secretary, rather than face up to Bellarmine's rightful accusation of duplicity. It led authorities in Rome to trump up charges against a scientist and indefatigably to persecute his memory for three centuries after his death. It led Bismarck to alter the Ems dispatch, and the Japanese to strike at Pearl Harbor. It has led present-day powers to do such things as Tamerlane himself would have boggled at. There is no question here; all this is in order. Provided, of course, it succeeds. What made Galileo "find this persecution very strange," as Niccolini says, is that he was given all sorts of juridical make-pretense, as we still are given today, but never, then or later, a clear and authoritative explanation of what that Reason of State could be. He knew what the Pope had said but admitted it made no sense to him, as it made none to the ambassador. In the explanations that were given after his time, artful confusion has continued to prevail. Many writers seem to believe that by taking the famous injunction for granted, with adequate persistence, they may get history to accept it. They have not been wholly unsuccessful. But it does no credit to their inventiveness. It may be said that Reason of State will stand being officially explained only after a long lapse of time. True enough. Three centuries have passed, and we are still waiting.

XII

THE TRIAL

Judex ergo cum sedebit
Quidquid latet apparebit...
"DIES IRAE"

I

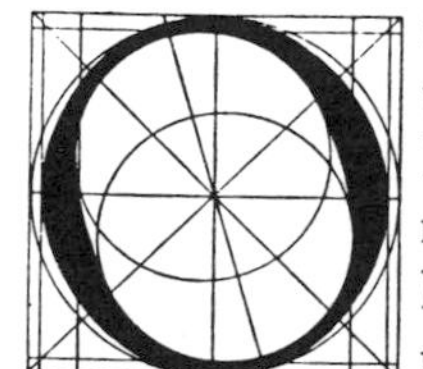

N THE twelfth of April, 1633, the first hearing took place before the Commissary-General of the Inquisition and his assistants. The Commissary's name was Father Vincenzo Maculano, or Macolani, da Firenzuola, which caused him to be currently called "Father Firenzuola" from the name of his home town. We know very little of this man whose career was to lead him later to the purple. He was, like all Inquisitors, a Dominican friar, but he had been singled out by the Pope (at least according to the talk of the town) not so much for his theological zeal as for the technical and administrative capacities he had shown in supervising the fortification of Castel Sant'Angelo. Urban VIII was no fanatic, and he liked to have humanists and executives in his entourage.

Galileo had officially surrendered to the Holy Office on that morning, for it was a standing rule that the accused were to be held imprisoned and in strict seclusion until the end of the trial. Out of consideration for his state of health and also for the Grand Duke's prestige, he was exceptionally allowed quarters in the Inquisition building itself, which was located close to the Vatican.

According to procedure, the defendant was put under oath and asked whether he knew or conjectured why he had been summoned.[1] He answered that he supposed it was on account of his last book. He was shown the book and identified it as his. They then passed on to the events of 1616. He said that he came to Rome in that year, and *of his own accord,* he specified,[2] in order to know what opinion it was proper to hold in the matter of the Copernican hypothesis and to be sure of not holding any but holy and Catholic views. These were soft words, but he had been advised to keep to the safe and submissive side. He was then asked about the conferences he had had with several prelates prior to the decree, and he explained that they had been due to the desire of those prelates to be instructed about Copernicus' book, which was difficult for laymen to understand. He could be glad now of his precaution to have put his arguments down in writing. The Inquisitor then asked what happened next.

A.: Respecting the controversy which had arisen on the aforesaid opinion that the Sun is stationary and that the Earth moves, it was decided by the Holy Congregation of the Index that such an opinion, considered as an established fact, contradicted Holy Scripture and was only admissible as a conjecture [*ex suppositione*], as it was held by Copernicus [*sic*].

Q.: Was this decision then communicated to him, and by whom?

A.: This decision of the Holy Congregation of the Index was made known to me by Cardinal Bellarmine.

Q.: Let him state what Cardinal Bellarmine told him about said decision, and whether he said anything else on the subject, and what.

A.: The Lord Cardinal Bellarmine signified to me that the aforesaid opinion of Copernicus might be held as a conjecture, as it had been held by Copernicus, and His Eminence was aware that, like Copernicus, I only held that opinion as a conjecture, which is evident from an answer of the same Lord Cardinal to a letter of Father Paolo Antonio Foscarini, provincial of the Carmelites, of which I have a copy, and in which these

---

1. See fols. 413 ff. of the Acts in Volume XIX of Favaro's National Edition of Galileo's *Works.* The questions are in Latin; the answers, in Italian.

2. It had become current, as we have seen from Riccardi's disclosures on p. 209, to say that he was summoned to Rome in 1616. Notwithstanding his denial here, it reoccurs in the official summary (see p. 280).

words occur: "It appears to me that Your Reverence and Signor Galileo act wisely in contenting yourselves with speaking *ex suppositione* and not with certainty." This letter of the Cardinal is dated April 12, 1615. It means, in other words, that that opinion, taken absolutely, must not be either held or defended.

This was neat. It was surely not the time to try to correct their obstinate preconceptions about Copernicus, if those preconceptions could be turned to some use. But Galileo was now requested to state what had been decreed in February, 1616, and communicated to him.

A.: In the month of February, 1616, the Lord Cardinal Bellarmine told me that, as the opinion of Copernicus, if adopted absolutely, was contrary to Holy Scripture, it must neither be held nor defended but that it could be taken and used hypothetically. In accordance with this I possess a certificate of Cardinal Bellarmine, given on May 26, 1616, in which he says that the Copernican opinion may neither be held nor defended, as it is opposed to Holy Scripture, of which certificate I herewith submit a copy.

Q.: When the above communication was made to him, were any other persons present, and who?

We can see Galileo suddenly getting suspicious. This was the first intimation that something more might have taken place on that day, for Riccardi, Serristori, and the Pope himself had mentioned only Bellarmine, and he was confident he knew exactly what Bellarmine had said. But Bellarmine had been dead these thirteen years, and he had only this piece of paper. He tries to be careful.

A.: When the Lord Cardinal made known to me what I have reported about the Copernican views, some Dominican Fathers were present, but I did not know them and have never seen them since.

Q.: Was any other command [*precetto*] communicated to him on this subject, in the presence of those Fathers, by them or anyone else, and what?

At this point the old man is becoming frankly scared. The Commissary is looking at a document in front of him; Galileo has no idea what the document may contain, and this is the mysterious Inquisition. He is afraid of falling into a trap; he is afraid of contradicting openly. We see thoughts racing through his mind. Was

Bellarmine's *precetto* something else, juridically, than what he thought it to be? He must have gone over it with Niccolini and his canonist friends. Could the whole decree be construed as a disguised bill of attainder? Had some words escaped his memory that made it a special command *ad personam?* Did anyone else make a move on that day? Could the presence of those Dominicans have meant something?

A.: I remember that the transaction took place as follows: The Lord Cardinal Bellarmine sent for me one morning and told me certain particulars which I had rather reserve for the ear of His Holiness before I communicate them to others.[3] But the end of it was that he told me that the Copernican opinion, being contradictory to Holy Scripture, must not be held or defended. It has escaped my memory whether those Dominican Fathers were present before or whether they came afterward; neither do I remember whether they were present when the Lord Cardinal told me the said opinion was not to be held. It may be that a command [*precetto*] was issued to me that I should not hold or defend the opinion in question, but I do not remember it, for it is several years ago.

Q.: If what was then said and enjoined upon him as a *precetto* were read aloud to him, would he remember it?

A.: I do not remember that anything else was said, nor do I know that I should remember what was said to me, even if it were read to me. I say freely what I do remember, because I do not think that I have in any way disobeyed the *precetto*, that is, have not by any means held or defended the said opinion that the Earth moves and that the Sun is stationary.

The Inquisitor now tells Galileo that the command which was issued to him before witnesses contained: "*that he must neither hold, defend, nor teach that opinion in any way whatsoever.*" Will he please to say whether he remembers in what way and by whom this was intimated to him.

A.: *I do not remember that the command was intimated to me by anybody but by the Cardinal verbally;* and I remember that the command was "not to hold or defend." It may be that "and not to teach"

3. No one has cared to go into this cryptic remark. Yet the fact that it implies information reserved for the Pope ought to mean that Bellarmine had told him of Maffeo Barberini's moderating intervention in the General Congregation in 1616. The "particulars" therefore

was also there. I do not remember it, neither the clause "in any way whatsoever" [*quovis modo*], but it may be that it was; for I thought no more about it or took any pains to impress the words on my memory, as a few months later I received the certificate now produced, of the said Lord Cardinal Bellarmine, of May 26, in which the order [*ordine*] given me, *not to hold or defend* that opinion, is expressly to be found. The two other clauses of the said command which have just been made known to me, namely, *not to teach* and *in any way*, I have not retained in my memory, I suppose because they are not mentioned in the said certificate, on which I have relied, and which I have kept as a reminder.

Q.: After the aforesaid *precetto* was issued to him, did he receive any permission to write the book that he has acknowledged was his?

The old man has stood his ground desperately, but he is obviously terrified. He has thought it better to concede that the notification in audience may have been some kind of command. He no longer knows where he stands, and this is no time to cite the Pope's ill-advised encouragements or to implicate the authorities. It might all fall back on his head. The only thing is to duck.

A.: I did not ask permission to write the book, because I did not consider that in writing it I was acting contrary to, far less disobeying, the command not to hold, defend, or teach that opinion.

[There follows a factual account of the negotiations concerning the printing.]

Q.: When asking permission to print the book, did he tell the Master of the Palace about the *precetto* which had been issued to him?

A.: I did not happen to discuss that command with the Master of the Palace when I asked for the imprimatur, for I did not think it necessary to say anything, because I had no doubts about it; for I have neither maintained nor defended in that book the opinion that the Earth moves and that the Sun is stationary but have rather demonstrated the opposite of the Copernican opinion and shown that the arguments of Copernicus are weak and not conclusive.

With this the first hearing was concluded. The very last statement is a poor job, for Simplicio's peroration could by no manner

---

were a brief account of the proceedings that were not disclosed and are alluded to in Buonamici's diary.

of means be construed as a "proof"; but by then Galileo was more dead than alive. His name below the proceedings is signed with a shaking hand. It cannot be said, however, that he lost his presence of mind. The statement that he had not told Riccardi about the *precetto* because he did not think it necessary may sound embarrassingly like Junior not telling Nurse what Mummy had told him to tell her, but it is not so at all. If we accept Galileo's undeviating position, that Bellarmine had simply notified him of the imminent decree, it would have sounded rather silly on his part to go and

SIGNATURES OF GALILEO ON THE PROTOCOLS OF THE TRIAL

The first signature comes after the interrogation of April 12 above. The second is to be found at the end of the protocol of April 30 (see p. 256), when he has regained some assurance.

solemnly remind Riccardi that he hoped he knew a decree had been issued in 1616. Riccardi would have answered jokingly: "I trust this is what your conversations with His Holiness have been about, or else what are we doing here?"[4]

---

4. That there *had* been a personal element in Bellarmine's convocation was obvious, but it has nothing to do with the case in point. The whole proceedings of 1616 had been taken *in causam Galilaei mathematici* and that was why Bellarmine had summoned him: to inform him by allusion of the considerations which were behind the published decree. He must have told him at the same time of the moderating action of Barberini on the Pope, as we can infer from Galileo's reserved statement at the interrogation, and only then explained to him that the forthcoming decree made it mandatory that the Copernican doctrine be "neither defended nor held" (although the book of Copernicus was expected to come out again after correction). It meant: "Before talking about it again, it is a good thing to make sure one has given it up as a commitment. Since you represent that commitment in the

It was quite another matter if there had been a formal injunction of the Inquisition in 1616 not to teach, defend, *or in any way discuss* the theory, for that involved a suspicion of heresy, or at least resistance, and would require an elaborate rehabilitation before the author could write again. And surely, even then, the Pope was at fault, for he should have known; the instructions of February 25, as we have seen (p. 125), prescribed, in case of recalcitrance, an injunction, and even arrest, and the report of Bellarmine on March 3 should have reflected those events. It actually did not, and that is the important point. So the Pope could not know. It was Galileo, he said, who should have come and told all in due obedience. Now he was under the odium of "having been found out."

All this is ridiculous and pitiful, of course. It was no time to be playing at Nurse and Mummy. A great and rigid authoritarian administration with a thought police which is supposed to know all should at least keep its records straight. Before granting permission to write the book, the Pope should either have remembered or have had his memory refreshed, or someone from the Inquisition might

---

public eye, we are telling you in advance of publication. Please be careful." The Cardinal must have added: "We know too well your pious sentiments not to trust, etc." Translated into a statement for public use, it becomes exactly Bellarmine's certificate. These simple facts had better be spelled out, to eliminate the confusion raised on this point by Berti, Gebler, Scartazzini, and others. Thus it was quite true that the whole content of the communication had remained impersonal and implied no more than the words of the decree. The Pope knew them well, and as he understood them he had not found it necessary to give Galileo special dispensation when he approved, in 1624 and in 1630, of his discussing the ideas hypothetically. What he had done was to issue a directive interpreting the policy of 1616 in the light of the requirements of 1630, which involved the writing of a book by Galileo under his high supervision. To assume that the Pope did not know about the summons would have been ridiculous, since he himself, as a cardinal, had sat in on the Congregation *in causam Galilaei* of February 24, 1616, which ordered the summons, and had obviously been informed, although he was not present on March 3, of Bellarmine's favorable report. Whatever personal intimation there may have been in Bellarmine's summons had thus been explicitly revoked by his directives of 1624 and 1630.

have told him. Worse: as a party to the secret deliberations of the Congregation of 1616, the Pope could not possibly have forgotten, if the injunction really took place, that he and the other members had been secretly directed to handle Galileo as a dangerous character; yet he had publicly favored and encouraged him in 1624, and now he was acting injured innocence, because there was no mention of an injunction in the *Decreta.*

About all of this Galileo was still in the dark. So far as he knew, all might have been in order, some kind of injunction might have been mysteriously made out in due form, and he might have been hanging himself by obstinately refusing to admit it. Yet he felt it safest to cling to what he knew. He remembered nothing else; he had never acknowledged anything else, except a simple notification not to hold or defend.

The Inquisitor had been dragging him along on an equivocal term. When he said *precetto,* he implied from the start a personal prohibition (see p. 239). For Galileo, it meant only the notification from the Cardinal. It is the text of that notification that seems to him to be challenged, until the Inquisitor asks insistently whether he remembers being addressed by anyone else. But he does not go beyond that, and down to the very end—that is, until the sentence—Galileo is never told that it *was* someone else and that it was the Commissary-General of the time. Hence his answer has to remain correspondingly indefinite. Was this done so he should not be able to deny explicitly that the Commissary had ever spoken? Was it in order to create the equivocation so cleverly exploited in the summary, as we shall see later? Was it because it was a principle never to disclose the charges? In any case, it is only when he understands that he is really being asked about a "command" that he replies anxiously: "It may be that a command was enjoined on me, but I do not remember." From that moment, he is on his guard. He is obviously trying to remember whether anyone said anything that he had better admit. He does not have a lawyer who could ask what kind of injunction they are talking about.[5] But, as the Inquisitor

5. Counsel for accused was excluded since the Council of Valence in 1245, on the grounds that "lawyers delayed the proceedings with their noise [*strepitus*]." There was an official called *advocatus reorum*

returns five times to the question of who had addressed him and tries to draw him out in various ways, Galileo answers again and again: "No one except Bellarmine."

In so doing, he has foiled the whole maneuver. For it had been clearly the Inquisition's intention to extract out of him, were it in a moment of bewilderment or fright, the admission that there *had* been a special command by the Commissary enjoined on that day. Such an admission in a signed protocol would have been a substitute for all the irregularities of the injunction. From that moment, the document of 1616 would have become fully legal. As it was, instead, Galileo had re-established consistently the fact that Bellarmine had informed him only of the contents of the coming decree; and thus the text of the decree remained the only legal directive to be considered both by him and by the censor. The injunction, on the other hand, if assumed valid, would have been a directive to the censor to suppress all and any writings of *this* particular person in the matter of Copernicus, or to prosecute them if published.

II

Where Galileo instead had walked into the delayed-action trap in his very attempt to play safe was in the last statement in his interrogation. To say that he had demonstrated the opposite of the Copernican opinion sounded very much like an attempt to fool the judges. It is not impossible that he should have reserved just such a line of argument, relying on some geometrical legerdemain and on his persuasive capacity. To say, however, that this was "why" he had not told about the notification made it worse. Like so many prisoners under questioning, he was protesting too much. It worked to his undoing, for five days after the audience the results of the official examination of the text came in, and they were not such as to make his plea look good. Three Counselors of the Inquisition, Augustinus Oregius (the Pope's theologian), Melchior Inchofer, and Zacharias Pasqualigo, delivered their reports, which came to the same conclusion: The author had not only "discussed" the for-

---

who functioned, however, only *in camera* if he did at all. The accused was never told the charges until the sentence.

bidden view; he had maintained and taught and defended it, and there was a "vehement suspicion" that he was inclined to it and even held it to this day. Inchofer and Pasqualigo gave a long list of passages which could leave no doubt. On the whole, their quotations were correct, in that they were faithful to the sense.

We shall summarize Inchofer's seven-page report, which is the most explicit.

1. The accused does teach, for, as St. Augustine says, what is teaching except to communicate knowledge? Now Galileo certainly does so and has done so since his pamphlet on the sunspots. It is of a teacher to hand on to his disciples first those precepts of a science which are easiest and clearest, so as to enlist their interest, and to present the science as a new one, which attracts curious minds wondrously. Moreover, defendant makes it appear as though a number of effects which have been already truly and authoritatively explained otherwise could be solved only by the motion of the Earth.

2. He does defend. One may be said to defend an opinion even if he does not refute the contrary one; all the more, then, if he tries to destroy that utterly. In law this is called an impugnation.—Copernicus only proposed a more convenient method for computations [this interpretation is, as usual, due to Osiander's Preface], whereas Galileo tries to confirm and establish it as a doctrine and with new reasons, which is twice to defend.—Because, if the intention had been disputation and intellectual exercise, he would not so proudly and arrogantly traduce and ridicule Aristotle, Ptolemy, and all the truths he will not acknowledge. And, if he does so in writing, there is no doubt he must have done it much more in conversation.

3. He does hold. He does so on two counts, through necessary conclusions and also through his assertiveness, for we need not consider valid the occasional pretended protestations that he interposes in order not to appear to go against the decree. As for the reasons given in his Preface, it is certainly not the "mutterings against Church Consultors" which could have moved a serious man to undertake such a work; and I did not come across a single publication of ultramontane authors in which this matter of the decree is as much as mentioned, not to speak of the Consultors. It is sure that of Catholics no one would have dared. And then, if this was the motive, why did he not undertake really to defend the decree and the Holy Congregation? But this is so far from his thoughts that he goes on to arm the Copernican opinion with new arguments that no ultramontane ever suggested, and he does so in

Italian, surely not the language best suited for the needs of ultramontane or other scholarship but the one most indicated to bring over to his side the ignorant vulgar among whom errors most easily take hold.

4. The author claims to discuss a mathematical hypothesis, but he gives it physical reality, which mathematicians never do. Moreover, if defendant had not adhered firmly to the Copernican opinion and believed it physically true, he would not have fought for it with such asperity, nor would he have written the *Letter to the Grand Duchess*, nor would he have held up to ridicule those who maintain the accepted opinion, and as if they were dumb mooncalves [*hebetes et pene stolidos*] described them as hardly deserving to be called human beings.[6]

Indeed, if he had attacked some individual thinker for his inadequate arguments in favor of the stability of the Earth, we might still put a favorable construction on his text; but, as he holds all to be mental pygmies [*homunciones*] who are not Pythagorean or Copernican, it is clear enough what he has in mind, especially as he praises by contrast William Gilbert, a perverse heretic and a quibbling and quarrelsome defender [*rixosum et cavillosum patronum*] of this opinion.

This last sentence affords a rewarding glimpse into the ways of thought of the thought police. The good Jesuit never stops to consider whether the magnetic phenomena discovered by Gilbert might not be highly relevant, as in fact they are, to a discussion of physical principles.[7] For him, the only point is that Gilbert is a perverse

---

6. "I have met with such arguments that I blush to rehearse them, not so much to spare the shame to their authors, the names of whom might remain perpetually concealed, as because I am ashamed so deeply to degrade the honour of mankind" (*Dialogue*, p. 291).

7. This Gilbert episode has a weird sequel that is worth recounting, were it only to show by one example among many how Galileo's person goes on forever being ground between the upper and the nether millstone. In the 1840's, Arago, then the great authority in French astronomy, wrote some comments about the affair. He stood, needless to say, for Science. But, being also a pillar of the state, he thought he had to strike an impartial note. After making out Galileo to be not much of a scientist (the Encyclopedist preconception, carried on by Delambre and Chasles), he remarked that he was even less of a moral character, witness his cowardly surrender before the authorities and the "base envy" he evidenced with respect to Gilbert. Now here is the relevant passage in the *Dialogue:* "Yes, I am whole-

heretic, and hence guilt by association is established. "Quibbling" and "quarrelsome" are hardly apt descriptions of Gilbert's scientific style; they are stock adjectives from Inchofer's Scholastic equipment, roughly equivalent to the present-day "subversive."

But if, intellectually, this expert is the *homuncio* whom Galileo had sized up well in advance, he is otherwise shrewd and competent enough. He pins down the quarry. His report in its relentless animus is well worthy of the hand that wrote the *Tractatus syllepticus*. The defendant is shown to have transgressed not only the questionable injunction but Bellarmine's direct notification "not to hold or defend."

One cannot but wonder what had happened to the previous deliberations hinted at by Monsignor Serristori: "All points have been allowed to drop, except one." Such helpful hints could have come only from the Commissary's office, and Galileo had seized on them for guidance in preparing his defense. The injunction alone provided a legal point, and Niccolini could confirm it, for Galileo knew himself triply protected against a trial of mere intention: by the Pope's authorization, by the explicit instructions to the licensers, and by the license itself. The first day of the questioning had not belied it, for the Commissary had insisted on nothing but the injunction. Hence Galileo had understood this to be still the dangerous point and felt that he was easing the task for any leniently disposed judge by making a stand on the injunction and by abounding

---

heartedly for Gilbert's magnetic philosophy, and I think that those who have read his book and tried his experiments will bear me company therein. . . . I extremely praise, admire, and envy this author that an idea so stupendous should have come into his mind touching a thing handled by infinite great intellects and hit upon by none of them. I think him, moreover, worthy of extraordinary applause for the many new and true observations that he made, to the disgrace of so many fanciful authors who write what they do not know." Needless to say, Arago had never read the *Dialogue*, as no one in France had done; he thought he could trust the word of some Inchofer of his time about its contents. There seem to have been a great number of such agents around, judging from the revolting lies they managed to accredit even among Protestant scholars.

otherwise in the sense of pious conformism. And, now that the reports had come in, it turned out that he had only been making a noose to hang himself.

Does this again imply Machiavellian duplicity on the part of the authorities? We have tried to show in the previous chapter what the situation seems to have been. The search for the point of indictment had led to a long-drawn-out fumble between different conceptions; and, as the first scene comes to a close, we see those conceptions embodied in two factions which are still far from agreeing on a common line. The Dominicans of the Inquisition, no longer the ruthless ones of a generation before, were still trying to handle the affair on a restrictive legalistic basis; but they had against them the will of the Pope and the plans of a curial group allied with the Jesuits, of whom men like Inchofer were the spearhead, who were pressing for judicial slaughter. The hints dropped by the officials, which were intended to help Galileo, had led him astray. The Jesuit faction had outmaneuvered its opponents and sprung its trap.[8]

This was in truth legal "railroading," as we have said, for in those times it was well understood that a man could go quite far in playing "double truth" and yet stay within judicial orthodoxy, as long as he covered himself with explicit clauses of submission—and an official license. At most he could have been asked to re-

---

8. On opening the proceedings, the authorities had to take two possibilities into account: either the defendant acknowledged the injunction, and then he was technically guilty of relapse and could be sentenced on that alone, but he could be conceded extenuating circumstances; or he denied it, and then he could be further prosecuted (*a*) for evasion and (*b*) for "holding" the condemned opinion. By sticking strictly to the letter of his instructions, Galileo might have contended that, however much he had erred in the language, he had never deviated from a hypothetical discussion. On this point it would have been difficult to break him down except by torture, which was against the rules for a man of seventy, and more, in his condition. But there was enough to make out vehement suspicion if required. Actually, through his last denial, the defendant had put himself into a worse position than that. At this point, as we have indicated, there appeared two opposing factions among the judges. This sketch may help us infer which course may have been advocated by either.

write in a "problematic" form.[9] One-half of the existing literature could otherwise have been condemned by such methods.

We must insist on this point, because Inchofer's report may look to the modern reader more objective than it really is. To demonstrate that Galileo considered the Copernican argument as convincing for human reason was to hit him below the belt, for that was exactly what he had been supposed to do under the Master of the Palace's written instructions of July 19, 1631: "Signor Galilei will have to add as a peroration the reasons from divine omnipotence dictated to him by Our Lord's Holiness, which must quiet the mind, even if there were no way out of the Pythagorean arguments [*ancorchè da gl'argomenti Pitagorici non se ne potesse uscire*]." That was why the Preliminary Commission, although summoned by the Pope in his anger, had found itself compelled to conclude lamely: "The faults that we have found might be corrected, if the book is deemed worth publishing." How little, how miserably little, correction could entail technically is shown by what happened more than a century later, in 1744.

In that year a Pope of great sense, Benedict XIV (still affectionately known in Italy as "Papa Lambertini"), gave permission to print a revised edition of the *Dialogue,* although Galileo and Copernicanism itself were and remained under condemnation. Now in this "revised" edition *not one word* of the text has been altered, and only a few marginal headings expunged or modified by the insertion of an *if* which makes them into "probable" statements. Such was, and had always been, the formal meaning of the command not to "hold" an opinion. It had a mile-long jurisprudence behind it. Gali-

---

9. As a matter of curious precedent, this was exactly the solution suggested by the Jesuit General Acquaviva to Bellarmine when the latter's *Controversies* were being put on the Index in 1590; not to retract any of his opinions but simply to change over the chapter headings from the negative to the problematical form: "Whether, etc." Yet Bellarmine's opinions had been declared erroneous by the Pope himself and not by a secondary Congregation, as was the case with heliocentrism. What had drawn the attention of Inchofer in the *Dialogue,* from the juridical point of view, were the few strictly affirmative passages, one of them a small marginal heading: "The Sun does not move."

leo had some right (if the story is true) to challenge the cardinals on the day of his sentence to show him what could be wrong with his book. But the Consultors' report had driven him to break on the rock that he had tried to avoid by steering the discussion around to real issues. As he lay there, day after day, in the building of the Inquisition, racked with acute sciatic pains and intestinal trouble, for all that he had fine rooms and Niccolini's own majordomo to attend him, he might as well have been confined like anyone else in the dark holds of the Castle.

III

Weeks passed, and nothing happened. The judges were deliberating. The Inquisition was always slow. But in this case we can guess why it was being slow. The Inquisitors had a clear case already, and they did not know what to do with it. In the exploratory phase they had been worried about the rather shaky personal injunction which was the keystone of the case as it had been handed to them. Now they could feel they had gotten past that, for the defendant's denials, in the light of the Consultors' report, made as clear an incrimination as anyone could need to put the machinery into gear—if this was what was really wanted. The Inquisition had been built into a dreadful apparatus in order to make terrifying examples whenever needed, so that no one should feel secure. Once the procedure had been turned on, a man was virtually at their mercy. This time they had been requested by the Pope to oblige with a political performance and a "limited example." It would be like administering a shampoo with a Bessemer converter. Some of the judges at least were balking at this point—perhaps even, at last, the Pope himself.

We know this from what followed, which does credit to all concerned. Cardinal Francesco Barberini, who was himself one of the ten judges, had put discreet pressure on the Commissary to find a way out. One day the Commissary walked into Galileo's room and sat down with him. It was Ivanov coming to Rubashov. The story is told in a letter written to the Cardinal, which was unearthed by Pieralisi in 1833:[10]

10. The text of the letter will be analyzed later on (see p. 293).

In compliance with the commands of His Holiness, I yesterday informed the Most Eminent Lords of the Holy Congregation of Galileo's case, the position of which I briefly reported. Their Eminences approved of what has been done thus far and took into consideration, on the other hand, various difficulties with regard to the manner of pursuing the case and of bringing it to an end. More especially as Galileo has in his examination denied what is plainly evident from the book written by him, since in consequence of this denial there would result the necessity for greater rigor of procedure and less regard to the other considerations belonging to this business. Finally, I suggested a course, namely, that the Holy Congregation should grant me permission to treat extrajudicially with Galileo, in order to render him sensible of his error and bring him, if he recognizes it, to a confession of the same. This proposal appeared at first sight too bold, not much hope being entertained of accomplishing this object by merely adopting the method of argument with him; but, upon my indicating the grounds upon which I had made the suggestion, permission was granted me. That no time might be lost, I entered into discourse with Galileo yesterday afternoon, and after many and many arguments and rejoinders had passed between us, by God's grace, I attained my object, for I brought him to a full sense of his error, so that he clearly recognized that he had erred and had gone too far in his book. And to all this he gave expression in words of much feeling, like one who experienced great consolation in the recognition of his error, and he was also willing to confess it judicially. He requested, however, a little time in order to consider the form in which he might most fittingly make the confession, which, as far as its substance is concerned, will, I hope, follow in the manner indicated.

I have thought it my duty at once to acquaint your Eminence with this matter, having communicated it to no one else; for I trust that His Holiness and your Eminence will be satisfied that in this way the affair is being brought to such a point that it may soon be settled without difficulty. The court will maintain its reputation; it will be possible to deal leniently with the culprit; and, whatever the decision arrived at, he will recognize the favor shown him, with all the other consequences of satisfaction herein desired. Today I think of examining him in order to obtain the said confession; and having, as I hope, received it, it will only remain to me further to question him with regard to his intention and to receive his defense plea; that done, he might have [his] house assigned to him as a prison, as hinted to me by your Eminence, to whom I offer my most humble reverence.

Your Eminence's most humble and
most obedient servant,

FRA VINC°. DA FIRENZUOLA

ROME, April 28, 1633

One wonders what the initial conversation between the two may have been like. It makes one regret that the tape recorder was not in existence; for, this once at least, it was Galileo who had something on the Commissary. He had received in October a letter in which Castelli reported a meeting with Firenzuola, whom he had known for a long time, he said, as a competent military engineer and "a decent person." Castelli had gone to Firenzuola when the first trouble was stirring and, as between monks, had talked to him as vividly and "heretically" as he knew how. "I told him I had no scruple in holding firmly that the Earth moves and that the Sun stands still and that I saw no reason for prohibiting the *Dialogue*. The Father told me that he was of the same opinion and that these questions should not be determined with the use of the authority of Holy Writ. He even told me he intended to write on the subject and would show it to me."

Thus, Galileo knew that the reluctant dragon who had been ordered to devour him held really the same opinion that he did; and there must have been much curious sparring between the two on the lofty subject of theological interpretation. After "many and many arguments and rejoinders," the Commissary must have felt that he was getting nowhere and told him the facts bluntly, somewhat like this:

"My dear Signor Galileo, you do not seem to realize your position. You insist on talking about your text, while I have not asked you about it. You still want us to believe both the rightness of your thought and the purity of your intention, allowing at most that you misundersood the instructions. You think you can make a stand on Bellarmine's certificate. But the Holy Office cannot be defied like that. It is desired from high quarters, as you realize, that we should make an example, and we are going to. The question is: How far do you want to push us?

"You may quote the licenses again. You may try to allege that the injunction we have was—shall we say—well, lacked your signature. You are going to say that you were encouraged by high quarters to discuss the doctrine and that one cannot discuss it without teaching the contents. But don't you see that in that case you compel us to go into your motives? Don't tell me that your intention is not in question. It is. And I am very much afraid that it might come out, God forbid, that you were, and are, a Copernican. Please—you are not talking to Firenzuola now; you are talking to the Commissary. That you held, as I was saying, the opinion all along and that you do even now—with dissimulation and pertinacity in the face of your inquirers—hold it. I might just as well tell you that this is the way it looks, now that the experts' report upon your book has come in. This would be quite enough in itself. For Cardinal Bellarmine left you in no doubt about the Church's intentions; you promised to obey and then chose to disregard them. You did try to outwit us and affirm your will, which has become contradictory to that of the Church on theological matters. May I add that you further used the freedom you had been given to slip in a couple of propositions which directly deny the transcendence of the Divine Mind. You know what that is called, don't you? A real procedure *de vehementi,* once started, cannot be so easily checked. We shall have to go through the routine of rigorous questioning, by regrettable means if necessary, and the admission will come out. After that there is only our mercy, which means perpetual incarceration in the prisons of the Holy Office. Nobody wants that.

"If you would only understand, you ought to see that a plea of disobedience is still your best bet. Admit it. Plead forgetfulness, complacency, pride, vanity, conceit—choose your own out of the catalogue of venial sins—and we shall have no need for inquiring further. You will get off with a light spanking, and everybody, please believe me, will be much the happier."

Whatever the words, this was the gist of it, as is clearly indicated in the letter, and it was well said. It was the stroke of lightning that rent the veil of Galileo's obsolete Renaissance convictions. He had been introduced to the modern state.

When he was called in two days later, April 30, he was asked whether he had anything to say. He spoke as follows:

In the course of some days' continuous and attentive reflection on the interrogations put to me on the twelfth of the present month, and in particular as to whether, sixteen years ago, an injunction was intimated to me by order of the Holy Office, forbidding me to hold, defend, or teach "in any manner" the opinion that had just been condemned—of the motion of the Earth and the stability of the Sun—it occurred to me to reperuse my printed *Dialogue,* which for three years I had not seen, in order carefully to note whether, contrary to my most sincere intention, there had, by inadvertence, fallen from my pen anything from which a reader or the authorities might infer not only some taint of disobedience on my part but also other particulars which might induce the belief that I had contravened the orders of the Holy Church.

Being, by the kind permission of the authorities, at liberty to send about my servant, I succeeded in procuring a copy of my book, and, having procured it, I applied myself with the utmost diligence to its perusal and to a most minute consideration thereof. And as, owing to my not having seen it for so long, it presented itself to me, as it were, like a new writing and by another author, I freely confess that in several places it seemed to me set forth in such a form that a reader ignorant of my real purpose might have had reason to suppose that the arguments brought on the false side, and which it was my intention to confute, were so expressed as to be calculated rather to compel conviction by their cogency than to be easy of solution.

Two arguments there are in particular—the one taken from the solar spots, the other from the ebb and flow of the tide—which in truth come to the ear of the reader with far greater show of force and power than ought to have been imparted to them by one who regarded them as inconclusive and who intended to refute them, as indeed I truly and sincerely held and do hold them to be inconclusive and admitting of refutation. And, as an excuse to myself for having fallen into an error so foreign to my intention, not contenting myself entirely with saying that, when a man recites the arguments of the opposite side with the object of refuting them, he should, especially if writing in the form of dialogue, state these in their strictest form and should not cloak them to the disadvantage of his opponent—not contenting myself, I say, with this excuse, I resorted to that of the natural complacency which every man feels with regard to his own subtleties and in showing himself more skilful than the generality of men in devising, even in favor of false propositions, ingenious and plausible arguments. With all this, although with Cicero "avidior sim gloriae quam sat est," if I had now to set forth the same reasonings, without doubt I should so weaken them that they should not be able to make an apparent show of that force of which they are really and essentially devoid. My error, then, has been—and I confess it—one of vainglorious ambition and of pure ignorance and inadvertence.

This is what it occurs to me to say with reference to this particular and which suggested itself to me during the reperusal of my book.

After this declaration, the defendant was dismissed; but he came back after a moment (*post paullulum*), asking to be allowed to make a supplementary statement:

And in confirmation of my assertion that I have not held and do not hold as true the opinion which has been condemned, of the motion of the Earth and stability of the Sun—if there shall be granted to me, as I desire, means and time to make a clearer demonstration thereof, I am ready to do so; and there is a most favorable opportunity for this, seeing that in the work already published the interlocutors agree to meet again after a certain time to discuss several distinct problems of Nature not connected with the matter discoursed of at their meetings. As this affords me an opportunity of adding one or two other "days," I promise to resume the arguments already brought in favor of the said opinion, which is false and has been condemned, and to confute them in such most effectual manner as by the blessing of God may be supplied to me. I pray, therefore, this holy Tribunal to aid me in this good resolution and to enable me to put it in effect.

By enlisting the co-operation of Galileo, the Commissary had obtained the admission he needed, and with it he had regained the initiative over his opponents.

IV

Historians have wept unrestrained tears over this final self-degradation of the great man. Nothing apparently would have satisfied them except his being roasted at the stake in Campo di Fiori, as Bruno had been thirty-three years before. In fact, it was a rational move, and it would have obtained for Galileo all that he really wanted—the circulation of the *Dialogue*. No doubt it was bitter to him. He skipped it in his first statement and then drove himself back to say it. He knew he had to say it. It was what Niccolini had advised, much earlier in the game, and what he suggested again now.[11] In an age which laid so much more weight than ours on formalities, everyone knew the difference between due form and intention. Kepler himself, the blameless and fearless Kepler, had thought well in 1619 to send to his bookseller in Italy a letter to be shown to the authorities, so they would not prohibit his *Harmonice mundi*. Although a fervid Protestant, he avowed himself to be "a son of the Church" and added: "As much as I have been able to understand of the Catholic doctrine I not only submit to but indorse it with my reason, and I have tried to show it in several passages of this work." The censor must have raised his eyebrows in wonderment over such a peculiar "son of the Church," but what Kepler lacked was only practice in the proper language. Anyway, on the Index forthwith did he go.

Moralist historians do not seem to notice that their perspective is that of believers in another religion. They would have Galileo behave like Jerome of Prague or like a prophet of Bruno's strange un-Christian God. They forget that he was a member of the Apostolic Roman communion and had to submit in some way. Quite apart from the personal inconvenience of being burned at the stake, it would have been a sin of diabolical pride on his part to push the Vicar of Christ into committing a crime.

He had gambled and lost. He was not a religious visionary being asked to renounce his vision. He was an intelligent man who had taken heavy risks to force an issue and to change a policy for the good of his Faith. He had been snubbed; he had nothing to do but to pay the price and go home. The scientific truth would be able to take care of itself.

He had realized at last that the authorities were not interested in truth but only in authority. They did not expect him to change his mind. They wanted, most illegally, to kill it; and he was going to consider his own interests henceforth. In this new clarifying spirit of mutual disrespect, he proposed a deal *in extremis*. But it

---

11. Dispatch of May 22. Niccolini, after seeing the Pope, is suddenly afraid again that it may come to the prohibition of the book, unless it is decided to have him write an apology, "as I suggested to His Beatitude." This means that, in his recent deal with Galileo, the Commissary had intimated that a corrected version would be allowed.

was too late. The reigning faction had decided it was not going to be outsmarted again.

His suggestion was allowed to drop. But, in any case, the dangerous passage had been negotiated: from now on, the Commissary was empowered to carry on interrogations only *pro forma.* True to his promise, Firenzuola released the prisoner in the custody of the ambassador, who was surprised and overjoyed to see him arrive back at the Villa Medici. "It is a fearful thing," he wrote to the Grand Duke, "to have to do with the Inquisition. The poor man has come back more dead than alive."

The next interrogation on May 10 had been obviously prearranged in the tête-à-tête, for Firenzuola, on opening it, informed the defendant, according to the rules, that eight days were allowed him to present a defense if he wished to submit one; and Galileo handed it in at once. It was as follows:

When asked if I had signified to the Reverend Father, the Master of the Holy Palace, the injunction privately laid upon me, about sixteen years ago, by the order of the Holy Office, not to hold, defend, or "in any way" teach the doctrine of the motion of the Earth and the stability of the Sun, I answered that I had not done so. And, not being questioned as to the reason why I had not intimated it, I had no opportunity to add anything further. It now appears to me necessary to state the reason, in order to demonstrate the purity of my intention, ever foreign to the practice of simulation or deceit in any operation I engage in.

I say, then, that, as at that time reports were spread abroad by evil-disposed persons to the effect that I had been summoned by the Lord Cardinal Bellarmine to abjure certain of my opinions and teachings and also to submit to penitence for them, I was thus constrained to apply to his Eminence and to solicit him to furnish me with an attestation, explaining the cause for which I had been summoned before him; which attestation I obtained in his own handwriting, and it is the same that I now produce with the present document. From this it clearly appears that it was merely announced to me that the doctrine attributed to Copernicus, of the motion of the Earth and the stability of the Sun, must not be held or defended; but that, beyond this general announcement affecting everyone, there should have been ordered anything to me in particular, no trace thereof appears in it.

Having, then, as a reminder, this authentic attestation in the handwriting of the very person who informed me of the command, I made no further application of thought or memory with regard to the words employed in orally announcing to me the said order not to hold or defend the doctrine in question; so that the two articles of the order—in addition to the injunction not to "hold" or "defend" it—to wit, the words "not to teach it" and "in any way whatsoever"—which, I hear, are contained in the order enjoined on me, and registered—struck me as quite novel and as if I had not heard them before; and I do not think I ought to be disbelieved when I urge that in the course of fourteen or sixteen years I had lost all recollection of them, especially as I had no need to give any particular thought to them, having in my possession so authentic a reminder in writing. Now, if the said two articles be left out, and those two only be retained which are noted in the accompanying attestation, there is no doubt that the injunction contained in the latter is the same command as that contained in the decree of the Holy Congregation of the Index. Hence it appears to me that I have a reasonable excuse for not having notified to the Master of the Holy Palace about the command privately imposed upon me, it being the same as that of the Congregation of the Index.

Now, if so be my book was not subject to a stricter censorship than that made binding by the decree of the Index, it will, it appears to me, be sufficiently plain that I adopted the surest and most becoming method of having it guaranteed and purged of all shadow of taint, inasmuch as I handed it to the Supreme Inquisitor at the very time when many books dealing with the same matters were being prohibited solely by virtue of the said decree. After what I have now stated, I would confidently hope that the idea of my having knowingly and deliberately violated the command imposed upon me will henceforth be entirely banished from the minds of my most eminent and wise judges; hence those faults which are seen scattered throughout my book have not been artfully introduced with any concealed or other than sincere intention but have only inadvertently fallen from my pen, owing to a vainglorious ambition and complacency in desiring to appear more subtle than the generality of popular writers, as indeed in another deposition I have confessed; which fault I shall be ready to correct with all possible industry whenever I may be commanded or permitted by Their Most Eminent Lordships.

Lastly, it remains for me to beg you to take into consideration my pitiable state of bodily indisposition, to which, at the age of seventy years, I have been reduced by ten months of constant mental anxiety and the fatigue of a long and toilsome journey at the most inclement season—together with the loss of the greater part of the years to which, from my previous condition of health, I had the prospect. I am persuaded and encouraged to do so by the faith I have in the clemency and goodness of the most Eminent Lords, my judges; with the hope that they may be pleased, in answer to my prayer, to remit what may appear to their entire justice the rightful addition that is still lacking to such sufferings to make up an adequate punishment for my crimes, out of consideration for my declining age, which, too, humbly commends itself to them. And I would equally commend to their consideration my honor and reputation, against the calumnies of ill-wishers, whose persistence in detracting from my good name may be inferred from the necessity which constrained me to procure from the Lord Cardinal Bellarmine the attestation which accompanies this.

The world will long remember the touching appeal for mercy. What it seems to have forgotten is that it concludes what amounts to a very strong defense, so confident and prompt indeed that one is led again to imagine some previous helpful hints from the Commissary himself. Galileo goes as far as he dares in calling his accusers a pack of liars. The expressions "not to teach it" and "in any way whatsoever" had struck him as "quite novel" and as "not heard . . . before." So they were indeed—and to the Pope himself for that matter. (The accused still had no word of a specific injunction by Father Segizi as separate from Bellarmine's command.) He ventured to suggest coolly that they be soft-pedaled henceforth. There is no mistaking the intimation. After politely granting that he might possibly have forgotten the full command, he goes on to dismiss that possibility in the sentence that we have italicized (in the original: "Che poi, stante che 'l mio libro non fusse sottoposto, etc.," which amounts to: "Enough of that nonsense") and proceeds from there to reaffirm his perfect regularity. Such a defense, clearly, could be effective only within the frame of the extrajudicial settlement that the Commissary had offered. It was there only to complete the record, and it must have been made clear that it would be acceptable.

XIII

THE PROBLEM OF THE FALSE INJUNCTION

Inter hos judices vivendum, moriendum, et quod durius est, tacendum.

BENEDETTO CASTELLI

I

WHAT can be the conclusion concerning that famous injunction of 1616? It is, and will remain to the end, the kingpin of the case. With it, from the legal aspect, the trial stands or falls. It came to our notice how everything connected with it was being surrounded all along with a screen of vague, reticent, or misleading language so as to protect it from indiscreet curiosity.

Some curiosity is therefore in order. We are going to review the evidence, starting from the two critical documents that we gave in chapter vi. One of them is the injunction; the other is Bellarmine's certificate.

Friday, the twenty-sixth [of February]. At the palace, the usual residence of the Lord Cardinal Bellarmino, the said Galileo, having been summoned and being present before the said Lord Cardinal, was, in presence of the Most Reverend Michelangelo Segizi of Lodi,

We, Roberto Cardinal Bellarmino, having heard that it is calumniously reported that Signor Galileo Galilei has in our hand abjured and has also been punished with salutary penance, and being requested to state the truth as to this, declare that the said

O.P., Commissary-General of the Holy Office, by the said Cardinal, warned of the error of the aforesaid opinion and admonished to abandon it; and immediately thereafter, before me and before witnesses, the Lord Cardinal being still present, the said Galileo was by the said Commissary commanded and enjoined, in the name of His Holiness the Pope and the whole Congregation of the Holy Office, to relinquish altogether said opinion that the Sun is the center of the world and immovable and that the Earth moves; nor further to hold, teach, or defend it in any way whatsoever, verbally or in writing; otherwise proceedings would be taken against him in the Holy Office; which injunction the said Galileo acquiesced in and promised to obey. Done at Rome, in the place aforesaid, in the presence of R. Badino Nores and Agostino Mongardo, members of the household of said Cardinal, witnesses.

Signor Galileo has not abjured, either in our hand, or the hand of any other person here in Rome, or anywhere else, so far as we know, any opinion or doctrine held by him; neither has any salutary penance been imposed on him; but that only the declaration made by the Holy Father and published by the Sacred Congregation of the Index has been notified to him, wherein it is set forth that the doctrine attributed to Copernicus, that the Earth moves around the Sun and that the Sun is stationary in the center of the world and does not move from east to west, is contrary to the Holy Scriptures and therefore cannot be defended or held. In witness whereof we have written and subscribed these presents with our hand this twenty-sixth day of May, 1616.

We showed then that the first document looks gravely irregular both as to form and as to its place in the file; that the instructions of the Congregation to Bellarmine, as well as Bellarmine's subsequent report on what he had done that day, agree with his certificate and *not* with the injunction; and that there was in fact no allowable ground for an injunction as things stood.

We have seen further that in his most carefully considered piece of writing, the Preface to the *Dialogue*, Galileo deliberately mentions the famous audience as a signal distinction. He is actually calling the authorities to witness against the rumors that had been spread of a secret recantation. This would have been to provoke them foolishly if he had not been quite assured that things stood, in fact, so.

The natural supposition is that the record was hastily fabricated in 1632 when the authorities were trying to get a case against Galileo. Since it was certain, however, that no new sheet had been inserted, Wohlwill suggested that the regular record had been fraudulently altered by deleting the last lines and by tacking a new ending onto it.[1] He supported his contention with a mass of evidence derived from inspection of the manuscript with a magnifying glass. The paper being in bad condition and corroded by the ink, that evidence remained very controversial. Gebler and then Favaro, also from direct inspection, held out for the authenticity of the document. It is true that Gebler's conclusion (Favaro refrains from drawing any) is hardly more flattering: the text was concocted, with careful deliberation and malice prepense, on that very day it was dated, February 26, 1616, and planted in the file in order to trap the unsuspecting scientist the moment he proceeded to discuss the Copernican system "in any way whatsoever."[2]

---

1. Wohlwill's contention is that the original document, as indicated by the spacing of the text (fol. 378^{v}), faint traces of erased letters, and other clues, ended, after Bellarmine's words, with the simple concluding statement that would be logically expected: "cui praecepto idem Galilaeus acquievit et parere promisit." This conclusion was carefully deleted and a sequel inserted, concerning the intervention of the Commissary, beginning with the words "et successive ac incontinenti" ("and immediately thereafter") and going on to the blank recto of the next sheet, fol. 379^{r} (see Appendix II of the second volume of his *Galilei,* p. 298).

2. We have indications that Galileo himself inclined to this opinion. In his letter to Peiresc he says: "If some power would bring to light the slanders, frauds, stratagems, and trickeries that were used eighteen years ago in Rome. . . ." This means something definite. Very definite, indeed, in the light of his subsequent words in that same letter (quoted *in extenso* on p. 324): "Against one wrongfully sentenced while he was innocent, it is expedient, in order to put up a show of strict lawfulness, to uphold rigor." Galileo is saying here something new with respect to what he had said in 1616. He wrote at that time to Picchena that he had "incredible tales to tell him about the workings of those three most powerful operators, ignorance,

Thus the matter stood for decades; it seemed suspended pending new evidence. This came eventually, not from any document, but from new physical means of analysis. In 1927 Laemmel, with the co-operation of the Vatican authorities, submitted the doubtful page first to soft X-rays and then to the much more rigorous test of the Hanau ultraviolet lamp.[3] The result left no doubt on one point at least: the pages had never been tampered with. Wohlwill's laborious inferences fell to the ground. They had never been very plausible to begin with, except on the surface, for Wohlwill had never stopped to consider that the document (we have seen earlier it is in the form of an unsigned minute) would hardly have been worth that amount of fuss. It would have been easy for anyone who wanted to do away with an early version to cut off the two pages containing it, as has been done elsewhere in the file and with no thought of concealment (fols. 342 and 343). He would still have had available in the right place a blank page, 377ᵛ, quite sufficient if used properly, on which to effect a new transcription.

Having settled that particular point, Laemmel thought he could draw the conclusion that the whole text had been added in 1632 when it was badly needed. But his reasons are curiously uninformed and of hardly any logical value. What could it mean, for instance, that the handwriting seems different on the second page? The supposedly altered text begins in the first one.

Against such arguments, one has to stand on Gebler's findings, confirmed recently by Jauch: the text is in exactly the same hand as other neighboring and certainly genuine documents; hence, it was

---

malice, and impiety, such that he dared not intrust to writing." But what he meant then, obviously, were the intrigues which had brought about the prohibition of 1616 and his being accused of blasphemy. (Of these "slanders" he had been cleared by the Inquisition.) The net result of the intrigues was the decree itself. Now he declares himself innocent of ever having violated the decree (as he is accused in the sentence); hence he ought logically to accuse the tribunal of sheer arbitrariness in what had become a trial of intention. Instead, he mentions "frauds, stratagems, and trickeries" going back to 1616. This ought to mean forged evidence, about which the authorities had to put on "a show of strict lawfulness."

3. H. Laemmel, *Archiv f. Gesch. d. Mathematik*, Vol. X (March, 1928).

written at or about the same time. To this we can add a clinching argument: the contemporary pagination shows that the original, if there ever was one, never got into the file; and therefore the decision to replace it with a falsification must have been taken then and there.

Still, there is something that remains hard to explain. The operation is curiously botched. The lack of an original alone might be construed as a mishap, for an inserted double sheet may drop out, but the wrong substitute job in the wrong place is painfully lasting evidence. A regular judge would have had to throw out the injunction on that evidence alone; even the judges of 1633 did not dare rely too much on it.

Should one see here plain cynical disregard for regularity? We would doubt it very much. Regularity was a fetish with the administration, and any such detectable irregularity always entailed a risk for its author. It would almost look as though the thing had been done by someone not in full control of events and having to make shift with what he had. Even so, from a Commissary-General able to arrange things at his will, one might expect more resourceful solutions. For instance, leaving the pagination open and referring to the injunction with seeming casualness but convenient explicitness somewhere else. A later investigation could then only have accused the archivist of negligence for losing the original.

So there might remain a point of doubt. Let us check our conclusions as they stand by assuming the opposite to be true, namely, that things happened as written and that Galileo really stands guilty of violating his instructions. We would then have to say that the protocol was accidentally lost as soon as made out; that the official doing the pagination never noticed its absence; that someone noticed it soon afterward; and that it was deemed sufficient to insert a transcription which can only have been done from memory, for, if the original had been available somewhere, it would have been put back into place. It does not sound very convincing.

Thus we are led back perforce to our version, and the question why the operation was carried out so and not otherwise turns out to be simply a statement of the Commissary's best judgment, based upon what he thought could be done and could not be done. The straight fact that emerges is that it was not held to be quite essential to have the protocol—or, rather. that, following Bellarmine's audience, it was deemed better to have no protocol at all rather than an authentic version of that audience. And so we may be led to conclude that the Commissary simply decided to do without one. Regularity has its limits. But, it would seem, falsification has too.

We know that there had been a strong tension in 1616 between the higher authorities who had decided on diplomacy and the Dominicans, bent at that time on repression. Vatican quarters several times hinted to Guicciardini that "the monks" were relentless. We may then reconstruct as follows: The Commissary, as he watched the scene (we know he was present), was disgusted with the easy way in which Galileo was let off, and he decided to omit the protocol, although his instructions were clear, and the witnesses already designated, obviously by the Cardinal himself. On going back to his office, he told his assistant to arrange a more helpful minute of the proceedings. "And," he may have added, "make it stiff, just in case. What they don't know doesn't hurt them; when trouble arises, it is we who have to take it on." Or it may be, of course, that the assistant, Father Tinti, did the job on his own initiative. But it seems very unlikely. This theory would have the merit of explaining naturally why the protocol was omitted from the pagination as well as accounting for the other facts in the case.[4]

To look at that silent sheet now, after three centuries, gives one a strange feeling, as though it were trying to tell us something. The

---

4. We should mention here a variant derived from an independent study of the documents and personally communicated by Professor C. Jauch. His idea is that the minute was written in advance of proceedings by officials who took the "second degree" for granted and then let the text stand in the record, even though events had gone otherwise. The idea is quite plausible. In that case, however, the text would have been easy to make out as a regular, if false, protocol, which it is not. Moreover, the names of the witnesses from the Cardinal's household, obviously designated by the Cardinal on the spot, could not have appeared, and the signature of a couple of the regular Inquisition officials would have been the natural thing, in addition to making it look more legal. Finally, we would expect to find in the text the clause: "the said Galileo having demurred," whose very lack in the actual document is so revealing. A man inventing the situation *ante factum* would not have omitted that clause, whereas, trying to arrange what had actually happened, he would have tried to keep down lies to the strict minimum necessary.

first part, which reproduces the papal decree, is dealt out with well-practiced smoothness. As soon as it comes to the injunction, the lines get closer, and the writing becomes less legible, as though the writer were unconsciously trying to duck.

The falsification as such is, then, beyond doubt—truly, by modern standards, an exceedingly modest one. Father Segizi would never have dared forge a protocol. He had done a little something, the least he could do, in order to provide a toehold for prosecution if that were needed. It was as much as, on the other side, Lancelot Andrewes proved quite willing to do when he altered the text of Father Henry Garnet's letters in order to implicate him in the Gunpowder Plot.[5] Our contemporaries cannot expect their authorities to be so considerate. Today, over one-half of the globe, the suspect is asked to forge the accusation documents himself, and to do it thoroughly, by inventing all the lurid details that can make his confession convincing and comprehensive. He is supposed to disavow, dishonor, and damn himself with all the fervor of progressive citizenship, if he is to take his last walk to the basement at peace with his conscience.

Going back to Galileo, we can see that the course of events agrees with our previous conclusion. For not only, as we have shown, did Galileo feel completely confident that the officials were mistaken when the matter was finally revealed to him (and that would have been rather the time for him to grovel) but those very officials demonstrated, by their manner of handling the procedure of injunction when it was really necessary (viz., in order to summon Galileo to Rome), the elaborate context of rules in which such an act is framed. Here was a man who had patently fooled them, who was now subtly evading and challenging them; and yet a whole contraption had to be worked out in order to have something that would serve for an injunction without a previous refusal to motivate it.

II

How this was done is a fascinating little story—and a short course in procedure—all by itself. It is provided by Francesco

5. Cf. Lingard, *History of England* (3d ed., 1825), Vol. IX, Appendix, Note D, pp. 433–35.

Barberini in two letters to the Nuncio in Florence, both of September 25, 1632, when Galileo was to be summoned to appear in Rome after the publication of the *Dialogue*. The first letter said:

The Florence Inquisitor is instructed to tell him that he must be pleased to come to Rome and exhort him thereto, explaining to him that he might with his presence repair many things and give and receive satisfaction. If he promises to do so, there is no need to go further; but if perchance he should refuse to come, or make difficulties, let the Father have a notary in readiness who will then enjoin on him the command [*facci precetto*] to come to Rome.

On reading the draft, which is in the hand of Benessi, a papal secretary, Barberini had this section struck out and replaced by the following, which was much more drastic:

[He] shall notify him of a *precetto* to present himself, etc., and he shall be made to promise to obey said *precetto* in the presence of witnesses, so that, if he refuses to obey, in any case they can be examined.

This altered version was signed and dispatched, but immediately afterward Barberini must have received the actual text of the Inquisition orders, sent out two days previously, for he wrote on the same day a second letter:

His Holiness has ordered that the Inquisitor should signify to Galileo, in the presence of a notary and of witnesses (not however qualified in his presence as such), that the will of the Congregation is that he should come to Rome for the whole month of October; if he declares himself willing to obey, he should be made to acknowledge in his own hand the communication and his intention to obey; this acknowledgment, once he has departed, shall be certified and authenticated by the notary and witnesses. If Galileo refuses to acknowledge or to come to Rome, then the Father Inquisitor shall make out the injunction in due form.

We have thus three degrees of the same action described; and it was the intermediate one that was adopted. Now we should consider that the proceedings of 1632 were being taken *ab irato* and by authorities who knew, as is said in the same letter, that Galileo was not respecting the suspension and was "thinking of sending" his book abroad (there are instructions to stop it at the border). Furthermore, we must suppose they assumed that he had violated the injunction of 1616. Yet they could not bring themselves, even at this point, to serve a regular injunction complete with the clause *sub poenis*. Benessi's early draft corresponds exactly in form to Bellarmine's instructions in 1616. It is full of soft words, which shows that it was assumed at the papal secretariat that the affair had to be handled with kid gloves and on the same level of social consideration as in 1616. Then there is a change of mind, but the authorities never go as far as the third degree, which is the strict regular injunction. They could not, apparently, because Galileo, however suspicious his thoughts, had always been regular and submissive; and the best they could do was to lay a trap. (But, then, had he or had he not violated the injunction of 1616 in their eyes? We are left with the same curious question.) Therefore, they evolved an intermediate procedure, whereby they could get a signed acknowledgment without serving the injunction. It was only if he refused that the Inquisitor was supposed to step forward and say: Very well, this is it, now, and these here are the witnesses. In this case, of course, a further refusal to acknowledge and submit would have meant rebellion, warranting immediate arrest. We have thus the three degrees mentioned in the decree of February 25, 1616, confirmed and spelled out in detail.

We have, indeed, more. These men, who had no sense of the ridiculous, had elaborately restaged the whole operation of 1616, including the deceit, but this time taking all the precautions to make it foolproof. Galileo was asked politely to state his acquiescence in writing. He did. Then, as soon as the commission was beyond earshot, the assistants, who had previously been in the next room, apparently under the pretense that they had come just for the outing, bore down on the paper, which was frantically signed, countersigned, sworn to, and then validated by the Secretary of the Inquisition. Galileo still thought that what he had given was a written assurance, but they had now, without a refusal to motivate it, what could serve for an injunction in case it were needed.[6] Clearly, the *extra ordinem* had its limits—and also a curious shape of its own in their minds.

---

6. A puzzle remains: why this fumble between three versions of the same act? We may begin to guess some reasons further on.

III

In the light of these later events it appears all the more incongruous that in 1616, when all was still clear, the Commissary should have sprung forward brandishing his threat *incontinenti,* as soon as Bellarmine had considerately informed Galileo that his theory had been found wrong, without even giving him the time to declare his acquiescence to the new ruling.

These problems really all reflect to the credit of the institution. In fear of its own absolute and unlimited powers, it had framed for itself such a rigid set of rules that, when the need came for cutting corners, it could not do so by merely stretching the interpretation. As a result, certain officials, who held the view that when a job has to be done it has to be done, did not shrink from altering the records without the acquiescence of their superiors. That they were not above such methods is well known; there is quite a number of precedents. The following is taken from a formal protest to the Cardinal Legates of the consuls of the city of Cordes in Languedoc in 1306:

> *Item,* seeing that the processes and books of the said Inquisitors are deservedly suspected by us, both by reason of change or burning or cancellation of writings in the said books, and also by reason of confessions extracted by the Inquisitors uncanonically and by force of torture, and written down (as it is said) otherwise than the matter stands in truth, and seeing also that this is reported in the district of Albi and in the regions round, therefore, we, the consuls of the city of Cordes, beseech and request you to inform yourself on this matter. Moreover, since it is publicly reported that certain witnesses, through whom you may gain clearer information concerning the alterations and burning and cancellation and injustice of the said records and processes, have at the command of those Inquisitors sworn certain prejudicial oaths, to wit, that they will not reveal that which they know of these matters, under pain of being condemned as relapsed heretics and burned—therefore the said consuls beseech and request, etc.

How widespread these conditions were is shown by the vain summons of Pope Clement trying to recall the Inquisitors to order. Things had changed considerably for the better since that time, and the central organs had enforced regularity. But it would appear that someone, at times, still took the law into his own hands.

To maintain that Bellarmine himself was a party to the deceit ought to be out of the question.[7] The operation seems to begin and end in the office of the Commissary-General of the time, Father Michelangelo Segizi, among those implacable Dominicans to whom Guicciardini alludes, "fired with holy zeal" like their own Lorinis and Caccinis and no more scrupulous, like them convinced that mathematicians are a tool of the Devil, who thought it an excellent precaution against the Adversary to put in this pretended registration. No one need be deceived by it if he did not want to, they thought; and, meanwhile, here was a trap to snare the Evil One in case of need. As it happened, it was Pope Urban and the Congregation who were to be snared in it.[8] Fouché, well versed in the ways of Old Nick, used to teach: *surtout pas de zèle.*

---

7. If needed, there would be evidence to help us. We have noted earlier how irregular the choice of witnesses is. It would be passing strange that in Bellarmine's own palace, with "a number of Dominicans standing around" as we know from Galileo's deposition, two servants of the Cardinal's household should have been commandeered by the Inquisitor himself to witness a secret injunction, instead of the ecclesiastic officials that procedure imposed. No one could have chosen and commanded them except the Cardinal. And he knew too well, as everyone did, that Inquisition procedure admitted of no lay witnesses to its acts. He had emphasized thus to Galileo, who was present, that no injunction was implied; that this was his regular private audience and not a visit of the Inquisition; and that, since Galileo had acquiesced, it was going to be handled formally like any public act, be it a notification or the granting of a title.

8. Some historians who want this ancient quarrel to be patched up and to have everybody live happily ever after have advanced a curious compromise suggestion. It is implied by Favaro, apparently, and made explicit by J. J. Fahie. The idea is that the Commissary pounced upon some bewildered question that came to Galileo's lips the moment Bellarmine had finished speaking (e.g., "What, not even discuss the theory?") and interposed quickly an explanation that it was not to be discussed in any way whatsoever. Subsequently, without either Galileo or Bellarmine (both declared to be present) having taken note of it, the event was set down as an injunction. The learned authors do not seem to have realized that this saves nobody's face. An injunction that escapes the notice of the enjoinee is a fraudulent injunction. Even only to omit the last threatening clause *sub poenis, etc.*, would make it such. We have seen from the other cases of regu-

If the document was actually predisposed in 1616, it might throw some light upon the insistent rumors that went around then of secret measures. Echoes come back from the diplomats' suspicions: "The monks are all-powerful"; "One of these days we shall hear that he has fallen over some incalculable precipice [*qualche stravagante precipizio*]." The kind of men who were capable of organizing the denunciations that we have seen, and the report on the proceedings that we shall soon see hereafter, can be credited with exactly anything. And they seem to have also implied it beyond the bounds of discretion. Some good brother must have gone around in guarded exultation, saying darkly: "Just wait and see."[9]

---

lar injunctions that elaborate formalities were taken to make them explicit. The compromise that is suggested amounts thus to another variant of the act of forgery. Also, we have Galileo's explicit and repeated declaration, under very dangerous circumstances, that no one except Bellarmine said a word to him. He does not remember, he specifies, whether those Dominican Fathers were still in the room when the Cardinal spoke to him. Apart from this, it is absurd. To suppose that Galileo was abruptly told that what Bellarmine had just explained to him was no longer valid, that he was no longer allowed a discussion *ex suppositione*—and that he did not even notice such words coming from the Commissary of the Inquisition, makes no sense at all. The theory had to be mentioned because it has been adopted by Fahie, who is among the very few reliable English authors on the subject whose work is currently available. We think our supposition is, on the whole, more charitable to all concerned. A strange note is struck by Father Brodrick in his *Bellarmine* (II, 370). After admitting the "discrepancy" between the two documents, which he explains through the "fussiness or excess of zeal" of the Commissary, who spoke or tried to speak out of turn (we have seen what this explanation is worth), he concludes: "The writer of the other report [the injunction] and the purpose for which it was intended are not known." This last sentence is hard to believe, but it stands there in black and white. It presents again as much of a mystery, written in our own time, as the whole of the proceedings of three centuries ago.

9. Those who used to maintain with Wohlwill, Cantor, Gherardi, Scartazzini, and others that the document was fabricated only in 1632 pointed to the fact that Galileo had come under the attention of the Inquisition apropos of the *Saggiatore,* and also of the *Letter to Ingoli,* and that the injunction would have been then brought up against him. This is

It might still be asked, finally: Why did Galileo in person never pronounce himself explicitly on the subject? He was the man to know. Well, we do have a fairly explicit statement from him—as explicit as he could make it without contempt of court. It is to be found in Buonamici's memorandum (scc p. 286). He told the judges that he would not recite the formula of abjuration, even at the risk of dire penalties, *if it contained anything implying that he had ever deceived his censors and specifically in the matter of extorting a license.* And in fact it does not, although the sentence was built upon this specific accusation, and hence a penitential admission was in order. But, if he does *not* admit that he did "artfully and cunningly" refrain from telling about the injunction, then Galileo is saying as clearly as he can, in the face of the authorities, that the injunction never existed. And this ought to answer the question.[10]

Even a century ago the question was hardly open to doubt. M. de l'Epinois, writing in 1877 as an accredited apologist for the authorities, was willing to grant that the document is "a note for a protocol which probably never was written," and, starting from there, the

---

no doubt a point. The Vatican authorities insist that the document has been there since 1616, and we incline to agree. It ought to imply, however, this: that the Inquisitors realized that either piece did not allow them to go beyond a pointed reminder; that this would have spoiled the game and allowed Galileo to retreat without damage; and that they decided to give him enough rope to make a solid noose for himself. That is, if the Inquisitors bothered to look up the file at all, which is the point where doubt is allowed.

10. Since Monsignor Marino Marini, almost all ecclesiastic historians have lamented his denials in the first interrogatory and considered them "childish evasions unworthy of such a great man." It is indeed plausible to suggest that Galileo at that point desperately refused to admit what might incriminate him and claimed that, "if it was so, he had lost all memory of it"; although, if he lied, he showed great consistency and adroitness in maintaining his point throughout the interrogations. But here the motivation would be reversed. The sentence had fallen, with the judges reserving the right to "moderate, commute, or take off" the imposed penalties. It would have been, therefore, in Galileo's interest to be co-operative, as we have seen at modern trials, and to make as ample a confession as possible.

case for the defense becomes hard to maintain. The best that this reputable scholar could do, in fact, was to ask why Galileo did not speak out: "After the trial, how could he not be revolted at the thought that he had been faced with a forgery, and how could he keep silent on this point? How can it be that, in the nine years which followed, this man so vehement in his expressions did not vent his indignation in letters to the Grand Duke and to his friends at home and abroad against the odious abuse of justice and the crime of the base falsifier of whom he had been the victim?"

It is still conceivable that M. de l'Epinois may not have known the letters we quoted above, which express the victim's feelings in no uncertain terms. But he could not be unaware (having published the record himself) of the famous incident of 1634 we recounted on page 222, when Galileo, having asked for some easements on grounds of illness, was notified by the Pope that, if he was ever again heard of, he would be taken back to Rome and jailed for good. It is under those circumstances that the author asks why he did not indict formally the Holy Office for a fraud to which he was the only surviving witness. Now really. Even published after his death, such a document would have called down implacable persecution on his family, which depended largely (as most of that class did) on ecclesiastical benefits or protection. When Galileo wrote, "If only *some power* would bring to light . . ."; when he said and repeated that he had been gagged forever—he meant it. If M. de l'Epinois had nothing better to suggest, it would have been wiser of him to have kept silent.

Buonamici wrote what was understood to be so in the embassy circle. It follows that it was clearly established among all concerned, with the possible lone exception of the Pope himself, who may still have stood there in the solitary unawareness of despots, that Galileo's trial was based on a judicial forgery, although it could not be stated explicitly without bringing about a diplomatic crisis.

XIV

CHANGE OF COURSE

Nil inultum remanebit
"DIES IRAE"

I

E THAT as it may, there was good cheer at the Villa Medici in those weeks of May, 1633. It was clear to Galileo after his release that the worst was over. The answers to his letters in those weeks give evidence of an optimism among his friends and relations which is positively chirping. They expect the case to die out quietly. Cardinal Capponi writes from Florence that the favorable issue of the trial had been a foregone certainty. Guiducci, Aggiunti, and Cini send in their congratulations. Archbishop Piccolomini asks when he can send a litter to convey his friend to Siena.

Sister Maria Celeste writes that she had been so stunned with joy at the good news that she was seized with a violent headache that lasted for a day and a night. This was one of the very few intimations of her anxieties. She had helped her father's friends to remove all the papers from the house for fear of an Inquisition raid and had braced herself for the worst, as she "cried to God without ceasing." But her correspondence all through the ordeal is sheer intelligence of the heart.

"My beloved Lord and Father," she writes, "your letters have come like the *zoccolanti* [the wooden-shod friars] not only in a pair, but like them with much noise, giving me a more than ordinary emotion of pleasure. As to your return, God knows how much I desire it, nonetheless it will be good for your health to stay a little while with the Lord Archbishop in Siena and enjoy the many exquisite pleasures he can provide you, before coming back to this your dear hovel, which truly laments your long absence; and in particular the wine barrels, one of which, envying the praise you give to the wine of those countries, has spoiled her wine, and the same would have happened with the other, except that we noticed it in time and sold the wine to a tavern through Mattio the shopkeeper. By way of punishment we drew them up in the loggia and knocked their bottoms off, as is the sentence of the more experienced wine-bibbers in these parts.

"The potted oranges have been damaged by a storm, and we have transplanted them in the earth until you tell us what must be done. The broadbeans are wonderful, from what Piera [the maid] tells me, and there will be about five bushels of them.

"Your little mule has become so haughty that she will be ridden by none, and she bucked even poor Geppo, but nicely, so he wasn't hurt. She disdains to be ridden by others, and no one can get her past the village, being without her true master.

"I have bought six bushels of wheat, so that as soon as it gets cooler, Piera can go about making bread. She says that her desire for your return is so much greater than yours, that if they were put on a balance, yours would just go high up in the air. Of Geppo I need not even say."

Niccolini was the only one whose happiness was not unclouded. In an audience of May 21 he had heard that the trial would probably be concluded by the Congregation Thursday week. "I very much fear," he writes in his dispatch, "that the book will be prohibited, unless it is averted by Galileo's being charged, as I proposed, to write an apology. Some salutary penance will also be imposed on him, as they maintain that he has transgressed the command issued to him by Bellarmine in 1616. I have not yet told him all this, because I want to prepare him for it by degrees in order not to distress him. It will also be advisable to keep it quiet in Florence, that he may not hear it from his friends there, and the more so, as it still may turn out for the better."

He had been told that in ten days it would be over. But weeks passed, and complete silence continued to reign.

II

What was happening was that the case, being concluded (*expedita causa*), had been sent up for decision to the higher authorities; and there, obviously, a crisis had arisen.

It had gone up in the form of a report which summed up the proceedings to date and which has been preserved for us, although unsigned, so that we shall never know its real author.[1] It is the *chiusura d'istruzione,* as such documents are still called today. This indecent and fascinating piece of judicial skulduggery has rarely been reproduced, and yet it is an essential part of the story. The judge who later wrote the sentence, as we shall see, went back to the original documents; but this report is apparently all that the

---

1. It has been shown by Wohlwill that the summary was sent up *without* the documents of the trial (*Galilei,* II, 337 ff.), and his conclusions are now confirmed by the analogous procedure followed in the trial of Giordano Bruno. The acts of that trial are lost, but the summary was recently discovered (A. Mercati, *Il Sommario del processo di Giordano Bruno* ["Studi e Testi Bibl. Apost. Vat." (1942)]). The fifty-nine-page document, equally unsigned and very similar to that of Galileo's trial, is addressed to the Assessor and, through him, to Bellarmine for decision (1597). The proceedings that followed were, first, the conclusions extracted by Bellarmine and the Commissary, consisting of eight heretical propositions, then a decree of February 4, 1599, in which Bruno was ordered to recant the propositions. After this, it becomes a matter of personal negotiation. Bruno recanted; then, obviously in a severe nervous breakdown, he challenged the authority of the Holy Office, appealing directly to the Pope. Such a move was natural in itself, and we have Galileo at least talking about it; but Bruno's memorandum simply reaffirmed his theses, which were certainly heretical, and he was given forty days to retract them again. Then, after a visit of the authorities in his cell, where he refused to retract, and a last attempt by his fellow-Dominicans, on January 20, 1600, the Pope signed the decree handing him over to the secular arm. As to the summary that we are discussing in Galileo's trial, it should be noted that L'Epinois, writing in defense of the authorities, agrees substantially with Wohlwill on its role in the procedure. The question is therefore beyond controversy.

Pope and the Congregation had to go on as they decided about the future course of the trial.

We give here the first two pages. The remarks in italics are ours.

AGAINST GALILEO GALILEI

In February, 1615, Father Nicolò Lorini, Dominican of Florence, forwarded here a letter of Galileo which was being circulated in that city and which, following the positions of Copernicus, contained many propositions that were either suspect or temerarious. Said Father informed that the letter was written to contradict certain sermons delivered by Father Caccini on Joshua X, to the words "Sun do not move." (*This is inaccurate as to time but of little consequence.*)

The letter is to Father B. Castelli, a monk of Montecassino, at the time mathematician in Pisa, and it contains the following propositions:

That in Holy Scripture there are many propositions false as to the strict meaning of the words. (*This is Lorini's careful forgery carefully highlighted.*)

That in natural disputes it should be given the last place. (*This is artfully truncated.*)

That Scripture, in order to accommodate itself to the incapacity of the people, has not abstained from perverting some of its essential dogmas, in attributing even to God Himself conditions very far from and contrary to His essence. (*This is the only direct quotation, and it is artfully lifted in order to bring into evidence the word "perverting," which had again been forged into the text by Lorini* [*see p. 46*].)

That in a way, in natural matters, the philosophical argument must prevail over the sacred.

That the command of Joshua to the Sun should be understood as having been made not to the Sun but to the *primum mobile*, if one does not hold the Copernican view. (*This is capable innuendo, as the reasons are left out and the statement made to look disrespectful.*)

Notwithstanding all diligence, it was impossible to secure the original of this letter. (*This is not so. The original had been forwarded by Galileo on February 15, 1615, but had never found its way into the file.*)[2]

---

2. This incident affords us one opportunity of scrutinizing the Inquisitorial policy. As soon as he heard that Caccini was going to Rome, Galileo wrote in haste his first letter to Dini and inclosed a copy of the *Letter to Castelli* "lest by inadvertence some words be altered." The *Letter* reached Dini on February 21, and he gave it to Prince

Examination was made of Father Caccini, who testified, in addition to the above, that he had heard other erroneous opinions uttered by Galileo:

That God is an accident, that He laughs, weeps, etc., and that the miracles said to be made by the Saints are not true miracles. (*This is a falsification. Even Caccini had not directly said that Galileo had uttered these opinions* [*see p. 48*].)

He named some witnesses, from whose examination it appeared that such propositions were not assertive on the part of Galileo and his pupils, but only disputative. (*This is again a falsification. Attavanti had stated explicitly that Galileo had never had anything to do with certain theses that he, Attavanti, as a theological student, had mentioned disputatively* [*see p. 50*].)

Having found further in the book on sunspots published in Rome by said Galileo the two propositions, etc. [Here follows the Latin text of the Qualifiers.] (*This is a false statement which may still be due possibly to carelessness* [*see p. 139*]. *The propositions were taken from Caccini's denunciation. It certainly aggravated the case to say that they had been taken from a printed work by the defendant.*)

They were qualified as absurd in philosophy;

and the first, as formally heretical, because expressly contradicting

---

Cesi, who promptly had "a great number of copies made," as he writes on March 7, and handed over to several people; he gave one personally to Bellarmine. It was unavoidable routine for the Cardinal, after having read it, to forward it to the Inquisition file that he himself had started on the suspect with so much forethought four years earlier. Thus we know that the *Letter* reached the Inquisition in early March. Now Father Segizi, the Commissary, on specific orders of the Congregation of February 25, had written to the Archbishop of Pisa requesting him to secure "in a skilful manner" an authentic copy, and the Archbishop had answered on March 7 that he was trying but that it was difficult because he had "to pretend to be friendly and interested merely in the subject." On March 22 he was to answer that he had failed and that "the easiest way ought to be to get a copy from Galileo himself." Hence, a copy arriving directly from Galileo about or after March 10 is sure to have received full attention. But the Inquisitor, instead of having it placed straightway into the file, obviously had it compared first with Lorini's version. As this last looked more toothsome and profitable, he must have destroyed the authentic copy.

Scripture and the opinion of the Saints; the second, as at least erroneous in faith, considering true theology.

Therefore on February 25, 1616, His Holiness ordered Cardinal Bellarmine to summon before him Galileo (*this leaves it implied that Galileo came to Rome under summons in 1615, which he had denied explicitly*) and to command him [*facesse precetto*] to abandon and not discuss in any manner said opinion of the immobility of the Sun and the stability [*sic*] of the Earth. (*This is false. The instructions to Bellarmine did not include the clause "not to discuss in any manner"* [*see p. 125*].)

On the twenty-sixth following, by the said Lord Cardinal in the presence of the Father Commissary of the Holy Office, notary, and witnesses, said command was intimated to him [*gli fu fatto il detto precetto*], which he promised to obey. Its tenor is that "he should wholly abandon said opinion, nor further hold it, teach it, or defend it in any manner whatsoever; otherwise proceedings would be taken against him by the Holy Office." (*This is a deliberately misleading account of the actual document, since the injunction above is described in the acts as delivered by the Commissary and not by the Cardinal.*)

No need to go on.

What has been done here deserves to be called in modern terms a "slick job." Whoever read this document could have no idea of the contradiction between the orders of the Congregation and their alleged execution in Bellarmine's residence as reported in the documents; he could not suspect that the defense had a strong point here. In fact, he was prevented from understanding Galileo's defense at all; and the further material was so arranged, including the *in extenso* reproduction of Galileo's calculated admission on April 30, to cause him to conclude that the defendant had pleaded guilty to a minor transgression, mainly in order to escape the accusation of heresy.

But there is something even more remarkable. Why, on what grounds, did the analyst have to exhume here, among so many data omitted, just the forgotten blasphemous nonsense that Caccini had planted into the file and which had dropped out of the case since the time it had been ignored and thrown out of court by the Inquisitors of the previous generation? There is no mistaking the care with which it is highlighted. It is also ascribed to Galileo directly and in person, which even Caccini had not dared to do. True, the analyst concedes that it was declared to have been uttered only disputatively, but the extenuation as it stands becomes the knife blade capably inserted below the fifth rib. For now, sixteen years later, Galileo had in fact maintained that his Copernican position had been purely disputative. By digging up the disallowed precedent, the accuser is suggesting this: "Defendant regularly invokes the disputative position whenever it suits him; but, whereas it might be imagined from the present case that his main interest is astronomy, we can show from his past that his intention is, and has always been, pure irreligion and blasphemy."

The general idea is clearly to cut out the juridical defense and to underline the defendant's last plea, whereby he throws himself on the mercy of the court. And then we are struck by a strange uniformity. This is the *n*th time, since Riccardi's earliest disclosure, that the injunction is constantly misrepresented as a command by Bellarmine alone. The Pope himself had described it thus to Niccolini on February 27, and we suppose in good faith. No mention is made anywhere of the intervention of Father Segizi. The only outsider to know otherwise was the defendant himself, for he had been able to guess it, at least, in the audience of April 12—but under the oath of absolute secrecy that covered all the proceedings, so that it could not reach the Pope through Niccolini. There is no fortuitousness involved here, as might have been supposed previously: the writer of the abstract was working on the actual documents; and yet he carefully misrepresents the events in the same way. Further on in the summary a full page is given to the first interrogation, with much picayune detail about the account of previous events connected with the licensing, obviously to convey the impression of an irregularity hidden inside them (there was none, as the sentence tacitly admitted later). But the esential phase of the questioning, when Galileo was stringently asked five times whether he remembered a statement delivered "by someone else"—and denied it—is brazenly fixed in one sentence: "He admits the injunction, but on the strength of the certificate, in which the words *quovis modo docere* are not registered, he says that he has no memory of them." Two lies in three words, a maximum of effortless efficiency. We have evidence, therefore, of a definite line of policy, followed consistently up to the time when the decision fell. Why is not entirely clear. Then comes the sentence, written probably by one of the cardinals on the Board acting as Judge-Extensor, which ignores the report and works out the case on a parallel but different line.

In one thing at least they agree: in deriving the whole merit of the case from Lorini and Caccini.

Caccini and Lorini. The machinery went on humming to the pitch set seventeen years before. It had been nimbly set by scoundrels, liars, and forgers of solidly established reputation, to which an imposing section of the clergy, both regular and secular, prelates, archbishops, cardinals even, were ready to bear witness. Father Maraffi, a Dominican authority entitled to bring judgment on the men of his Order, had put it in no uncertain terms at the very outset of the affair: "We should not open the door for every impertinent individual to come out with what is dictated to him by the rage of others and by his own madness and ignorance." The door had been thrown wide open and kept open. Certain Eminentissimous Lords of the Congregation seemed to feel at home only within the orbit of thought of their police informers, and beyond it the case appeared very obscure. History has indorsed this unassuming appraisal of their own mental capacities.

Someone else was obviously doing all the thinking, who had taken over from where the scandalous pair and their associates had left off in 1616. But what took place exactly? On this we have only a few leads. From Firenzuola's letter we know that the Pope and the Congregation allowed him to pursue the compromise line he had suggested but that several members at first "found this idea too bold." Since it cost nothing at least to try, it shows again in this second phase that the faction pressing for rigorous punishment was well represented inside the Congregation as well as outside, wherever certain disparate elements could work hand in glove. They must have had considerable latitude of action.

The *affaire Galilei,* which looms so large in the eyes of posterity, was really a very secondary problem for the authorities at that time, beset as they were by a multiplicity of ordinary and extraordinary business that looked far more important to them. Even for the Florentine secretariat of state, it was coupled with other minor difficulties with the Inquisiton, such as the well-forgotten Alidosi case. As for the Pope, he had granted it only the most inadequate attention. Riccardi had never been able to talk about it when he was trying to extract a permission. Later, troubles had piled up for the Holy Father such as would have given an ordinary man a nervous breakdown. To the bad news from abroad had been added, as we have said, after Cardinal Borgia's challenge in Consistory, the discovery of a cabal aimed at establishing the Spanish faction in power in Rome; and Urban VIII had had to stamp it out with drastic measures. He was "living in fear of poison." It was rumored that one of the reasons for his displeasure against Galileo, never admitted, was that the luckless one had been negotiating about his method for longitudes with the Spanish Admiralty.

In all these affairs of high policy it was the Jesuit staff that held the threads. To think that the Pope was really informed about the details of the case would be not to know the ways of top executives: in his crowded schedule of appointments, pressures one way or the other were most of what he got to hear. It was the Assessor and the Commissary who were intrusted with the continuity of the case; and the Commissary-General of the Holy Office was, he too, an executive beset by a vast number of cases and problems running concurrently. Under these conditions it is quite possible that the Pope may never have known at all how things stood. The only documents that he surely saw, as far as we can make out, were the early report of the Preliminary Commission and then the summary of the interrogations. It is significant that both manage to gloss over cleverly the events in Bellarmine's palace.

III

We are left, then, with the question: Was the Commissary, Firenzuola, a major party to the conspiracy? As far as blurring out the action of his predecessor went, we might see his motivation. He would be theoretically at least coresponsible for the incredible abstract. But it does not bear his explicit signature. To credit him with its direct authorship implies a degree of duplicity for which there is no warrant. That he was trusted by Castelli may mean little, for Castelli had always been a trusting soul; but he was apparently trusted also by Francesco and Antonio Barberini, whom Niccolini in his turn considered reliable. Those three men were in a position to know who was what.[3]

It should also be noticed that the document is a hasty, sloppy, and inferior, although shrewd, compilation, such as a competent Commissary-General would not make himself responsible for. It is in the anonymous hand of the same secretary who wrote down the interrogations, of which we have the original. But who did the dictating? It ought to be, in good reason, the prosecuting attorney, "The Magnificent Carlo Sinceri, Doctor of both laws, Proctor Fiscal of this Holy Office," as he is mentioned in the sentence. His name makes him a most inviting candidate for this piece of character assassination.

But, saving the more-informed advice of canonist experts, we would not leave out of this the Magnificent's direct superior, namely, the Assessor of the Holy Office. We have said previously that above the Commissary-General there was an Assessor of high ecclesiastical rank. We know from the Bruno trial that it was normal for the Assessor to approve and hand on the final report. His name was Monsignor Paolo Febei of Orvieto; he had succeeded just in that spring the friendly Monsignor Boccabella. He had listened politely enough to Galileo when the latter called on him; but earlier, when Niccolini had submitted the medical certificate of sickness, he had indicated in true Vatican manner, "by movements of the head and also by noises," that he considered it worthless. In a word, he was one of "them." That is all we know. And, we may notice, the Assessor was the only official in the Inquisition who was not a Dominican. His office had been set up in that way for purposes of check and control. He may very well have played a key role in this conflict. Above him there were only the cardinals of the Board.

---

3. We must admit that there were ugly rumors against the Commissary, as shown by some remarks of Peiresc; but they are third hand. There is also, inevitably, the other question: Supposing that Barberini had not trusted him, to whom else could he have addressed his request? Firenzuola was the man in charge. This, however, would be spinning out suppositions. From all that we can feel, Firenzuola was saying what he thought. This was also the impression of Niccolini: "The Commissary shows an intention to have this case settled and to have it die out quietly" (May 1).

The chief powers in the Congregation itself seem to have been Desiderio Scaglia, the senior professional Inquisitor among the cardinals[4] (we have seen that he had gone over the *Dialogue* personally, and Niccolini pinned some vain hopes on him); Guido Bentivoglio, who held the title of Chief Inquisitor; and Marzio Ginetti, who presided at the time in his capacity as Cardinal-Vicar. Francesco Barberini, as "Cardinal-Nephew," was Secretary ex officio.

There are two stray pieces in the puzzle for whose reliability no one could vouch but which ought to go on the record. One of them is a passage out of Guido Bentivoglio's later *Memorie:* "God knows how much I regretted to see this Archimedes in such a sorry pass, and all by his own fault, for having wanted to bring into print the new opinions about the motion of the Earth against the true accepted sense of the Church. It is these opinions which brought him before the Holy Office here in Rome, where I was filling at the time the office of Supreme Inquisitor-General, and where I tried to help him out as much as I could." This attitude seems to be borne out by another passage in the same memoirs, where the Cardinal takes the Pope to task for wanting to legislate in all matters, even philosophical.

The other piece is from a go-between. Many years after the events a certain Canon Gherardini wrote a brief *Life of Galileo.* It was published first by Targioni and begins as follows:

"I came to know Signor Galileo in the year 1633, when I lived in Rome. As I had a close acquaintance with one of the chief ministers of the Holy Office, I offered my assistance, which indeed could not go beyond giving him some helpful hints to guide him. I was prompted to do this by the official himself [Bentivoglio? Barberini?], who not only was moved by the urgent pressures of Galileo's protectors but also wanted to counteract in part the evil intention of another personage who had great authority in that Tribunal and wanted to save him from an impending and far too severe humiliation.

"Galileo professed himself grateful for my services, but, either because he did not think enough of his helper or because he sus-

4. We know he was that already in 1624 from a letter of Giovanni Faber to Cesi on the trial of Marcantonio de Dominis.

pected some deceit or because he trusted too much in his innocence, he was not willing to listen to certain suggestions of that prelate, whose name I could not reveal to him without indiscretion; and it is perhaps this forced silence of mine which caused him to disregard the warnings, from which came the consequences that everyone knows. Even so, they were less than had been feared by those who had known the origin of such fierce persecution. In a word, the wound was small if we consider the force behind the dart; and it was an effect of the protection with which the Grand Duke had surrounded him."

That there actually were implacable elements among the judges is shown by the Commissary's letter. By elimination they can be tentatively located (besides Scaglia) within a group of three: Ginetti, the president; Gessi; and Verospi—all of them Romans and prejudiced against Florentine influences. They may be considered to be "the Pope's faction" in this affair. Of Verospi, the Pope had told Niccolini reassuringly that he "knew about mathematics," but that might well be taken in a sinister sense. As for the helpful prelate, it might be Bentivoglio, or Francesco Barberini, or Zacchia. The "evil intentions" certainly went far, for the decision, harsh as it is, bears the documentary mark of a compromise (see n. 10, p. 304). There were obviously forces which wanted the *Dialogue* burned as the work of a confirmed heretic, and Galileo confined for the rest of his days in the holds of Castel Sant'Angelo, which had never been the Pope's intention. They had left no means untried. They were the same who had spread the rumors that those dolphins on the imprint were a sinister Masonic symbol and that Galileo had astrologically predicted the death of the Pope in 1630. Their apologetic manifesto is the Jesuit Inchofer's *Tractatus syllepticus.*

It should be mentioned that we have what looks like Galileo's own inferences at the time, for what they are worth, from the Buonamici memorandum.[5] They point bitterly to the Commissary him-

---

5. See Ed. Naz., XV, 343. G. F. Buonamici, of whom more later, writes in September, regretting Galileo's sudden departure which prevented him from submitting the text of a memorandum that he has sent to correspondents abroad. The paper had therefore been agreed on and probably also the line to be followed. As it stands, however, it is an

self. According to that paper, Firenzuola was a black soul who engineered the proceedings in alliance with the Jesuits out of "monkish hatred" for Father Riccardi. This seems too pat, and, besides, the search for someone on whom to fix the blame while exonerating the hierarchy has its obvious motives. But the choice of Firenzuola as the villain shows at least that Galileo for a time had drawn the worst conclusions from what he had seen of his behavior.

We say "for a time," and it must have been under the impression of those last days, when he felt he had been double-crossed in the deal he had made with the Commissary. Earlier, he had written his brother-in-law that he trusted his promises more than those of anyone he had met so far, and his impression was confirmed by Niccolini. In after years, as new information reached him, he concluded that the operation had been master-minded by the Jesuits alone.[6]

Those who knew the Commissary speak of him as a practical, sensible man and a decent soul. We might even suppose this: That

---

odd mixture of talk of the town, inaccurate personal reconstruction, and factual data that can come from none other than Galileo himself. These have proved valuable. (Nor should the obviously wrong account of the interrogations be held against it, because that was a point where Galileo could not help, being under oath of silence.) Otherwise the intention is too clear not to have to be discounted. It is significant, however, that he too remarks that this sudden reconciliation of the Jesuits with the Dominicans after the quarrel *de auxiliis* made them into strange bedfellows.

The memorandum was dismissed as apocryphal by T. H. Martin and Gebler and maintained to be such by G. Guasti in the *Archivio storico italiano* (1873). These doubts are no longer possible since Favaro's National Edition, which not only authenticates the document but shows its repercussions at home and abroad. The question of its reliability is another matter. But the fact that Buonamici himself did have important confidential information from Galileo is established beyond doubt.

6. Quite independently of these impressions, it is difficult to see, on the face of it, how the Commissary-General could be exonerated entirely. Too many elements come straight from his own desk. On no one else did it devolve to "discover" the injunction, to inform the Pope, to brief the Preliminary Commission, to organize the trial, and to report its course to the Congregation. He had, in fact, to run the show. So much is implied in his letter to Barberini. If one or the other move

he went along at first with the proceedings, expecting them to turn eventually against the Master of the Holy Palace, whom he disliked, according to insistent rumors, and who certainly was on the spot; and that, when the Consultors' report came in, he suddenly realized that Galileo was in a grave position (notwithstanding the fact that he had successfully denied the injunction) and rushed

---

took place without his consent, they all finally had to come to his knowledge.

But how much was the result of his own planning? All we can say is that several stages are discernible in the proceedings. The early campaign which aroused Urban VIII took place outside, and it ended up in the report of the Preliminary Commission. When the affair was handed to the Commissary, there was a sudden lowering of tension in the exploratory phase, which tended to minimize the case, and in fact to drop it altogether, had it not been for the injunction. We can conceive that the Commissary was on the spot, for it was hard for him to admit that his predecessor had forged a record. Loyalty is strong in the great services. Then comes the report on the *Dialogue* which is the work of the Consultors appointed by the Pope (under whose influence we do not know), and with it the anti-Galileo faction has a new powerful weapon. The Commissary steps in, helped by Barberini, and, in the absence of the Pope, who is at Castel Gandolfo, negotiates an extrajudicial settlement. This holds until about the middle of May, when, the Pope having returned to Rome, the case is sent up to the Congregation. Galileo's defense, which was really supposed to conclude the trial, had taken place on May 10. At that point, however, the case seems to have been taken entirely out of the hands of the Commissary. We say so because he had expected to conclude the case himself in his own way, and he did not; because the summary of the trial should have been along his lines, and it was not. It is as though the Proctor Fiscal and the Assessor had confiscated the case, arranged it as best they could so as to get an unfavorable decision, and handed it on for sentencing, because the sentence obeys the higher instructions but disregards many of the falsifications of the summary. We have to say "as though," because, in the absence of further documents, it is impossible to decide how far the Commissary himself may have obeyed, or connived, or compromised, or been overruled. We have thus even less than before the right of branding the Commissary with infernal duplicity, although many will still say that he, as the "black-and-white hound of the Lord," had to consider first the *salus Ecclesiae* and only in the second place his conscience.

to get him out of it before it was too late. But who will ever know? He remains an undecipherable figure, wrapped in the hood of his Order and the mystery of his service.

IV

One remaining piece of the puzzle ought to be of interest. It is provided by a lone page of Buonamici's diary. G. F. Buonamici was a friendly "intelligencer" who was in close contact with Galileo during that period and performed many services and informal errands on his behalf. As soon as Galileo was sent back to the embassy on May 1, he came to visit; and Galileo must have gone over the whole situation with him, for, on returning home, he started under the date of May 2 a careful account of the affair, going back to the events of 1616. It is there that we learn of Maffeo Barberini's moderating intervention in the Congregation under the influence of the *Letter to the Grand Duchess*, of his sensible remarks to Cardinal Hohenzollern in 1624, and of other such things that Galileo had never disclosed before. But the story breaks off at the end of the first page in the middle of a sentence, and the next pages are gone. There must have been good reasons for disposing of them. From the general tone, it can be inferred that the sequel was a reconstruction of the intrigues against Galileo as the latter could see them at this point and of the successful settlement of the affair up to date. The logical conclusion in this happy mood ought to be an account of Galileo snatched from the jaws of death by the strong intervention of his sponsors, of the Pope and of Francesco Barberini and not last of the Commissary, who had just made the deal with him. We should remember that on that day it seemed that even the *Dialogue* had been saved pending correction. Iniquity stood reproved, and the two men must have felt free to discuss the influences which had been at work.

Later, in July, Buonamici composed his memorandum to be sent abroad, of which we have spoken already, and it was of course in the blackest mood. Galileo was then in the state of a man who has been hit with a blackjack and does not know what happened. Everyone had betrayed him. But in this account meant for the public, it was wise to leave out the hierarchy entirely, for they had Galileo at their mercy. This explains why the sequel of the diary was torn off as a precaution against informers. It must have contained a very different and compromising version. It was decided in the later document that all the guilt of the executives could be concentrated on the Commissary, whom they no doubt at that point considered a party to the Dominican-Jesuit plot. Once the documents are seen in the proper light, the accusation loses much of its weight.

One thing can be concluded for certain: that an extremely capable outfit of "hypocrites without Nature and without God," as Micanzio calls them, was operating effectively inside the hierarchy. Some of them were undoubtedly fanatics like Inchofer; others, mere power politicians. Some were even scientific renegades like Scheiner (at least if we believe Father Kircher), who had chosen to commit the Church to what they knew to be ultimate discredit for the sake of personal revenge and of currying favor with the authorities. The rest is lost in the mists of time. Were the events even contemporary, it would be hard to reconstruct them. The working of great administrations is mainly the result of a vast mass of routine, petty malice, self-interest, carelessness, and sheer mistake. Only a residual fraction is thought. To try to look into them is as unprofitable as to stare at the wall of Plato's cave.

As to Galileo, he had no doubts at all. He never thereafter deviated from cold implacable contempt for his judges, and he took considerable risks to express it. He repeatedly speaks of a masterly conspiracy of "hatred, impiety, fraud, and deceit" which would startle the world if he could tell. And he might have known a few things which we do not. One statement at least we have through his correspondence, and it is "straight from the horse's mouth." In a conversation which he expected would remain confidential, Father Grienberger said: "If Galileo had only known how to retain the favor of the Jesuits, he would have stood in renown before the world, he would have been spared all his misfortunes, and he could have written what he pleased about everything, even about the motion of the Earth."[7]

---

7. Calileo's letter to Diodati, July 25, 1634. After the Galileo trial in 1633 the venerable Father Athanasius Kircher confided himself to Peiresc: "He could not hold himself from admitting, in the presence of Father Ferrant, that Father Malapertius and Father Clavius him-

Unnumbered tons of learned and ingenious apologia have flowed from the presses since that day to obliterate that phrase from the memory of posterity, and they have in a large measure succeeded. But then one opens the records, and there it is.

---

self did not really disapprove of the opinion of Copernicus; in fact, that they were not far from it themselves, although they had been pressed and ordered to write in favor of the common doctrine of Aristotle, and that Father Scheiner himself followed only by order and through obedience" (letter to Gassendi, September 6, 1633). Peiresc admits that this casts an extraordinarily sinister light on the figure of Scheiner, whom he had tried himself to reconcile with Galileo.

XV

THE SENTENCE

Quomodo sedet sola civitas plena populo; ecce facta est quasi vidua domina gentium.

LAMENTATIONS I

I

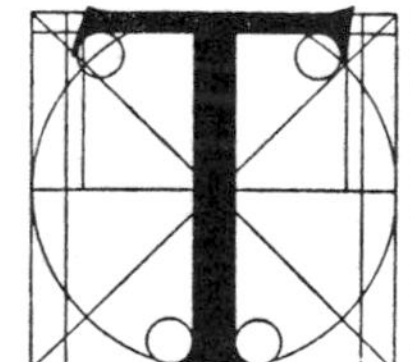

HE Acts of the investigation, represented by the inquisitional abstract we have reproduced in the preceding chapter and by the report of the experts, were sent up for decision to the Holy Congregation in early May, 1633, but had to wait for the return of the Pope from Castel Gandolfo. The affair was on the docket for the first meeting in June but was twice postponed. So that it is only under the date of June 16 that we find the decision entered in the *Decreta:*

Sanctissimus decreed that said Galileo is to be interrogated on his intention, even with the threat of torture, and, if he sustains [the test],[1] he is to abjure *de vehementi* [i.e., vehement suspicion of heresy] in a plenary assembly of the Congregation of the Holy Office, then is to be condemned to imprisonment at the pleasure of the Holy Congregation,

1. The text says *et si sustinuerit.* Some, reading *ac* instead of *et* (the manuscript is in bad shape), have translated: "as if he were to sustain torture." It is a forced translation, and, besides, the *et* has been generally accepted. Hence, it means: "and if he sustains it," which does not refer to torture (otherwise it would be *cum*) but to the examination itself.

and ordered not to treat further, in whatever manner, either in words or in writing, of the mobility of the Earth and the stability of the Sun; otherwise he will incur the penalties of relapse. The book entitled *Dialogo di Galileo Galilei Linceo* is to be prohibited.[2] Furthermore, that these things may be known by all, he ordered that copies of the sentence shall be sent to all Apostolic Nuncios, to all Inquisitors against heretical pravity, and especially the Inquisitor in Florence, who shall read the sentence in full assembly and in the presence of most of those who profess the mathematical art.

The Commissary's deal with Galileo had been overruled.

What the Commissary had outlined in his letter to Barberini, as we remember, was this: "It will only remain [after the confession] to interrogate him with regard to the intention and enjoin him formally; that done, he might be granted his house as a prison, as your Eminence suggested."[3] The statement might have been more explicit, but the general idea can hardly be misunderstood. The Commissary had suggested a settlement out of court. Once he had the confession he needed, he would receive the defense plea, also prearranged, as we saw; he would go *pro forma* through an examination of intention in which the defendant would repent and reaffirm his obedience; and after that he would enjoin on Galileo to go home and stay home, avoid writing about cosmology, and perform salutary penitential recitations.

This is also how Niccolini understood it from what the Commissary told Galileo, for he wrote: "He seems to be of intention to have the case quashed and silence imposed on it." The last clause here means clearly that the Commissary's plan involved no public sentence or abjuration. The Congregation's role would be limited to authorizing the settlement and suspending the book

---

2. There are here in the Gherardi manuscript the words *publice cremandum* fore, which are struck out and replaced with *prohibendum fore*. Hence, the first decision had been to have the book burned in the public square by the executioner, as was done in cases of confirmed heresy; after discussion it was toned down to a prohibition of the book.

3. This is what we can make out of the passage: "non mi restarà altro che interrogarlo sopra l'intentione e dargli le diffese; e ciò fatto, si potrà habilitare alla casa per carcere, come accennò V.E." We understand here *diffese* in the sense of the more correct *diffide*.

pending its correction. It was planned, in other words, to deal with the case on the general lines laid down for the second stage ("demurring") in Bellarmine's instructions of February, 1616. This time, and justifiably, there would be all the steps that Bellarmine had certified had *not* taken place in 1616: there would be a retraction in the hands of the Commissary, for Galileo had disobeyed rashly; there would be a formal injunction, personal restriction for a while, and salutary penances.

This in turn implies something fairly definite. If the Commissary intends to serve *now*, with its proper corollaries, the injunction that is supposed to have been served in 1616, it ought to mean that he believes that it was never served. Otherwise his plan would be as pointless as a twice-told tale and certainly derogatory to the dignity of the court.

We notice, at this point, that there is no mention of that first injunction in the letter—and yet it has been the whole subject of that critical session of questioning which had taken place. For Firenzuola, the "crime" is beginning to shape up only now, with the defendant's unfortunate behavior in the interrogations. It is as though the writer and Barberini were tacitly agreed that the earlier crime is to be disregarded. It might help us understand why Barberini later refused to sign the sentence. We noticed, also, that the defense plea, which had certainly been agreed on in the interview, as it had to fit with the confession, is a straight challenge of the old injunction as "never heard before." It would not carry far with a court that stuck by its documents.

If we follow the hypothesis, we might even imagine with some plausibility the "grounds" on which the Commissary persuaded the cardinals to let him try. The actual words of the letter are disingenuous enough: "This proposal appeared at first too bold, not much hope being entertained of accomplishing this object by adopting the method of argument with him; but, on my indication of the grounds upon which I had made the suggestion, permission was granted me." This has always been understood to mean that several of the judges wanted rigorous punishment and would have liked to stop the pacifying attempt. For how could they have doubted that Galileo would agree with any "argument" that could let him off? His answers in the first questioning indicated not an arrogant heretic but a helpless and frightened man. The question that has never been answered is rather: How did Firenzuola manage to give pause to these implacable men and win at least their temporary assent? By telling them that the defendant had aggravated his position by refusing to acknowledge the injunction? Hardly, for in the afternoon of that same day he was to tell him quietly to go ahead and impugn the injunction in his defense. By showing them what might happen now that he had been caught lying about his intention? They knew it as well as he, and they apparently did not mind. Some of them even looked forward to it.

Still, the fact is that he gave them reasons that took the ground from under their feet. This ought to mean that he did as a last resort what he hoped he would never have to do and admitted that the records left by the previous Commissary, of blessed memory, did not look too good. He intimated (nothing need be stated in those circles) that, especially after the interrogation, he did not feel he could insist too much on the injunction of 1616; that this, however, left the road open to a settlement by serving one now; and that it would be better for everyone's prospects in Purgatory to let that old injunction go back to whence it came, so long as it had not yet been revealed to the public.[4] It was enough, apparently, of a surprise effect to carry the court, at least for that day.

This last part of the story, of course, is only inference. What is certain from the letter is that a settlement had been worked out on the basis of a new injunction to replace the old one. We assume that this was the Commissary's own policy. What happened after that? We can only carry on again with inferences. We have really nothing to go by, except a passage in the Buonamici memorandum, and the explanation there is obviously fumbled.[5] But, however much

4. Only four men on the outside know about it at that point, viz., Galileo, Niccolini, Cioli, and the Grand Duke; they could be trusted to keep it quiet.

5. Buonamici places at this late date the discovery of Ciàmpoli's release note: "They turned then the prosecution against the Father Monster, who excused himself with having had direct orders from H.H., and, as the Pope denied it with irritation, produced a note from Ciàmpoli which said that H.H. (in the presence of whom the note was assertedly

Buonamici may have misplaced this or that event in the telling (he apologizes for not checking his manuscript with Galileo), he was expressing the point of view of the embassy circle, whose members knew more than we do. We had better therefore not disregard the main line of his reasoning, and it is this: The Jesuits had moved to the attack in 1632, finding this an excellent tactical opportunity both to ruin Galileo and to damage the Dominicans, with whom they had an old grudge since they had been bested in the quarrel *de auxiliis*. The Dominicans had found themselves compelled to join forces, for they were in a delicate position as the licensers. Someone still hoped (maybe it was the Commissary) to make Riccardi the individual scapegoat. Hence the Commissary chose the right moment to check the pro-Jesuit cardinals, who were pressing for a heresy trial, and negotiated a settlement with Galileo. But that faction came back with a threat, perhaps to try Ciàmpoli and thus put the Pope himself in an embarrassing position. At this point the change of course took place. The Dominicans had been beaten in their attempt at preserving control of theological policy.

II

We now resume the all-too-well-known chronicle of events.

When the case came up for decision, the Pope and the Congregation decreed, as we have seen, a full-dress sentence *de vehementi*, complete with rigorous examination, public abjuration, and "formal prison." The defendant had been led to admit that his intention had been wrong because of conceit. It was now resolved not to accept his plea and to consider his intention contrary to the Church (i.e., criminal). Apparently the résumé submitted to the judges had eased the job not only by its commissions but also by

---

written) gave orders for the approval of said book; seeing then that the Father Monster could not be involved, and in order not to look as though they had run the tilt for nothing, etc."

This is obviously wrong as to dates, for the discovery of Ciàmpoli's note and the exculpation of Riccardi had taken place months earlier (see p. 198). Ciàmpoli was already in disgrace, and the very fact that nothing worse happened to him shows that the Pope saw his own responsibility involved more than he cared to admit.

its omissions, which nullified whatever defense Galileo had put up.

The threat of torture was only a formality, since it would have been an infringement of the rules to apply effective torture to a man of Galileo's age and health (in Rome it was rarely applied anyway);[6] but it meant that the interrogation could go as far as the *territio realis,* or the showing of the instruments of torture. This question, however, is a minor point, although it has become the subject of song and legend. The *et si sustinuerit,* which leaves

---

6. We have in the Acts, although it has little to do with the case, an interesting report from Desiderio Scaglia himself at the time when he was still a provincial Inquisitor in Milan (1615). It is of a very routine character, but it gives a complete outline of the procedure as it was later used in our case: "I understand the Bishop of Sarzana complains that I give orders to the Vicar of the Holy Office in Pontremoli to come to tortures and sentences without communicating with the Ordinary on the merits of the proceedings, against the form of the Clementine *Multorum de hereticis.* I can reply that said Rev. Bishop is badly informed, because I never gave such orders. When the Vicar of Pontremoli sends trials or summaries here, I take the opinion for the expedition from the Consultors of this Holy Office, and then I write to him the resolution that has been made and the decree that has been formed so he may carry out in the tortures and sentences there what has been found right here, with the proper participation of the Ordinary there." Here at least is an Inquisitor more law-abiding than Bernard Gui, who openly scoffed at the Clementine Decretal.

In any case, the application of torture, or even of *territio realis,* was accompanied by circumstantial formalities, as we know from the *Sacro Arsenale.* If it was applied in this case, we would have to suppose that the whole protocol of June 16 is falsified, as Wohlwill suggested (*Ist Galilei gefoltert worden?*). Later, he revised some of his inferences (cf. *Galilei,* II, 321 ff.). We give only his last conclusion as it stands: "On the sheet that is considered authentic on good grounds, the pagination is correct; the decree [of relegation to Siena], which is here in its proper place, is also in the usual handwriting. On the sheet which is suspect because of its contents, the pagination is interpolated in a completely different handwriting; the decree, which is here absolutely out of place, is of an unknown hand." That is all. It might be something. Later (1907), Favaro decided that it is not enough, and we incline to stand by Favaro. We say this simply because, whatever the state of the Acts, it seems very improbable that more was done to Galileo than the protocol implies.

open frightening possibilities in the case of the defendant's *not* sustaining the test, may also be considered a necessary formal clause. The really serious point, which a modern might fail to appreciate, was that of a solemn abjuration, which was a social dishonor and a brand of infamy in the Catholic society of the time.

In the light of this all the physical easements and comforts granted the prisoner, of which so much has been made, show up as frivolous amenities directed mainly at the Grand Duke and at public opinion, which was getting clearly resentful of all this excess of authority. They are not even so exceptional as all that. Prior to the regime of Gian Pietro Carafa, it had been current practice of the Italian Inquisition to release prisoners not considered dangerous in the custody of their families or even of themselves. A powerful personage like Cardinal Morone could be thrown into the dungeons of the Castle, in order to give an example; but when Ulisse Aldovrandi, the naturalist, who had abjured heresy in Bologna, was ordered to Rome for his sentencing in 1549, he spent three years there visiting the monuments and came home, like many others, with his sentence remitted. The Italian branch of the Holy Office, even at its strictest, had been nothing to compare to the Spanish or even to the Languedocian.

It should be clear that we are trying not to inject any extraneous standards into the appraisal of the crisis. The proceedings that we have described fall short of the normal standards of the Roman Inquisition, which were high. In the central organs at least we know that procedure had been meticulous, and judgment correct. The terrifying apparatus had been there for very adequate reasons, namely, holy terror; but it had never been used casually or brutishly, and it was not now.

In the Galileo trial the Inquisition was suborned into a command performance by an unscrupulous group of power politicians; even so, the behavior of the judges compares most favorably with that of the famous Justice Jeffreys, or with Henry VII's judges in a treason trial; better still, with Cecil's judges in the Gunpowder Plot. Yet that was lay procedure.[7] The Inquisition must be compared

---

7. The Abbé Morellet, who was certainly not prejudiced in favor of the Inquisition, writes: "When M. de Malesherbes read my *Inquisitors'*

to a military tribunal or a people's court in times of revolution. It is an organ of repression conceived for situations of emergency. There was a time when the corporate religious unity of Christendom, the communion of those who pray, was conceived to be at least as important as territorial or political unity is thought to be today. In the light of that idea, such men as Peter Martyr, Torquemada, and Ghislieri appear as scrupulous judges and as ardent compassionate souls.

Cardinal Newman once wrote, in a strange blend of ancient and modern feelings: "Contrasting heretics and heresiarchs I had said: the latter should meet with no mercy; he assumes the office of the Tempter, and so far as his error goes, must be dealt with by the competent authority, as if he were evil embodied. To spare him is a false and dangerous pity. It is to endanger the souls of thousands, and it is uncharitable toward himself. I cannot deny that this is a very fierce passage; but Arius was banished, not burned; and it is only fair to myself to say that at no time of my life could I even cut off a Puritan's ears." Such thoughts are unwittingly justified by H. C. Lea himself, the great denouncer of the Inquisition, who finds himself strangely in accord with Loyola on this one point: "Had it existed in Germany in good working order, Luther's career would have been short. An Inquisitor like Bernard Gui would have speedily silenced him. . . . In France the University had taken the place of the almost forgotten Inquisition, repressing all aberrations of faith, while a centralized monarchy had rendered the national Church in a great degree independent of the papacy. In Germany there was no national church; there was subjection to Rome, which was growing unendurable for financial reasons, but there was nothing to take the place of the Inquisition, and a latitude of speech had become customary which was tolerated so long as the revenues of St. Peter were not interfered with."

It is all a matter of optic. Voltaire could dedicate his life to avenging the wrong done to Calas, but the ferocity of lay penal law which aroused Beccaria left him unconcerned. Today, when

---

Manual, he remarked: Such facts and such procedures may seem new and incredible to you, but the jurisprudence is no more than our own criminal jurisprudence as it stands."

juridical safeguards have been exterminated in one half of the world and are gravely threatened in the other, it might behoove us not to feel overly virtuous in reading of these ancient errors. The Curia of Urban VIII stand out as great gentlemen compared to their modern lay counterparts. Caccini rides again among us, and his name is legion. He is no longer an itinerant monk; his place is in the senates of great nations. Electronic computers are slowly closing in on the citizen's uncertain course. Deviations from what is considered the essential orthodoxy have never, of course, escaped punishment since the beginning of history; but, once search converges on the "thought crime" in its double aspect of something theoretically intangible and concretely dangerous, the way of the inquirer is bound to become again and again that of the Inquisitor. A man may be belabored without defense by investigating committees, deprived of a living, or at best kept, as happened in Inquisition surveillance, under *praeceptum non discedendi* or *non accedendi,* which may mean that he is cut off from his family, his friends, or his future, without any reason whatsoever having to be given by the authorities. We have come very close indeed to inquisitional conditions without realizing it and without even the moral justification. Even less could the Catholics of the seventeenth century have reproved them. But still they found the Galileo trial very strange.[8]

---

8. Writes Cini from Florence on March 26: "In the house of Orazio Rucellai, where all the nobility meets, there is not one who would not give of his blood to see you vindicated of these indignities. They hope that Cardinal Scaglia will read your *Letter to the Grand Duchess.* Everyone exclaims, 'Let them *read* the *Dialogue* for once! Has the book been read? Has it really been considered?' "

   Later comments become sharper: "Si aulcun la pouvoit avoir meritee [la prison] pour l'edition de ses *Dialogues,* ce debvoient être ceux qui les avoient chastrez a leur poste, puisqu'il avoit remis le tout a leur discretion. ... je pense que ces Peres peuvent aller à bonne foy, mais ils auront de la peine à le persuader au monde" (Peiresc to Dupuy, May 30, 1633, and Holstein, June 2, 1633). Peiresc said it again a year later, in more diplomatic language but no less explicitly, in a long letter addressed to Francesco Barberini himself. He pointed out that this unprecedented behavior could not but damage the

As to the causes of this extraordinary reversal to a crime of intention, which dismayed the public, the mind loses itself in conjecture. It had taken place on the return of the Pope from Castel Gandolfo, and it bears the mark of his decision. One plausible reason of policy is clear, namely, that it was considered essential to take action, not against the doctrine, but against the man. We have seen why. We cannot see, however, why the effect could not have been reached by a more correct procedure. Once they had the defendant's admission of partial guilt, it was possible to put the whole weight on that (according to the Commissary's suggestion), which made a clear-cut case, and then to mention the contradiction of Scripture as an aggravating circumstance. It would have spared the authorities the odium of a rigorous examination and of the suspicion of torture on a man of seventy.[9] This line, however, would have led to punishment but not to abjuration. This is where the mendacious inquisitional abstract possibly turned the scales, by blackening the figure of the accused. It is as though the Pope had decided that what he really wanted was not simply repression but humiliation. It was his enemy's mind that had to be shamed, and his name dragged in the mud.

III

Two days after the decision had fallen, Niccolini was again ushered into audience. He had come to ask for a speedy release as implied by the Commissary, and he was not a little taken aback when the Pope informed him that the case had been concluded and that within the next few days the defendant would be summoned to hear his sentence before the Holy Office. To the ambassador's urgent pleas for clemency, the Pope replied that they really could do no less than prohibit the opinion, because it was erroneous and contrary to Scripture, dictated *ex ore Dei;* as to Galileo's person, he would, according to usage, be imprisoned for a time, because he had transgressed the mandate issued to him

---

prestige of the Church. See also the remarks of Descartes quoted on pp. 317 and 319.

9. Cf. L. Garzend, "Si Galilée pouvait, juridiquement, être torturé," *Revue des questions historiques,* XLVI (1911), 353 ff.

in 1616. "However," added the Pope, "after the publication of the sentence We shall see you again, and we shall consult together so that he may suffer as little distress as possible, since it cannot be let pass without some demonstration against his person." In reply to Niccolini's renewed pressing entreaties, he said that "he would at any rate be sent for a time to some monastery, like Santa Croce, for instance; for he really did not know precisely what the Holy Congregation might decree, but it was going along unanimously and *nemine discrepante* in the sense of imposing a penance."

This was said diplomatically. We know that there was at least a certain amount of "discrepancy," since three cardinals out of ten eventually refused to sign the sentence. But nothing was left for Niccolini except to go and break the news to the accused as gently as he could. He did not mention the prison sentence, for he still hoped it would be remitted.

The final phase of the trial now proceeded strictly according to the rules laid down. On the evening of Monday, June 20, 1633, Galileo received a summons from the Holy Office to appear the next day. In this final hearing the accused was to be questioned under threat of torture about his intention, that is, as to his real conviction concerning the two systems. On the morning of the twenty-first Galileo appeared before the Commissary. After he had taken the usual oath, he was asked whether he had any statement to make, and he answered: "I have nothing to say."

Interrogated as to whether or not he holds or has held, and how long ago, that the Sun is the center of the world and that the Earth is not the center of the world and moves, "and also with a diurnal motion," he answered:

> A long time ago, i.e., before the decision of the Holy Congregation of the Index, and before the injunction was intimated to me, I was indifferent and regarded both opinions, namely, that of Ptolemy and that of Copernicus, as open to discussion, inasmuch as either one or the other might be true in Nature; but after the said decision, assured of the wisdom of the authorities, I ceased to have any doubt; and I held, as I still hold, as most true and indisputable, the opinion of Ptolemy, that is to say, the stability of the Earth and the motion of the Sun.

Being told that from the manner and connection in which the said opinion is discussed in the book printed by him subsequently to the time mentioned—nay, from the very fact of his having written and printed the said book—he is presumed to have held this opinion after the time specified, and being called upon to state the truth freely as to whether he holds or has held the same, he answered:

As regards the writing of the published dialogue, my motive in so doing was not because I held the Copernican doctrine to be true, but simply, thinking to confer a common benefit, I have set forth the proofs from Nature and astronomy which may be brought on either side; my object being to make it clear that neither the one set of arguments nor the other has the force of conclusive demonstration in favor of this opinion or of that; and that therefore, in order to proceed with certainty, we must have recourse to the decisions of higher teaching, as may be clearly seen from a large number of passages in the dialogue in question. I affirm, therefore, on my conscience, that I do not now hold the condemned opinion and have not held it since the decision of the authorities.

Being told that from the book itself and from the arguments brought on the affirmative side, it is presumed that he holds the opinion of Copernicus, or at least that he held it at that time; and that therefore, unless he make up his mind to confess the truth, recourse will be had against him to the appropriate remedies (*remedia juris et facti opportuna*), he replied:

I do not hold and have not held this opinion of Copernicus since the command was intimated to me that I must abandon it; for the rest, I am here in your hands—do with me what you please.

Being once more bidden to speak the truth, otherwise recourse will be had to torture, the old man repeated dully:

I am here to submit [*fare l'obbedienza*], and I have not held this opinion since the decision was pronounced, as I have stated.

In the protocol of the trial the concluding sentence follows immediately after this last response of Galileo's: "And as nothing further could be done in execution of the decree [of June 16], his signature was obtained to his deposition, and he was sent back to his place." If Galileo had maintained so much, and no more, in his first interrogation, instead of saying that he had really intended to defend the Ptolemaic system, he might have been better off. The Commissary, on his side, had been as sparing as he could. The whole thing had taken less than an hour and was handled as a mere formality. If he had confronted Galileo, one by one, with the passages excerpted by Pasqualigo and Inchofer from the *Dialogue*, he would have had him on a cruel spot, even without recourse to the trestle and the rope. Worse, he might have brought out passages (see p. 211) noted by the Preliminary Commission, which went considerably beyond the overworked issue of Copernicanism and which might have been reasonably defined as at least *proxima haeresi;* and Galileo, as the inceptor of those thoughts, would have found himself worse than a heretic and very close indeed to the position of a heresiarch. But the dangerous issue of heresy had been settled. In fact, the sentence had been written out already on that assumption, for it was ready and signed within twenty-four hours.[10]

---

10. A point might be raised, under the correction of experts in inquisitional procedure. There was no more questioning about the injunction; it had not even been mentioned in the decree of June 16. One wonders why. There were two points on which Galileo had been officially found insincere, as later declared in the sentence. One of them was the injunction; the other, the intention. For the injunction, of course, the document itself was enough to establish the truth without further ado. Also, Galileo had pleaded forgetfulness, which is hard to challenge. But forgetfulness is hardly an excuse in such matters. The sentence says: "You represented that we ought to believe that you had forgotten," and goes on to other matters without insisting—but, as it comes out later, without accepting the excuse. We submit that a man could hardly be "absolved" in the end unless he confessed. It would have been logical, were it only for regularity, to ask Galileo to "recollect" in a hurry. But the subject is never touched upon, either in the decree or in the questioning. Yet, intention or no intention, the matter of transgression of an injunction is of the kind that should not go unmentioned in the Congregation and its *Decreta,* as indeed it had been discussed in that of February 25, 1616. Many curious things must have happened in that sitting of June 16, which, we may remark, had been twice postponed notwithstanding pressures from both sides. There must have been a hot fight of some kind, but probably with bashful and total silence being preserved in the delicate matter of that command.

IV

One wonders what Galileo's thoughts must have been in those stunned hours of the night as he lay there in the Inquisiton building, uncertain of what the morrow would bring in the way of a sentence.

As he measured the extent of the spectacular repression for which he had been made the pretext, he could measure for the first time the depth of the catastrophe. That his own career as a public figure was finished, he had known for a long time. But he guessed now that this was the end of the whole scientific movement in Italy and, worse, of Florence herself. Although research went on in Florence after Galileo's death in the "Accademia del Cimento," the decay could be noticed within a few years: "I have sat among their learned men," writes Milton in *Areopagitica*, "and been counted happy to be born in such a place of philosophic freedom as they supposed England was, while they themselves did nothing but bemoan the servile condition into which learning amongst them was brought; that this was it which had damped the glory of Italian wits, that nothing had been there written now these many years but flattery and fustian. There it was that I found and visited the famous Galileo, grown old, a prisoner of the Inquisition."[11] His city had lost her freedom on the field of Gavinana a century before; now she had lost her intellectual life at the hands of the Holy Office. We can date back to that day, indeed, the time when Florentine civilization, which had carried the world since the thirteenth century, practically vanished from history. As he was able to realize it, Galileo must have rued his own fateful imprudence and the hour when he obtained permission to print his work;[12] and he must have called himself again and again the curse and destruc-

---

11. This decay of culture in Italy was used as an argument by Leibniz—but in vain—to try and persuade the Curia to release the *Dialogue* (cf. his letter to Magliabechi, October 30, 1699). The *Dialogue* was released from the Index only in 1822.

12. That feeling stayed with him. Two years later Father Fulgenzio Micanzio writes: "Please do not go on reviling and cursing the *Dialogue*. You ought to know it is wonderful."

tion of his own motherland. As for the fate of science itself, his concern was justifiably less.

V

On the next day, Wednesday, June 22, 1633, in the morning, Galileo was conducted to the large hall used for such proceedings in the Dominican convent of Santa Maria sopra Minerva, built in the center of Rome out of the ruins of an ancient temple to the Goddess of Wisdom. Clad in the white shirt of penitence,[13] he knelt in the presence of his assembled judges while the sentence was read to him:

> Noi, Gasparo del titolo di S. Croce in Gerusalemme *Borgia;*
> Fra Felice Centino del titolo di S. Anastasia, detto *d'Ascoli;*
> Guido del titolo di S. Maria del Popolo *Bentivoglio;*
> Fra Desiderio *Scaglia* del titolo di S. Carlo detto di Cremona;
> Fra Antonio *Barberino* detto di S. Onofrio;
> Laudivio *Zacchia* del titolo di S. Pietro in Vincula detto di S. Sisto;
> Berlingero del titolo di S. Agostino *Gessi;*
> Fabricio del titolo di S. Lorenzo in pane e perna *Verospi,* chiamati Preti;
> Francesco del titolo di S. Lorenzo in Damaso *Barberini;* e
> Martio di S. Maria Nuova *Ginetti,* Diaconi,

by the grace of God, cardinals of the Holy Roman Church, Inquisitors-General by the Holy Apostolic See specially deputed against heretical pravity throughout the whole Christian Commonwealth.

Whereas you, Galileo, son of the late Vincenzo Galilei, Florentine, aged seventy years, were in the year 1615 denounced to this Holy Office for holding as true the false doctrine taught by some that the Sun is the center of the world and immovable and that the Earth moves, and

---

13. This detail has been hotly contested by L'Epinois, who claims that the whole etiquette of the Holy Office was against wearing a shirt on this occasion, and Gebler feels compelled to accept his reasons. It is too bad, but we have the word of a witness, G. G. Bouchard, writing on June 29: "come reo, in abito di penitenza." The conclusion, from what L'Epinois himself contributes, would be that Galileo was actually treated as a pronounced heretic. What he was spared was the second half of the trip on the Inquisition mule, which Bruno had to take, from the Minerva to Tor di Nona and then to Campo dei Fiori.

also with a diurnal motion; for having disciples to whom you taught the same doctrine; for holding correspondence with certain mathematicians of Germany concerning the same; for having printed certain letters, entitled "On the Sunspots," wherein you developed the same doctrine as true; and for replying to the objections from the Holy Scriptures, which from time to time were urged against it, by glossing the said Scriptures according to your own meaning: and whereas there was thereupon produced the copy of a document in the form of a letter, purporting to be written by you to one formerly your disciple, and in this divers propositions are set forth, following the position of Copernicus, which are contrary to the true sense and authority of Holy Scripture:

This Holy Tribunal being therefore of intention to proceed against the disorder and mischief thence resulting, which went on increasing to the prejudice of the Holy Faith, by command of His Holiness and of the Most Eminent Lords Cardinals of this supreme and universal Inquisition, the two propositions of the stability of the Sun and the motion of the Earth were by the theological Qualifiers qualified as follows:

The proposition that the Sun is the center of the world and does not move from its place is absurd and false philosophically and formally heretical, because it is expressly contrary to the Holy Scripture.

The proposition that the Earth is not the center of the world and immovable but that it moves, and also with a diurnal motion, is equally absurd and false philosophically and theologically considered at least erroneous in faith.

But whereas it was desired at that time to deal leniently with you, it was decreed at the Holy Congregation held before His Holiness on the twenty-fifth of February, 1616, that his Eminence the Lord Cardinal Bellarmine should order you to abandon altogether the said false doctrine and, in the event of your refusal, that an injunction should be imposed upon you by the Commissary of the Holy Office to give up the said doctrine and not to teach it to others, not to defend it, nor even discuss it; and failing your acquiescence in this injunction, that you should be imprisoned. And in execution of this decree, on the following day, at the Palace, and in the presence of his Eminence, the said Lord Cardinal Bellarmine, after being gently admonished by the said Lord Cardinal, the command was enjoined upon you by the Father Commissary of the Holy Office of that time, before a notary and witnesses, that you were altogether to abandon the said false opinion and not in future to hold or defend or teach it in any way whatsoever, neither verbally nor in writing; and, upon your promising to obey, you were dismissed.

And, in order that a doctrine so pernicious might be wholly rooted out and not insinuate itself further to the grave prejudice of Catholic truth, a decree was issued by the Holy Congregation of the Index prohibiting the books which treat of this doctrine and declaring the doctrine itself to be false and wholly contrary to the sacred and divine Scripture.

And whereas a book appeared here recently, printed last year at Florence, the title of which shows that you were the author, this title being: "Dialogue of Galileo Galilei on the Great World Systems"; and whereas the Holy Congregation was afterward informed that through the publication of the said book the false opinion of the motion of the Earth and the stability of the Sun was daily gaining ground, the said book was taken into careful consideration, and in it there was discovered a patent violation of the aforesaid injunction that had been imposed upon you, for in this book you have defended the said opinion previously condemned and to your face declared to be so, although in the said book you strive by various devices to produce the impression that you leave it undecided, and in express terms as probable: which, however, is a most grievous error, as an opinion can in no wise be probable which has been declared and defined to be contrary to divine Scripture.

Therefore by our order you were cited before this Holy Office, where, being examined upon your oath, you acknowledged the book to be written and published by you. You confessed that you began to write the said book about ten or twelve years ago, after the command had been imposed upon you as above; that you requested license to print it without, however, intimating to those who granted you this license that you had been commanded not to hold, defend, or teach the doctrine in question in any way whatever.

You likewise confessed that the writing of the said book is in many places drawn up in such a form that the reader might fancy that the arguments brought forward on the false side are calculated by their cogency to compel conviction rather than to be easy of refutation, excusing yourself for having fallen into an error, as you alleged, so foreign to your intention, by the fact that you had written in dialogue and by the natural complacency that every man feels in regard to his own subtleties and in showing himself more clever than the generality of men in devising, even on behalf of false propositions, ingenious and plausible arguments.

And, a suitable term having been assigned to you to prepare your defense, you produced a certificate in the handwriting of his Eminence the Lord Cardinal Bellarmine, procured by you, as you asserted, in order to defend yourself against the calumnies of your enemies, who charged that you had abjured and had been punished by the Holy Office, in which certificate it is declared that you had not abjured and had not been punished but only that the declaration made by His Holiness and published by the Holy Congregation of the Index had been announced to you, wherein it is declared that the doctrine of the motion of the Earth and the stability of the Sun is contrary to the Holy Scriptures and therefore cannot be defended or held. And, as in this certificate there is no mention of the two articles of the injunction, namely, the order not "to teach" and "in any way," you represented that we ought to believe that in the course of fourteen or sixteen years you had lost all memory of them and that this was why you said nothing of the injunction when you requested permission to print your book. And all this you urged not by way of excuse for your error but that it might be set down to a vainglorious ambition rather than to malice. But this certificate produced by you in your defense has only aggravated your delinquency, since, although it is there stated that said opinion is contrary to Holy Scripture, you have nevertheless dared to discuss and defend it and to argue its probability; nor does the license artfully and cunningly extorted by you avail you anything, since you did not notify the command imposed upon you.

And whereas it appeared to us that you had not stated the full truth with regard to your intention, we thought it necessary to subject you to a rigorous examination at which (without prejudice, however, to the matters confessed by you and set forth as above with regard to your said intention) you answered like a good Catholic. Therefore, having seen and maturely considered the merits of this your cause, together with your confessions and excuses above-mentioned, and all that ought justly to be seen and considered, we have arrived at the underwritten final sentence against you:

Invoking, therefore, the most holy name of our Lord Jesus Christ and of His most glorious Mother, ever Virgin Mary, by this our final sentence, which sitting in judgment, with the counsel and advice of the Reverend Masters of sacred theology and Doctors of both Laws, our assessors, we deliver in these writings, in the cause and causes at present before us between the Magnificent Carlo Sinceri, Doctor of both Laws, Proctor Fiscal of this Holy Office, of the one part, and you Galileo

Galilei, the defendant, here present, examined, tried, and confessed as shown above, of the other part—

We say, pronounce, sentence, and declare that you, the said Galileo, by reason of the matters adduced in trial, and by you confessed as above, have rendered yourself in the judgment of this Holy Office vehemently suspected of heresy, namely, of having believed and held the doctrine—which is false and contrary to the sacred and divine Scriptures—that the Sun is the center of the world and does not move from east to west and that the Earth moves and is not the center of the world; and that an opinion may be held and defended as probable after it has been declared and defined to be contrary to the Holy Scripture; and that consequently you have incurred all the censures and penalties imposed and promulgated in the sacred canons and other constitutions, general and particular, against such delinquents. From which we are content that you be absolved, provided that, first, with a sincere heart and unfeigned faith, you abjure, curse, and detest before us the aforesaid errors and heresies and every other error and heresy contrary to the Catholic and Apostolic Roman Church in the form to be prescribed by us for you.

And, in order that this your grave and pernicious error and transgression may not remain altogether unpunished and that you may be more cautious in the future and an example to others that they may abstain from similar delinquencies, we ordain that the book of the "Dialogue of Galileo Galilei" be prohibited by public edict.

We condemn you to the formal prison of this Holy Office during our pleasure, and by way of salutary penance we enjoin that for three years to come you repeat once a week the seven penitential Psalms. Reserving to ourselves liberty to moderate, commute, or take off, in whole or in part, the aforesaid penalties and penance.

And so we say, pronounce, sentence, declare, ordain, and reserve in this and in any other better way and form which we can and may rightfully employ.

Then come the signatures. They are only seven, as Cantor was the first to observe in 1864. Three judges did not sign: Francesco Barberini, Borgia, and Zacchia. It may well be that Caspar Borgia's reasons were political, for he had exchanged hard words with the Pope as head of the Spanish faction, was not on speaking terms with him, and probably saw no reason to do him this favor. But for Francesco Barberini and Laudivio Zacchia no extraneous motives could be found, even by diligent apologists. They simply did not sign that sentence. Physical absence on that day is not a sufficient explanation. The inference ought to be that they found it "an excess of authority and an injustice," in the words of a learned French priest, Abbé Bouix, who studied the question. On the other hand, Bentivoglio, known to be rather friendly to Galileo, had signed. For all we know, however, his signing may have been part of a bargain in favor of the accused. We may see, on the other hand, how Barberini, whose solution had been flatly rejected, had good reason not to sign.

After the sentence had been read, Galileo was presented with the formula of abjuration. But at that point the proceedings lost some of their mechanical solemnity, if we are to believe Buonamici, and there is good reason to do so, since he saw Galileo soon after the event and was told facts, such as his talk with the Commissary, which only later research discovered again. "As Galileo saw himself constrained to what he would never have believed possible, the more so as in his talk with Father Firenzuola he had never had a hint of such an abjuration, he begged the cardinals that, if they insisted on proceeding against him in such a manner, they should at least leave out two points and then have him say whatever they pleased. The first one was that he should not be made to say that he was not a good Catholic, for he was and intended to remain one despite all his enemies could say; the other, that he would not say that he had ever deceived anybody, especially in the publishing of his book, which he had submitted in full candor to ecclesiastical censure and had it printed after legally obtaining a license."

An eighteenth-century version of Buonamici's memorandum (the above is from a copy corrected in his own hand) carries the following sequel: "He added that, if Their Eminences wished it, he would build the pyre [for the book, obviously] himself and touch the candle to it, and make public declaration thereof and bear the full expenses as well, if they would give him any good ground against his book." This may be an insertion of the copyist, but it does not sound like one. It rings true somehow. It might have been added by Buonamici himself to a second version after the death of Galileo.

Having won out on his two points, Galileo now dutifully knelt again and read aloud the corrected version of the formula:

I, Galileo, son of the late Vincenzo Galilei, Florentine, aged seventy years, arraigned personally before this tribunal and kneeling before you, Most Eminent and Reverend Lord Cardinals Inquisitors-General against heretical pravity throughout the entire Christian commonwealth, having before my eyes and touching with my hands the Holy Gospels, swear that I have always believed, do believe, and by God's help will in the future believe all that is held, preached, and taught by the Holy Catholic and Apostolic Church. But, whereas—after an injunction had been judicially intimated to me by this Holy Office to the effect that I must altogether abandon the false opinion that the Sun is the center of the world and immovable and that the Earth is not the center of the world and moves and that I must not hold, defend, or teach in any way whatsoever, verbally or in writing, the said false doctrine, and after it had been notified to me that the said doctrine was contrary to Holy Scripture—I wrote and printed a book in which I discuss this new doctrine already condemned and adduce arguments of great cogency in its favor without presenting any solution of these, I have been pronounced by the Holy Office to be vehemently suspected of heresy, that is to say, of having held and believed that the Sun is the center of the world and immovable and that the Earth is not the center and moves:

Therefore, desiring to remove from the minds of your Eminences, and of all faithful Christians, this vehement suspicion justly conceived against me, with sincere heart and unfeigned faith I abjure, curse, and detest the aforesaid errors and heresies and generally every other error, heresy, and sect whatsoever contrary to the Holy Church, and I swear that in future I will never again say or assert, verbally or in writing, anything that might furnish occasion for a similar suspicion regarding me; but, should I know any heretic or person suspected of heresy, I will denounce him to this Holy Office or to the Inquisitor or Ordinary of the place where I may be. Further, I swear and promise to fulfil and observe in their integrity all penances that have been, or that shall be, imposed upon me by this Holy Office. And, in the event of my contravening (which God forbid!) any of these my promises and oaths, I submit myself to all the pains and penalties imposed and promulgated in the sacred canons and other constitutions, general and particular, against such delinquents. So help me God and these His Holy Gospels, which I touch with my hands.

Having recited, he signed the attestation:

I, the said Galileo Galilei, have abjured, sworn, promised, and bound myself as above; and in witness of the truth thereof I have with my own hand subscribed the present document of my abjuration and recited it word for word at Rome, in the convent of the Minerva, this twenty-second day of June, 1633.

I, Galileo Galilei, have abjured as above with my own hand.

This, for once, was receipt of an injunction in due form.

Two days after the ceremony was over, Galileo was released in the custody of the ambassador and went back to the Villa Medici. Wrote Niccolini: "He seems extremely downcast over the punishment, which came as a surprise; for as to the book, he showed little concern over the prohibition, which he had long foreseen."

VI

It must be said that the Judge-Extensor, whoever he was, had made the best of a bad job. The sentence shows the hand of a competent jurist. He has discarded the official résumé and worked over the original sources. They are, inevitably, Lorini and Caccini forever, but at least the facts are presented correctly. It looks even as though the magistrate had consulted the original of the *Letter to Castelli* instead of Lorini's copy, for otherwise those words "false" and "perverting," forged into it by Lorini, would have seemed too good not to be used. The judge goes on from there, piling up grounds for crime of intention assiduously, and even sideswipes the Pope in his zeal, for he defines as a "grievous error" that very policy of indeterminate discussion which had received papal indorsement.

The text of the Qualifiers is there, indeed, published for the first time. He needs it for those words, "*formaliter haeretica,*" applied to the immobility of the Sun. Unfortunately, it is only the opinion of eleven learned gentlemen, without papal indorsement. But he must make shift with what he has.

The famous personal prohibition of 1616, the cynosure of the case, is not glossed over. It is revealed at last to the world, and the proceedings connected with it also disclosed, just enough to imply, even at a little risk, that Galileo had always had bad intentions (a neat job). It has to be there, because it is the only thing that can get the judge past the licenses. Once it is there, it might as well be used for a bit of innuendo and to make Galileo out in the public eye as a perversely rash and obstinate character; but the judge is obviously not comfortable about it. Instead of dwelling on it as the basic point of incrimination (which it ought to be),[14] he manages to shift the center of gravity quickly to the Bellarmine certificate, where he feels on firmer ground.

In good logic either the injunction was not true, in which case Galileo was guilty at most of impertinence, or it was to be considered true and based on an article of faith; and the inescapable question for an Inquisitor would be: *an sit relapsus*—carrying with it something more than vehement suspicion. The word "malice" is there in all letters and is not taken back in what follows. But the contradictory orders of the Pope and the operations of Galileo's enemies had brought about proceedings based on a kind of three-valued logic whereby Galileo was brought to trial as though the injunction were true and was then sentenced as though, in a way, it were not very serious. A couple of imaginary (or rather faked) factors had been multiplied by each other to give an arbitrary real culpability. The acrobatics of the text were bound to give it away as soon as it came under the inspection of dispassionate jurists.[15]

The shift of ground is effected in the curious "but" section, which we are going to quote again in context. Although prepared

---

14. The Pope had said to Niccolini that some kind of prison sentence was inevitable *because of the injunction.* Which was reasonable enough.

15. C. J. Jagemann, in his book on Galileo which appeared in 1784, having nothing to go by except the text of the sentence published by Riccioli (the Acts were published only in the nineteenth century), surmised that there had never been a special prohibition and suspected Riccioli of having invented the passage where it is mentioned. The fact is that the authorities did not dare have the sentence scrutinized in Florence. Guiducci writes on August 27 that, after it was read to the assembled public by Father Egidii, the local Inquisitor, he and others asked to peruse it but were refused. Father Egidii must have acted on orders, because he personally would have liked nothing better than to have the text taken apart by Cardinal Capponi and his circle. He was the man who had granted the license, and his personal feelings were strong. During the trial he had let Galileo know that he was praying "night and day" for him. After the sentence, we have his reply to a lost Inquisition letter: "I receive the sharp reprimand of your Lordship concerning my faulty service in licensing the *Dialogue.* I might have quite a number of things to

by a previous "declaration of His Holiness," dexterously slipped in to blend with the precedents,[16] it remains a judicial mare's nest:

> . . . And all this you urged not by way of excuse for your error but that it might be set down to a vainglorious ambition rather than to malice. But this certificate produced by you in your defense has merely aggravated your delinquency, since, although it is there stated that the said opinion is contrary to Holy Scripture, you have dared to discuss and defend it and argue its probability; nor does the license artfully and cunningly extorted by you avail you anything, since you did not notify the command imposed upon you.[17]

Two points are made: (*a*) (*stressed*) Bellarmine's certificate aggravates the case, because it does mention the contradiction with Scripture; (*b*) (*added quickly*) as to the licenses, they are no good because of the injunction that you maliciously pretend to forget.

The insistence on the first point is really extraordinary. How could the certificate "aggravate" what is already declared in the

---

say, but, since you judge the fault to be mine, I prefer to accept it in full humility."

16. The text reproduces, no doubt literally, Bellarmine's certificate (official documents avoid verifiable misstatements), but it tends to imply here that the decree of the Congregation was of dogmatic importance, which it was not. All decrees began with *Sanctissimus decrevit* or *mandavit,* but they were really Cabinet orders. In order to commit the Pope's sacred authority, the decrees had to carry the formula: "SS. confirmavit et publicare mandavit." Even so, it was not equivalent to a formal declaration *ex cathedra.* In fact, we know that Paul V wanted to declare the Copernican doctrine heretical and that he was restrained by Maffeo Barberini and Caetani. It was brought out later that the importance of the pronouncement had been further attenuated by having it issued, not by the Holy Office, but by the secondary Congregation of the Index. Hence, the doctrine could still be considered "undecided" (cf. Abbé Bouix, *La Condamnation de Galilée*).

17. The original Italian (Inquisition proceedings were always in the language of the accused) is: "Ma da detta fede, prodotta da te in tua difesa, restasti magiormente aggravato, mentre dicendosi in essa che detta opinione è contraria alla Sacra Scrittura, hai non di meno ardito di trattarne, di difenderla e persuaderla probabile; nè ti suffraga la licenza da te artefitiosamente e callidamente estorta, non avendo notificato il precetto ch'havevi."

previous sentence to be malice, unless it showed that the Pope had made a fool of himself with his highhanded instructions? The ominous roll of the big drum is obviously there to divert attention from the concluding sentence, which has to mention *a* command; and it is hoped that the reader, carried along by the whole sixteen lines preceding, will take the personal prohibition as an integral part of Bellarmine's notification—as, indeed, had been not hinted but brazenly affirmed in all previous informal statements. The ambiguity had to be kept whirling on a pinpoint. But now the judge has re-established the ground under his feet. "What is really damning," he thunders, "is this paper which you brought here in your defense."

The situation *ex parte objecti* has been carefully ignored, and we have instead a configuration of heresy *ex parte dicentis,* trying to look as though it had been there all the time.

If there had been a counsel for appeal—but there was not even a court of appeals—it might have been asked: "And why, pray, is this impersonal note, which simply repeats the terms of a public decree and which is superseded anyway by explicit papal instructions to the contrary, so much more serious than a stringent personal prohibition to write in any and whatsoever way? Would you mind *showing* us that prohibition? It begins to sound a little like the Donation of Constantine."[18]

From that point on, in fact, the injunction is lost sight of. The sentence goes downhill in a formal mumble about "seeing and considering all that has to be seen and considered" and comes to a conclusion based on the theological points alone, which are juridically the weakest. The accused is actually sentenced for sus-

---

18. There was a widespread notion in the Middle Ages that the sovereignty of the Pope over Rome and its territory had its origin in a charter of the Emperor Constantine to Pope Sylvester. Dante still believed it. The idea had had strong and not always tacit encouragement from official quarters in Rome, and it was allowed to drop only after a decisive exposé by Lorenzo Valla (1440). When the people of Ancona, in the fourteenth century, received an ultimatum from the Holy See about certain disputed territories, they replied blandly that the title was theirs and that it could be found registered on the back of the Charter of Constantine.

picion of heresy, namely, suspicion of having "believed and held" (this is strictly within Bellarmine's "hold or defend") a doctrine never proclaimed heretical but simply found wrong by some cardinals, as the respectful Descartes was to write;[19] and for having believed and held that said opinion may be considered open to discussion, which the Congregation implied it was, up to a point, and the Pope subsequently said that it actually was so, and even empowered his Master of the Holy Palace to confirm it officially.

If we compare the sentence—and the decree of the Congregation which determined it—with the report of the Preliminary Commission, we find that the picture has changed a good deal. It remains withal what a serious sentence should be—a mirror of the truth. From it, jurists were able to conclude two centuries ago what we have derived from the documents of the Secret Archive. The injunction was really the only thing that could invalidate the official and quite specific permission; but, rather than stand the ground of the injunction to the last, the judge is led to disavow Riccardi's written instructions to the Inquisitor in Florence as they stood in the Acts:

> I remind you that it is the intention of Our Lord's Holiness that the title and subject should not be on the flux and reflux but absolutely on the mathematical consideration of the Copernican position concerning the motion of the Earth, so as to prove that, except for the revelation of God and of Holy Doctrine, it would be possible to save the appearances with this position, solving all the contrary arguments that experience and Peripatetic philosophy could advance, so that the absolute truth should never be conceded to this opinion, but only the hypothetical, and without Scripture [May 24, 1631]; the author must add the reasons from divine omnipotence dictated to him by His Holiness, which must quiet the intellect, even if it were impossible to get away from the Pythagorean doctrine [July 19].

---

19. "Il aura sans doute voulu établir le mouvement de la terre, lequel je scay bien avoir esté autrefois censure par quelques cardinaux; mais je pensois avoir ouy dire, que depuis on ne laissoit pas de l'enseigner publiquement, mesme dans Rome: et je confesse que s'il est faux, tous les fondemens de ma philosophie le sont aussi" (letter to Mersenne, end of November, 1633).

Any superior court would have had to reverse the sentence and order the defendant freed and proceedings started against the Master of the Holy Palace. We may guess now why the facts about the injunction had to be constantly misrepresented, and even to the Pope himself, by the people who were determined to "railroad" Galileo into an Inquisition trial. We can see also, in retrospect, why Galileo was so confident in the face of the storm that there was not the shade of a legal case against him. To get one, he reasoned, it would take not only false documents but also the Pope's going-back on his word; either of these actions was to him beyond the bounds of the conceivable. As a matter of fact, the authorities had managed to achieve both. Even for the zinc-lined curialist stomach, it had taken quite a bit of juggling to get it past.

VII

Through his proceeding the judge has simply highlighted the careful equivocation which had been laid in the groundwork of the whole case by the Index prohibition of 1616. Through the prudent suggestion of Maffeo Barberini himself, the decree had been organized as a flexible weapon. To the public (in case the authorities might have to change their mind) the official text presented only the statement that the new ideas were wrong and unscriptural. That was the flat of the sword. But, whenever it suited them, the authorities had in reserve the cutting edge provided by the Qualifiers, the *formaliter haeretica* applied to the stability of the Sun. (The Earth was allowed to move somewhat *à la rigueur,* provided the Sun did too; such is the comic conclusion of their wisdom.) Now you see it, now you don't.

But you cannot have it forever both ways. If the authorities had been bold enough to stick by their dubious injunction, they might have sentenced Galileo on clear if limited grounds. By flourishing the prohibition itself, they brought out the cold query: "Which heresy are you talking about, anyway?" This query was promptly raised from the Gallican camp, at least privately. Descartes writes to Mersenne in 1634: "As I do not see that this censure has been confirmed either by a Council or by the Pope, but proceeds solely from a committee of cardinals, it still may happen to the Copernican theory as it did to that of the antipodes, which was once condemned in the same way."[20]

Once raised, the question had only one answer. And, as the mass suggestion of blind obedience induced by the Jesuits began to subside, it became clear, and most of all to the authorities themselves, who were by now eager to get themselves out of a jam, that there had been no heresy whatever involved. What a baker's dozen of cardinals sitting in executive committee may decide cannot become a matter of faith and salvation. Since the Pope had cozily refrained from ever pronouncing himself *ex cathedra* on the subject, he had never been entitled to brandish the sword forged for the extermination of heretical pravity.

If Galileo, standing in the hall of the Minerva, had raised this point, he would have brought the roof crashing down on his head. Yet he would have had the whole of jurisprudence on his side.

But he had to keep his peace,[21] and the rest of the Catholic world with him. For the Pope, not unlike that Queen of Spain who

---

20. In 1642 Gassendi remarks that, in the absence of papal ratification, the negation of the Copernican theory is not an article of faith; and ten years later the good Jesuit Riccioli, who was obviously getting nervous notwithstanding his own monumental refutation of Galileo, reproduces his statement word for word in the *Almagestum novum*. Everywhere theologians were already preparing to cushion the fall. Father Fabri, a French Jesuit, wrote in 1661, while defending the geocentric passages of Scripture: "If ever any conclusive reasons are discovered, which I do not expect, I do not doubt that the Church will say that they are to be taken figuratively." Father Caramuel Lobkowitz wrote in 1676 in his *Theologia fundamentalis* that, if it ever should be proved wrong, "it never could be said that the Church of Rome had been in error, as the doctrine of the double motion of the Earth had never been condemned by an Ecumenical Council or by the Pope speaking *ex cathedra*."

21. Another one who thought it better to keep his peace, although far from Rome, was Descartes. (It is true that Richelieu was hardly more liberal than the Pope on that point.) He decided that a challenge to the authorities was not worth the trouble and gave up writing about cosmology. He wrote to Mersenne on January 10, 1634: "Vous savez sans doute que Galilée a esté repris depuis peu par les inquisiteurs de la foi, et que son opinion touchant le mouvement de la terre

told her husband, "I can make princes of the blood without you, but what you can make without me has quite another name," was able to turn the Copernican opinion into a heresy by infallible pronouncement at any time; and that would have settled the question for good.

He did not, and that leaves the Galileo trial as a curious inconclusive oddment in history. Such thundering theological persecution combined with dogmatic timidity, this dragging and kicking a man for suggesting his scientific conviction while they dared not formally assert the contrary, left the authorities twice stultified in the end. They could not very conveniently broadcast the real motives, which were that Galileo had taken to writing in Italian and that he had made them look foolish, or that the political meaning of it was that the Jesuits had evened up a score with the Dominicans by way of the new game of cosmological football. They never revoked the sentence of formal prison, and the last recorded words of the Congregation in 1638 are: "Sanctissimus refused to grant anything [*nihil concedere voluit*]"; on the other hand, they never revoked the small pension that the prisoner had been granted in happier days. The whole performance is in tune with the magniloquent papal arches of the period, leading into a dump that was once a road, or with those imposing Baroque gateways of the Campagna

---

a esté condamnée comme hérétique; or je vous dirai, que toutes les choses, que j'expliquois en mon traité, entre lesquelles etoit aussi cette opinion du mouvement de la terre, dépendoient tellement les unes des autres, que c'est assez de savoir qu'il y en ait une qui soit fausse pour connoistre que toutes les raisons dont je me servais n'ont point de force; et quoique je pensasse qu'elles fussent appuyées sur des démonstrations très certaines et très évidentes, je ne voudrois toutefois pour rien au monde les soutenir contre l'autorité de l'Église. Je sais bien qu'on pourroit dire que tout ce que les inquisiteurs de Rome ont decidé n'est pas incontinent article de foi pour cela, et qu'il faut premièrement que le concile y ait passé; mais je ne suis point si amoureux de mes pensées que de me vouloir servir de telles exceptions, pour avoir moyen de les maintenir; et le désir que j'ai de vivre au repos et de continuer la vie que j'ai commencée en prenant pour ma devise 'bene vixit qui bene latuit,' fait que je suis plus aise d'être delivré de la crainte que j'avois d'acquerir plus de connoissances que je ne désire, par le moyen de mon écrit, que je ne suis fâché d'avoir perdu le temps et la peine que j'ai employée a le composer."

Romana, unexpectedly opening out from a drowsy walled-in road onto a field of thistles. It, too, has that persuasive Roman air of having a purpose, where none is visible.

Roman society hardly took notice of the whole affair, except for the usual pious conversational sighs about the wickedness of new philosophies. There were more absorbing subjects to talk about, in that summer of 1633, such as Bernini's enormous and magnificent black baldachin with the twisted columns which had just been inaugurated in St. Peter's. As for the Eternal City itself, anonymous and unseizable, it had never been much impressed with the action of its authorities and it intimated again as much through its official spokesmen, Pasquino, Marforio, and the Foot, whose age-long diplomatic immunity had never been questioned, due to their being of stone.[22] The idea of a man having to promise that the Earth would not move if he could help it was too interesting not to be taken up. More explicit was a note which, some time later, was found inserted right up under the tail of that absurd and most decorative elephant supporting an obelisk, which still turns both its backside and its worried gaze toward the monastery of the Minerva. The note said in good Latin: "Fratres Dominici, hic ego vos habeo" ("Brothers of St. Dominic, this is where I hold you"). The words came, as it were, from the heart.[23]

---

22. Pasquino and Marforio (so the people have called them for no assignable reason since the Middle Ages) are two pieces of ancient statuary stuck in a street near Piazza Navona and facing each other. The Foot is the last remnant of a colossal imperial statue of the time of Constantine. Pasquino and Marforio are the Martin Marprelates of Rome, although often good-humored and easygoing. Most satirical flyleafs and anonymous tracts took the form of a dialogue between the two characters. We have given a sample in the epigraph to chapter vi. Marforio usually acted "straight man," and Pasquino was, as Rabelais calls him, the "marble doctor."

23. There ought to be more of the affectionate legend in this than of the truth, for the elephant was not set up until 1657, as the inscription on the pedestal shows. That inscription, however, is quite a good unintended joke in itself. It suggests in ample Latin hexameters that, even as it takes an elephant to carry the weight of the wisdom of mysterious Egypt, it takes a strong mind to carry the weight of true science. The elephant looks as though he could not make up his mind to stay or go.

XVI

AFTERMATH

But for your fault the wine
Were sweet as water is:
No taint of taste, no sign,
No promises.

But for your sin no tongue
Had tasted, salt as blood
The certainty among
These grapes of God.

ARCHIBALD MACLEISH,
"WHAT THE VINE SAID TO EVE"

I

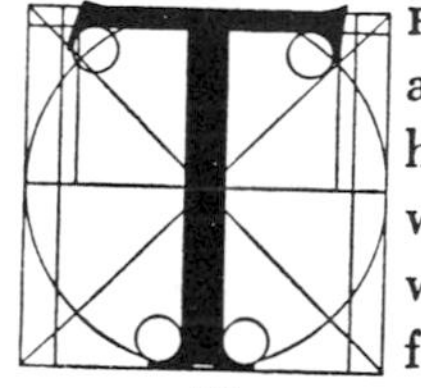

THE abjuration itself is not at all the surrender and moral disgrace that self-appointed judges have made it out to be. Galileo knew exactly what he could say and what he could not say without committing the mortal sin of perjury, for he was better trained in moral theology than we are. That was why, as we know from Buonamici, he had stood firm on refusing two points even at the risk of the stake. He was never going to say that he had deceived anyone during the negotiations for the license or that he had ever deviated from Catholic orthodoxy. These would have been acts of the will. The rest was not.

His real statement then amounted to this: "If the Vicar of Christ insists that I must not *affirm* what I happen to *know*, I have to obey. I herewith declare that at no point should my will have consented to my knowledge. Not even God can prevent my reason from seeing what it sees, but by His Vicar's explicit command I can withdraw my public adhesion from it to avoid scandal among the faithful. You most illegally condemn my truth and want submission. I give you submission and keep my truth. As to that matter of a 'judicial injunction,' it is your lie, not mine, that you ask me to recite, and let it be on your own heads. On this I can stand —that my will was not and will never be consciously contrary to that of the Holy Apostolic Church. For the rest, obedience compels me to say publicly whatever you please."

This is very different from what a modern reads into it. It is illuminating that Castelli, who had been tortured from afar by the thought that his master had consented to commit perjury, breathed more freely when he read the formula. This did not prevent him from thinking of the judges what he thought and even writing it on the spot, although he had to be careful about spies:[1] "My brother was sentenced on the deposition of a witness who testified falsely for a doubloon and a dinner. And yet it is among such judges that we must live, that we must die, and, what is yet harder, we must keep silent. *Inter hos judices tamen vivendum, moriendum, et, quod durius est, tacendum.* Keep me in your grace."

To have recanted was not considered a moral degradation. It was a deliberate *social* degradation, and it was as such that it broke the old man's heart.

II

It did not break his spirit, as time was to show, for, although despairing that he would be allowed to publish, he was to go on from there to his greatest scientific achievement, the *Two New Sciences.*[2] It did not even check the ironic and caustic flashes which

1. Castelli, at the time "Father Mathematician of His Holiness," intrusted with Galileo's defense by the Grand Duke, had been ordered off to Brescia, on his Benedictine vow of obedience, before Galileo arrived in Rome, and was allowed to return only after the latter's departure.

2. When the Duke of Noailles, ambassador of the King of France, insisted on visiting Galileo as a prisoner, he could not be refused, and on their meeting he accepted the dedication of the coming work. The manuscript was smuggled out of Italy by Prince Mattia de' Medici and ultimately printed by Elzevir in Holland.

broke out at times and drove his enemies to fury, even though they knew he was gagged and helpless in the face of their triumphant refutations. He made no mystery of what he thought of his judges and their judgment, nor did he feel that this scornful appraisal made him insincere in his submission and withdrew him from the communion of the faithful. He went on praying and asking his friends to pray for him. He had even planned a pilgrimage to Our Lady of Loreto to repeat the one he had made after 1616, and only his health prevented him from performing it. But to men like Peiresc he could write:

> I do not hope for any relief, and that is because I have committed no crime. I might hope for and obtain pardon, if I had erred; for it is to faults that the prince can bring indulgence, whereas against one wrongfully sentenced while he was innocent, it is expedient, in order to put up a show of strict lawfulness, to uphold rigor. . . . But my most holy intention, how clearly would it appear if some power would bring to light the slanders, frauds, stratagems, and trickeries that were used eighteen years ago in Rome in order to deceive the authorities! . . . You have read my writings, and from them you have certainly understood which was the true and real motive that caused, under the lying mask of religion, this war against me that continually restrains and undercuts me in all directions, so that neither can help come to me from outside nor can I go forth to defend myself, there having been issued an express order to all Inquisitors that they should not allow any of my works to be reprinted which had been printed many years ago or grant permission to any new work that I would print. . . . a most rigorous and general order, I say, against all my works, *omnia edita et edenda;* so that it is left to me only to succumb in silence under the flood of attacks, exposures, derision, and insult coming from all sides.[3]

This makes his position clear. He had sworn before Christendom that he would never consent to any heresy; but he considered himself in no way bound to recognize as of the faith the arbitrary and wilful decision which broke all Church constitutions. They had

---

3. Letters to Peiresc, February 22 and March 16, 1635. He had known about the reserved orders to the provincial Inquisitors from Micanzio in Venice. On September 8, 1633, the Pope had further reprimanded the Inquisitor of Florence for giving permission to reprint some past works.

forced on him a dishonoring obligation; he was not going to honor the extorted promise. They wanted to destroy him and "extirpate even his memory." He was going to fight back with all the means at his command. Within a month of his leaving Rome, a copy of the *Dialogue* was on its way to Matthias Bernegger in Strasbourg, through trusted intermediaries, so that a Latin translation was ready for the European public in 1637.

There is no clearer sign of the anarchic situation brought about by the authorities through their travesty of legality than the resistance of the public to the prohibition.[4] Pious believers who would never have touched a Protestant tract, priests, monks, prelates even, vied with one another in buying up copies of the *Dialogue* on the black market to keep them from the hands of the Inquisitors. A friend writes scornfully from Padua that Messer Fortunio Liceti has handed in his copy to the authorities, with the clear implication that he would be the only one to do that. As Micanzio says, most readers would face the "greatest indignations" rather than part with a copy, and the black-market price of the book rises from the original half-scudo to four and six scudi (almost a hundred dollars in our currency) all over Italy.

This degenerates into an undignified chase reminiscent of the

4. Ascanio Piccolomini must be singled out as a man who was not impressed by pontifical thunderbolts. When Galileo, after his sentence, was intended to spend a long period of penitence in the monastery of Santa Croce in Gerusalemme, Piccolomini, with the help of Cardinal Barberini, obtained custody over him for five months, with strict orders to see no one. As soon as Galileo had arrived in Siena as his guest, he forthwith proceeded to open the archiepiscopal palace to a steady stream of visitors. It was there that the French poet Saint-Amant saw the scientist "dans un logement tapissé de soye et fort richement emmeublé," at work together with Piccolomini on his theory of mechanics, with papers scattered all around the room, "et ne se pouvoit lasser d'admirer cez deux vénérables vieillards, etc." The inevitable informer wrote in anonymously: "The Archbishop has told many that Galileo was unjustly sentenced by this Holy Congregation, that he is the first man in the world, that he will live forever in his writings, even if they are prohibited, and that he is followed by all the best modern minds. And since such words from a prelate might bring forth pernicious fruit, I herewith report them, etc."

Keystone Cops: as soon as the *Discourses on Two New Sciences* is licensed in Olmütz by the bishop, and then in Vienna, obviously under direct imperial orders, by the Jesuit Father Paullus, the other Jesuits start in hot pursuit after the book. "I have not been able," writes Galileo to Baliani in 1639, "to obtain a single copy of my new dialogue which was published two years ago in Amsterdam [it should have been "Leiden"]. Yet I know that they circulated through all the northern countries. The copies lost must be those which, as soon as they arrived in Prague, were immediately bought up by the Jesuit Fathers, so that not even the Emperor himself was able to get one." The charitable explanation would be that they knew what they were doing. Some one at least may have understood that Galileo's work in dynamics went on quietly establishing the foundations of the system that he had been forbidden to defend. But they were like that gallant man of whom Milton speaks who thought to pound in the crows by shutting the park gate.

There is perforce no longer any question here of spiritual authority or obedience but simply of administrative abuses by a thought police whose decrees are ignored and dodged by each citizen as he can, in a manner that cannot but remind one of the "lawbreaking" under the Volstead Act. We know that Galileo regularly went in for confession and received communion. This shows that he was absolved by his spiritual counselor for ignoring the potential excommunications of Rome.

We realize the story at this point might look passing strange to a modern Catholic, especially one from Anglo-Saxon countries, who, being used to the strict separation of church and state, can hardly imagine what his reactions would be were his church endowed with secular as well as theological authority. To such an onlooker, Galileo might appear as a crypto-Protestant who is driven gradually to rebellion but does not have the courage to come out in his true colors. This is an error in perspective. Galileo belongs to a very specific type, the anticlerical Catholic, such as is common even today in countries where the resistance to the encroachments of the priesthood in temporal matters has to come from a Catholic population; a community obedient in matters of doctrine but ready to challenge the Pope acting as a sovereign, as their ancestors did who had to fight the armies of the Papal State. How far resistance and disobedience could go even inside the Counter-Reformation system is shown by the passion of the Jansenist controversy a few years later, down to the razing of Pont-Royal. Had Galileo lived in the generation of Pascal, he, too, probably, would have been driven into the Jansenist camp by the action of the Jesuits. But his figure, poised between two eras, should be seen more rightly in the perspective of the sixteenth century, to which his youth belongs.

Like Erasmus, like Copernicus himself, who lived and worked unconcernedly among the tidal currents of the early Reformation, he belongs to the ecumenic, ancient, and easygoing "Christian Commonwealth"; he cannot bring himself to see the Protestants as "pestilent heretics," segregated in the outer darkness, but rather as intemperate reformers, riding a wave of political change in their own countries, who would eventually find their way back to the Mother Church once their aims were achieved.

How much of a Catholic, indeed, was Francesco Guicciardini, who wrote that he would have dearly loved to have Luther exterminate the whole Vatican system with its "reign of infamous priests," had it not been that his personal career was involved in it? How much of a dissenter, on the other hand, was Father Paul Sarpi, Galileo's bosom friend, the excommunicate, the implacable fighter for Venetian sovereignty? He was driven beyond the pale, yet he did not break loose. Sir Henry Wotton's hopes of bringing him over into the Protestant camp came to nought. "I have come to the conclusion," writes Diodati sorrowfully back to Paris, "that it will never come to his blowing up the works [*qu'il ne soit jamais pour donner le coup de pétard*]." Both as a Venetian patriot and as a believer, Sarpi could never bring himself to sever his tie with sacramental apostolic Catholicity, and he kept to it even beyond excommunication. His last words on his deathbed were: "Esto perpetua." They certainly refer more to the Ecumenic Church than to the Most Serene Republic. No doubt he, like Galileo, considered that a time would come when sobered Protestantism would be reunited sacramentally with a chastened pontifical authority in a world of free states.

In Galileo himself there was nothing of the little old Irishwoman in the story, who refused an Ulsterman's proffered umbrella in a downpour, saying: "Thanks very much, and ye're a kind soul; but what good could be comin' to me of a Protestant umbrella?" Galileo's letters to Bernegger and Diodati, the best of his later years in their quiet dignity and frankness, bespeak the trust he laid in men whom he considered the bearers of the future. Had not France, Diodati's adopted country, set up with the Edict of Nantes a symbol of this coming era of reconciliation? Many must have felt that way in Italy during that somber close of the Thirty Years' War. The dedication of the *Discourses on Two New Sciences* to the Duke of Noailles is in itself an act of legacy to the French "ultramontanes," now that the Italian republics were no more.

Thus Galileo's resignation and acceptance could still remain unyielding both in scientific certainty and in what he knew to be the unalterable content of his faith. Although he had been ordered not to write or converse in any manner about cosmology, at the risk of being treated as a relapsed heretic, and the local Inquisitors watched his visitors and correspondence through their informers, he could write in 1641 to Francesco Rinuccini with thinly disguised irony:

> To be sure, the conjectures by which Copernicus maintained that the Earth is not at the center all go to pieces before the fundamental argument of divine omnipotence. For since that latter is able to effect by many, aye, by endless means, what, so far as we can see, only appears practicable in one way, we must not limit the hand of God and persist obstinately in anything in which we may have been mistaken. But, as I hold the Copernican observations and conjectures to be insufficient, so much more do those of Ptolemy, Aristotle, and their followers appear to me delusive and mistaken, because their falsity can clearly be proved without going beyond the limits of human knowledge.

There was enough of undisguised "intention" here to have caused him to be hauled in again by the Inquisition and end his days in its dungeons. After all, he had formally declared under "rigorous questioning" that he believed Ptolemy to be right.

Nineteenth-century scholars found this letter regrettable and undignified, which again goes to show how far a mere century or two of impunity can corrupt judgment. If, let us say, in 1951 a Russian scientist had written that he repudiated all Morganite-formalist-cosmopolitan-reactionary genetics, in obedience to the directives of the party, which is infallible in its leadership of the rising masses in their struggle, but that he was quite sure at least that Lysenko is beneath notice—if he had written thus, we would describe it as irresponsible heroics. The style that it was (and is) wise to adopt under similar conditions can be seen in a letter from Rome of Carlo Rinuccini to Galileo in August, 1633. After some chatty references to the ambassadress' night concerts in the garden, he goes on as if casually: "Wonderful things and musics are being prepared, and a great personage, who is at the head of it, has told me that he will come and sing whenever I like, so long as I can promise some conversation too. Your Excellency can see from this how many would put on your clothing and then speak for themselves. Well, I shall say no more." This is obviously a message in code, and this is how things had to be said by people mindful of their personal safety. One wonders who that great personage could have been.

Far from following his example, we see Galileo in 1641, already blind and near death, but not beyond the reach of Urban's undiminished rancor,[5] writing to Fortunio Liceti, not to a friend this time, but to an important pedant whom he had already provoked with his ironic criticism:

> Now your Honor may see what a hard task it will be for those who want to make the Earth the center of the planetary circles. A place which could be, as it were, a center to all planets except the Moon befits more the Sun than anything else. This is not to say that the centers of the planets must a priori tend exactly to its center; rather, they appear *hinc inde* located around the Sun, but with anomalies infinitely smaller than those which they would have around the Earth.

The man who wrote this may well, for all we know, have muttered the legendary "Eppur si muove" right in the hall of abjuration. The Commissary-General, we trust, would have done his best not to hear.

---

5. After Galileo's death in January, 1642, the Grand Duke wanted to erect a monument over his grave in Santa Croce. But the Pope warned him that he would consider this a slight to his authority. Galileo's body was to remain for almost a century laid away in the basement of the bell tower.

On June 30, 1633, Galileo was released in the custody of Archbishop Ascanio Piccolomini in Siena. After five months it was intended that he should go to the Charterhouse of Florence. This was later commuted, and he was allowed to move to his own little farm in Arcetri, where he was to face the remaining eight years of his life, and oncoming blindness, under perpetual house arrest.

INDEX

The chapter initials in this book are reproductions of illustrations in *Sette Alphabeti di Varie Lettere*, a manual by Ferdinando Ruano dealing with the geometric construction of Roman capital letters which appeared in Rome in 1554. The copy from which these initials were reproduced is in the collection of the Newberry Library.